Tick

"John is a legend. Throughout my 30-year career in sustainability leadership, he has been a source of insight and inspiration. By extension he has influenced the thinking of thousands of senior executives on our programmes. This book offers a wonderful and personal reflection on the evolution of the sustainability movement and glimpses of what might be to come."

—**DAME POLLY COURTICE**, founding director, Cambridge Institute for Sustainability Leadership

"Read *Tickling Sharks* if you care about the world around you. Actually, read it if you DON'T CARE about sustainability, ESG, climate, and all that stuff. Because this book is about being a happy person in a not-always-happy world, and everyone needs that."

—**SOLITAIRE TOWNSEND**, cofounder, Futerra; author of *The Solutionists*

"Thank you, John, for being our godfather, soothsayer, advocate, provocateur, and—ultimately—inspiration."

—**HANNAH JONES**, CEO, The Earthshot Prize

"By coaching the enlightened—and confronting the laggards—John has helped put the issues and opportunities firmly on the top tables of some of the world's largest and most impactful businesses."

—**SIR DAVE LEWIS**, former CEO, Tesco PLC; chair, WWF-UK

"Readers, may I have the privilege of introducing you to a man I'm proud to call friend, a man who has shaped the direction of travel for so many, a man whose twinkling smile and bookish eyebrows can light up any room. I give you John Elkington, the ultimate pragmatist with a heart of gold."

—**SIR TIM SMIT**, cofounder, The Eden Project

"John has seen farther, sooner, and better than anyone how commerce could reimagine the world and has done so with modesty, eloquence, and kindness."

—**PAUL HAWKEN**, environmentalist, entrepreneur, author of *The Ecology of Commerce*, *Drawdown*, and *Regeneration*

"From the first page, you feel like you are sitting at John's dinner table in a conversation that you never want to leave. He is a giant whose shoulders we all stand on. Here is to riding that 100-foot wave of regeneration ahead of us—with this book as our compass."

—**JEAN OELWANG**, founding CEO, Virgin Unite; author of *Partnering*

"John Elkington has been a key player in the world of corporate sustainability for decades, and *Tickling Sharks* provides us with a very personal, highly entertaining account of this constantly evolving world and of his fascinating life. As a fully paid-up 'stubborn optimist,' John Elkington remains both realistic and refreshingly upbeat."

—**JONATHON PORRITT**, former co-chair, Green Party; former director, Friends of the Earth; cofounder, Forum for the Future; author of *Hope In Hell*

"*Tickling Sharks* invites us to delve into the fascinating mind of John Elkington. Curious and independent-minded, John has always been ahead of his time. I share his view that the next wave of change in business and markets will be about regeneration—environmental, social, economic, and political."

—**GUILHERME LEAL**, cofounder and co-chair, Natura &Co

"Tackling society's grand challenges, both for present and future generations, requires us to transform business, markets, and capitalism. John's leadership on all three has often been ahead of its time."

—**PROFESSOR MARIANA MAZZUCATO,** founding director, UCL Institute for Innovation and Public Purpose; author of *Mission Economy*

"Today, sustainability, climate risk, health and safety, culture, and diversity are front and centre of every corporate annual report—thanks for that, John. The valuing of People, Planet, and Profit are core to MBAs, risk matrices, credit risk ratings, and lending criteria across the globe—thanks again. And thank you, too, for this story of discovery, determination, and the art of befriending those we considered enemies."

—**PAUL GILDING,** former executive director, Greenpeace International; fellow, Cambridge Institute for Sustainability Leadership (CISL); author of *The Great Disruption*

"John's work has been key—his provocations and criticisms of companies, his advice for business leaders, and, above all, his sharing of inspiring stories that help us keep believing that big change is possible. We need more 'Johns'!"

—**CRISTIANO C. TEIXEIRA,** CEO, Klabin S.A.

"John gives us the memoir that we would hope for and expect from his unrivalled role in originating what we now call 'business sustainability.' It's erudite, entertaining, challenging, and optimistic about what can be achieved in the years to come."

—**TANYA STEELE,** chief executive, WWF-UK

"Cometh the moment, cometh the book. Candid, insightful, and inspiring, *Tickling Sharks* is testimony to a remarkable life lived at the foaming edge of change."

—**JOHN O'BRIEN,** founder, Anthropy

"For so many of us in sustainability, John Elkington has been both an icon and iconoclast, a deep thinker and gifted storyteller who marries wit and wisdom, insight and inspiration, and a deep well of experience and expertise that would rise to the top of any profession. In *Tickling Sharks*, it all comes together, the personal and the professional, seamlessly woven into a captivating story that reveals not just the history of sustainability and business, but also its future."

—**JOEL MAKOWER**, chairman and cofounder, GreenBiz Group

"*Tickling Sharks* is essential reading for anyone who believes that business can contribute to a more just and sustainable future and who wants to play a role in making that happen."

—**JANE NELSON**, director, Corporate Responsibility Initiative, Harvard Kennedy School

"In the galaxy of ESG superheroes, John Elkington is the Incredible Hulk."

—**FELIX ARROYO PUJOL AND MONICA RICO**, cofounders, ESG Summit Europe

"I once asked John what it took to lead a sustainable business. He said, 'imagination and stamina in equal measures.' Well, there is no one who has more of these qualities than he. More importantly, he and his team know how to bring these alive in any organisation. He's truly the Godfather of Sustainability."

—**ALANNAH WESTON**, former chair, Selfridges Group

"John Elkington's was probably the earliest—and is still the most important—voice to listen to on corporate sustainability. And as *Tickling Sharks* is his first-person narration of his journey, it's a must-read for anyone wanting to understand the past, present, and future of the business of system change."

—**PAVAN SUKHDEV**, CEO, GIST Impact; former president, WWF International; study leader, The Economics of Ecosystems and Biodiversity (TEEB) initiative

"With his patented mixture of humor and ardor, the father of the triple bottom line distills the most important lessons learned during a long career spent at the bleeding edge of ESG."

—**DENIS HAYES**, organizer of the first Earth Day in 1970; former head, Solar Energy Research Institute; president, Bullitt Foundation

"Building the regenerative economy is the ultimate learning challenge and opportunity. John's intellectual restlessness and insistence on continually challenging mainstream views [including his own through a 'product recall' of an early idea] have extended the boundaries of what's possible for decades. Here he recounts with humility and humour his personal journey and shows that courage and curiosity are the essential attributes of the systems change agent!"

—**NIGEL TOPPING**, former CEO, We Mean Business coalition; UN Climate Change High-Level Champion, COP26

"In his poem 'Dotei,' Japanese poet Kotaro Takamura mused about feeling that his future path was not clear. But as he kept going, he had the sensation that a path had appeared behind him as he walked. In that spirit, this magnificent book describes the leadership journey of one of the founding fathers of the global sustainability movement. A must-read for tomorrow's leaders."

—**DR. TOMO NODA**, founding chair and president, Shizenkan University Graduate School of Leadership and Innovation; co-initiator, IESE-Shizenkan Future of Capitalism Project

"John took me under his wing at the start of my career, and it was the steepest learning curve I've ever been on. Many people know him as an agitator within boardrooms, but those lucky enough to have met him know he's humble, funny, and insatiably curious."

—**CLOVER HOGAN**, climate activist and founding executive director, Force of Nature

"John Elkington is unusual in that he has ridden—and helped shape—so many waves of change. But perhaps his central contribution has been in helping to ensure that the tremendous opportunities offered by responsible and sustainable business models are increasingly understood by CEOs and boards."

—**PAUL POLMAN,** former CEO of Unilever, campaigner, and co-author of *Net Positive: How Courageous Companies Thrive by Giving More Than They Take*

"John Elkington has been both our sage and our visionary, guiding EcoVadis as we grew from a handful of people in Paris to 1,700 based in 14 countries, covering over 130,000 businesses worldwide."

—**PIERRE-FRANÇOIS THALER, FRED TRINEL, AND SYLVAIN GUYOTON,** cofounders and chief rating officer, EcoVadis

"Few have so tactfully and tactically tickled as many corporate sharks as John. This book is essential reading for anyone with the ambition to engage the sharp-toothed business end of business in the cause of making positive change."

—**ED GILLESPIE AND MARK STEVENSON,** The Futurenauts

"John hates being cast as a guru, but the word means 'one who shines light into darkness'—and that is what he has long done for us."

—**SHANKAR VENKATESWARAN,** chair, Oxfam India; founder, ECube Investment Advisors; former chief, Tata Sustainability Group

"A masterly account of how sustainability has evolved into the mainstream. John has always taken the road less travelled with humility and humour. His latest book is packed with stories and lessons from which we can all learn."

—**RICHARD BRASS,** managing director and co-head, Sustainable Capital, Wealth Management UK, Rothschild & Co

"One key piece of advice I was given as I took the reins as CEO and co-owner of Volans in 2017 was 'Don't let John write any more books; it distracts him.' Yet I would argue that John's appetite for distraction is one of the characteristics that helps him notice what others don't, to see the future before others do."

—**LOUISE KJELLERUP ROPER,** CEO, Volans Ventures

"With significant support from John, and over a number of decades, we formed models and experimented with them. Reflecting on our successes and failures is the critical next step by which we all learn and move forward."

—**PATRICK THOMAS,** chair, Johnson Matthey PLC; former CEO, Covestro AG and Bayer MaterialScience at Bayer AG

"*Tickling Sharks* is quintessentially John—meeting leaders where they are as he schools new generations of change agents. With his contrarian-yet-collaborative worldview, he has inspired many in the impact space."

—**CAROLINE SEOW,** founder and director, B Lab Singapore; former head of sustainability, Family Business Network International

"Since John first became an RSA fellow in 1983, the sustainability agenda has been mainstreaming in politics, policy, and, crucially, economics. Our challenge now is to make sure that the coming changes are both positive and systemic."

—**ANDY HALDANE,** chief executive, Royal Society of Arts; former chief economist, Bank of England

Also by John Elkington

The Ecology of Tomorrow's World: Industry's Environment, Environment's Industries

Sun Traps: The Renewable Energy Forecast

The Poisoned Womb: Human Reproduction in a Polluted World

The Gene Factory: Inside The Biotechnology Business

The Green Capitalists: How Industry Can Make Money and Protect the Environment, with a concluding chapter by Tom Burke

Green Pages: The Business of Saving the World, with Julia Hailes and Tom Burke

The Green Consumer Guide: From Shampoo to Champagne—High Street Shopping for a Better Environment, with Julia Hailes

The Green Consumer's Supermarket Shopping Guide, with Julia Hailes

A Year in the Greenhouse: An Environmentalist's Diary

The Young Green Consumer Guide, with Julia Hailes, Douglas Hill, and Tony Hill

The Green Business Guide, with Julia Hailes and Peter Knight

Holidays That Don't Cost the Earth, with Julia Hailes

Cannibals with Forks: The Triple Bottom Line of Twenty-First Century Business

Manual 2000: Life Choices for The Future You Want, with Julia Hailes

The New Foods Guide: What's Here, What's Coming, What It Means for Us, with Julia Hailes

The Chrysalis Economy: How Citizen CEOs and Corporations Can Fuse Values and Value Creation

The Power of Unreasonable People: How Social Entrepreneurs Create Markets That Change the World, with Pamela Hartigan and a foreword by Professor Klaus Schwab

The Zeronauts: Breaking the Sustainability Barrier

The Breakthrough Challenge: 10 Ways to Connect Today's Profits with Tomorrow's Bottom Line, with Jochen Zeitz and a foreword by Sir Richard Branson

Green Swans: The Coming Boom in Regenerative Capitalism, with a foreword by Paul Polman

Tickling Sharks

HOW WE SOLD BUSINESS
ON SUSTAINABILITY

Tickling Sharks

JOHN ELKINGTON

FAST
COMPANY
Press

This publication is designed to provide accurate and authoritative information in regard to the subject matter covered. It is sold with the understanding that the publisher and author are not engaged in rendering legal, accounting, or other professional services. Nothing herein shall create an attorney-client relationship, and nothing herein shall constitute legal advice or a solicitation to offer legal advice. If legal advice or other expert assistance is required, the services of a competent professional should be sought.

Fast Company Press
New York, New York
www.fastcompanypress.com

Copyright © 2024 Volans Ventures Ltd.

All rights reserved.

Thank you for purchasing an authorized edition of this book and for complying with copyright law. No part of this book may be reproduced, stored in a retrieval system, or transmitted by any means, electronic, mechanical, photocopying, recording, or otherwise, without written permission from the copyright holder.

For permission to reproduce copyrighted material, grateful acknowledgment is made to the following:
Jane Martinson and Peter Brabeck-Letmathe, "Smooth Defender of a Tainted Brand," © 2006 Guardian News & Media Ltd. Reprinted with permission.

This work is being published under the Fast Company Press imprint by an exclusive arrangement with *Fast Company*. *Fast Company* and the *Fast Company* logo are registered trademarks of Mansueto Ventures, LLC. The Fast Company Press logo is a wholly owned trademark of Mansueto Ventures, LLC.

Distributed by River Grove Books

Design and composition by Greenleaf Book Group
Cover design by Greenleaf Book Group
Cover images used under license from ©Adobestock.com

Publisher's Cataloging-in-Publication data is available.

Paperback ISBN: 978-1-63908-088-5

Hardcover ISBN: 978-1-63908-090-8

eBook ISBN: 978-1-63908-091-5

Audiobook ISBN: 978-1-63908-089-2

First Edition

John Elkington has helped make business sense of perhaps the most important global social movement of the past fifty years. *Tickling Sharks* is the candid memoir of a change champion who has worked tirelessly to transform business, markets, and capitalism. He wrote the book as a witness statement for change agents of all ages—and for future generations wanting to know what the hell we were thinking. Now, the Godfather of Sustainability is preparing to surf tomorrow's waves of change—and urges us all to "step up—or get out of the way."

To Elaine, Gaia, Gene, Hania, Jake, and Paul;

To my siblings, Caroline, Gray, and Tessa;

To Volans—past, present, and future;

And to those long-ago elvers.

Contents

FOREWORD 1: by Hannah Jones xix
FOREWORD 2: by Louise Kjellerup Roper xxv
INTRODUCTION: Capitalist Jaws 1

PART 1: SPAWNING GROUNDS
CHAPTER 1: Nuclear Families 23
CHAPTER 2: Learning Curves 45
CHAPTER 3: Accidental Capitalist 77
CHAPTER 4: Surfing Tomorrow 95

PART 2: FEEDING FRENZIES
CHAPTER 5: Embracing Gaia 115
CHAPTER 6: Going Green 141
CHAPTER 7: Selling Sustainability 165
CHAPTER 8: Valuing Impact 195
CHAPTER 9: Regenerating Tomorrow 227

PART 3: SCHOOLING DOLPHINS
CHAPTER 10: System Change 255

CODA AND MANIFESTO: TACKLING SHARKS
AFTERWORD: by Sir Tim Smit 285
ACKNOWLEDGMENTS 289
NOTES 295
INDEX 319
ABOUT THE AUTHOR 355

FOREWORD 1

Hannah Jones

Sometimes, you only see transformation in hindsight. It is often far harder to see in real time. Looking back on the last quarter century, I am awed by the shifts. The sustainability-in-business agenda has gone mainstream, new purpose-led organizations are being birthed and many are thriving, sustainability MBAs and classes are jam-packed, almost every major company has a chief sustainability officer, and our work has gone from being an oddity on the fringes to a mainstream reality for leading businesses.

But for all this activity and change, the climate science and data are clear and alarming: the urgency and scale of the work ahead is ever more pressing and daunting. Meanwhile, today's systems are still hamstrung by the legacy of policies and incentives that give an unfair advantage to twentieth-century extractive linear systems.

Viewed from that angle, you might conclude that the mainstreaming of sustainability into business functions has become mired in incrementalism, with early ambitions distracted by activity masquerading as progress, and with leaders dogged by competitive pressures and a sense of limited power when there seems to be no end to the wider distractions—be they COVID-19, war, inflation, or the potential for deglobalization. Stand back and it would be easy to succumb to defeatism, fatalism.

Paradoxically, perhaps, I am more optimistic than ever. "Urgently Optimistic," as we like to say at the Earthshot Prize. I am optimistic because I believe that the last quarter century of change in business, so influenced by John Elkington and his teams at SustainAbility and Volans, has laid the groundwork for transformation.

Change is rarely linear. Instead, it builds in waves, often proceeding via a series of tipping points before exponentiality hits like an express train. Most people then see overnight success, but the reality is that transformation is messy—relying much more than you might imagine on coincidences, on timing, and on those rare innovations that change everything. Time and again, we see real-world transformations build on hard-earned incremental gains achieved over years and decades.

So, what will it take, in this decade, to bend the arc of history toward a just, repaired, and regenerative world?

The answer is no longer either/or but both/and. When I was sixteen and a rebellious teen, I was fortunate to have some great mentors. One of them took me to one side and said, "Hannah, one of these days you will have to decide whether it is more effective to shout from the outside or to change things from the inside."

I've done both—and now I believe there is also a third option. And that is to disrupt systems with innovation that can make the incumbent models obsolete. Building tomorrow's regenerative business models will take innovation and disruption. Incremental change will be a necessary condition for success, of course, but it is a long way short of sufficient.

At the Earthshot Prize, founded by William, the Prince of Wales, we act as a beacon for innovators around the world. We were inspired by President John F. Kennedy's Moon Shot challenge. By posing a seemingly impossible goal, he triggered a wave of economic and social progress—while also successfully landing men on the Moon and getting them home alive, safe, and healthy.

That first Moon Shot was made possible by more than four hundred thousand dreamers, disruptors, inventors, and doers, collaborating across many different industries, sectors, and geographies. We conclude that this must now be the Earthshot Decade—in which we make twentieth-century models and mindsets obsolete by mainstreaming twenty-first-century regenerative mindsets and business models.

To that end, we must look for the edges, the mavericks, the soothsayers, and the visionaries who will disrupt business from the outside and inside, helping build new value creation models from scratch. To accelerate the process, we must collaborate furiously, generously, and relentlessly with the empathy needed for any transformation to happen, given that such momentous periods can both excite and terrify.

I first met John in 1999, having recently joined the nascent Nike Corporate Social Responsibility team. Today, every company worth its salt has a chief sustainability officer, or CSO, alongside a sustainability report series and linked targets. At times it seems that every employee I meet wants a career in "purpose."

But travel back with me to the nineties. The negative impacts of globalization were under intense attack at the time, with Nike on the front lines of the issue of labor rights in factories. I joined during an inflection period for the company and the industry. Having been on the defensive, in rebuttal mode, Nike's leadership decided to pivot and lead, doing everything necessary to address what were increasingly recognized as real issues.

Back then, there was no ESG—or environmental, social, and governance framing. No scope 1, 2, and 3 in terms of greenhouse gas emissions. No standardized sustainability reporting. No university courses in sustainability. No playbooks or case studies mapping the path ahead.

None of us had qualifications for the roles we performed because the roles had never been played before. We made up titles. We made up new rules, broke old rules, and fit in with no one very well. Our business colleagues had no frame within which to place us—at best, we were seen as oddities, at worst, a source of continual provocation, harassment, and irritation.

Our agenda could be a bitter pill for conventionally trained businesspeople to swallow. But the medicine began to work. Understanding the unintended negative social impacts of globalized supply chains opened our eyes to the seismic challenge that business was going to have to confront when it came to the environment, human rights, and so on.

It was daunting—and it's still daunting. Social and environmental impacts rarely fit neatly into the balance sheets and balanced scorecards taught in Ivy League colleges and elite business schools. Indeed, the very design of a linear value chain was predicated on ignoring the impact of extraction and consumption.

The design and baked-in incentives of our financial systems required never-ending growth at all costs, with the extractive industries often supported via skewed policy, regulation, and incentives. Environmentalists were demonized, ridiculed, ignored. According to some of my colleagues, they certainly had no place inside a business.

That was the prevailing reality when I met John in Portland, Oregon. At that time, you could name-check most of the people working in this space, whether they were working inside far-sighted businesses or advancing the cause as campaigners or policymakers.

John had recently launched his book *Cannibals with Forks*, which introduced his term *triple bottom line* to a wider audience. He was, as ever, prescient. He could see the system for what it was, for what it needed to become, and he helped map out the pathways to get us there.

He became a guide to us, often carrying a lone candle into the dark, walking ahead, beckoning us to have courage and step forward. He created space and legitimacy for bold moves, sketching out frameworks and language we could use to justify our next steps into the unknown.

Ultimately, he helped us build trust with key actors in the system. He saw systems when others got stuck in silos. He spoke with compassion and empathy while others grew polarized or entrenched. He sought solutions but never gave us a soft way out of the uncomfortable situations in which we often found ourselves.

I remember one moment when we were setting targets and John challenged us: "You're being incremental. If you don't set an audacious, seemingly impossible goal you won't innovate. It's either a hundred or zero. But ten percent won't get us there."

That is how I have come to see the author of this book, which documents the accidents and incidents that helped shape John. You begin to see why he has championed those working at the edges of the current system—the visionary, disruptive, generous, and collaborative people who have also refused to accept the world as it is. There are important lessons here, set in a rich tapestry of experiences, battle scars, and hard-won wisdom. Thank you, John, for being our godfather, soothsayer, advocate, provocateur, and—ultimately—inspiration.

Hannah Jones
CEO, The Earthshot Prize
non-executive director, Oatly
former CSO and president of
Valiant Labs, Nike Inc.
https://earthshotprize.org

FOREWORD 2

Louise Kjellerup Roper

One key piece of advice I was given as I took the reins as CEO and co-owner of Volans in 2017 was "Don't let John write any more books; it distracts him." Yet I would argue that John's appetite for distraction is one of the characteristics that helps him notice what others don't, to see the future before others do.

In fact, his flitting from one interesting domain to the next is a key part of what makes him such an impactful thought leader and effective cross-pollinator. That has been one of the reasons why Volans, since its inception, has been at the forefront of a series of movements and change waves.

Early on, the team championed social entrepreneurship and intrapreneurship, a phase in our evolution marked by *The Power of Unreasonable People*—the book that John co-authored with Volans cofounder Pamela Hartigan. That book went into the hands of all three thousand delegates attending the World Economic Forum in Davos in 2008.

Later, Volans backed purposeful business in the shape of the B Corporation movement, which I have been involved with since 2007 with US companies like method and gDiapers and London-based ENSO Tyres. Several years before John hooked me in, Volans incubated the UK end of B Lab for nine months as it got ready for launch in 2015.

More recently, we have backed the regenerative economy movement, which is still emerging and which came into sharper focus for our team during our Tomorrow's Capitalism Inquiry. This has aimed to answer the question of how a business might be a catalyst for systems change. One output was John's twentieth book, *Green Swans: The Coming Boom in Regenerative Capitalism*.

A key conclusion of all this work has been that if it is to have systemic impact, the triple bottom line (People, Planet, and Profit, or the 3P's) concept, coined by John in 1994, must be seen through an additional filter, the three R's. These are responsibility (doing less harm to other parts of the system), resilience (protecting your organization from stresses in other parts of the system), and regeneration (acknowledging that only if the various systems of which we are part thrive can your own organization enjoy long-term success).

Over the years, we have dug deep into living systems thinking—and are now working to make business sense of it, making it practical. Our aim is to help business organizations pioneer and apply regenerative principles. Among those we have worked with are Spanish infrastructure and energy group Acciona and Ireland's Electricity Supply Board, alongside public sector projects like the Leven Programme, led by the Scottish Environment Protection Agency.

We aim to help spur a shift in our paradigm and in linked systems, helping business use its power to shape a better, more resilient, and increasingly regenerative future. Whatever they produce, businesses, industries, markets, and economies must now undergo a major transformation if they are to survive, let alone thrive.

This will mean engaging well beyond their current supply systems, pulling in policymakers, nongovernmental organizations, financial institutions, and private individuals in new ways—and engaging with those helping to build the new systems the world needs so urgently.

As we work to help transform organizations, we provide both the leadership and those deeper in the organizational structures with new practices and tools to influence change, supporting the formation of new networks and injecting courage to expand the necessary agency for change.

For the team at the heart of the evolving Volans constellation, this requires us to stretch into new areas, too, growing the range of our strategic conversations—a core activity at Volans from the outset. John always insists that he thinks and works best in conversation, something I have seen up close. I have enjoyed our own evolving conversation, and in the same vein, his books can be seen as conversations—most obviously with those he talks to and interviews, but also with you, his reader.

It is through such conversations that John weaves his magic, "tickling" the human sharks of the corporate world, encouraging them to open their eyes, ears, and minds, and to take timely and effective action toward a resilient, net-zero, and regenerative future.

Despite all the well-intentioned advice, I encouraged John to write this book, to turn the spotlight inward, illuminating his half a century of experience that stretches back to the early seventies. His highly unusual journey as a pioneer of the global environmental, green, sustainability, impact, and regeneration movements makes this book a valuable witness statement.

It may seem that now that most of these movements are mainstreaming, our job is almost done, but as John argues here, the most challenging and exciting years still lie ahead. As the world wakes up to the nature and scale of the emergencies facing us, it will also begin to understand the extraordinary opportunities now opening up. Join us on the journey, helping—as they say—to make the impossible first possible, then inevitable.

Louise Kjellerup Roper
CEO, Volans
cofounder and non-executive member of the board, Bankers for Net Zero
member of Exeter Business School Advisory Board
https://volans.com

INTRODUCTION

Capitalist Jaws

I have spent most of my adult life in or close to the jaws of capitalism. They're predatory jaws, particularly since economist Milton Friedman, half a century ago, persuaded generations of businesspeople that their prime mission was to pursue a single bottom line—as long as they didn't break too many laws along the way.*

Whereas some brave people tame lions and tigers, my aim has been to rein in market man-eaters—or "the future eaters," as Tim Flannery dubbed them in his book of the same name.¹ That is, powerful people, businesses, and sectors able to dictate the fates of thousands, even millions, of people. Market actors able, with scarcely a second thought, to send mighty shock waves roiling through the natural world, oceans, and atmosphere. In some cases, you might even see them as market equivalents of the great white shark that dominates Steven Spielberg's blockbuster film *Jaws*, which launched in 1975, just as I was starting the journey that I describe in this book.

---

* Milton Friedman is easy to caricature—with catchy phrases like "the business of business is business" and "the social responsibility of business is to increase its profits"—but he was subtle in his thinking. The problem is that such people can attract and inspire zealots who push things to extremes. Mix in a degree of religious fundamentalism, as in the United States; a Party-knows-best mindset, as in China; or corruption and criminality—name your countries—and you unleash levels of economic, social, and environmental predation that can put sharks to shame.

The experience has been far from pleasant at times—and sometimes decidedly risky. *Tickling Sharks* is the story of how this began for me, what life is like inside the maws of some of the world's biggest corporate predators, and what I learned along the way as we tried to work out how to speak tomorrow's truth to today's power.

Cue the *Jaws* soundtrack.

Once heard, it's virtually impossible to get the music from Spielberg's film out of your head—the ominous, two-note score that accompanied a series of full-blooded shark attacks projected into darkened cinemas worldwide and later into our homes. It proved to be the ultimate earworm. One unintended consequence: a testosterone rush among shark catchers along the United States' Eastern Seaboard, with thousands joining a frenzied hunt for the living incarnations of Spielberg's mechanical models.[2]

In the years following the film's release, the number of large sharks off the East Coast plummeted by around fifty percent—a cameo of the wider story in which life on Earth has found itself sucked into and shredded by the jaws of capitalism. During my fifty-year working life, the diversity of life on Earth has fallen by some seventy percent. Scientists warn that we are now living through—and causing—the planet's sixth great extinction event.

Appalled, Spielberg apologized for his role in all of this, as did Peter Benchley, who wrote the novel on which the film was based. Indeed, in an ironic twist, Benchley later became a leading shark conservationist.

That said, even before the movie surfaced, few people in their right minds would have wanted to get into the water with big sharks, let alone great whites. *Galeophobia*, or fear of sharks, existed long before Captain Quint and his ramshackle shark-fishing boat, the *Orca*, hove into view.

There have been exceptions to this rule, of course, including someone I very much wish I had met in her heyday but who sadly died in 2015. She was Eugenie Clark, "the Shark Lady." The only child of Japanese descent in her New York school before World War II, she spent a great deal of time in the New York Aquarium, later becoming both an oceanographer and ichthyologist (shark scientist), fighting for the conservation of these extraordinary cartilaginous fishes.

Clark also inspired Sylvia Earle, the marine biologist and explorer who later spoke in terms of "hope spots." These are areas critical to the health of the oceans for a variety of reasons, whether that be "an abundance or diversity of species, a unique habitat or ecosystem, or significant cultural or economic value to a community."[3] Among the hope spots she spotlighted were some of the submarine seamounts now targeted by mining companies in a feeding frenzy triggered by the growing global hunger for precious metals that will be make-or-break for tomorrow's—hopefully greener—economy.

Anyone who has seen underwater film footage of such seamounts will recall their huge concentrations of marine predators, among them goblin, hammerhead, and sixgill sharks. Hammerheads are by no means unusual in using these extraordinary features in the submarine landscape as navigational and refreshment points along what biologists now see as marine superhighways. We disturb such dynamics at our peril.

Stand back from the water's edge, though, and the diversity of sharks around the world is still striking, involving perhaps 250 species—ranging from tiny, 30-centimeter-long pygmy sharks to giant whale sharks, the largest of which can reach nearly 20 meters. All are part of a family of cartilaginous fish that has been evolving for more than four hundred million years. And all underscore the diversity of life that our species and civilization have so poorly served.

Happily, galeophobia is not something I suffer from, although in truth I have not encountered a shark outside an aquarium, except in wildlife documentaries or horror films. Perhaps that's why, when people ask me what I do, I sometimes reply that I tickle sharks for a living. I have done so for decades, without yet losing a digit, let alone a limb. But I add that I have no interest in tickling the sort of predatory giants that attracted the likes of shark ladies Clark and Earle, or that have been portrayed in films like *Jaws*, *The Reef*, or *The Shallows*.

Instead, the targets of my tickling have been human sharks. Or Sharks, as I will style them from here on. These are formidable people with Shark-like tendencies, often possessed of immense power, prestige, and wealth;

people running some of the most successful, dominant, and aggressive institutions of our time; and people, many of them, who would happily skewer their colleagues' careers or chew up their competitors, spitting out indigestible bits along the way as they move on in pursuit of new prey.

Like sharks, however, human Sharks are not all cast in the same mold. Indeed, research has shown that shark species show distinct personality types, with some being quite social and others more solitary. They build social networks and hang out with favored companions, you might even say friends.[4] So anyone insisting that all sharks—or all Sharks—are the same is, to put it politely, misguided.

In engaging Sharks, clearly, we have been playing a "truth to power" game. For those who insist on goals and targets, it may be disappointing to hear that while the game's purpose was often clear, the desired outcomes weren't—beyond opening closed minds to new realities. In my mind, the stakes ran as high as the future of our planet, though other players saw things differently. Crucially, and unlike players of well-known games like chess, golf, gomoku, or poker, we had no option but to make up the rules as we went along.

Ticklish Fish

Some humans pursue dangerous livelihoods by choice, becoming miners or deep-ocean fishers, for example, or even high-rise constructors, commandos, or astronauts. But I declare from the outset that my high-risk career was not planned; rather, it evolved.

At no point did I plunge into the world of work expecting to tickle predators for a living. Nor was this something my family had done for generations, as you might expect had I wanted to be a lion tamer or tightrope walker. If I ever received career advice, I don't recall anything like this being listed as an option. If anything, the opposite was true—challenging powerful people, from head teachers to policemen, was actively discouraged, with obedience an absolute virtue.

Capitalist Jaws

If you challenged authority in school, you expected a whack; in the working world, the sack.*

At no point have I tickled Sharks for fun, although sometimes, I admit, it does have a certain amusement value. I have occasionally wound them up simply to watch their reactions—all, please understand, in the interests of research, not of sport. I detest the baiting of any animals, be they bears, lions, or sharks—and the same goes, within limits, for their human equivalents. Instead, I worked out how to tickle human predators because someone had to do it. In the process, I discovered that I had at least some talent in the area, rather as some people have discovered when trying to tickle fish like trout or catfish.

The art of tickling fish has a long and often illegal history. Practiced by boys, poachers, and out-of-work men in hard times, it requires no net, no rod, and no line. Instead, it requires local knowledge, patience, and a steady hand. The tickler introduces an upturned hand beneath a fish as it hovers in the stream, using a forefinger to tickle first the tail, then the belly, and lastly the head under the gills. If things go to plan the fish falls into a trance, at which point it can be scooped from the water, dispatched with a quick blow, and pocketed—with no other evidence of the crime.

My grandfather-in-law used to *guddle* for trout in Scotland. Meanwhile, in the United States, people in the southern states still tickle, or noodle, catfish. This can be fatal, though, because venomous snakes like the cottonmouth sometimes share the holes that catfish shelter in.

Not that tickling real-world sharks is for the fainthearted. Among those who have tickled large sharks, including great whites, is South African shark whisperer Andre Hartman. He is renowned for tickling the noses of great whites to send them into a dreamlike trance. The nasal areas of sharks

---

* The notion of speaking truth to power has long roots. Most people track the term back to a 1955 Quaker document titled *Speak Truth to Power: A Quaker Search for an Alternative to Violence*. But one of the co-authors, Bayard Rustin, said that he had adapted the phrase in the early 1940s from a saying of the Prophet Muhammad (see: https://quaker.org/legacy/sttp.html). Mahatma Gandhi, too, spoke of *satyagraha*, or the "truth-force." And tracking the concept back even further, in classical Greece the approach was known as *parrhesia*. So, there's nothing entirely new under the sun here.

are generally so rich in nerve endings that they either find the sensation pleasant or experience sensory overload. As a result, they end up behaving very much out of character—or at least out of the character we understand them to have.

One reason why many of us have such a grim view of sharks may be that they are often seen—or filmed—when there is blood in the water, often dumped there by people wanting them to put on a show, a process known as *chumming*. However triggered, feeding frenzies are not pretty to watch, and the same is true, I discovered, of human feeding frenzies.

Processes of boom and bust seem to be hardwired into our psychology, with the economic version of chumming triggered by the discovery of gold or other precious metals; great runs of fish like cod, herring, or other prey animals; or the emergence of new technologies, business models, and market valuations.

As an environmentalist from my earliest days, I found myself drawn to the bleeding edges of the economic system—areas where the Shark-like behaviors of our economies and political systems can savage the health of people and the planet. Given the scale of such challenges, you may conclude that the best way to handle human Sharks is to treat them as you might a real shark—harpooning them or, at the very least, punching them in the nose. By contrast, I have taken paths somewhat less traveled.

This has not escaped comment. I recall one conversation, back in the nineties, with Peter Melchett, then executive director of Greenpeace UK. An effective champion of such causes as youth clubs, music festivals, wildlife conservation, and the legalization of cannabis, Peter was also a thoughtful opponent of nuclear power and genetic engineering. I grew to admire and like him, but we agreed to disagree when it came to the benefits of engaging business leaders as human beings. (This even though his own father had been chairman of the British Steel Corporation, which is why Peter found himself a hereditary member of the House of Lords upon his father's death.)

He insisted that it was fine with him if I wanted to engage individual businesses but argued that the only way forward involved ever-tougher regulation, ever-tighter rules, and ferocious enforcement. My response, in the language of this book, was that this made sense when you were dealing with human Sharks, but what, I asked, if you were dealing with the human equivalents of orcas or other forms of dolphins? That is, with people who are perfectly happy to play along once you tell them what the game is.

If you pin people down to the point where they have little freedom to maneuver, as Jonathan Swift's Lilliputians did when roping down Gulliver, you risk strangling the creativity needed to achieve true transformation. We were both right, of course—yet another case of both/and. The threat of new laws can help at least some leaders open up to new realities, while business brains can also help shape new rules and incentives so that they deliver the desired results without crashing the economy.

Corporate Jester

Consider the US company 3M, based in Minnesota and perhaps best known as the maker of Post-it notes. It woke up early to the need for change; indeed, I began tracking the company back in the mid-seventies. Its Pollution Prevention Pays program launched in 1975, spurring a wave of internal innovation—and helping save or make 3M well over one billion dollars in short order.

But now it was 2005, thirty years later, and 3M's world was in flux. One of the company's biggest customers had just been whacked around the corporate head by Hurricane Katrina, a category 5 storm that tore through the United States' southeastern states, flooding New Orleans and surrounding regions.

That customer, the giant retailer Walmart, lost scores of stores overnight as the storm drove inland, finding itself unable to serve its customers. Keen to take urgent climate action in the aftermath, Walmart was now rattling its supply chains, pushing change faster and further on energy efficiency than had been the case when the main driver had been government regulation. That had been slow, predictable, and too easily gamed by lobbyists wanting to stall change.

That's how I found myself, in the summer of 2006, talking to 3M's top team at a grand lodge in Nisswa, Crow Wing County, Minnesota—population less than two thousand at the time. The community lay astride the Paul Bunyan Trail, named after an American folk hero, the superhuman lumberjack, though I never got to see the trail, or him.

After we had finished the session, a distinguished, well-coiffured woman approached. A member of 3M's top team, she began to quiz me. Why, she asked, did I use humor in such situations? Slightly taken aback, I said it had evolved naturally, in the doing, without my giving it very much thought. I never told jokes, partly because I could never remember them—I instead did what court jesters once did, responding in the moment, on the fly.

I said nothing about tickling sharks, but she was mulling her own theory. She had trained as a psychologist, she explained, and it had struck her while listening to me that even if I pursued a high-risk strategy, the approach worked well for a couple of reasons.

First, she noted, senior people saw my willingness to be playful with my own agenda as a sign that I wasn't a total missionary, hell-bent on saving the souls of poor corporate sinners. That helped them relax. But second, the use of situational humor, playing off what these leaders said as they said it, took top team brains in a very different direction.

No one from the outside world would normally tease people at this level in the company, she said. And that potentially triggered another thought train in these powerful brains: if he has the confidence to treat us like this, the army behind him must be *huge*.

To be clear, I have always been careful to point out that I represent no one but myself and my organization, plus my reading of the trends underlying what other changemakers were thinking. But don't take it from me, I would urge; talk to them. Let me introduce you.

In some ways, this approach shares elements of what jesters used to do to earn their crust. They tended to be honest, sometimes overly so, which distinguished them from most other people who would show up at court. The jester's allegiance was to the king, the emperor, the big cheese. My own allegiance, I would explain, extended well beyond the confines of the room and the ongoing discussion; instead, I was trying to channel the interests of a wider stakeholder universe, and of the future. At one point, I even attracted the tag "ambassador from the future."

Hammerhead in Cashmere

Another striking example of how this approach could play out in practice involved Nestlé, specifically its then-CEO, Peter Brabeck-Letmathe. When you saw him being chauffeured around Davos during World Economic Forum summits or riding ski lifts to elite gatherings, he was an imposing, even forbidding figure. Tall, muscular, majestic, and in winter draped in cashmere from neck to ankle. Here's how the *Guardian* described meeting the man in 2006, in a profile titled, "Smooth Defender of a Tainted Brand":

> Politely pouring a cup of tea into a bone china cup in his sumptuous Claridges suite, Peter Brabeck-Letmathe is an unlikely bogeyman. Yet ask many food campaigners to name their least favourite corporate executive and the silver-haired Austrian at the head of the world's largest food company, Nestlé, would come high on many lists. Ever since the baby milk scandal in Africa first prompted a boycott of its products 30 years ago, the producer of Kit-Kat, Nescafé and Perrier has been the byword for corporate arrogance and even malice.[5]

I went head-to-head with Peter several times. First came a Davos breakfast for some one hundred World Economic Forum delegates, hosted by the Indian IT company Infosys. He was the main speaker, with a follow-on discussion chaired by BBC news anchor John Humphrys, himself a challenging interviewer. I posed the first question, couched in friendly terms but with a clear, blunt challenge at its core. Peter responded remarkably well, but apparently, behind the scenes, the Infosys team frantically instructed Humphrys through his earpiece to shut the discussion down. Their reasoning, I heard later, was that if this was the first question, who knew what might come next?

The next time I met Peter was several months later at the London Business School, where we were part of a three-person panel at an event attracting some two hundred people. I was asked to speak first, then Peter followed—and partway through his remarks he said something factually incorrect. I wondered how to react: Should I delay saying anything to the end, at the risk of everyone forgetting what he had said?

Instead, I waded in, touching him on the elbow and saying, so that the room could hear, that he was wrong. He turned, inviting me to explain. I did, and he gracefully accepted the correction, then resumed his talk.

Later, as the session wound down, one of his Nestlé colleagues raced up to me, protesting that "Mr. Brabeck" did not like being treated like that. I shrugged, replying that Peter's response had been well judged; indeed, had probably won over some people in the room. I soon forgot about the exchange, perhaps concluding that the Nestlé CEO was little more than a sophisticated hammerhead in an exquisite cashmere coat.

But then, some months later, Peter called me out of the blue, inviting me to join a new advisory board Nestlé was forming.

Ah, I said, pretty much verbatim, this is what establishments do, isn't it? If they can't kill, lock up, or otherwise silence their opponents, they pull them in close to their corporate chests—and attempt to suffocate them. Co-option, I stressed, was not an option. But, out of curiosity, I asked who else had agreed to join—and was told that their number already included several strategy gurus, among them Michael Porter, C. K. Prahalad, and Jeffrey Sachs. Quite the pantheon.

So, after asking for time to consider, I took the plunge, concluding that I could learn a lot—and would always have the option of resigning. In the end, I would serve nine years on Nestlé's Creating Shared Value Council. Most sessions were chaired by Peter and attended by other senior Nestlé people, including the company's next CEO, Paul Bulcke, as Peter took over the chairman's role. Those involved later told me that my voice was routinely the most provocative, though my style was to ask questions rather than make assertions.

Over the years, the sessions took us to such places as Brazil, Colombia, India, Indonesia, and in my last trip with Nestlé, the Ivory Coast. During the Colombian event, held in Cartagena, Michael Porter turned to me and said, "You ask great questions!"[6] This was something of a surprise, given that he and I had fought an extended battle through a series of council meetings over whether the concept of shared value (pioneered by Nestlé and championed by Porter and his colleague Mark Kramer) trumped (as he argued it did) that of sustainability—with my arguing the reverse. Finally, Nestlé decided to focus on "shared value *and* sustainability."

It struck me as a lot of fuss to add two words, "and sustainability," but language shapes thought—and thought can shape action.

Stockholm Syndrome

With any Shark-tickling, there is a real and growing risk of falling victim to so-called Stockholm syndrome, where those taken hostage fall under the thrall of their captors, developing emotional bonds when in forced proximity. Aside from the fact that I have always had a fiercely independent streak, I have also sought to counter that threat by being open about any businesses we are working with—and about what is working and what is not, at least so far. All of which might suggest that the theme—and title—of this book, my twenty-first, was obvious to me from the outset.

Not remotely. Indeed, at times, the process reminded me of a striking, grisly feature of shark biology. Something grotesque often happens inside the wombs of a pregnant shark (an interesting side note is that female sharks have two uteruses). This also happened in megalodons, the gigantic shark ancestors that terrorized ancient oceans.[7] Over time, scientists realized that the shark embryos they were studying were too big to have grown simply by feeding on the nutrients in their egg sacs. They concluded that, instead, the babies' growth was—is—fueled by their cannibalism of unhatched siblings.

Embryos that are early to hatch eat the surrounding eggs, and in some cases, as with the sand tiger shark, they devour other embryos too. Nor is this grisly survival technique unusual: we know that great white, mako, and thresher sharks use the same cannibal strategy.

In very much the same way, earlier titles for this book were overtaken by later ones, a repeat of what happened when I was writing books like *Cannibals with Forks* and *The Power of Unreasonable People*. So, titles like *Surfing the Future*, *An Accidental Capitalist*, and *Running Up the Down Escalator* came and went. Then an idea that had been lurking in the depths as a section title surfaced and cannibalized the others—with several earlier titles digested and excreted as section titles.

As the book's title settled into its final form, *Tickling Sharks*, my purpose remained more or less the same. The basic idea has been to produce a candid memoir of the first fifty years I have spent in driving the environmental and sustainability agendas into business, all in the context of a series of huge societal pressure waves that have swept around the world.

The book is topped and tailed by a foreword and afterword written by two people whose judgment I value enormously: Hannah Jones, CEO of the Earthshot Prize, whom I first met when we worked together at Nike; and Sir Tim Smit, cofounder and executive vice chair at the Eden Project, a key anchor point in the rapidly developing regenerative economy. A second foreword, contributed by my colleague and good friend Louise Kjellerup Roper, sets all of this in the context of the evolution of our small London-based system change agency, Volans.

Along the way, it became obvious that I needed to expand the spotlight well beyond sharks, human or otherwise. It struck me that many of the business leaders and other senior figures I had engaged with over the decades were not Sharks, even if they sometimes demonstrated Shark-like mindsets, priorities, and behaviors. Most of them were highly successful competitors, of course, to the point where some of their less successful rivals probably saw them as merciless predators. But as the change agenda penetrated deeper into the public consciousness, and then into boardroom priorities, the best of these people had become at least curious about what we were doing and— in a growing number of cases—increasingly supportive.

Predatory Quartet

To keep track of who my colleagues and I were trying to convert, the businesses we were aiming to transform, and any progress we were achieving along the way, some form of compass was needed. So, I resurrected a framework that I had created a couple of decades earlier to map the mindsets of activists and campaigning groups.

It spotlights four types of marine animal—each symbolizing a different type of human and organizational behavior—and it seemed to work well in the world of Shark-tickling, too. This predatory quartet is categorized in terms of the risks each type poses to human beings from low to high, alongside their potential, again low or high, to serve as partners in driving longer-term sustainability.*

	Low potential	**High potential**
Low risk	*(seal)*	*(dolphin)*
High risk	*(shark)*	*(orca)*

Silvio Rebêlo for Volans, 2024

---

* The damage that we cause to such species is hugely greater than any risk they pose to us. It has been estimated that some one hundred million sharks are killed every year, or around three sharks every second. Many die during the horrific process of shark finning. By comparison, the International Shark Attack File recorded just fifty-seven unprovoked and thirty-two provoked shark bites on humans in 2022. Just five deaths were reported, in line with annual averages.

No surprise, then, to find that **Sharks** rank highest in terms of risk, but very low when it comes to partnership potential. They are monomaniacal, reflexive, driven by immediate environmental signals suggesting that other animals are in distress, play zero-sum games, and succumb to feeding frenzies. Leaders and institutions showing Shark-like behaviors must be handled with extreme caution. They dominated the early years of the sustainability transition—and many are still in reasonably good health.

Among those showing Shark-like behaviors have been the fossil fuel industries, thought to have invested at least $9.77 billion into climate denial between 2003 and 2018 alone.[8] A small price to pay, they concluded, for an implicit license to wreck the planet—imposing costs worth trillions of dollars on others, including future generations.

Even the nicest people can change when given power. Recent research suggests that power makes people less likely to take advice, even from experts.[9] They struggle to see the world through other people's eyes. They are less likely to say "I don't know," even if they sense that doing so would signal honesty and inclusivity. Intriguingly, too, powerful people are more likely to see themselves as taller than they are and to rate their own stories as more inspiring than those told by others.

Human—and organizational—nature being what it is, there will always be Sharks. Intriguingly, there is even now a novel, *Shark Heart*, tracking the Kafkaesque transformation of a man from Texas into a great white shark.[10] He suffers from a genetic mutation for which there is no cure. Our challenge, in contrast, is to transform Shark-like leaders into something more human.

Tickling sharks in the wild is at the very edge of the possible. Indeed, it's hard to think of anyone who has managed to train these creatures to do anything particularly useful for us humans. That said, science is waking up to the fact that sharks play a crucial role in ensuring the health of the world's oceans—and, if you think of it in that light, perhaps we might accept that their human equivalents provide much of the motivating force behind the success of capitalist economies.

Orcas, a.k.a. killer whales, are a different matter. With shame, I recall watching some performing a long time ago at Florida's SeaWorld—even then knowing it was outrageous to keep such intelligent animals in captivity. The psychological impact of their imprisonment was underscored in the tragic case of Tilikum, an orca first caught off Iceland—and then thought to have suffered repeated trauma as he was abused by higher ranking but also captive female orcas.[11] He is said to have suffered from psychotic rages during his thirty years in confinement and ended up killing two of his trainers, at different times, alongside a SeaWorld visitor who somehow got into his tank.

Orcas are mammals, not fish. In fact, they are an aggressive form of dolphin: highly intelligent, curious, adaptive, and excellent team players, at least when playing with their own kind; they do attack other sea life. But beware: leaders dubbed Orcas in the human world can eat all our other players, be they Dolphins, Sea Lions, or Sharks. Leaders showing Orca-like behaviors can achieve real progress, if it suits them—and with a close eye on the menu. They can be tickled, but only with empathy and great care.

Despite claims that orcas have attacked surfers, mistaking them for seals or other prey animals, the evidence is inconclusive. So, consider orcas symbols of a more thoughtful approach to interspecies engagement. Intensely social, they represent the more thoughtful approaches adopted by leading businesses, even if they are still some way from full-throated collaboration with all key stakeholders.

Next, expanding the spotlight to the lower risk cell in the top line of the compass, we have **Sea Lions**—moderately intelligent and perfectly sociable but not given to behaviors that would make them particularly useful to us. Unlike the other three predators, sea lions move between land and sea, so are not at great risk of stranding, as sharks, orcas, and dolphins are. They are also eminently trainable and happy to perform in return for the odd bucket of fish. They are beautiful to watch, but—at least in the wild—no sooner in view than gone.

Looking back, I can think of many CEOs and other business leaders I have encountered who slot in well here. These are people largely driven by reputational concerns, by how they and their organizations are likely to be seen by the wider world and by a desire to boost the trust and loyalty of a narrowly defined set of stakeholders, while—behind the scenes—changing very little.

Sea Lion leaders can be useful partners at the lower ends of ambition but tend to be unreliable when things get more challenging. Such problems can be aggravated when, as such people and organizations often do, they operate behind smoke screens of public relations people and media consultancies. The lines of communication can become dangerously overextended, risking new forms of the old Chinese whispers game—or, as Americans know it, the telephone game.

Before I learned how to avoid such dynamics, they caused us grief a couple of times. In one case, where we were working with the food giant Heinz, of "57 Varieties" fame, we ended up in a cartoon showing two shoppers gossiping, featured on the front page of the *Times*. Heinz had pulled out of a big green consumer initiative we were planning. The cartoon's caption read, "I bet they gave 57 excuses!"

By contrast, the human and organizational equivalents of **Dolphins** swim in an expanding range of sweet spots, both lower risk and higher potential. In nature, dolphins are deeply intelligent, curious, playful, collaborative, and non-zero-sum team players—willing to accept lose-win outcomes for longer-term gain. They are interested in other species, and not just as lunch. The number of leaders showing Dolphin-like behaviors is growing, and they are likely to be our best partners for long-term change initiatives.

When I started out, the business world was full of Sharks and, to a limited degree, Orcas. Over time, though, the Orcas began to grow in number, as did the number of leaders with Sea Lion tendencies. You will have encountered Sea Lions in abundance if you have attended award ceremonies in areas like wildlife conservation, corporate citizenship, or social responsibility.

Things can go horribly wrong when corporations play at being Dolphins but continue to have pronounced Shark-like tendencies. A case in point was the Volkswagen "Dieselgate" scandal.

I had served for many years on an advisory board for the Dow Jones Sustainability Indices (DJSI), a leading corporate ranking scheme that began life in Switzerland. This was the Dow Jones empire's first venture into sustainability, and we were excited to see it gaining real traction with business—which saw the DJSI platform as a major mainstreaming of the change agenda. But in 2015, well after I had left the advisory board, the DJSI rankings celebrated Volkswagen as the world's leading auto company in terms of sustainability.

A few weeks later, Dieselgate broke, with the company discovered to have criminally distorted the monitoring of emissions produced by cars undergoing testing. The loss of reputation was immense, the ensuing fines enormous. It was a striking example of greenwashing by a company that was old enough to know better.

The Dolphin will be most people's favorite of the quartet. Although related to killer whales, species like the bottlenose dolphin are hugely popular. The smiley shape of their jawlines doesn't hurt, either.

Among the earliest business leaders with Dolphin characteristics that I worked alongside was Anita Roddick, cofounder of The Body Shop International, who is discussed in the book. Then, while I was drafting this introduction, I flew to Munich to do a session with the board of a sustainability-focused private equity firm, EQT. The board members were joined by a considerable number of partners and sustainability staff, and the resulting conversations struck me as being very much like swimming among a superpod of Dolphins.

Indeed, when people ask how I have kept going over the years, one part of the answer must be that wonderful sense of swimming alongside other intelligent, motivated people bound in the same direction. Judging whether that is the right direction requires a compass, ideally more sophisticated than the one I have sketched here.

Of course, any such compass risks missing out on all sorts of behaviors that could help shape successful business and market strategies. Where, for example, are the corporate examples of jellyfish, octopi, tuna, and those consummate if hideous and slime-wreathed bottom-feeders, the hagfish?

Still, our four lenses—Shark, Orca, Sea Lion, and Dolphin—have helped me navigate over the years and provide potentially useful labels for the mindsets and behaviors of leaders in all sectors of our economies.

Step Up Or...

Like marine biologist Sylvia Earle, I have spent decades trying to identify and explore the economic versions of her hope spots, places where new business priorities, technologies, and business models are already in play or surfacing. Strikingly, though, the nature, size, and location of such hope spots have shifted every time a new wave of societal pressure has crashed through. That story comes later, in part 2 of the book.

First, though, I must try to answer several questions that have been endlessly asked of me through the years. Who—and what—am I? How did I become what I became? What factors shaped me, in terms of family background, education, or early working experiences? What went wrong along the way—and how did we cope with the ensuing fallout? What went right, and why? Who did we collaborate with—and with whom did we compete? And, by no means finally, knowing what I now know, what makes me pessimistic—and what gives me hope?

These elements of my story are told in part 1, **Spawning Grounds**. Like many baby boomers, my character and priorities were powerfully influenced by the historically unparalleled conditions in which we grew up in the wake of World War II. In the process, we provided fertile spawning grounds for new memes; new ideas about society, politics, the economy, and technology; and—perhaps the biggest single differentiator from earlier generations—new thinking about the importance of protecting our small, blue planet.

In what follows, I outline the family and educational background that helped turn me into a Shark tickler in part 1, then sketch the five main themes of my work to date in part 2. So anyone wanting to focus on the professional rather than personal aspects of this story should now skip directly to part 2.

For those staying the course, chapter 1 recalls what it was like growing up under the threat of atomic extinction, particularly with a father involved in early A-bomb and H-bomb tests; chapter 2 recalls the somewhat unusual circumstances in which I gained an education, at the schools I was sent to and the universities I chose to go to; chapter 3 explains how I found my way into the working world and specifically into the embryonic environmental industry; and then chapter 4 introduces the series of societal pressure waves that I have mapped and learned to surf since 1960.

Titled **Feeding Frenzies**, part 2 tracks that series of societal pressure waves outlined in chapter 4. Chapter 5 explores the environmental wave, which started building in the early sixties and peaked in the early seventies. Much of my work at the time involved helping this new agenda penetrate parts of the business world that it would not otherwise have reached. Chapter 6 expands the spotlight to the green wave, which peaked at the end of the eighties, this time with much stronger political overtones. Again, I helped give the emerging agenda a market focus, introducing terms like *green growth* and helping to mobilize what we dubbed the "green consumer." Chapter 7 tracks the sustainability wave, which really began to take off in the late eighties and early nineties. I had more of an impact here than on any of the earlier waves, coining terms like *triple bottom line* and the linked term *People, Planet, and Profit* (3P's). Again, they went into the language. Chapter 8 recalls the environmental, social, and governance (ESG) boom of the early twentieth century—and the linked world of impact investment. Chapter 9 then dives deep into the regeneration wave, which is only just beginning to build.

Part 3, **Schooling Dolphins**, draws together threads from earlier sections, considering some of the challenges—and opportunities—that the rising tide of awareness, concern, and outright terror will bring. As a result, it concludes that we will see more change in the next fifteen years than in the last fifty. That said, the outcomes will very much depend on us.

In what follows, I am less interested in blowing my own trumpet than with spotlighting other people who have shaped the sustainability revolution. And one person who had a huge influence on me was James

Lovelock, inventor of the Gaia hypothesis, discussed in chapter 5. In 2010, he concluded that humankind is too stupid and too venal to ward off the threat of climate catastrophe.[12] On current evidence, sadly, he seems to have been right. But if I have learned anything, it is that the sort of exponential change now exploding all around us can take us further—and faster—than most people imagine to be possible. The key question now is whether such changes drive us toward breakdown outcomes or accelerate the development and diffusion of the breakthrough solutions we now so urgently need.

In my previous book *Green Swans*, I flagged the risk of pandemics—but failed precisely to predict COVID-19, which burst on the scene soon after. So what have I missed this time? An even more infectious pandemic, perhaps engineered by bad actors? Peace in the Middle East? New waves of conflict and ethnic cleansing? A second Donald J. Trump presidential term in the US? Politicians rediscovering the centrality of public service in their work? The COP (Conference of the Parties) series of climate summits producing real step change? A quantum leap in nuclear fusion? Artificial Intelligence (AI) surprising us all by cracking some of our most pressing problems? Right-wingers suddenly waking up to the magic of pure science? The discovery of life on distant planets? Or perhaps the baby boomers (I am one), consenting to an extraordinary death tax to fund the regeneration of the planet that has been so ravaged on their watch?

Who knows? But what is now blindingly clear is that our future has been injected with the scientific, technological, economic, and political equivalents of steroids. To my mind, *Tickling Sharks* is ultimately a hopeful book, but if you have a safety belt, consider fastening it, both for yourself and those you care for.

PART 1

Spawning Grounds

Nature—and nurture—made me do it.

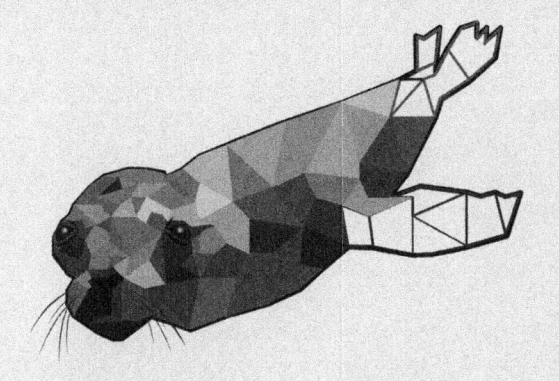

CHAPTER 1

Nuclear Families

Your parents fuck you up, lamented Philip Larkin, dubbed "England's *other* Poet Laureate" because he consistently ducked such honors. His poetry echoed the grim dreariness of much of postwar England. In "This Be The Verse," published in 1971 as I was trying to find my own feet in the world, he accepted that in most cases they didn't intend to do so, but concluded that typically parents cascaded their issues—and added some special ones, designed just for you.[1]

If Larkin intended this as advice, I ignored it, and looking into the rearview mirror now, my experience has been different. From the smoldering ashes of war something unexpected took root, spiraling toward the light. Millions of baby boomers, including me, found ourselves swarming up a set of beanstalks that simply didn't exist for most of our parents' generation.

Today, at a time when we are increasingly urged to confess our privileges and decolonize our thinking, it is clear that I was privileged to be born as part of that postwar boomer generation; to grow up on the ragged and often bleeding edges of the British Empire; to be sent to one of the most liberal public (read, private) schools in the known universe; and to become involved in a couple of the world's most powerful social movements when they were still embryonic. But it was an even greater privilege, in retrospect, to be born to the parents whose firstborn son I became.

In some brave new future, the rearing of human beings may happen in test tubes and fermenters, but for the moment, human life typically involves a womb and the subsequent embrace of a family. Mine did, and no question, my parents had the greatest early impact on me—an influence that extended over some seventy years, given that they died at either end of 2019, Tim aged ninety-eight; Pat, ninety-seven.

Whatever some people may believe, none of us chooses our parents. But if I could have done, I'm not sure I could have done better. Still, as I busily took my first breaths, I had not the slightest inkling that I had been born into a very particular nuclear family—and, as it turned out, it was nuclear in several senses.

Mildly Radioactive

Sociologically, we were nuclear in that the family unit consisted of my parents and their growing number of children. In terms of birth order, I was followed by three siblings over the next eleven years. Our sense of being a tight family unit was intensified by the fact that we were a Royal Air Force (RAF) family, constantly on the move, used to seeing temporary homes filling up with former tea chests as packing began for the next posting.

You might also say that we were nuclear, or at least mildly radioactive, because of our exposure to fallout from the growing number of open-air nuclear bomb tests. As a result, our teeth and bones were increasingly marked by elements like iodine-131, strontium-90, and cesium-137. We tend to forget that hundreds of thousands of people died as a result of the residual fallout from such tests in the United States alone.[2]

Nor were we simply passive victims of other people's tests. Our family was also professionally nuclear. My father, Tim, flew to Christmas Island (now Kiritimati in the Pacific) for four months in 1957 to patrol the exclusion zone around British bomb tests during Operation Grapple. Later, too, he was involved in civil defense preparations for safeguarding British leaders in the event of a nuclear attack, likely mounted by the Soviet Union. As a result, he probably knew more about the nation's secret bunkers than most members of government who hoped to shelter underground when, to use the charged language of the time, "the Bomb drops."

Nor, I discovered years later, did the nuclear story end there. Several miles upstream from Padworth, England, where I was born, was Aldermaston. This village achieved notoriety a decade after I arrived when the nearby Atomic Weapons Research Establishment became the target of protest marches by the Campaign for Nuclear Disarmament (CND).[3] The reason for the protesters' ire was that the site was—and still is—ground zero for the design, operation, and disposal of nuclear weapons, including warheads for Britain's Trident nuclear deterrent program.

CND had a considerable impact on popular opinion in the UK but ultimately failed to achieve its declared goal of nuclear disarmament. Still, those involved helped lay the foundations for later protest movements—including those I was more actively involved in. The disarmament issue, as CND itself would later recall, would be elbowed aside by concerns about the Vietnam War.

I went on only one anti-Vietnam march but was conspicuous as the only person in subsequent newspaper coverage who, while sporting shoulder-length hair, was also wearing a suit. Maybe I thought it would help me be taken more seriously? And, just maybe, there might have been advantages when it came to avoiding police snatch squads and truncheons?

All of which said, I have read enough about seven-year wars, thirty-year wars, and even hundred-year wars to have split emotions on nuclear weapons. Although I clearly recall the terrors of the Cuban Missile Crisis while away at school as a child, and even though today, at the time of this writing, Russia's President Vladimir Putin was rattling his nuclear arsenal over Ukraine, I still recognize that the threat of atomic warfare has helped maintain one of the longest periods of relative peace in history.

When I was younger, too, I dug into the history and science of A- and H-bomb tests and of the Hiroshima and Nagasaki bombings. Unspeakable though their impact was, it is now clear that they saved considerably more lives than they took. These included those who would have had to invade (and defend) the Japanese mainland, plus those imprisoned in Japanese prisoner-of-war camps. It emerged later that the Japanese had imminent plans to liquidate all surviving inmates in the camps.

There were echoes of this in our family memory bank. Our mother, Pat, served as a driver in the Auxiliary Territorial Service, the women's branch of the British Army during World War II. Her duties ranged from transporting pig swill to chauffeuring senior officers, among them the brilliant, eccentric Chindit special operations leader Orde Wingate.[4] One thing she regretted later was her innocence, as the war ended, when ferrying survivors of the Japanese prisoner-of-war camps from airfields and ports to reception points across Britain. She said, "You only needed to look at them to know something unspeakable had happened to them." But like so many others, she was oblivious to the details. The public had been kept in the dark—and she didn't feel able to question those keeping their own counsel in the back seat.

The one time I did get to Hiroshima, traveling on a *shinkansen*, or bullet train, I was shocked to see how the story told in the city's museum was a "poor me" one. It was as if the bomb had come out of the blue, in a different sense. No mention of what Japan had done in Manchuria, or elsewhere, to trigger such cataclysmic retribution.

That said, as I sped south to Hiroshima, I was also forcibly reminded of just how much wrenching change societies like Japan's had endured as they recovered from the war. As we flashed through the outskirts of Osaka, I fell into a kind of conversation with a white-haired man sitting opposite. He had been staring out of the window, his face blank. I spoke no Japanese, he no English. But he managed, somehow, to communicate that he had grown up in a world of rice paddies and egrets, isolated remnants of which were whizzing by. Nowadays, though, any remaining paddies were tightly hemmed in and overshadowed by factories, infrastructure, and cities.

Then, to my surprise, he began crying.

Maybe it was old age: I, too, find myself more prone to tears as I age. But equally, it may also have been a symptom of the immense pressures experienced by ordinary Japanese people as their country recovered from the war and modernized at breakneck speed.

The Shrapnel Within

Many veterans who survived the war tried desperately to forget. Or, where that failed, they stayed mum—trying not to impose their grim memories on their children. As a result, most of us boomers knew a lot less about what our parents and grandparents had gone through than we should have known.

Too often, our limited sense of war came from comics, with my favorite reading in preteen years including Frank Hampson's fabled *Eagle* comics. Their colorful Dan Dare adventures—celebrating the "Pilot of the Future"—appeared to be straight-line extrapolations of what Tim and his comrades-in-arms had gone through in the Battle of Britain and later campaigns. At times, ultimate victory must have been almost inconceivable.[5]

I don't think Tim tried to keep us in the dark, but as with many veterans, he thought it best to draw a veil over the conflict. Still, over time, I managed to winkle out some stories. One notable breakthrough came when I was sitting on a laundry chest while he enjoyed a hot bath—and was struck by the rasping noise his towel made as he dried his back.* Challenged, he showed me pieces of shrapnel, fragments of his exploded fuel tank, still buried in his body—migrating over time until they popped out through his skin. Black, oxidized fragments of a very different reality.

Much later, celebrating the fiftieth anniversary of the Battle of Britain, I pulled together everything I had learned about the incident that peppered him with red-hot shrapnel. The story began when Tim, aged nineteen and flying in the exposed top weaver position in a formation of Hurricanes from No. 1 Squadron, was bounced by three Messerschmitt Bf 109s—just one day after he had shot down another of these fighters.

I recalled how his mother, Isabel, had unwittingly watched the attack from her seaside apartment on Hayling Island, Hampshire, not knowing he was involved. Later, she responded to a telephone call and raced into a

---

* The full story can be found here: https://johnelkington.com/2015/08/a-battle-of-britain-whodunnit.

nearby hospital to be told that her only child was dead. Later, this proved to have been another pilot, in the next bed.

But the nub of the story was how Tim's flight leader, the significantly older Flight Sergeant Fred Berry—already a seasoned veteran of the earlier Battle of France, saved his life by doing something that had never been done before, nor since, as far as we know. Fred flew several flypasts, using his slipstream to nudge the parachute carrying the unconscious Tim back over West Wittering Beach. As the unconscious teenager drifted toward the beach, Home Guard volunteers on the ground added insult to injury. Tim already had several machine gun wounds in his legs before Home Guard soldiers opened fire on him; they were apparently angered by the Luftwaffe's growing habit of strafing Royal Air Force (RAF) pilots as they jumped for safety. So they mistook my dad, Tim, for a German pilot.

Ironically, the incident saved Tim's life, in several ways. After a young nurse, whose freckles lodged in his memory, cut away his trousers to inspect his wounds, he was taken to hospital. Out of harm's way for several critical weeks, and already tall, he grew two inches while confined to bed. Meanwhile, as the Battle of Britain reached its blistering peak, his squadron was decimated.* One sad indication of the scale of those losses was the saga of how Tim later tried to find Fred Berry to thank him for saving his life, only to find that he had been killed just days later. Despite further checks when the war ended, Fred seemed to have disappeared without a trace.

Then, decades later, when the wrecked fuselage of Tim's Hurricane was found deep underground by an archaeological team, I blogged about the discovery. Next, the BBC—having seen the blog—got in touch when making a documentary that covered No. 1 Squadron's (and Fred's) time in France. That ultimately allowed me to help bring Tim together with Fred's daughter and granddaughter. It turned out that they had known nothing

---

* When I used the term *decimated* in a *Guardian* article in 1990, Tim protested that the squadron hadn't been wiped out. I explained that the term was appropriate. In Roman times, a force that was decimated lost one in ten of its men—and No. 1 Squadron had lost a higher proportion of its pilots.

about Fred because his widow had so resented his death that she had never mentioned him again.

When Tim himself died, in February 2019, he received a full-page obituary in the *Times*, substantially built around the story that I had helped rescue. In Copenhagen as the news broke, I responded to several telephoned media requests for background even as my flight to London was lining up for takeoff. One of those newspapers reported my comment that Tim had stressed that, while he was one of The Few, "they in turn were supported by The Many. The ground crew, radar plotters, the merchantmen and tanker crews running the gauntlet of the U-boat wolf-packs. And, critically, the ordinary Britons who endured the Blitz."[6]

These days, the crushed, corroded altimeter from Tim's shattered Hurricane enjoys pride of place in the small study where I have written most of my books. It serves as a mute, mangled reminder of a moment when the fate of his future family tree winked in and out of existence, like a scene from 1985's sci-fi blockbuster *Back to the Future*.

A reminder, too, of the luck that I seem to have inherited from my father. He survived being shot down in the Battle of Britain as the battle reached its deadly peak; he trained to fly rocket-powered fighters off convoy ships as part of a program during which many pilots died; he was sent on convoys to and from Russia, escaping unscathed both ways; he was posted to Asia ahead of D-Day, during which thirty-eight of forty pilots in his squadron were lost; and then, when posted to India with another pilot, he survived while his friend was shot down and beheaded by the Japanese. By no means finally, he was sent on what he was told would be a suicide mission scouting for Operation Zipper, the invasion of Burma (now Myanmar); but the atomic bombs were dropped on Hiroshima and Nagasaki as he was en route—and the war ended.

Tim was probably in his late eighties when, as the memories flooded back, he grabbed a piece of mount board used in his art framing business and scribbled down for me some of the events where he believed that Lady Luck had intervened on his behalf—sometimes to an extraordinary degree.[7] Indeed, the *Daily Express* obituary would later speak of his "charmed life."

Still, after the war, he would insist that his luckiest break happened in 1946, after he was repatriated from India. Offered five options, he chose to command the RAF base at Turnhouse, on the fringes of Edinburgh—and now subsumed into the city's main airport. Standing rather grandly at the edge of the airfield, but inconveniently close for pilots trying to take off and land, was Castle Gogar. Built in 1625, it was home for more than two hundred years to the Steel-Maitland family, who once owned the land the aerodrome now stood on.

As commander of the base, Tim duly visited Gogar to pay his respects to the laird, Sir James Steel-Maitland. "Uncle Jimmy," as I came to know this most exotic of godfathers, was married to one of three sisters, one of whom—Marjorie—later became my maternal grandmother. Of the other two, Brenda was married to Jimmy for many years before handing him over—don't ask me how—to her sister Dorothy. Accustomed to receiving letters at prep school from Uncle Jimmy and (Great) Aunt Brenda, I was intrigued when the signature line changed to "Uncle Jimmy and (Great) Aunt Dorothy."

At one point, the kilt-wearing Jimmy collected wild animals, particularly for the Edinburgh and London zoos. In this spirit, his first gift to me was an engraved silver christening tankard sheathed in a section of elephant tusk. Later, he would give me something even more grotesque, at least when viewed through today's eyes. This was a pair of hairbrushes whose backs were fashioned from elephant ivory, their bristles made from whale baleen. I still have both the tankard and the brushes—and the sense of guilt has never quite left me.

Pagan or Pantheist?

On the day Tim arrived to meet Uncle Jimmy, who emerged blinking from a coal bunker clad only in sooty underwear (his kilt being elsewhere, to keep it clean), he also met Pat Adamson, my mother-to-be. She was visiting her aunts. With her dark-haired beauty and Tim's good looks, it now seems somehow predestined. In any event, they married in 1948 and, with the inevitable ups and downs, remained so until they died.

I owe an immense debt of gratitude to my mother, Pat, too. If I inherited some of my taste for adventure and stamina from Tim, he was no reader—and no writer, either. By contrast, she was very much a writer, like her younger brother, Paul, though while he wrote books (notably his autobiographies, *None the Wiser*[8] and *Still None the Wiser*[9]), she wrote long letters. First and foremost, my mother was a born storyteller.

I absorbed a great deal from that side of her. She was loving, forceful when necessary but mainly calm—though with four children, constant moves, and challenging postings, she clearly had much to contend with. Nor was she shy of disciplining us. One linked memory suggests a more violent childhood than was the case. I no longer remember what I had done to offend, but Pat was beating my rear end with a Mason Pearson hairbrush. Its handle snapped in her hand. As one did in those days, she wrote to the company, protesting that she had always beaten her children with Mason Pearson hairbrushes—and complaining that this was the first time one had broken in the act. They replaced the brush without comment.

Different times.

Unsurprisingly, given his service background, Tim was the greater disciplinarian, but things changed when he flew off to the Pacific on March 6, 1957, to join Operation Grapple. Pat was left to fend for herself—and us—for four months. As we lived on one of an isolated pair of farms near Limavady, Northern Ireland, where there was no phone and the Irish Republican Army (IRA) posed a constant low-level threat, Tim organized for a hand-cranked landline to be installed days before he left.

On the first night after he departed, ominously, the line went dead. Pat, on her own with three children, later recalled a sleepless night. In the morning, when the police came, they discovered a flock of sheep had entered a culvert through which the cable had been laid and had gnawed through it.

One unexpected benefit of our father being elsewhere was that I was kept on a looser rein. Indeed, Pat would encourage me to go and have a late tea with a farm laborer and his family, who lived in a cottage not far away. On one particularly damp evening, when darkness had fallen without our noticing, I insisted that I could find my way home alone. There was no moonlight, and I had to walk some way across fields featuring at least one disused flax retting pond.[10] I knew the lay of the land but certainly didn't expect what happened next.

Suddenly, all around my ankles, there was wriggling. After a moment's shock, in complete darkness, I lowered my hands until whatever surrounded me was writhing through my fingers. It took a moment to realize that I was standing amid a vast elastic sheet of elvers, or baby eels, migrating between water bodies.

Tens of thousands of them.

But beware: our memories can betray us. You can never really know what is a real memory and what has been re-created or remolded based on what we learned later. Scientists say that our memories are regenerated—and thus potentially mutated—each time we recall them. I long knew that this encounter happened, but after some years, I began to doubt details of the memory. Then, decades later, among books I was asked to review for *New Scientist* magazine, there was one written by a poacher who had haunted the Somerset Levels in the southwest of England. Halfway through the book, he described going out on a damp, dark, moonless night and experiencing the exact same phenomenon I had. Almost the same story, except that mine predated his by perhaps twenty years.

Less happily, I got a strong whiff of the communal tensions in Northern Ireland when Mrs. Mullen, the Irish woman who helped my mother in the house, took me down the main street of Limavady one day. She kindly pointed out the Catholics for me. "She's a Catholic," she hissed, "and he's a Catholic—and you can smell them at half a mile!" This from a woman, as Pat later pointed out, who lived in a single-room cottage with a dirt floor, her pig sleeping under her bed.

As for bleeding edges, I have never been able to shake off the memory of an autopsy on an ailing cow that had been fed buckets of molasses, turning her entrails black. She was dead, upended on her back in the muddy farmyard next door. Her legs projected into the air, her belly massively distended. The vet sliced her open in front of our horrified, fascinated eyes. The blood and molasses mingled together, at which point the vet turned to me and my brother Gray and, brandishing the bloody blade, growled, "Now, you're next!"

We fled, the deathly smell seeming to linger on our clothes for days.

Or there was the time Gray and I were playing cowboys and Indians around a huge fire of old tractor tires on that same farm. A roiling cloud of black rubbery smoke staggered up into the sky. Next, a whooping Gray, aged perhaps five, tripped over a coiling, white-hot wire from one of the giant tires—and, somehow, was dragged into the blaze. The wire ate deep into his flesh, the melted rubber flowing into the wound, leaving him with the most spectacular spiraling black scars.

It took several men to carry him home.

Still, given that I never actually saw the eels that rocked my life on its axle, because that happened in total darkness, the image that lives on most powerfully from that time is that of the threshing machine making its annual visit to the farm across the way. Crops stacked in stooks (or, in American English, shocks) in the fields were brought in by trailer and formed into ricks. The thresher thundered like a mechanical brontosaurus, its belts whizzing, its entrails wheezing, and its looming chimney vomiting clouds of coal smoke, sparkling with embers. A Vesuvius on wheels.

All about us, farmhands hurled great pitchforks of the crop into the engine's clattering maw. Unspeakably exciting. The dramatic peak, however, came when the ricks began to run out, their base of stacked logs now plain to see—rocking edgily as the men trod on them to get at the last of the crop. At this point farm dogs seemed to congregate out of the blue, forming an expectant ring. As terrified rats flew out in a furry Catherine wheel, the dogs snapped their necks left, right, and center. When you were my height, at the level of the action, this was a scene plucked from a Hieronymus Bosch painting: medieval, primal, bloody.

Given all of this, and the fact that the farmworkers took me to a slaughterhouse when I was six, and that at least one of the people we knew—Marcus McCausland—would later be shot dead by the Official IRA, it may seem odd that I have maintained such a deep affection for this part of the world. But I have.

Looking back, at least in terms of anthropologist Joseph Campbell's version of the hero's journey, those migrating eels provided the first part of my "call to action." And the second installment came the very next morning, when I had an equally shocking encounter with the Mother Superior who ran our Catholic convent school. Gray and I were two of a handful of notional Protestants in the school. So already suspect, I imagine.

Struck by my encounter with the eels the previous day and wondering what happened to such animals when they died, I innocently asked an obvious question in this heaven factory: "Mother Superior, do animals go to heaven?" Innocent enough for me, perhaps, but heresy to her. She erupted. I only know the words she used because, when I got home, I asked Pat what they meant. As best as I could remember them, Mother Superior's words had been, "You're either a pagan or a pantheist—and I don't know which is worse!"

I subsequently discovered that being called a pagan, someone who worshipped multiple gods, generally with bloody sacrifice thrown in for good measure, was akin to being called an infidel or heretic. Pantheism, which involves worshipping nature and life, would prove to be closer to the mark, though I didn't know it then.

Most of this went way over my head, unsurprisingly, but I have always had a vivid visual imagination—and my main memory of that heated exchange with God's closest representative on Earth is that, at least in my mind's eye, clawed fingers ripped through a set of red velvet curtains, shredding them. Any religious faith I might have had evaporated in that instant.

Into that vacuum, I have come to see, environmentalism, sustainability, and the like would later flow. Even so, the Northern Ireland experience would live on powerfully for me. Perhaps that was why I long thought that my earliest memory dated back to our time in Ireland.

Mini Amazon

Most of us have been asked to recall our first memory. I used to refer to something I thought I had experienced near our Limavady home in Northern Ireland. I recalled a semi-paradisiacal environment, like a working model of the Amazon, with water braiding everywhere, dragonflies and kingfishers darting back and forth. So, imagine my shock when, on June 23, 2018, my sixty-ninth birthday, my wife, Elaine, and I walked into that very world—but in England.[11]

I literally found myself walking through that memory all around Mill Cottage, where I was born. We found ourselves beside a wide river flowing over a waterfall, alongside several smaller tributaries, and a speeding mill race. This, clearly, was the source of my earliest memory. But I had been told by my parents that we had left the area—Padworth—when I was just eighteen months old. I had never been back, until that day. Memories can be powerful indeed.

Two other Padworth tales Pat later told me featured kingfishers and, separately, blue underpants. In the first of these, she recalled that I would sit enthralled while watching a family of kingfishers perched on a branch outside our kitchen window, overlooking the mill stream at the back of Mill Cottage. In the second memory, Pat recalled looking out of a window while shaking a duster to see with horror that I, aged around twelve months, had overturned my pram. Wearing blue toweling pants over my nappy, I was headed energetically into the reeds—and, beyond them, the churning mill race.

Curiosity seems to have been hardwired in me, with everything seemingly linked. A striking example of the sort of connection that my brain surfaces constantly came to mind when we arrived at the site of Custer's Last Stand in Montana, with our daughters not yet in their teens. I already knew that one of the Oglala Sioux warriors who fought in the Battle of the Little Bighorn, alongside Sitting Bull and Crazy Horse, had been called Long Wolf. I had discovered that fact when I went to Hammersmith Registry Office in the summer of 1977 to register the birth of Gaia, our first-born daughter.

I duly reported that her third name was Onawa, meaning, in the language of the Choctaw, "bright-eyed, alert maiden, the one who saves the tribe." The registrar's eyes lit up as he noted that this was only the second Native American name he knew of in the Hammersmith register of births, marriages, and deaths.

The first one, in 1892, had been Long Wolf.

After the Plains nations were defeated, it turned out, Long Wolf (by then known as Lame Warrior) joined Sitting Bull in William "Buffalo Bill" Cody's itinerant Wild West Show. Visiting London while performing with the show, he contracted pleurisy and died in Hammersmith. Because his wife was worried, with good reason, that his body might be dumped overboard if he were shipped home, he was buried in Brompton Cemetery—his grave marked by a carved wolf. I was profoundly moved years later when his story was rediscovered, his descendants contacted, and his body repatriated in 1996 to the Pine Ridge Indian Reservation in South Dakota.[12]

Time and again, everywhere I have looked, everywhere I have gone, there have been these twinklings of unseen connections, deeper realities.

Sweeping Decks

After Ireland, in November 1957, Tim was posted to Cyprus. By then I was beginning to pay real attention to the wider world, which proved to be full of interesting hazards. Again, memories are fallible, but I distinctly recall seeing the orange flash of an exploding bomb on the ceiling of our hotel bedroom a week or so after our arrival in the capital city, Nicosia.

Tim was involved in intelligence operations designed to disrupt the shipment of banned weapons into Cyprus, mainly for the EOKA movement. That acronym stood for Ethniki Organosis Kyprion Agoniston, or the National Organization of Cypriot Fighters. They were fighting for an end to British rule in Cyprus, plus eventual union with Greece. As a child, there was no way I could have forecast the Turkish invasion of 1974. But some small clues were already there—for instance, when our

Turkish nanny, Aisha, was routinely stoned (in the traditional sense) by Greek Cypriots as she cycled to our home.

Tim routinely carried a Browning automatic in a shoulder holster, and even Pat was armed—legally or not—with a tiny pistol carried in her purse. That said, the bullets were so tiny that I doubt they would have had more than a momentary deterrent effect.*

Guns were at a premium during the Cyprus emergency. We got a visceral sense of that fact while we were playing with a friend—Johnny Sanders, the son of the American consul. A group of local youths seized his somewhat realistic toy pistols and ran off with them. The result: our collective interrogation, followed by a police dragnet. Apparently, toy weapons could be used in holdups or, on occasion, adapted to fire real bullets. I have no idea whether the toy guns were recovered, though I doubt it.

Whatever the rights and wrongs, we were regularly exposed to different facets of Britain's armed presence on the island. Aged nine, I spent several days with Gray, aged seven, no parents in tow, on a minesweeper circumnavigating the island. Our job, we were told, was not to fall overboard and to keep our heads down in the event of a firefight. This was HMS *Fiskerton*—and at one stage, we were tasked with sweeping down the decks with brooms and buckets of water. Somehow, we managed to sluice the water through a skylight, into the captain's cabin. Happily, the British navy no longer practiced keelhauling.[13]

Or there was the time when a cutter ferried us from a beach out to the immense aircraft carrier HMS *Eagle*. I vividly remember standing on the carrier's flight deck and being struck by the hues of the surrounding

---

* When Pat's brother, Paul Adamson, reviewed this section of the book, he commented: "Being something of an antique arms collector, I also have a passing interest in more modern curiosities. [Pat's gun] was one of the very smallest automatic pistols ever made, a 4.25 mm Kolibri Liliput, dating from the 1920s, manufactured in Germany. It was barely capable of inflicting a trivial flesh wound, which if untreated might have led to mild blood poisoning. By the time your father sold it, it was no longer even considered a 'firearm' in the UK—appropriately, perhaps, as Kolibri (translating as *hummingbird*) were better known as makers of cigarette lighters."

Mediterranean: deep blue, veined with lighter blues and greens, all fading to the deepest indigo. My favorite color, it would later transpire.

For the first and last time, we were packed off to an RAF school outside Nicosia. Here, one memory is of our school bus being rammed by a truck that was being towed. We promptly crashed off the road, across a ditch, through a wall, and into a massive stack of empty soda bottles. I have no idea whether this was a planned attack, but it certainly gave us something to talk about.

Another time, as the family drove back into the city, I heard an extraordinary clattering as we passed the main prison. When I asked Tim what was going on, he said it was the prisoners rattling their metal plates against the bars of their cells—in protest against the impending execution of some of their comrades. I dreamed of hangings for years afterward, my head being slipped into the noose.

But there were wonderful times, too. Among our friends in Nicosia were the March family, more Americans. Years later, I discovered that the father, also Pat, spoke Russian, wrote books on the Soviet Union, and had been involved in setting up US intelligence operations on the island. The Marches helped feed my growing fascination with the United States—later helping kick-start, among other things, my enduring love of surf music and, in particular, the Beach Boys.[14]

Even more than Ireland, Cyprus permeated my soul. Then in 2021, I was introduced to novelist Elif Shafak in our local bookstore, Barnes Books. We discussed her latest book, *The Island of Missing Trees*—that island being Cyprus.[15] The horror of the partition that split the island in 1974 is underscored by the fact that one hundred and sixty thousand Greek Cypriots living in the north were forced to move south of the new Green Line, while some fifty thousand Turkish Cypriots had to move north into the Turkish-controlled zone.

The result was rival community narratives, as Shafak put it, "that run counter, without ever touching, like parallel lines that never intersect." As the exiled fig tree at the heart of her story muses, "There is one thing I have learned: wherever there is war and a painful partition, there will be no winners, human or otherwise." And, as Shafak noted, nature generally suffers too.

Returning Home

Then came the final family posting. In 1959, we headed home to England, though it didn't much feel like home. At the ages of four, eight, and ten, Caroline, Gray, and I had only fleeting memories of our home country. For us, home had been our nuclear family: within nine years, we had lived in nine different places. For us, then, this was just one more move.* As we left Cyprus, our Jaguar loaded in a great net onto the MS *Messapia*, a small Italian passenger and cargo ship, I stood at the rail watching the island fade into the distance, heartbroken that I would never see those landscapes—those friends—again.

I was wrong on both counts, it turned out.

My parents eventually purchased Hill House, our longstanding family home in Little Rissington in the Cotswolds,[16] and it proved to be a wonderful anchor through my early teens as well as a springboard from which I moved back into a wider world. Soon, there were close friendships in nearby villages, particularly with the Keays and Palmers in Icomb. The mothers were sisters from Australia—and both families had lived in far-flung places like Nigeria and Bahrain.

When it came to affairs of the heart, I first met Jane Keay (later Davenport) at a dance in a friend's home, on a hill overlooking Icomb, and she dazzled me by dancing the Charleston. As a poor dancer myself, I was in the happy situation of having just had my appendix removed, so was confined to a chair. Perhaps I got the sympathy vote that evening, but Jane (then perhaps sixteen) and I (fourteen or fifteen) fell in love and remain close friends to this day.

Meanwhile, however, the stars were shifting into new configurations.

---

* During one such move, Tim had checked off seventeen pieces of luggage loaded onto a train on his list of eighteen items: the eighteenth proved to be Gray in his cradle, left on the platform.

"She's a blonde!" Pat exclaimed when Elaine first visited Hill House, early in 1968. Like Jane, Elaine was a couple of years older than me. I was eighteen when we met, whereas she had just celebrated her twenty-first birthday. I was just finding my feet at university, while she was taking her finals later that year. Still, we were young, and time seemed to stretch out forever.

We moved in together six days after meeting—living in sin, as Elaine's mother would have put it, had she known—and have been together since. After five years, we got married in 1973 at St. Peter's Church in Little Rissington.* We did so partly because it was simpler and cheaper for Elaine to travel to the States as my wife when I landed a University College London travel fellowship. And, of course, there were more romantic reasons, with that mind-bending trip also serving as our honeymoon.

We met extraordinary people—in New York, Arizona, and Washington state. They included the team building Paolo Soleri's seemingly space-age city, Arcosanti, in the Arizona desert. This visit, as described in chapter 2, helped launch both my writing and public speaking careers.

In Washington, we stayed with a first cousin of my father's mother. We had already met Hollister Sprague in England—and discovered that he lived in a stunning wooden house, Forestledge, roofed in cedar shakes and overlooking Puget Sound. Built by his father, it had an immense 60-foot ballroom-cum-music room, with a grand piano and a series of small rooms full of workings for what had once been the biggest pipe organ on the West Coast.

A captain in the United States Air Force in France during World War I, Hollister Sprague had wanted to become a musician, but his parents had refused to fund that because another family member had become an alcoholic after studying music in New York. So he went into law, eventually serving as the private lawyer for the founder of Boeing for several decades. When Elaine and I visited Hollister in Washington, he proved the

---

* The church would later serve as a time portal in my sister Caroline's novel about the English Civil War, *A Very Civil War* (Self Published, Amazon Kindle Direct Publishing, 2021).

perfect host, among other things taking us around the Sound in a Republic RC-3 Seabee floatplane that was like an upended Volkswagen Beetle on stubby wings, before driving us north into the temperate rainforests of the Olympic Peninsula.

Later, after Hollister had driven us across the Cascade Mountains to Yakima, and through the good offices of Hollister's sister, Joan Gilbert, we visited the extraordinary home of painter Leo Adams,[17] a member of the Yakama Nation. Leo's triptych of a golden-brown desert landscape, hung on the rough-hewn wooden walls of his home, still ranks as one of the most engaging works of art I have seen.

A day or two later, we had an opportunity to experience that landscape firsthand when Joan's husband, Elon, took Elaine and me riding around their ranch and nearby Cowiche Mountain.[18] We rode for hours through scrubland, with Elaine almost thrown from her horse when a rattlesnake spooked it.

My own steed was a finer beast, an Arab. When we finally trotted back down into the grassy bottoms of the valley among the apple orchards, he took off like a bullet—and ran for what seemed like miles as I relaxed the reins, going with the flow. Or rather *to* the flow: we ended up under irrigation sprays, drenched to the skin. If horses can laugh, and I could feel him shaking, my Arab was laughing his head off.

Joan and Elon didn't play it up, but among the friends they regularly hosted was history's longest-serving (and wildly liberal) United States Supreme Court judge, to that point at least—Justice William O. Douglas. He was a staunch opponent of the Vietnam War, even traveling to Vietnam to meet Ho Chi Minh. His views were at right angles to those of some of Hollister's other friends we met—including one power couple whose home was full of photographs of them with public figures like former President Richard Nixon and celebrities like Bob Hope. This couple's Etruscan-style house, complete with a moat you had to cross by a little bridge, was carpeted in white throughout. That seemed appropriate, since when they took us to dinner, they proudly declared that "no Blacks and no Jews" were allowed in their country club.

I discovered that Douglas—dubbed "Wild Bill" for his views on conservation—was part of the landmark decision in 1972 that said objects like trees could have legal standing, meaning that people could sue on their behalf. It has taken a long time for that notion to take root, but for example, New Zealand now accords legal standing to rivers, treating them as legal persons.[19] Justice Douglas would sometimes sleep over in the Gilbert barn, whereas we slept in a delightful octagonal guest block alongside a creek that chuckled and muttered to itself through the night, conjuring up the voices of long-ago peoples trying to catch our attention.

In later years, with our girls, we would stay with our cousin Jeanne Branson and her husband, Chuck, in the next house along from Forestledge, and on Vashon Island with Charlotte, my second cousin, and her husband, Clark Turner, who also worked with Boeing. One memory of the Turner house, with its great plate-glass windows overlooking Puget Sound, was of watching our daughter Hania down on the foreshore, where she hooked a wild salmon. She was immediately in tears, and that was even before a neighbor noted that the beautiful creature was out of season—though he suggested we keep it now it was hooked.

Illegal. Delicious.

We visited Hollister at Forestledge several times over the years. But we couldn't have imagined, despite all the musical associations, that Hollister's "dream house," as the media would describe it later, would one day become home to Sean Kinney, the drummer of the grunge band Alice in Chains.[20] Had Hollister still been around, I am sure he would have welcomed the grunge tribe in with his usual grace—courteous, calm, intrigued, working out the chords.

A Hole Vanishes

Once we were back in London, Elaine worked with publishers like Oxford University Press and Heinemann. Thanks to her ability to find flats in upmarket places, we lived in a series of less expensive abodes in places like

Belgravia and Knightsbridge.* Then we upped sticks and moved to Barnes, in South West London, a couple of blocks from the Thames. There, in 1975, we bought the semidetached house we live in still.

I worked for four years in my spare time to restore the building, alongside a wily and often cantankerous old builder, Dick Sharp. His family had lived in the area for generations. Somehow, despite his Ali Baba persona, or maybe because of it, we got on famously. To keep the project supplied with materials, Elaine and I often returned by train from Covent Garden, where she and I both ended up working in the same building in Floral Street, albeit for different firms, before staggering across Hungerford Bridge with lumber salvaged from skips during the area's reconstruction.

At one point, a kindhearted district nurse expressed horror that we were raising Gaia in a ruin. She may have been exaggerating the dangers slightly, but I had taken up all the floorboards in the front room, with a tottering fridge only approachable by a plank spanning piles of bricks. The sharp, dry smell of soot and cement was inescapable.

Gaia's upstairs bedroom also had a sizeable hole in its floor. I encouraged her to walk around it, rather than risk crashing through the ceiling into the hallway. She probably didn't want to break her legs, I suggested. Still, when I finally filled in the hole, she wept—insisting it had been her friend.

Our small house, easily visible as you fly into Heathrow, with all the acoustic joys that has involved, has expanded outward and upward over the years: first to house our daughters, then to accommodate the growing team that formed when I set up on my own in 1983—before expanding further when we launched SustainAbility in 1987.

Throughout, I felt real tensions between my life as a global villager and my obligations to my nuclear families. These were underscored when my youngest sister, Tessa, got married. I had asked that the wedding date avoid just one weekend that year, having promised to take Gaia and Hania

---

* For Elaine's recollections, see: https://elaineelkington.com/biography/.

to the Glastonbury music festival, by way of partial recompense for all my traveling. For whatever reason, that weekend was chosen.

As what seemed a reasonable compromise, I suggested that the girls and I go formally clothed to the wedding and attend the reception for an hour or so, before driving on. A few people, including my beloved mother, considered this monstrous. So, in the spirit of being hung as wolves rather than sheep, I suggested the three of us turn up at the reception in full festival gear, including—in at least one case—facial warpaint. Several older friends and relatives later confided that this had been a highlight of the proceedings.

After family, in terms of early influences, comes education—much of it acquired at one remove from the schools to which I was sent and the universities to which I chose to go. Nelson Mandela, who knew a thing or two about the power of learning, once said, "Education is the most powerful weapon which you can use to change the world."[21] So that's where we head next.

CHAPTER 2

Learning Curves

Perhaps the warnings were already there when I overturned my pram and crawled off into the reeds. I have overturned various prams since, heading off into areas of greater interest. Looking back, I have been a connection junkie, using schools, universities, and later working roles as springboards from which to explore the edges of a wider, weirder world.

That dash into the reeds signaled something else, too—a growing interest in nature. Sent away to school, I spent much of my spare time at the margins, exploring woods and river, observing fish and kingfishers alike. This was Glencot School near Wookey Hole in rural Somerset, in the southwest of England. I was entranced by an ornamental pool on the grounds that featured a constantly upwelling spring. Here dragonflies and damselflies flitted, while grass snakes basked in the sun. One boy brought a snake into the classroom and kept it alive, if disconcerted, in his flip-top desk. The smell from its anal gland was foul; before long, he was forced to release it back into the wild.

Not content to sit back and simply be taught about nature, I would taste and eat the roots, stalks, branches, shoots, flowers, berries, and seeds of plants I discovered around the school's extensive grounds. Sometimes, inevitably, this experimentation landed me in trouble. One day, I walked in for the evening meal and sat down at one of the long tables—only to have our immense and formidable headmistress, in retrospect an only slightly softer version of Agatha Trunchbull from the Roald Dahl musical *Matilda*, demand to know who had been eating *garlic*.

I don't think I even knew what garlic was; there wasn't much of it in English cuisine back then.

When there was no reply, she stalked around the tables, sniffing the breath of each of eighty nonplussed boys. Eventually, she got to me and erupted in fury. Was I hoarding garlic sausage in my tuck box? I denied it. "So, what have you been doing?" she demanded. "Eating plants in the wood," I replied—among them, though I didn't know it at the time, must have been ransoms, or wild garlic.

Beautiful flowers. Delicious, too.

"Why, in God's name," she roared, "are you risking imminent death by eating weeds, most of them poisonous? What will your parents think when you are found dead?" And, unsaid perhaps, what would be the legal and reputational consequences for her school?

Perhaps my answer should have been that I am driven by curiosity. Indeed, at times, I have joked that my real superpower is that I get bored easily. I must expand my interests and horizons, just as—we are told—some types of shark must keep swimming or suffocate.

Even if I struggle to recall what I was taught long ago, my education did a lot more than simply fill my brain with facts. If our family travels had weakened my ties with my home country, and they had, and Mother Superior had severed my ties with the major religions, which she had, then the logical next step was to loosen my ties with my nuclear family.*

That was something that Glencot helped initiate. I was lucky, given that I was nine at the time of dispatch, whereas my father, Tim, had been

---

* No accident, perhaps, that the person I got on best with in the Church of England was Justin Welby, first as Bishop of Durham, later as Archbishop of Canterbury. No accident because he didn't come up through the holy orders but had previously been chief financial officer for Enterprise Oil. He chaired a Friends Provident socially responsible investment advisory council when I was a member—and seemed to use me as a human battering ram to ask questions he wanted asked, as when we grilled both the chairman and the CEO of the banking group HSBC.

packed off solo to prep school by train, aged just six. Maybe kind by the standards of Sparta, and no doubt helpful in forging functional cogs for the imperial machinery, but it is hard not to see this as inhumane for most of those sent away.

Years later, Glencot enjoyed a new incarnation as a boutique hotel, with online reviewers swooning that it was in grand Jacobean style with mullioned windows, ancient trees, and a dreamy green sward leading down to the River Axe. It was also surrounded by high walls. No barbed wire that I remember, but the intention was not simply to keep criminals out but us in.

Dreamy now, perhaps, but often nightmarish when we were there.

The headmaster, who may have been a retired Indian Army colonel, seemed kindly to parents; clearly, he was on his best behavior with those paying the bills. He also proved to be a wonderful teacher—schooling me on four key subjects and getting me through the relevant exams. But he was also an industrial-strength alcoholic and hardwired sadist to boot.

He kept a cabinet of some fifty canes, some with split ends to increase their bite, some filled with lead to increase their kinetic impact, and several burned at their tips—because one aggrieved pupil once set fire to the whole cabinet of horrors. Sadly, the flames were extinguished before taking a real hold.

"Ned" Adams was eventually locked up in an asylum, and his school shuttered.

Seeing Stars

In their heyday, Ned's wife, Dorothy, had, as one former pupil later described her behavior to me, "oscillated from being a benevolent grandmother to a volcano in a flick of a switch." When I discussed elements of the story via my blog, the floodgates opened. One former pupil recalled our headmistress this way: "Humongous fat woman who could land such a hefty blow I saw stars!"

Once the dam of memory was breached, a surprising number of

former Glencot students—from around the world—began to share long-suppressed horrors. One exchange, between two old school friends who had rediscovered each other via my blog, recalled how one of them had been waiting in line to be caned when he became totally incensed on seeing a friend being beaten. "Brave as a lion," he promptly burst into the headmaster's study to try to interrupt the savagery. Failing in that, he raced the full length of the school to find the Gorgon-like Mrs. Adams. She erupted in fury and was described as galloping along the corridor, driving all before her, howling "not again, you fool!" Colliding full tilt with our apparently all-powerful headmaster, she sent him tumbling backward into his study.

True, eighty boys, however angelic some of us may have been, would drive many older people to distraction. At times, too, a *Lord of the Flies* reality simmered. One halcyon summer day when the teachers were away, our sole semi-adult guardian was snoozing. Some of us began building small fortifications out of hay bales ejected from a baler onto the sports ground, beyond the river. Then we fashioned bows in the bamboo grove—and began firing makeshift arrows at one another. Immense fun, but—perhaps inevitably—one of us ended up with an arrow impaled in his knee.

You might imagine that we would learn from such mistakes. Perhaps we did, but some years later, back in the Cotswolds, we made more powerful bows out of Tim's garden canes—and proceeded to loose goose-feather-fletched arrows high into the sky from the pasture in front of St. Peter's Church. So high that some disappeared. Inevitably, again, one plunged out of the blue and straight into the side of a village friend's head, where it anchored to one side of his eye socket.

Our Battle of Hastings moment.

Luckily, Robert Hamilton didn't lose his sight, though the Furies were already snapping at his heels. A couple of years later, we were at the village fête, hosted by the local manor house, when some of his other friends ran in to say he had drowned in a quarry on the edges of Bourton-on-the-Water. He couldn't swim and had been dragged down by weeds.

Robert Hamilton's was the most grief-stricken funeral I have attended.

So, the Glencot Adamses must have been sorely tested at times. But they were about as dysfunctional as they could have been without torturing and murdering the children in their care. Still, I owe them a huge debt of gratitude. In retrospect, they got me into my true alma mater, Bryanston School, despite at least one report from a Glencot teacher insisting that "John sets himself low standards—and consistently fails to achieve them."

While in benevolent grandmother mode, Dorothy Adams also gave me permission to do something that proved to be a key stepping stone. The memory came back to me twenty years later when I was driving down to the headquarters of the World Wildlife Fund (WWF), near Godalming, with one of its founders, Max Nicholson. Along the way, he asked me the inevitable question: "What first got you started in the environmental area?"

I kicked off with the eel story, then said there was this other thing, too. When I had been at Glencot, I had lobbied Mrs. Adams for permission to speak to all the boys, asking them for two weeks' worth of their treasured pocket money for the fledgling WWF. This was 1961, the organization's first year. Although I was paralytically shy at the time, something had propelled me to act.

Max said he knew what that catalyst had been.

Nonplussed, I asked him what he thought it might have been. And how could he possibly know? He explained that he and his WWF colleagues, including Sir Peter Scott and Guy Mountfort, had managed to get their story onto the front page of the *Daily Mirror*. The headline was a single word: "DOOMED."

This was designed as a "shock issue" to launch the new organization, with a number of pages inside on related themes. As soon as Max said that, the memories flooded back. Aged eleven, I had walked into the school library and leafed through the newspaper on a reading stand—then decided I had to act. So, there we have it: further impetus for my lifetime odyssey. The boys coughed up the money, I got a nice letter from Buckingham Palace, and we all then went back to the normal round of cramming and caning.

Car Crash

One day while I was still at Glencot, Mrs. Adams surged into the common room where we were permitted to watch carefully monitored television. She then hissed to me that Tim had been involved in a serious car crash. Always in a hurry, he had been driving his Rover 3-Litre literally at 100 miles per hour, as was his way, when a small van full of crockery pulled out of a side road, unable to gauge the banshee speed of the oncoming car.

When the vehicles collided, Tim had been thrown clear, as the car had no seat belts, and it then proceeded for a while on its own. It ended up crashing through a farm gate in the next county, which wasn't far away, releasing a herd of horses that cantered off down the road.

The van driver survived; his crockery, not so much.

My father, Tim, was taken to a nearby hospital, then loaded into an ambulance for the long trip home. Over the following days, Pat looked anxiously at her injured husband, eventually sending him back to a nearby hospital. His head looked strange to her, she insisted—hardly surprising, given that he proved to have a nine-inch crack in his skull.

Nor was that the end of the saga. When the police opened the Rover's glove compartment, they discovered Tim's Browning automatic pistol, the one he had worn in a shoulder holster while we were in Cyprus. A remarkable weapon in widespread use by armed forces worldwide, but the police were not amused. The gun was illegal in Britain, they protested. Tim insisted that he had planned to sell it. Whatever the truth, he escaped with little more than a slapped wrist—and that cracked skull.

Cracked, indeed severed, heads were central to another story that had long intrigued me, that of the Crusades. Growing up in Cyprus, we were surrounded by Crusades-era ruins like St. Hilarion Castle, whose flanks we scrambled up as children. Oddly, perhaps, I was much more interested in the lives of people like Salah al-Din (a.k.a. Saladin), the notional enemy, than in our own man in the Holy Land, Richard the Lionheart.[1] (Even if the latter would subsequently prove to be my uncle, twenty-six generations removed.)

Similarly, I would become much more interested in the lives of Crazy

Horse and Sitting Bull than I was in George Armstrong Custer or, later, in Ho Chi Minh and General Giáp, rather than Lyndon Johnson or his defense secretary, Robert Strange McNamara—whom I would later meet, a tale I will tell further on in the book.

Looking back, I was always peering around the edges of the history we were being taught, whether in schools, on TV, or in cinemas. So, when I was decanted to Bryanston School, I continued investigating civil and religious wars on my own account. It struck me that such periods, horrific though they were, provided a useful X-ray view of what a society had been—and might yet become. The future in embryo.

Learning to Say No

It was awe at first sight. Bryanston occupies a palatial country house built in the 1890s by Richard Norman Shaw—modeled on a château at Menars, in the Loire Valley. It has long been coeducational, but when I—and later Gray, he having ended up as head boy (student body leader) at Glencot—went there, it was single-sex. Still, it was pretty much nirvana after Glencot.

For one thing, there was no corporal punishment. Instead, you would be sent on morning or (more arduous) afternoon "runs." The boys wore shorts even into their late teens, though I left at sixteen—having gone through the system rather speedily. Ultimately, though, Bryanston was the making of me. And there were extraordinary people among the pupils: I remember being hugged goodbye on the morning I finally left by my head of house, Mark Elder, the future orchestral conductor. He was in a check dressing gown, while I was wearing a suit as I scrambled into the family Land Rover.

This liberal education, with pupils given a tutor and allowed a considerable degree of flexibility in what they studied, suited me down to the ground. I had also been posted to a wildly independent senior house, Forrester, located in what had once been large stables. Its decorations included reproductions of impressionist paintings.

Forrester has long since been disbanded, however. Even at the time, it had a slightly edgy feel, partly because it was a physical outlier from the main school, but also because our class size was very large—designed to flush out an earlier Forrester culture apparently symbolized by one boy having his hand speared to a dining table with a knife.

Still, Forrester was tailor-made for the outsider in me. I was showing a considerable degree of independent thought by now. Indeed, I ended up having a huge fight with my widely respected tutor in one of the most silence-mandatory libraries. I felt stifled by his academic ambitions for me, protested vigorously, and was reallocated to a more placid science teacher, who subsequently caused me no great trouble.

In retrospect, I seemed to say no whenever possible. No to Latin, no to being confirmed, no to joining the Sea Cadets, no to cutting up a live frog in a biology lesson. Still, there were things I would have said yes to, but they were denied to me. Among them were the Spanish lessons I had started taking with instructor Edward "Eddie" Renton, a veteran of the International Brigade in the Spanish Civil War. I loved the subject, loved him—and particularly enjoyed studying Miguel Delibes's book *El Camino*, about a young man who must leave home to get an education. But only a couple of us wanted to learn the language, so after the year that door closed abruptly.

Navigating the Future

The school project that influenced me most involved studying the development of John Harrison's chronometer—a device I later encountered at the Greenwich Observatory on the outskirts of London. The story illustrated the astonishing centrality of technology to the evolution of our economies. His work was inspired by the Longitude Prize, a huge sum of money offered by the British government to solve one of the most intractable problems facing the British Empire at the time.

The story is well known these days, thanks to Dava Sobel's brilliant book *Longitude*.[2] One sequence that stuck in my brain was her account of a sailor hung from a yardarm for daring to challenge the misguided orders of the admiral of a major fleet, Sir Cloudesley Shovell. Because the admiral was clueless as to where he was, so the story ran, the fleet promptly ran aground on the Isles of Scilly along Cornwall, drowning thousands of sailors including the ill-fated Shovell. Whatever the facts, and the recent evidence that raises a question mark over Sobel's account of the suspended sailor, it made a great morality tale.

Powerful people—or powerful societies—unable to see what is coming at them end up paying the ultimate price. Think of the hospital authorities deaf to warnings from doctors and consultants that a British neonatal nurse, Lucy Letby, was murdering the babies in her care in 2023.[3] Institutional survival and equilibrium often trump the duty of care, whether that be to patients or to the future.

In this context, I was also fascinated to read Arnold Toynbee's multi-volume *A Study of History* in the school library, charting the rise and fall of great civilizations—all with the apparent inevitability of the rise and fall of tides. This was a theme that Jared Diamond picked up later in his book *Collapse: How Societies Choose to Fail or Succeed*. As with Sobel's book, though, I was intrigued to see other historians arguing for rather different interpretations of at least some of these declines and falls.

Technology, I learned, evolves—indeed, I had already absorbed elements of that lesson through my fascination with aviation while at Glencot. There, I would write to US aerospace companies for their annual reports and catalogs, receiving exhilarating packages by airmail, in huge envelopes blazing with exotic stamps. Still, however far we might have roamed in search of extracurricular adventures, education was the main business of the day. And books were central to that, at least for me—with three I read during the Bryanston years having a profound, even disorientating, impact.

The first was Rachel Carson's *Silent Spring*. She opened my mind to the ways in which our species was tearing apart the fabric of nature that I had taken for granted until I read that "DOOMED" issue of the *Daily Mirror*. She was an exquisite writer, a poet. By contrast, Thomas Kuhn, to be blunt, was not.

His book, *The Structure of Scientific Revolutions*, was—and still is—heavy reading, but it still blew my young mind. He introduced the now much-misused term *paradigm shift*. True, few parents at the time sent their child to school to have their paradigm shifted. Instead, I suspect, they pictured us studying how others had had their worldviews upended. If they thought about it all, they probably expected us to learn about people like Copernicus, Galileo, Darwin, and Einstein.

In Kuhn's view, scientists usually practice "normal science," using the same, well-honed mindsets, frameworks, and tools repeatedly. Every so often, though, "extraordinary research" suggests that the existing paradigm is flawed—and a new one begins to emerge. For those steeped in the old worldview, this is shocking, nauseating even. Which was exactly the reaction of many of those occupying the world's boardrooms at the time when environmentalism and then sustainability began to push into the global consciousness.

And the third book that irreversibly shaped my thinking was E. H. Carr's *What Is History?* published in 1961. It argued that we shape history through what we choose to pay attention to or ignore. This chimed with my own experience. History proved to be my best subject at Bryanston, by far.* Happily, my eventual results also made university a real possibility, though it had never been on my to-do list and my results in economics and French were decidedly lackluster.

Something Illegal

Once I left Bryanston, I spent a few months at Cheltenham Tech to brush up my results, particularly in economics. I took up with Peter Jacobs (whose Mini Estate got us to and from Cheltenham), en route

---

* I scored high marks in key history exams after spending a week in the school sanatorium with acute chickenpox, blisters even erupting in my eye sockets. I nonetheless managed to read *Gone with the Wind*, Margaret Mitchell's 1936 novel on the American Civil War and its aftermath. I then bent several questions in two separate exam papers to the theme, the narrative ensuring the facts stayed in my mind.

to his becoming a lawyer and marrying a Milk Marketing Board model, and with Dudley Russell, en route to his marrying poet and broadcaster Pam Ayres.

I also spent a fair amount of time with Irene, the Countess of Effingham. I was in my early teens when we first met, while she was over forty. She was known as Kerry, the surname of her first husband, whom she had married in India. That was where she had been raised, too, before being abused by a stepfather and running away with the water buffalo *wallahs* until retrieved. Her estranged second husband, the Earl, would eventually receive one of the most damning obituaries I ever read in the *Times*—and deserved every word of it.

Among other things, he was closely involved with the murderous Kray Twins, who ended up referring to him as "Effing Effingham."[4] He once sent a huge truck to Kerry's home, long after they had divorced, and while she was away, stripped it of everything valuable to pay off his gambling debts.

I was enthralled by Kerry's tales of her early life in India. Among other things, she had caught the eye of—and gone riding with—the future (and frightful) Edward VIII, who was at the time the Prince of Wales. It struck me later that she had the same dark-haired looks as Wallis Simpson. I shared her passion for bees; surprising on her part, given that she had once ridden into a bee's nest dangling from a tree in India and had been stung within an inch of her life. Her cottage smelled of beeswax, which she made into a furniture polish with turpentine and applied liberally to everything, including an oak kitchen table—which she later left to me, scarred by the spurred boots of generations of men.

Hideous now to think of all those vigorously spurred horses.

Kerry was also a highly skilled weaver and dyer, arts she began to teach me. She remained a friend until she died, aged almost ninety. When it happened, I was in Australia, so Elaine kindly stood in for me at the funeral. Later, when I was back in England we gathered a few of Kerry's friends for a celebration of her life, congregating at Hill House before heading down to a small bridge over the River Dikler, a tributary of the Windrush. I went down into the stream to release a couple of handfuls of Kerry's ashes into the stream. Before I did so, however, I cautioned the mourners that this was probably illegal—so they should not mention it in public.

One older woman promptly fell backward on the slippery grass bank by the bridge, as if poleaxed. She cracked her head, spilling a prodigious amount of blood. We raced her across to the cottage hospital in nearby Bourton-on-the-Water. When the medical staff asked her what we had been doing, to get her talking, this distinguished woman kept saying she didn't know—but that she did know that it had been illegal. Mercifully, the nurses put it down to a concussion.

Something Fierce

Still, all of that lay in the future. Back in 1967, my period of treading water ended when I was offered a place at the University of Essex, outside Colchester, one of seven new plateglass universities.* My top choice had been the University of Sussex, but it turned out that the University of Essex was the perfect place to further hone my outsider status and the mindset to approach power from unusual angles.

I certainly dressed the part. Among other things, I sported self-assembled and heavily patched white jeans with "Love" and "Hate" spray-painted on the back of the opposing legs, beneath a heavily bejeweled Dior waistcoat inherited—or purloined—from one of our great-aunts at Castle Gogar. No question, I stood out—even in those days. One of Elaine's friends, Marie-Gabrielle Blanchet, had dubbed me "Henley Regatta" before any of

---

* A good deal of industrial plate glass was used in building these universities. And one of the first company visits I made when we set up Environmental Data Services in the late seventies proved to be the glassmaking company Pilkington, in St. Helen's, Merseyside. Pilkington pioneered the production of float glass: see https://www.pilkington.com/en-gb/uk/about/heritage/invention-of-float-glass#.

us had met, referring to a wildly colorful rowing contest held each year in Henley-on-Thames.*

In later years, businesspeople would routinely dismiss us as hippies—and our change agenda as "beads and sandals stuff." Just as well that there was no internet back then from which they could have trawled up images of me at the time. Their worst suspicions would have been confirmed.

By contrast, the campus—originally intended as Britain's answer to the Massachusetts Institute of Technology[5]—sported several brutalist buildings including the Albert Sloman Library and the Hexagon, created by architect Kenneth Capon, who insisted he didn't want his designs to be "shaggy and soft," aiming instead to create "something fierce." Inevitably, *Something Fierce* would become the title of a major exhibition about the university's founding.

By the time I returned to Essex to receive an honorary doctorate in 2014, the reviled buildings had become architectural icons, at least by the university's own account.[6] I didn't know at the time, but the original plans for the university as envisioned by Albert Sloman, the school's first vice chancellor, had been so groundbreaking that he had been asked to give the BBC's Reith Lectures in 1963, the year before the university opened. His thinking was that Essex would break the mold, challenging expectations about what a university could be.

So it proved, though not quite in the way he imagined.

I arrived in 1967 to study economics, though I would give that up the following year because the dismal science struck me as virtually useless when it came to tackling the social and environmental issues that were increasingly in the headlines. Then, in May 1968, the university itself exploded in protest. A visiting chemical warfare scientist was the proximate trigger. He was shouted down—and possibly also had mustard powder

---

* Something Elaine and I only realized decades later was that one of Elaine's ancestors was a so-called regicide after the English Civil War, one of fifty who signed King Charles I's death warrant. On the restoration of the monarchy, he fled to Barbados, which is where Elaine's father, Stanley Waite, returned from the UK centuries later. So, given that Charles I was in my family tree, it seems that her ancestor helped commit mine to the executioner's block.

thrown at him. As vice chancellor, Sloman suspended three ringleaders, and the campus was promptly shut down by the students.[7] Wildly educational times.

Someone we knew while at Essex, Anna Mendelssohn, later became a member of the Angry Brigade, a far-left British terrorist group—and would be sent to prison for ten years for conspiring to blow up British government ministers. Danny the Red, the face of the student revolution in Paris, showed up on campus, too, and my new girlfriend's previous (if fleeting) boyfriend, now in the House of Lords, was one of the three ringleaders who had tried to silence the Porton Down chemical scientist.

An early example, perhaps, of what we might now call "canceling"—and of the Establishment's facility in either crushing challengers or pulling them into a close, and here ermine-coated, embrace.

Looking back, you could scarcely have designed a better laboratory in which to learn how society works, or at least how ours did. The events of 1968 left me profoundly dissatisfied with what I was learning, even if there were entertaining moments, as when our Canadian economics professor, Dick Lipsey, was in full flow in the biggest lecture hall. One entire wall of the theater was blackboard, up to a high roof. Tankard of beer in hand, as was his style, he leaned back against the blackboard, oblivious that there was a small door in it. As he waxed lyrical, the door slipped open—and he disappeared into the darkness.

For me, it served as an allegory of how his discipline was shot through with wormholes, some of which I was now keen to investigate further—from behind the scenes, so to speak. So, I switched to sociology and social psychology. Here, Professor Peter Townsend ruled the roost, though once again I was soon exploring the wilder fringes of his discipline. The year 1968 has sometimes been called "The Year That Shattered America"[8] and "The Year That Changed History,"[9] among other taglines. It was the year that saw that extraordinary *Earthrise* image of our home planet from behind the lunar horizon. And it was the year when I met that girlfriend, Elaine, who would become my emotional anchor through the next fifty years—and counting.

The soaring political temperature of the times was heavily underscored when, early on in our relationship, I took Elaine to dinner with my cousin, Eve Henley-Welch, at her family home near Colchester. By way of context, the town hosted both the university and a major army garrison. Matter and antimatter, you might think, tank and gown.

Eve was at least twice my age, from a very different generation, but was beautiful, intelligent, and immense fun. Hers was a rather grander family—and one guest at the dinner table that evening proved to be a general from the nearby base. As the discussion became more heated, he talked of sending in tanks to take over the campus, at which point I felt I should declare an interest. There was a different side to the story, I suggested. To be honest, I was much more interested in protecting the environment than blowing things up.

Yes, I read radical magazines, subscribing for a while to the left-wing American magazine *Ramparts*, an early opponent of the Vietnam War. Unlike most left-wing magazines, though, it was well designed. An early portent, perhaps, of my longer-term habit of buying armfuls of science, technology, and business magazines in airports around the world and then devouring them on long-haul flights.

Indeed, my wide interests were underscored when I was invited back to the University of Essex in 2014 to receive that honorary doctorate. The university noted that the sheer range of my work meant that I could be hosted by the economics, sociology, environment, or biology faculties, or by the business school—which hadn't even existed when we were there. In the end, I plumped for biology, the keystone science I didn't study, either at school or at Essex, but often wished I had.[*]

Throughout those years, the Vietnam War proved to be a seismic fault line between the generations, particularly in the United States. The Marches, the US naval family we had grown up with in Cyprus, had by

---

[*] Indeed, if I could have read one book back in the sixties, it would have been E. O. Wilson's *Genesis*, published in 2019, a short overview of how life evolved and led to our increasingly complex societies.

now been transferred from the States to London—where I remember having a heated exchange with Pat, the father, on his way to becoming a vice admiral in the United States Navy. Sadly, there was no way we were going to see eye to eye on the war. You could almost smell ozone as the sparks flew across the breakfast table.

So it was quite a shock years later to meet Robert Strange McNamara, who played such a pivotal role in escalating the presence of the United States in Vietnam. We only exchanged a few words at a dinner in London, but he seemed chastened and thoughtful—as he did when I later heard him speak at the John F. Kennedy School of Government at Harvard.

Meanwhile, the opposite of the military-industrial complex that people like McNamara represented was the counterculture and boomer music—everything that eventually bubbled up at Woodstock and its evil twin, Altamont. It was no accident that US soldiers in the war zone played music that their seniors considered actively seditious, as portrayed in the Robin Williams film *Good Morning, Vietnam*. Like many people of my age, I was enraptured by the new sounds. They held meaning to which most of our elders seemed deaf.

Under the Influence

One of my favorite courses at Essex was the sociology of religion, taught by Andy Tudor. It helped me understand my seismic collision with Mother Superior all those years before. Critically, one of the books Andy set us was Frank Herbert's *Dune*—because Herbert had built aspects of his Fremen religion on the fictional planet of Arrakis around the real-world religion of Africa's Dinka people.

Sometimes ranked as the best science fiction novel ever, *Dune* pulled me deeper into the sci-fi world—sparking a multiyear quest to meet its author, an adventure I describe in chapter 5. On first reading, it took me forty pages to penetrate the *Dune* world, but then I was completely, irretrievably hooked. This was a radically different reality, but one shot through with ecological themes.

Simultaneously, I was devouring publications like the many editions of Stewart Brand's *Whole Earth Catalog*. Alternative realities were also readily available through hallucinogens. In fact, one of my favorite musical tracks at the time came from Jefferson Airplane's *Surrealistic Pillow* album: "White Rabbit."[10] In 1969, having sampled hashish, I finally took LSD. The experience lasted two days, the flashbacks another four years. I wouldn't recommend drugs, of course, but the experience proved transformative.

One particularly memorable moment was when I drank water from a pottery mug handcrafted by my cousin Eve. It was made from clay coils, so that when you looked down into its ribbed, flesh-colored depths, it was like peering into a human throat. Under the influence, I was suddenly tumbling down that throat, very much like Alice falling down the Rabbit Hole. As I fell, the throat formed from a continuous sequence of all the throats, tongues, and voice boxes that had ever spoken a particular word of Norman origin that someone had just used, perhaps in a song. The throat extended downward and outward, eventually stretching under the English Channel, well before the Chunnel was built. Eventually it surfaced in Normandy—at the very moment when someone spoke the word for the first time.

This was not a reality that my parents' generation would have understood, let alone embraced. But my father's mother, Isabel, was a different matter. A beauty in her time, she was joyous, open, free-spirited. A week after that hallucinogenic trip, I visited her in her Knightsbridge, London, apartment. She asked me what I had been up to, so I told her. She was fascinated, wanted to know more. Among other things, I recalled the moment where part of me had separated out and floated up against the ceiling, anchored back to my body by a long shining thread—an out-of-body experience, but it seemed totally real.

Isabel, whom I had called by her first name since I was four, said she knew exactly what I was talking about.* When she was twelve, she said, her family had been living in South Africa, as her father tried his luck as a gold miner. She became seriously ill with a chest disease, possibly pleurisy. She remembered finding herself up against the ceiling, at the end of a long silver thread. Then, she heard the doctor come into her bedroom and tell her parents that there was nothing more he could do, that they must get used to the idea of losing their daughter.

Isabel told me that she became angry, winding herself back down that long thread, back into her body. From that moment, apparently, she began to recover. How remarkable to have been able to share that experience with her, albeit with very different root causes to mine.

Or were they? An interest in those different causes, physiological and psychological, soon sent my university thesis spinning off the university rails. Originally, it was meant to explore Latin American militarism, or how the armed forces end up running governments in the southern continent. But I had just met Elaine, so the attractive young lecturer I was meant to travel to Venezuela with was now out of bounds. So, without telling my tutor, I switched the focus of the project to the ways in which mental breakdowns, religious ecstasy, and hallucinogenic drugs can trigger similar experiences.

Crucially, I explored how these experiences can be interpreted very differently, depending on whether you are seen to be mad, possessed by spirits,

---

* Isabel would have been remarkable in any age but was strikingly modern in her own era. She began as Isabel Griffin, then became Elkington, then Coaker. The divorces that characterized her life, and Pat's parents' too, led Elaine's parents to conclude that I had genes for divorce. Isabel's diaries during World War I could have been written by a highly intelligent young woman today. At one point she recalled making love in 1916 to one of her paramours, a naval officer, in St. James's Park in the dark with searchlights and flak seeking out Zeppelins growling overhead and dropping bombs on Park Lane.

She later proposed by telegram to Tim's ultimate father, Durham, who was distinctly older. As World War I ended, Durham was fighting the Bolsheviks in the same region, Murmansk, and Archangel, where Tim would find himself in World War II. Durham's reply said he didn't think he was good marriage material. How right he was, but World War I casualty rates squeezed women's options. Pat and Tim would later host a succession of Durham's former wives at Hill House. At least one of the relationships may have been bigamous. Still, I enjoyed a close relationship with his last wife, Kay, also my godmother. In her later years, she lived in Solva, Pembrokeshire, where we spent wonderful summer holidays with the children.

intoxicated, or in touch with God. By the grace of whatever gods, the thesis passed muster—and I left Essex with a good degree, something that would have seemed unimaginable a few years earlier. But I was still drifting.

Greece on Wheels

Time for something different. Six of us—Elaine; me; Martin Lindsay and his wife, Jan; Rex Gowar; and Ian Lovell—took my family's Land Rover and headed off through Europe to Greece for a couple of months. Our adventures along the way were many and various, including being shot at in the former Yugoslavia. Mercifully, the bullet had been fired at long range, so it was slowing and hit a crossbeam at the back of our vehicle.

Four people we met along the way who still live on in memory were the musician Shawn Phillips, a female café owner in Skiathos, an American calligrapher called Gail, and the artist Giorgos Varlamos. We met Shawn, hippie to hippie, as we drove into Positano, Italy, somewhere I hadn't been since 1959 but loved both times. He was striking to look at, even for the day: American, gauntly handsome, bearded, and with long blond hair reaching down to his waist. This Texas-born musician was later described by rock music impresario Bill Graham as "the best kept secret in the music business." Shawn Phillips invited us to his home high on the slopes overlooking the town. Exhausted, Elaine, Martin, and Jan chose to catch up on sleep in the small hotel we had booked into, while Ian, Rex, and I took the bait.

Thank heavens. What an extraordinary evening that was. In a large space with a gothic window looking down over the moonlit Mediterranean, Shawn played us the open reel tapes of the music he had just recorded with some of the best-known musicians of the day. His music melded many styles, including folk, rock, jazz, funk, progressive, pop, electro, and classical. Then, partway through the evening, as an energetic bass line thrummed through huge speakers, Shawn's black cat got to its feet and started to dance.

I swear.

The second memorable person was an older Greek woman reminiscent of Eli Wallach, the striking male actor who featured in films like *The Good, the Bad, and the Ugly*. We illegally pitched our tents on her beach for a month, eating at her café. Each morning, she would string out freshly caught octopi to dry on a washing line.

Along the same beach, we also met a third memorable character, an American calligrapher called Gail, who lived on her rowboat. She and I got on rather well, to the point where, when our group was leaving by boat, she surprised us on the jetty with a vast lump of halva, which she knew I loved. By then, however, we shared a criminal record, of sorts.

Late one night, we had taken Gail's boat to visit a nearby fish farm owned by a prominent Greek shipping family who were not immensely popular at the time. The Milky Way stretched above our heads, so bright against the darkness that you felt you could put your hands over it and swing. Golden puddles of phosphorescence spooled out on either side of our gleaming wake, and as the seawater ran back down the oars, it also illuminated our hands and wrists. I shall pull a delicate veil over the nature of the operation, which resulted in a small haul of lobster and *sinagrida*, the most prized fish in Greece, the "fish of kings." All of this had been quite some distance from our beach, and for perhaps obvious reasons, we said nothing about it to anyone.

But when we walked into the café for breakfast the next morning, "Eli" quipped that she had heard we had done "a good job" the previous night. Island grapevines are quite something.

As for Giorgios Varlamos, the fourth memorable encounter, we met him at his gallery in Athens, where Elaine and I bought our first piece of art together.[11] A highlight of the visit was Giorgios taking us through his photograph albums, almost exclusively black-and-white images of, among other things, his student days in Paris. These proved to be an inspiration for my own photography efforts, largely created in huge albums produced by bookbinding expert Tessa Fantoni, who had been married to the cartoonist and jazz musician Barry Fantoni.

Giorgios told us about how he had developed the large image we had bought, which depicted hunters and their dogs in a forest clearing. It was printed from a woodcut, for which he had used crunched up newspapers as a visual reference, the crosshatch echoing newsprint—with a strong suggestion of deeply encoded meaning.

Remarkable times. One overarching memory: wherever we went in Greece, mostly off the beaten track, we enjoyed remarkable hospitality. In northern Greece, we woke up one morning, having slept in the open air, each of us with a watermelon by our head—with the farmer in his oxcart trundling off into the distance, unheard and unthanked. That happened twice in different places.

In traveling through the Peloponnese, we put up our tents outside Nafplio in what we thought was an open field. It turned out to be an open prison. Elaine woke up from a nightmare in which someone was chopping off her feet. And there, standing by the tailgate of the Land Rover, from which our legs protruded, was a man with an ax. When we spoke, mainly in French, we learned that he was a murderer, having killed his wife and her lover. We had stopped for the night in his prison. He was perfectly pleasant and hospitable, but we soon decamped.[*]

When we got to Yugoslavia, close to the Albanian border, we were robbed. Our fault: it was illegal to camp outside official campsites, so by settling down by a stream in a magical little valley, we set ourselves up. Elaine and I were sleeping in the back of the Land Rover again, on rugs bought in Greece. She and I had disagreed energetically the night before as to whether we should be sleeping on them. Happily, I had prevailed. Everyone else had their belongings stacked on the front seat of the vehicle. In the night, one or more locals quietly opened the Land Rover door and made off with all the rugs that weren't being slept on.

More kindness came the next day, however, when Anglo-Argentine Rex and I climbed into the mountains to see if we could find any trace of

---

[*] When we visited Nafplio in 2020, just as the COVID-19 pandemic hit, the open prison was pointed out to us. "Yes," we said, "we slept there in 1970. And were woken up by an ax murderer—holding an ax."

the thieves. Early on, we came across a logging camp, where they fed us aromatic sourdough bread, just out of their wood-fired oven, accompanied by thick-skinned yogurt. Higher up the mountain, we found a shepherd's log cabin, sunk deep into the earth. A formidable drooling dog, a mastiff, was chained to his kennel outside—and came bounding at us, dragging chain and kennel behind.

Mercifully, he was called off by the shepherd's wife, who offered us glasses of what may have been salty mare's milk—strangely delicious. Then, as we sat by the fire, she sat alongside me, neither of us speaking a word of each other's language, as she counted off the pattern of my thick Norwegian jumper. Cultural diffusion in real time.

Smuggling Genes?

When we returned from Greece, I moved to London to be with Elaine, while she began working with Oxford University Press in Dover Street, in the former town house of the bishops of Ely.[12] Mention of the good bishops, gatekeepers to Heaven and Hell, reminds me that my own life sometimes ran perilously close to the guardrails of legality, and sometimes beyond.

When Elaine and I were hitchhiking back from seeing a former Swedish boyfriend of hers in Stockholm in 1969,[13] we accidentally ended up in the Reeperbahn, the red-light area of Hamburg, Germany. Here we bumped into a short, owlish German, Peter Siemer, who became a friend. He turned out to be a dealer in ancient gold coins but had become too well known in the London auction houses. Whenever he arrived, the prices went up. So, I ended up bidding for specified lots for him, then traveling across to Hamburg with the coins on ferries sailing to and from Harwich. No tax was paid, as far as I know, so already we were crossing the line.

Then I met a friend of Peter's, Frank Stop, a towering student with long blond locks and a beard. A German Viking. At his suggestion, Frank and I began buying lefthand-drive Volkswagens in Germany, which I would then ship back to London, selling them through the *Evening Standard*, for around twice what we had paid for them. Most were bought by American students wanting wheels for road trips across Europe. I recall one German count from a well-known noble family who arrived and paid for a car for his son in cash—and Elaine insisted we sleep on the loot until the banks opened in the morning.

On the subject of lawbreaking, perhaps there are genes for smuggling? I later learned from my mother and her youngest brother Paul that their brother Peter had been a ringleader in a smuggling racket after World War II. That said, Uncle Peter's prior service in the Fleet Air Arm had not been without incident. On one occasion, he had steered a Harvard training aircraft into the station commander's married quarters—and been asked whose side he was on.

When the European phase of World War II ended in 1945, Peter, a qualified naval fighter pilot, was back in the UK still training for the final push in the Pacific. When the atomic bombs in Japan brought the war to an end, the founders of the smuggling gang—"Pete," "Gus" (Adam Thomson, later founder of British Caledonian Airways), and "Hank" (MacArthur—as befitting a smuggling group, his first name could not be confirmed)—were still together as chief petty officer pilots, kicking their heels until "demobbed," or demobilized.

As my Uncle Paul recently recalled: "Wanting to earn more money, they set up their own air transport company, using old Walrus seaplanes, previously used in whaling operations. They smuggled in freely available and relatively cheap contraband from France: cognac, nylon stockings, perfume, branded cigarettes, etc.—all scarce to the point of non-existence in postwar, poverty-stricken Britain. One flight ended close to total disaster: when flying back from Caen, they made their UK landfall in thick fog on the last few drops of fuel sputtering in the Auster's single engine."[*]

Eventually the trio were forced to sell the Walruses for their scrap value. Compared to such entrepreneurial exploits, ours were more modest affairs. But I have often wondered about any genetic links between the appetite

---

[*] See *High Risk* by Sir Adam Thomson (London: Sidgwick & Jackson, 1990).

for entrepreneurial risk-taking and for pushing the law to—and sometimes beyond—the limits.

In the same spirit, something that I am not remotely proud of is that, like some other students at the time, I periodically stole books from bookshops. There was even a book at the time by counterculture activist Abbot Howard "Abbie" Hoffman called *Steal This Book*.[14] But, really, no excuse. Inevitably, I was caught red-handed at a large London bookshop, charged, and fined £10 at the local magistrates' court. Asked why I had done it, I replied that I had never done it before (not true), didn't know why I had done it (though I did, and in retrospect books had become—and remain—something of a mania), and would never do it again (at least I didn't lie there).

Meanwhile, by her own account, Elaine "cooked and cleaned and bottle-washed at our flat in Ebury Street for John, his brother Gray, and a huge number of visitors who often stayed, some for extended periods."* One of the latter was someone we had grown up alongside in the Cotswolds, who came to stay after being released from prison in Austria. He had been in Iran for some time, eventually driving homeward in a car packed with cannabis. He had been arrested after he ran out of money to pay for petrol and tried to sell drugs to a plainclothes police officer at Vienna's central railway station. Sentenced to twelve years in prison, he had spent much of his time playing chess with the prison governor, only getting out because his father, an international judge, had pulled strings—though he cut off his son from that day forward.

Among this friend's guests when he stayed with us was a mother and sometimes also her daughter. He had been sleeping with both, though I'm not sure either knew the full story. I had just returned from Germany and had brought back a bottle of whisky from duty free, something we usually

---

* Crucial to that period were John Bennett and Charles Logan, more than twice our age and living around the corner in Eaton Square. Our ground flat at 91 Ebury Street was theirs. Gloriously gay, in Noël Coward fashion, they had picked up Gray when he was hitchhiking to Oxford—and, in hindsight, offered us the flat in the hope that Gray would play the piano with John in the basement flat at Ebury Street. He did—and we reaped the rewards, until the ninety-nine-year lease ran out. The flat came with a wonderful little garden.

never had in the flat. The mother arrived and polished off the whole bottle in a single sitting. Anesthetic?

Up Each Other Like Knives

Meanwhile, I was still drifting. Indeed, in the two years between leaving the University of Essex and starting a postgraduate degree at the University College London (UCL) School of Environmental Studies (now the Bartlett School of Architecture), I had a wide range of temporary jobs. These included nine months with Industrial Facts & Forecasting (IFF) in Argyll Street, right by Oxford Circus, where we did endless telephone and door-to-door surveys on everything from bulk purchases of toilet paper to new types of ceramic cladding for buildings.

Next came six months with the General Nursing Council near Broadcasting House—using microfilm cameras to miniaturize the records of nurses around the world. At both IFF and the General Nursing Council, I worked with "resting" actors and actresses. The company was delightful, the language colorful. I remember one attractive actress telling us how a landlady on the south coast had viewed her suspiciously when she was looking for digs during a local run. "I know you lot," the landlady had snorted. "As soon as the curtain hits the deck, you're up each other like knives!"

I was not idling the time away as I microfilmed nurses' records, however. During lunch breaks I would sprint across Portland Place to the libraries run by the Royal Institute of British Architects and Royal Town Planning Institute. There I read everything I could lay my hands on about the environment, city planning, and architecture. Some of what I was reading was slightly far-fetched for most people, including the visionary work of Paolo Soleri, with his exquisitely drawn plans for arcologies, or self-contained and ideally self-sufficient cities.[15] What attracted me to his work, though, apart from the designs themselves, was the idea that, if we could super-concentrate cities, almost like termite colonies, we could dispense with most road traffic, with all its multitudinous health and environmental impacts. And maybe then we could also free up land to hand back to nature.

As I mentioned in chapter 1, when I landed a travel bursary from UCL in 1973, Elaine and I got married and flew to the United States. As part of our trip, we headed to Scottsdale, Arizona, north of Phoenix, to visit Soleri's Cosanti Foundation. The place was alive with windbells of his own devising, and we had a delightful exchange with his wife, Colly. Then we drove further north into the Sonoran Desert to see Arcosanti—Soleri's first attempt at an arcology.

That visit became the subject of my first published article, in *Architectural Association Quarterly*. It also became the subject of my first public speech in 1974 at the Architectural Association School of Architecture in London. Having had many article submissions rejected, I had said to Elaine that if this one was rejected, I would give up entirely. Somehow, the threat worked. The twelve-page article, with photographs I had taken as we explored the site, concluded (prophetically, as it turned out) by suggesting that Arcosanti would one day make magnificent ruins—and "perhaps sooner than most people might imagine."[16]

Apart from the sheer magic of Arcosanti, and of our first immersion in desert ecosystems—one of the cooks had been bitten by a black widow spider the week before—I was intrigued by the clash between Soleri's ultradense vision for future cities and the thinking of his former mentor, Frank Lloyd Wright. The latter had promoted a vision of cities based around one-acre lots for each family, a vision called Broadacre City. The influence of that car-based vision was painfully visible as we drove through the endless sprawl of nearby Phoenix.

Once back at UCL, I found most courses of relatively little interest, though there were exceptions, including an early lecture by Professor Gerry Wibberley of Wye College; he was a lovely man and a Quaker. He began by saying that he knew some of us would be thinking of cities as cancers in the environment. Spot on, exactly what I believed—and still largely do. But he went on to say that well-designed cities could be a much more environmentally acceptable way of housing billions of people—which was what made Soleri so appealing to me.

Two other powerful influences were Jane Jacobs, the urbanist and activist who wrote *The Death and Life of Great American Cities*, and Joan Davidson, one of our UCL lecturers. She was a strong champion of my writing, encouraging me to become a writer rather than a planner. I was greatly influenced by field trips she took us on to London's increasingly raddled Green Belt around Heathrow Airport, and along the Grand Union Canal, exploring the evolution and impact of linear forms of development—and the ways in which wildlife can colonize such corridors into the cities where most of us now live.

Again, as at Essex, my dissertation went seriously off-piste. We were limited to twenty thousand words, but mine came in at eighty thousand, and got within a squeak of being published as a book by Heinemann. Still, I was beyond lucky that it passed muster with the examiners. It could have been read—and at least one examiner did read it—as a full-frontal assault on the thinking and work of the school's head, Lord Richard Llewelyn-Davies. While he was gung-ho for system building, having been involved in developing the new city of Milton Keynes based on the Los Angeles car-based model, I was more interested in exploring urban regeneration in places like London's Covent Garden and Docklands, and—an extreme case—Venice.

Ultimately, UCL convinced me that, even if I emerged as a full-fledged member of the Royal Town Planning Institute, there was one thing I really didn't want to be—and that was a planner. So, if not that, then what?

Slow Boats to China

Happily, more seductive worlds beckoned. A longstanding friend of my grandmother Isabel's, Daphne Young, used to invite us to her cocktail parties in Cadogan Square—featuring glamorous folk like actress Eleanor Bron, who had appeared in the Beatles' 1965 film, *Help!*. There I also met Daphne's son, Gavin Young. The family were direct descendants of the privateer and Jamaica sugar plantation owner Sir Henry Morgan, and sometimes it showed.

Gavin invited me for a long weekend in Paris, where we stayed in a vast house owned by the Rothschilds in the Place des Vosges. Israeli premier Golda Meir was visiting Paris that weekend, so grim-looking CRS special police officers were patrolling everywhere, the streets ghostly. Even so, we had a stirring time visiting restaurants like La Coupole and enjoying the Marx Brothers in *A Night at the Opera*.

A longstanding foreign correspondent for the *Observer* and a deeply experienced war correspondent in the Middle East and Vietnam, Gavin then invited me to travel with him on a series of ships and boats around the world. That journey later turned into his magical pair of travelogues, *Slow Boats to China* and *Slow Boats Home*. Sadly, I had to decline, partly because I suspected he would be better off traveling alone—and partly because I had UCL to finish.[*] Even more importantly, there was Elaine to consider. Her brother Charles had just been in a near-fatal car crash and was in a coma that would last for two months, after which he would need to learn to walk and speak again.

Then, once again, the fates blew forcefully into my sails. I had picked my UCL tutor, Professor Peter Cowan, on the basis that he was running a leading-edge, futures-based research unit. I thought he might shrink the degrees of separation between me and the future I was aching to embrace. Happily, it worked. Two weeks before I left UCL, I discovered an unsolicited letter in my pigeonhole from a John Roberts—inviting me to visit his small Covent Garden–based consultancy called Transport & Environment Studies, or TEST.

There was no internet to look him up on, so I went sight unseen. More on that story later, though my time with John proved pivotal. Many things

---

[*] Another road not taken, but I packed my bags and went back to London—catching a glance of, and only then understanding, Gavin's disappointment in the taxi's wing mirror. He was gay; I wasn't.

I have done since, including the early configuration of both SustainAbility and Volans, harked back to lessons learned at TEST.

Meanwhile, Elaine and I toyed with moving to a restored warehouse in Rotherhithe but decided to move somewhere greener instead. Roger McGlynn, a colleague at TEST, invited us to see where he and his wife lived in Barnes, and we moved there in 1975. As already mentioned, we spent four years living in a ruin as we rebuilt it, a good deal of it with my own chapped hands. Our two daughters, Gaia and Hania, were both raised there, three social businesses have had their origins there, and I have now written twenty-one books, many hundreds of articles, and thousands of blog posts in various parts of that house.

Meanwhile, anyone who has had children knows that it also tends to be an ongoing education, on all sides. To summarize our daughters is beyond me, but let me try. Both went to St. Paul's Girls' School and both got firsts at Edinburgh University, but they were otherwise from different species.

Gaia became an antimotorway campaigner during an era best remembered for campaigners like "Swampy," briefly ending up in a Glasgow prison. Next, she set up an all-female tree surgery company, The Lumberjills. But that came to an end when one of her partners flew to New Zealand to work on the *Lord of the Rings* films. Later, Gaia moved back to London to work in film herself, spending fourteen years alongside director Danny Boyle and his producer Christian Colson, joining them from the earliest days of their Oscar-winning *Slumdog Millionaire* project.

For a short period before that, in pre-Danny days, she had worked with the now-notorious Harvey Weinstein. One memorable day, he fired her three times. He subsequently fell seriously foul of the #MeToo movement and, at least at the time of this writing, was serving a twenty-plus-year sentence in a maximum security prison in New York state as a serial sex offender. Gaia was the only one among Weinstein's UK staff who, through an oversight, had not signed a nondisclosure agreement—allowing her to talk to the media when the storm broke.

Later, she blossomed further, literally, expanding into high-end floristry for the likes of BAFTA, Harvey Nichols, the Serpentine Galleries, and the Globe Theatre while promoting seasonality, recycling, and plastic- and waste-free solutions.

Hania, on the other hand, often seemed distinctly less interested in my agenda. That was until a young whale shark lifted her bodily out of the water during an Earthwatch turtle conservation project in Baja California. Coincidentally, three weeks later, while hitchhiking solo around the west of Scotland, Gaia was marooned by a rising tide while exploring a small island, so decided to go swimming in the nude in the murky waters—and bumped into a giant basking shark. So, in less than a month, Hania had encountered the world's biggest fish, and Gaia the second biggest. Nature, it seemed, was trying to give us a helping hand.

When Hania was a child, her mind often seemed to be elsewhere, something her teachers would comment on—and not approvingly. Still, it was clear that she was highly creative, winning several writing awards, including the Monica Dickens Prize. Having found her feet in screenwriting, Hania cowrote and executive-produced her own original series for Netflix, *The Innocents*. At the time of this writing, as well as being a phenomenal mother to our grandson Gene, she was show-running her new series for Amazon, *Fifteen-Love*.

Don't Fence Me In[17]

I have learned so much from my daughters over the decades, but what have I learned about myself? Perhaps most importantly, I learned how lucky I am to have been born curious—it's far from typical. In that context, I came to see how important my father's spirit of independence and inquiry and my mother's love of words and stories have been.

I also learned a good deal from an exercise we went through a couple of times at SustainAbility. There are many competing frameworks for probing people's characters, including the Myers-Briggs Personality Type Indicator approach. Sometimes, this sort of analysis reminds me of having one's horoscope told. But other times the results feel amazingly accurate.

As far as Myers-Briggs was concerned, I initially came out as an INFP, where *I* stands for introverted, but was told that I had learned how to be more extroverted (or ENFP).* INFPs, I discovered, feel a higher calling, an urge to deliver some greater good. That ticked a box. INFPs also struggle with two competing characteristics: curiosity and shyness. That nailed it, accounting for the tension I had experienced when I stood up to ask those boys at prep school to hand over their treasured pocket money for the embryonic WWF.

We INFPs also tend to be positive, optimistic, and future-oriented, but we do not like to be categorized. That's me to a T: I have always resisted pressure to come up with an elevator pitch. If people have only a few minutes to spare, good night and good luck to them.

Cutting across organizational hierarchies and structures, INFPs prize their autonomy, insisting, "You can't put me in a box." I have never used those precise words, but the line captures my strong streak of independence, as in when I "sacked" my tutor at Bryanston.

Facts and details tend to bore most INFPs—who often ignore them in favor of bigger pictures and chances to explore the future and, shot through everything they do, engage in a quest for deeper meaning. But what happens when you then mix in the *E*, reflecting a growing degree of extroversion? ENFPs are typically driven by the new, have insatiable curiosity, and seemingly endless energy. They love to be surrounded by creative people if the overall spirit is open and collaborative. More boxes ticked.

On the downside, however: few things irritate them more than having to measure progress, report against organizational metrics, or fill in time sheets. So, with apologies to all the teams and clients I have worked with, this is what is behind my aversion to capturing any impact and value created by the hour.

Those who have studied ENFPs say that giving them targets or rules simply encourages them to concoct inventive ways of breaking them. Another characteristic I recognize is the love of spontaneity, meaning that

---

* The Myers-Briggs approach is disputed, but this summary of the personality type rang true to me: https://www.16personalities.com/infp-personality.

we are not really planners, preferring to fly by the seat of our proverbial pants. We also tend to be good at getting things started—piling in with energy, enthusiasm, and zeal. On the downside, and keen to see good in others, ENFPs often struggle with making the tough decisions needed to run organizations. They are very far removed from the Trumpian "You're fired!" world. Typically, too, they don't deliberately buck the system, instead simply withdrawing and doing things their own way. But corner them and push them too hard on their core values and you may have lit a blue touch paper. Stand well back.

Still, if we are to crack the climate and biodiversity emergencies, alongside the many other existential challenges we face, we must get much better at talking to each other, whatever our personalities, values, and priorities—at a time when social and political divides are growing more pronounced. We must engage people and interests we would normally ignore. This means asking better questions, both of ourselves and of others. It means making sure that we listen to, understand, and learn from the answers.

And, crucially, it means that we must carve out the time to take part in the right sort of constructive conversations and exchanges—with people of all ages, all backgrounds, and all persuasions. Sensing the tug of the future, people like me often feel the urge to move on to the next big thing before the previous big thing is done. Colleagues will recognize this version of me, for better or worse. An experimentalist, I ache to try new things. Often, I try many things before, if I am lucky, something works. Which is part of the reason why in the next chapter I describe myself as an accidental capitalist.

CHAPTER 3

Accidental Capitalist

If someone had told me when our little start-up was gestating in my London home that someday it would be acquired by the "Barbarians at the Gate"—the tag stuck on private equity giant KKR after its notorious hostile buyout of Nabisco, I would have said "Impossible!" and then, having thought about it a bit more, "Over my dead body!" But SustainAbility, the pioneering change agency I cofounded in 1987, was acquired in 2019 by ERM, itself now majority-owned by KKR.

All of this might suggest that I was a capitalist from the outset. Hardly. Three of the four businesses I cofounded over the decades may have been limited companies, but that was primarily to ensure their independence and freedom to maneuver, and secondarily to make them look business-friendly—not to prepare them for ultimate acquisition.

But perhaps there's another way to look at it. Perhaps we could view the SustainAbility acquisition as a signal that business, markets, and capitalism itself are finally buying into some elements of our change agenda—if not yet full-blown system change. Markets are beginning to step forward, if not yet up.

At SustainAbility, the idea of profiting from the sale of the firm was totally alien to me. When one cofounder suggested the possibility early on, to my mind it was a black mark. Before long, he was gone. And when another key member of the team suggested it some years later, my response was, "It's like saying you want to sell your family."

At best, then, I was an accidental capitalist.

Money was not a strong driver. Instead, SustainAbility's three-fold mission was to make a difference, to make a profit (to give us independence and to reinvest in our future), and to have fun and learn along the way.

But I was never a Marxist either, even when it was the height of fashion. Karl Marx was surprisingly popular when I was at the University of Essex. This surprised me at the time, given what I had learned about Marxism and Soviet history. But then I dug deeper into the things Marx himself had said and concluded that some of it made sense—at least in theory.

Capitalist production, Marx argued, grows by sapping the original sources of wealth: "the soil and the worker."[1] These days, perhaps we can see the soil as symbolizing not just farmland but also the wider natural environment, while the worker represents the ever-evolving social agenda. Whichever way I looked at it, though, Marxism left me feeling queasy.

Yes, I was impressed by the way it inspired the Vietminh and Vietcong coalitions in the seemingly endless Vietnam War, though I suspect that national identity was more important; and I saw overwhelming evidence that it could cause mayhem in the wrong hands.[2] As can any ideology, including capitalism.

Marxism was no fun either—though, every so often, you caught a slight twinkle. "Not every problem someone has with his girlfriend is necessarily due to the capitalist mode of production," quipped Herbert Marcuse, the "Father of the New Left" and a patron saint of the student movements of the late sixties.[3] Having struggled with Marcuse's books, I was startled to find that momentary flash of playfulness.

A Little Green Book?

A core insight on all of this has been attributed to Martin Luther King Jr. "Capitalism does not permit an even flow of economic resources," he warned. "A small privileged few are rich beyond conscience, and almost all others are doomed to be poor at some level. And since we know that the system will not change the rules, we are going to have to change the system."[4]

But whether or not he actually said this, it made sense to me then—and still does. At the time, though, watching angry students take to the streets waving copies of Mao Zedong's *The Little Red Book*, I did wonder how we might get them all brandishing a *Little Green Book*. And just in case you imagine that this must have been too early for anyone to be talking about "greening," the concept was already in the air—as signaled by the title of Charles A. Reich's 1970 book, *The Greening of America*.[5]

A key part of what put me off Marxism and its variants was the zealotry. Mao is reputed to have said that "the weeds of socialism are better than the crops of capitalism." If he didn't actually say that, he would have, had he thought of it. But the mindset proved cataclysmic at times. As when he ordered the Chinese into the streets, not to protest but to bang pots and pans until the birds fell exhausted from the sky. After all, he reasoned, birds competed for food. The fact that they also devoured pests was forgotten until it was too late. Harvests were decimated.

A different logic underpinned my own quest for a sense of openness, curiosity, and humor among those who wanted to work with us. A playful spirit can help immensely if you are looking for creative solutions to challenging—even apparently impossible—problems. But it also signals a range of other characteristics that can help keep things moving.

Once upon a time in China, I was speaking at a World Economic Forum event in Dalian and was asked while on stage how I could tell whether an organization was ripe for change. I replied that it was a bit like coming across a Ming vase in a high-end gallery or museum. To test its quality, you might flick it with a fingernail (intake of breath in the audience). If it sounded dull, you knew there were flaws. If it chimed, you knew there was a deeper integrity. For me, playfulness played a similar role when testing human beings and their organizations.

In the Mao era, Ming vases in China were deeply suspect, routinely smashed. But a society that smashes key elements of its culture is on a slippery slope to total anarchy. Most of Mao's student followers seemed oblivious, however—all they knew was that it was time to smash things, from priceless vases to economic systems. As student protests raged across Europe and the United States around the same time as the Chinese Cultural Revolution, I tried to get a better sense of what was going on—and of where things might be headed.

Along the way, I found myself at a key event at London's Roundhouse, a performance space converted from an old railway turntable building, where notables of the New Left were holding forth. Many wore army surplus greatcoats, perhaps because it was cold, perhaps to give them a revolutionary air. Whatever the truth, I couldn't help concluding that at least some of them were playacting, though perhaps revolutionaries often are.

Several Western societies were teetering on the edge of a political precipice at the time, with combined protests by students and workers threatening to bring down the French government. As I watched leading activists like Tariq Ali and Robin Blackburn stalking around the Roundhouse, I felt increasingly repelled. However much such people might call for change, I concluded, their revolutionary turntable would not be able to rotate our economic juggernaut.

I didn't shout it out—instead, like any self-respecting INFP, I slipped away into the night. Though I didn't know it then, I was becoming what Mao would have castigated as a "capitalist roader." The Chinese Communist Party had huge numbers of such people executed, often without trial. Again, I was lucky to be alive when and where I was.

Willy Wonka's Planes

Beyond capitalism, I was interested in business and markets—which are very far from the same thing. There had been plenty of entrepreneurial people in my family but not many real capitalists, as far as I could discover. My own family was not in any way capitalistic, though they all depended to some degree on the success of capitalism in the face of its enemies, both before and during the Cold War.

One great-great-grandmother, Clara Witter, traveled several times back and forth across the American prairies in covered wagons, eventually settling in the Rockies. There, she and her family set up a provisions store and post office. The miners would pay in gold they'd extracted, and at the end of each week, Clara would sweep the dirt floor and pan the sweepings for gold dust. Eventually the family made enough money to start a bank in Denver—and it still seemed to be there when I visited the city in the early 1980s.

Others from the same side of the family mined for gold and silver up and down the Rockies. Among other incidents and accidents, they had a number of tailings dam failures, one of which wiped out part of a nearby settlement.[6]

But as the reunified United States prospered after the American Civil War, a darker character appeared in the family tree. Later in Clara's diary a certain Schuyler Colfax appeared, a close friend of the Colorado branch of the Witters and a half-brother of hers. He is now notorious for being one of the most corrupt politicians in US history. As vice president to President Ulysses S. Grant, he was part of an immense corruption scandal linked to the construction of the transcontinental railway system and payment for votes.

At the same time, I later discovered, he broke with precedent to cast his vote, as Speaker of the House of Representatives, in favor of the Thirteenth Amendment to the United States Constitution. That vote ended slavery in the United States, but the Speaker would normally only have used the deciding vote when there was a tie in the House. An example, perhaps, of how people can be both good and bad at the same time, though you do wonder whether he was paid for that vote, too.

Still, I was less interested in trains than in aircraft, from the earliest days of birdman Otto Lilienthal through to Louis Blériot, the Wright Brothers, and Spitfire designer R. J. Mitchell. In the process, I became hooked on the history of companies that made both planes and rockets. I was particularly intrigued by Lockheed's famous "Skunk Works" in World War II. It has been described as aerospace's equivalent of Willy Wonka's chocolate factory.[7]

I also read assiduously about how Rolls-Royce's Merlin engine evolved, powering many of the aircraft that Tim had flown. I followed its history from the early efforts to win the fabled Schneider Trophy races, which the Merlin-powered Supermarine seaplanes eventually won outright for Britain, through to fighters like the Hurricane and Spitfire, fighter-bombers like the Mosquito, and heavy bombers like the Lancaster.

In 2015, Tim went to Rolls-Royce's Derby headquarters to rededicate a Battle of Britain stained-glass window. Accompanied by my youngest sister, Tessa, he spoke at the dinner, saying:

> I'm here today to join with you in remembering those who fought in the Battle of Britain, and your contribution to its outcome. But more especially, I've come to say thank you, Rolls-Royce.
>
> I thank you, first, for the "R Type" engine which powered the Schneider Trophy aircraft and Campbell's Bluebird, which kick-started my career in the Royal Air Force.
>
> And I'm grateful, too, for the hundreds of hours I have flown behind Kestrel, Merlin, Griffon, and Derwent engines—in Europe, Russia, on Atlantic Convoys, in India and the Pacific—without a failure.
>
> You have never let me down. A tribute surely to good design—and the work of your hands?
>
> Thank you.[8]

The stained-glass window they were rededicating showed rows of heavily smoking chimneys, symbolizing both the effort that went into making the machines that helped win the war and the damage done to human health and the wider environment by all that industrial activity—an interesting reflection of our very different generational challenges.

What I learned from all of this was that coming up with the right design is only part of the challenge. More important, generally, is the capacity to manufacture any product at scale. And that lesson was reinforced for me by an account featuring the Republic P-47 Thunderbolt, which Tim once told me had been his favorite aircraft among the many scores of British, American, German, and Japanese models he had flown. Perhaps because it had an ashtray?[*]

The story dates to 1945—and captures the critical role of industrial muscle power.[9] A German fighter pilot shot down during a surprise attack on the US 365th Fighter Group, the "Hell Hawks," pointed proudly to the considerable number of Republic P-47 Thunderbolts burning across the airfield. As he was led away into captivity, he said, in perfect English, "What do you think of that?" But American industry had churned out nearly 100,000 warplanes in the year just ended—and within days the airfield was swarming again with factory-fresh Thunderbolts. The American who had captured the German pilot went back to see his captive, still held at the base, and asked, "What do you think of that?" The German replied, "That is what is beating us."

Like it or not, the challenges we face in the twenty-first century will only be solved with the sustained application of the right technology, in the right way, and in the right places. Wherever you look—renewable energy, batteries, electric vehicles—the story is the same.

Inside the Gherkin

So how, I wondered, might we scale and replicate sustainability-oriented solutions? Two people powerfully influenced my thinking here. The first was R. Buckminster "Bucky" Fuller; the second, Lester "Les" R. Brown, whom I first met when he ran the Worldwatch Institute, based in Washington, DC.

I met Bucky through my writing for *New Scientist*. We had breakfast together in Reykjavík, Iceland, during an event I was covering for the magazine in 1977.[10] No one had done more than he to promote the idea

---

[*] Reading this section, Gray reminded me that Tim also said that the Hawker Typhoon was his favorite aircraft.

of "Spaceship Earth." He advocated the need to switch our economies from "weaponry" to "livingry." Later, I came across his influence in many places, including in the Thames-side studios of "starchitect" Sir Norman Foster, another of my longstanding heroes. There were photos of Fuller and his geodesic structures.

Foster, whose motto ran "The only constant is change," built some of my favorite buildings.[11] They include the British Museum's Great Court, which for years was a couple of blocks away from the Volans office in Bloomsbury; the new Reichstag dome in Berlin; and London's Gherkin.

I was taken around the Gherkin by site director Sara Fox while it was still under construction. The graceful building, nicknamed the "Erotic Gherkin," was eminently feminine, but Texan Sara had something of the Wild West about her. Her desk featured a photograph of her as a young girl, brandishing a very large revolver. When I asked about her job, managing a couple hundred men in high-risk situations, she replied: "It's about maintaining momentum when many people are saying this is such a stupid idea. Opening windows in a forty-story skyscraper? A circular floor plan? Are you nuts?" As a result, she said, getting some sustainability features into the building seemed to take "for fucking ever!"

But back to Bucky, whom I like to imagine rarely swore. When we had breakfast together, I had already read his books, loving his central idea of doing more with less, or "ephemeralization," as he liked to call it. This concept was embodied in his geodesic domes. At one stage they seemed to be everywhere I went, from dropout communities to the strategic radar domes of nuclear attack early warning systems. Today, some of the biggest geodesic domes in the world are at the Eden Project, developed by my friend Tim Smit, spotlighted in this book's afterword.*

Which brings us to Lester Brown. After an initial encounter at the Worldwatch Institute sometime in the nineties, I ran into him at a World

---

* Another touchpoint was when I helped judge the Buckminster Fuller Institute Challenge. My favorite Buckyism: "You never change things by fighting the existing reality. To change something, build a new model that makes the existing model obsolete."

Economic Forum summit in the noughties and visited him a couple of years later at his Earth Policy Institute in Washington, DC. His thinking powerfully shaped my own ideas about the business end of sustainability—and the wider context. "There are many things we do not know about the future," he said in his 2008 book, *Plan B 3.0: Mobilizing to Save Civilization*.[12] "But one thing we do know is that business as usual will not continue for much longer. Massive change is inevitable. Will the change come because we move quickly to restructure the economy or because we fail to act, and civilization begins to unravel?"

That question, again. Over time, sadly, the second option has begun to seem the likelier.

Brown went on to warn, "Saving civilization will take a massive mobilization, and at wartime speed. The closest analogy is the belated US mobilization during World War II. But unlike that chapter in history, in which one country totally restructured its economy, the Plan B [his branding for the impending economic transition] mobilization requires decisive action on a global scale."[13]

The key to building a global economy that can sustain economic progress, Brown insisted, "is the creation of an honest market, one that tells the ecological truth. To create an honest market, we need to restructure the tax system by reducing taxes on work and raising them on various environmentally destructive activities, to incorporate indirect costs into the market price. If we can get the market to tell the truth, then we can avoid being blindsided by a faulty accounting system that leads to bankruptcy."[14]

The US entry into World War II offered an inspiring case study in rapid mobilization, Brown argued. Initially, the United States resisted involvement and responded only after it was directly attacked at Pearl Harbor on December 7, 1941. But then it responded in the most extraordinary way. Political leadership was make-or-break. One month after the bombing of Pearl Harbor, Brown noted, President Roosevelt announced the country's arms production goals. Already, the US was planning to produce 45,000 tanks, 60,000 planes, 20,000 anti-aircraft guns, and 6 million tons of merchant shipping.

The Allies invested in and built a massive serendipity engine that ensured that the dice increasingly fell in their favor. The Lockheed Skunk Works, which I was fascinated by early on, was part of that, turning out top-notch fighters like the Lightning in record time. It was what we might now call an incubator. All those instruments of war eventually swung the balance of power.

Political stamina was more important still. No wonder Winston Churchill drank so prodigiously.

Now, in very much the same way, we must exert every sinew to swing the balance from planetary degeneration, the pattern of the last couple of centuries, to a worldwide push for regeneration across our economies, societies, and natural environment. Regeneration, in turn, requires a fervent embrace of new disciplines such as biomimicry, which is, among other things, the study of how life creates the conditions for more life.

Someone else who had a profound early impact on how I see our world was Stewart Brand. Once an American military parachutist, Brand later became a member of the legendary counterculture pioneers the Merry Pranksters, and the editor of the even more legendary *Whole Earth Catalog*, which inspired Apple's Steve Jobs and whose successive editions were essential reading for people like me from 1968 on. Mindbogglingly, too, he was among the instigators of NASA's famous *Earthrise* photo.

When I eventually met Brand, he was president of the Long Now Foundation.[15] At a time when attention spans are shrinking drastically, the foundation has built a ten-thousand-year clock that tells deep time, ticking once a year. As for that selfie of Earth from space, Brand had been immersed in an LSD trip back in 1966 on the roof of his home in North Beach, San Francisco. He became convinced that seeing an image of the whole Earth would forever change how we think about the planet and ourselves. He campaigned to have NASA release a rumored satellite image of the entire Earth as seen from space.

To that end, he distributed buttons for 25 cents apiece, each asking, "Why haven't we seen a photograph of the whole Earth yet?" During that campaign, he would meet Bucky Fuller, who offered to help. In 1967, a satellite took the photo. Shortly afterward, it would adorn the first edition of the *Whole Earth Catalog*. Then, in 1968, NASA astronaut Bill Anders took what became the *Earthrise* image, from the Moon orbit, and it became the cover image of the *Catalog*'s spring 1969 edition. The image may have become hackneyed over time, but for my generation it was both eye- and mind-opening.

During a 2003 interview, Brand explained that the image had given "the sense that Earth is an island, surrounded by a lot of inhospitable space. And it's so graphic, this little blue, white, green, and brown jewel-like icon amongst a quite featureless black vacuum."[16]

The first time I set eyes on Brand was on March 23, 2006. I was visiting the Global Business Network (GBN) in Emeryville, California, a think tank he had cofounded. This was an event for the defense industry, and even though I had arrived ridiculously early for a meeting with GBN CEO Peter Schwartz, I was invited in anyway. My blog entry that day reads as follows:

> Arrived way too early, but—to my amazement—Peter invited me into a closed session on future trends in the areas of security, borders, and boundaries. Utterly fascinating, with those taking part including former NASA astronaut Rusty Schweickart, ecologist Peter Warshall and one of my all-time heroes, Stewart Brand, who I first came across via *The Whole Earth Catalog* . . . I brought up the notion of "bodily trespass" [used against the chemical industry] as an interesting example of the ways in which our thinking on boundaries is changing.[17]

I would later have the pleasure of meeting Brand properly at Gaia scientist James Lovelock's hundredth birthday party, at which he and his wife, Ryan Phelan, were at our table. In this case, he completely disproved the old saying that you don't want to meet your heroes.

The work Ryan was doing also underscored the way the couple had routinely been ahead of the curve. She had been working to restore extinct mammoth populations,[18] later telling me that my "triple bottom line" thinking had informed her work on protecting threatened horseshoe crabs, a keystone species whose blood is used to develop vaccines, including ones for COVID-19, and all sorts of products implanted in the human body, including pacemakers.[19] The crabs, which have roamed the oceans for about four hundred fifty million years, are now under intense threat from destruction of their habitat and over-harvesting by the fishing and biomedical industries. Campaigners want the pharma companies to use synthetic substitutes like recombinant factor C.[20]

Meanwhile, the idea of *de-extinction* has been gaining traction. Dallas/Fort Worth-based Colossal Biosciences, which has been working to bring the mammoth and Tasmanian tiger, or thylacine, back from the dead, also recently announced plans to bring back the dodo. The good old hype cycle. Headline-grabbing, no question, but highly unlikely to provide practical answers to the global loss of species.[21]

Curiosity Didn't Kill This Cat

Serendipity can be a wonderful ally, though you must work at it. In that spirit, I have gone out of my way to meet people who were evolving new ways to think, work, and live. In 1973, it was Paolo Soleri's Arcosanti in the Arizona desert. That same year, in Shropshire, England, along Offa's Dyke ancient earthwork, I also worked for a short time at Biotechnic Research and Development, or BRAD.

This alternative technology commune was cofounded by Robin Clarke, a former editor of *Science Journal*, which later merged with *New Scientist*. Robin had done key work at the interface of peace and security, writing a book called *The Science of War and Peace*, published in 1972, the year before I landed on his doorstep—having been introduced by my friend and best man, Ian Keay.

At the time, people like us were inspired by publications such as *Whole Earth Catalog* and E. F. Schumacher's book *Small Is Beautiful: A Study of Economics as if People Mattered*. Housed in an in-conversion farmhouse under a massive, just-installed solar roof, BRAD was exciting and disconcerting in equal measure. The idea was to prototype and test technologies and lifestyles that could deliver what we might now call *sustainable outcomes*. When I arrived at BRAD, the solar roof had not yet been properly plumbed in and was capturing so much heat that it was boiling the sap out of the new roof beams. As a result, the attic floor was covered in conical masses of yellow sap.

More disconcerting still, the unpainted plasterboard walls of the room where I slept were covered in pen drawings of the hallucinations of a troubled brain, produced by the young son of one of the founding members. Given the unease I had felt about hanging since those Nicosia executions in the late fifties, it was disconcerting to have hanged and gibbeted people dangling all around me as I tried to sleep.

Many years later, Elaine recalled in a brief biography on her own website, "I remember [John's] descriptions of a giant boar breaking out of its pen and eating a live cockerel; his milking of a rectangular-pupiled goat in a broken-roofed byre, under the glittering stars, with a brown rat washing its whiskers nearby—like milking the Devil himself, John said later; and at the end of all this, he came back with a severe, chronic case of sinusitis, cured a couple of years later by a faith healer we found through Oliver 'Olly' Caldecott, a director of Wildwood House. But that's another story."

Indeed. Founded by former Penguin editors Oliver Caldecott[22] and Dieter Pevsner,[23] Wildwood House published the most extraordinary authors, exploring many aspects of the alternative economy. Among the more memorable was Jolan Chang, the Chinese Canadian sexologist who wrote books like *The Tao of Love and Sex*. As Elaine also recalled many years later about her years in the Wildwood team—

> Chang looked Chinese but I'm not sure what he was. He used to come to the office on a bicycle. He lived in Sweden and told us he had sex ten times a day. One day he arrived with a large bag of pumpkin seeds, which he said were an aphrodisiac and proceeded to offer them to Helen, Beverley,

and myself. Beverley announced that she was married and very much looked down her nose at Chang and his antics. Helen and I ate a handful of the seeds but, sadly for Chang, did not feel able to oblige him in his regime of ten times a day. Chang went off, saying that English girls were frigid and that was why he lived in Sweden.[24]

Other authors published by Wildwood House, which occupied the floor below TEST, included Fritjof Capra (*The Tao of Physics*) and Garry Trudeau (of the *Doonesbury* cartoon strips), alongside people like Buryl Payne (*Getting There Without Drugs*). Others coming through included people who had a significant impact on my thinking, among them Pulitzer Prize winner Studs Terkel (who wrote memorable oral histories such as *Working*, *Hard Times*, and *The Good War*) and the strikingly tall Alvin Toffler (*Future Shock*, *The Third Wave*).

Extraordinary people.

Terkel had been massively impacted by the McCarthyism witch-trial atmosphere of the 1950s in America, not least because he had refused to give evidence against other left-wing activists—and had been blacklisted and blocked from appearing on television. I adored his attitude: he suggested that his epitaph should read "Curiosity did not kill this cat."[25]

Another intriguing Wildwood author was Godfrey Boyle, with his book *Radical Technology*.[26] He produced one of my favorite magazines of the era, *Undercurrents*, dubbed the "house journal of the alternative technology movement." To begin with, it was circulated as photocopied pages in an envelope, evolving later into a more formal magazine format. *Undercurrents* provided rare windows into the world of ultralocal and renewable energy-powered development that Godfrey believed could provide workable solutions to the great challenges of the day.

As I dug deeper into the various configurations of the emerging alternative economy, I came away persuaded that people like the New Alchemy Institute's John Todd, who had inspired Robin Clarke's approach, could innovate and pilot future technology. But little of what I saw at BRAD persuaded me that I was yet seeing the seeds of tomorrow's economy striking root. Perhaps inevitably, sadly, the BRAD experiment ultimately failed.

Meanwhile, undaunted, I continued diving into different aspects of the alternative technology world, among other things helping to organize the People's Habitat Festival in London's Docklands in 1976—a counterblast to the United Nations' Habitat conference on sustainable human settlements of the same year held in Vancouver, Canada.[27] It was great fun but again something of a shambles.

We managed to get windmills and solar panels into the obsolete, aching-for-redevelopment Surrey Docks, but my main memory is of racing back and forth between Docklands and Covent Garden on crutches, having broken an ankle by falling down the steps at Barnes railway station. At one point during the festival, I was tearing back through Covent Garden to TEST, when one of my crutches smashed through a windowed pavement grid in Floral Street, shattering my plaster cast.

That, for me, symbolized the flying-by-the-seat-of-our-pants nature of so much of the alternative economy. One result was that I consciously decided to focus on business. My *New Scientist* articles increasingly zeroed in on what companies like British Petroleum (BP) and English China Clays (ECC) were doing, whether in using environmental impact assessment and auditing tools, in the case of BP, or regenerating industrial wastelands, in the case of ECC.

An Eye for Business

When I visited Cornwall to see the vast ECC opencast mine that would later become the Eden Project, the regeneration process was confined to a flock of Soay sheep used to punch grass into the sandy surface of vast soil heaps. This was an attempt to avoid the sort of collapse that had wiped out a school in the Welsh coal town of Aberfan in 1966, killing 28 adults and 116 children.

The sheer number of disasters at the time made people even more suspicious of what we then called "industry," though it became increasingly known as "business." And that's why a fair number of people saw my growing focus on business's role in developing and deploying environmental solutions—and later sustainability—as suspect.

Paradoxically, our limited company status, first at Environmental Data Services (ENDS), then at SustainAbility and later at Volans, set us to one side of nongovernmental organization (NGO) politics. It also had another unintended effect: it helped growing numbers of businesspeople to see us as probusiness, encouraging at least some of them to open up and engage.

The fact that I was writing books about the evolving business agenda also helped me get into places denied to many activists. My first book, *The Ecology of Tomorrow's World*, published in 1980, drew on what we were discovering through ENDS, where I was visiting numerous companies in the UK and elsewhere.[28] Later books dug deeper, as with *Sun Traps* in 1984[29] (focusing on the renewable energy forecast) and *The Poisoned Womb* in 1985[30] (focusing on the challenging subject of reproductive toxicology).

I also dug into the rapidly emerging areas of biotechnology and genetic engineering. For around fifteen years after leaving ENDS, almost as a hobby, I wrote a newsletter on the booming biotech sector, *Biotechnology Bulletin*. I learned a huge amount, visited scores of genetic engineering and biotechnology companies around the world—and wrote a book on the subject, *The Gene Factory*.[31] Years later, I spotted a copy of that book in New York's Museum of Modern Art, showcased as an example of excellent book cover design. I have Gail Rebuck to thank for that, the fabled editor who commissioned and edited the book. Meanwhile, *Biotechnology Bulletin*—largely written in the evenings and on weekends—funded our daughters' education.

The Sales Manager's Letter Book

This much I know: I am singularly poor at taking orders, which would have sunk any military career. So maybe business, with its alternating mix of market discipline and disruption, was always going to be my best bet. Still, early efforts to engage me in business struck me as profoundly unappetizing. I recall Tim suggesting I either take up military flying or, for some reason, merchant banking.

Given that I suffer from vertigo, the first was unlikely to take off, though Tim did send me up in a Tiger Moth biplane to loop a few loops with a trained pilot. Later, when I decided I wanted to try parachuting, he—having parachuted in anger in 1940—suggested I try gliding first. I did so on a sunny but stormy day; the stomach-churning movements of the glider rammed that idea firmly onto the spike.

As for merchant banking, I loathed men's social clubs, detested pin-striped suits, and—the clincher—was pretty much blind to numbers. Paradoxically, though, the as-yet-invisible societal pressure waves beginning to build all around would eventually carry me into the boardrooms of major businesses and financial institutions worldwide, including merchant and investment banks.

One book Tim gave me, which still sits unread on our shelves in London, represented his efforts to nudge me in the direction of management, if not yet capitalism.* While I appreciated the fact that the book's margins contained his own penciled notes, the book was about as far removed as possible from what I wanted to do and become.

This was *The Sales Manager's Letter Book.*

Its first line reads as follows: "No letter written for business purposes can be called unimportant, but the relation of sales to profit makes the sales letter stand out above the rest."[32] The author's aim was to generate a "sales pull" of ten percent. This would be "considered good in the average instance," he argued, "but what if it is twenty, thirty, or even higher? Then indeed, the writer's cup of joy runneth over." Well, my cup did not runneth over. I had already imbibed too much of the counterculture agenda for that. As a result, I had no interest whatsoever in concocting successful sales letters. Or sales pitches.

Instead, I have instinctively done things that actively disrupted the

---

* I remember Tim's joy, years later, when I had a couple of long-form articles (one of six thousand words) published in one of his favorite magazines, *Management Today.*

market and, counterintuitively, nudged at least some potential clients in our direction. In that spirit, the same *Green Consumer Guide* that would get SustainAbility sued by McDonald's Corporation would also help pull in clients like Dow Chemical Co., Novo Nordisk A/S, The Procter & Gamble Company, and Unilever PLC.

The dynamic is very different when a client approaches you, rather than vice versa. You can negotiate based on values, not just value. But to succeed in this way over time, you need a finely honed ability to spot—and then surf—incoming societal pressure waves.

CHAPTER 4

Surfing Tomorrow

It was one of those moments when you realize, too late, that you have made a painful mistake. The water was bone-shatteringly cold as my hands pierced the surface, translucent jellyfish wobbling away in confusion. This was May 2015, hardly the best time to be swimming off the Norwegian coast. Yet, as my body adapted to the cold, I considered how lucky I was to be on this island, Arøy, with some of the people I admired most in the world.

We had convened for a *Festschrift*, or celebratory conference, to mark the seventieth birthday of Jørgen Randers—one of the authors of the 1972 *Limits to Growth* study and a towering figure in environmental science and sustainable development. After the conference, Jørgen and his wife, Marie, had kindly invited ten of us to spend the weekend at their summer home, with its own private harbor.[1]

There, Elaine and I found ourselves alongside several longstanding friends. They included Paul Gilding, who had run Greenpeace International, with his wife, Michelle, also a former Greenpeace activist. And Mathis Wackernagel and his wife, Susan Burns, who had cofounded the Global Footprint Network and helped launch Earth Overshoot Day to ram home the grim reality that our degenerative economies are overwhelming our planet's ability to repair and regenerate itself.

There in the water, as I turned back toward the jetty, elbowing jellyfish aside, it struck me that each of the guests on the island represented different stages in the evolution of our agenda, each having caught—and worked out how to surf—successive waves of change.*

Most of us know how waves work. Foaming and hissing, a wave races in. When it hits—lifting us off our feet—we fight to keep our balance. Many of us recall this experience from our younger years, so wave metaphors have real power. Partly as a result, they have spread into every corner of our language. They have informed science, as with sound, electromagnetic, and plasma waves. They have shaped our thinking about the spread of pandemics. They have penetrated deep into economics in the form of long- and short-wave cycles. And they also surface in politics, as when American commentators comment on the potential for a "blue wave" of Democrat voters to sweep away a "red" incumbent, or vice versa.

Similarly, the term *surfing* has embraced new meanings—as in "surfing the internet," a phrase coined by a librarian, Jean Armour Polly, in 1992.[2] People also refer to young men riding the roofs of India's trains as "surfing." I use the word in a different context, though it's still inspired by the real-world exploits of big-wave surfers. I use it in the sense of surfing oncoming paradigm shifts of the sort discussed in chapter 2.

Duck-Diving

One surfer I reconnected with while developing this book was Chris Hines, a founder of the brilliantly effective group Surfers Against Sewage. I have known and admired him for almost thirty years—since he brought his surfboard and wetsuit along to London's Portland Baths to help us launch our 1992 book, *Holidays That Don't Cost the Earth*. His board was decorated with used condoms recovered from the sea.

---

* Jørgen Randers pioneered the environmental wave discussed in chapter 5, Paul and Michelle Gilding surfed the green wave sketched in chapter 6, and Mathis Wackernagel and Susan Burns helped inform the sustainability wave covered in chapter 7. I was perhaps the odd one out, having surfed all five of the waves mapped in part 2 of this book.

At the time, he was already campaigning against sewage pollution. Indeed, shortly after we caught up by Zoom in 2020, Chris sent me a note reminding me of just how polluted the seas off Britain's coasts had been back then. He recalled the day he went "duck-diving under a wave" and ended up with a discarded panty liner wrapped around his face. "The sea was literally fizzing and bubbling after a big set of waves, smelling of sickly-sweet sewage, mixed with washing up liquid detergents and washing powder," he wrote. "At the time, four hundred million gallons of crude sewage were being discharged untreated every single day."[3]

Sadly, such bad days are back now that more than seventy percent of Britain's water and sewage companies are owned by poorly regulated foreign investment groups. Clearly, there is nothing guaranteed about this ongoing revolution of ours.

When I asked him about any leadership lessons to be gained from surfing, Chris promptly introduced me to Easkey Britton.[*] A professional surfer, she had been Irish National Surfing Champion no less than five times when we spoke. As Chris suggested, she had thought deeply about the leadership lessons that surfing can offer the wider world. To my mind, Easkey also represents several other things: curiosity about what happens at the edge of things; a celebration of the power of conversations with strangers, surfers or not; and as the youngest of the surfers I had yet talked to, she also signposted the growing need for an accelerated generational handover.

Among other things, I was blown away by her efforts to teach Iranian women to surf in modern versions of the hijab. The picture this last sentence conjures for me is one in which everyone learns to surf the future—and does so in the spirit of a better future for all forms of life.

Once I had rumbled the fact that the future tends to come in waves, I tried to work out how to get ahead of the wave crests and stand upright on the racing edges of change. In the process, I worked out how to negotiate

---

[*] Easkey Britton has written two books: *Saltwater in the Blood* (London: Watkins, 2021) and *Ebb & Flow* (London: Watkins, 2023). She concludes in the second of these, "Our relationship with water is broken." She talks in terms of "blue health" and surveys the work of water protectors around the world. Inspiring.

upwaves and downwaves—the peaks and troughs—though not without frequent spills, or wipeouts, as surfers call them. Similarly, the entire history of our civilization has moved in waves: constructive and destructive waves; physical, political, cultural, and technological waves; large waves and small ones; visible waves—and those that our senses cannot detect. Tomorrow's waves, today's—and yesterday's.

Out of the Blue

Pottery crunched underfoot where no pottery should have been. It was Friday, April 20, 2007, and Elaine and I were walking across a windswept headland on the northern coast of Crete. There are varying views among scientists about what had happened there and how, but those shards high above the shoreline were unsettling—suggesting a tsunami had carried them there a long time ago.

This giant wave, or more likely waves, helped collapse the extraordinary Minoan civilization. And, just maybe, the archaeological evidence of the cannibalization of children after the tsunamis hit may have had something to do with the enduring myth of the child-unfriendly Minotaur. True or not, we were told on Crete that the ultimate fall of the Minoan civilization followed the destruction of Thera. The devastation of this extraordinary island, once known as Kalliste ("the most beautiful one") and a possible source of the enduring legend of Atlantis, caused grief in all directions. There is evidence of widespread tsunamis after the original island's cataclysmic destruction by volcano.

Today, a different type of monster wave has been elbowing its way into the spotlight. The best book I have read on such "freak waves" is *The Wave* by Susan Casey, given to me by our daughter Gaia.[4] Casey became fascinated by ship-swallowing waves, and by the scientists and surfers who risk their lives to study or ride them. These freak waves are useful models for the industry-swallowing waves we focus on in our own work.

For a long time, such monster waves were dismissed as fanciful, akin to the mermaids and sea monsters fringing early nautical maps. Some people considered them to be impossible, delusional, the product of overwrought imaginations and poor diets at sea. But, as Casey notes, "New technologies began to reveal startling information. 'Ship-Devouring Waves, Once Legendary, Common Sight on Satellite,' read a *USA Today* headline on July 23, 2004, describing how radar could now measure waves from space: '. . . a new study based on satellite data reveals the rogues are fairly common.'"[5]

Casey concluded: "Given the lack of survivors or evidence, exact statistics of ships scuttled by giant waves are impossible to come by, but every year, on average, more than two dozen large ships sink or otherwise go missing, taking their crews along with them. (If you also consider smaller vessels, the numbers are vastly higher.)"[6]

You would think that most sane people would steer as far away as possible from such waves. Yet, following the offer of a $500,000 prize for the first person to surf the face of a 100-foot wave, Casey tracked the efforts of surfers to extend their range from the previous limit of 40-foot waves to 60-foot, 80-foot, and even 100-foot waves.

The new art of tow-surfing, where surfers hitch themselves onto a jet ski or helicopter to be pulled into position to catch these ocean giants, enables them to do things that would be impossible if they still had to paddle out. Indeed, some of my favorite images of all time are of surfers slicing down the faces of such monsters.[*]

Over time, surfers have become ever more sensitive to what is going on around them. Casey again: "I had noticed that any tow surfer worth his foot straps [used to anchor surfers to their boards] was also a closet meteorologist, able to translate buoy readings, spectral analyses, swell periods, wind directions, and bottom features in the waves that would likely result."[7]

By contrast, the big waves I have got used to surfing are different. They are the societal pressure waves that can also appear out of the blue, rearing

---

[*] Including the image on the cover of the first LP I ever bought, back in 1963: the Beach Boys' *Surfin' U.S.A.*

up from the midst of lesser patterns and disturbances in human affairs—and frequently overwhelming the ill-prepared.

Marked Man

If any single person can be blamed, or credited, for my fascination with waves, it is Nikolai Kondratiev. I never met the man, given that by the time I was born, he had already been dead for eleven years. But he had an extraordinary life—and death. Unfortunately for him, his thinking flew in the face of the ideology of his ultimate boss, the stupefyingly brutal Josef Stalin.

In the heart of the Great Depression, the despotic Soviet leader was utterly convinced that capitalist nations were down and out for good. In stark contrast, the implication of Kondratiev's work was that those failing economies would eventually bounce back, likely stronger than ever. No matter how renowned Kondratiev may have been as an economist, this was tempting fate to a mind-boggling degree.

To prove his intuition that capitalist economies were subject to recurrent depressions and recoveries, Kondratiev analyzed, in depth and over time, the price of goods in the German, French, and British economies. His economic cycle theory suggested that there were long cycles ranging between forty and sixty years, involving periods of intense investment and disinvestment. But his conclusion that capitalism might survive in the long term despite wild excursions along the way made Kondratiev a marked man.

He was removed from the directorship of the Institute of Conjuncture in 1928 and arrested in 1930, then accused of being a member of a "Peasants Labour Party," a nonexistent party conjured up by the secret police to ensure his conviction. Kondratiev was sentenced to eight years in prison and was held from February 1932 onward at Suzdal, near Moscow. While his health deteriorated markedly under the wretched conditions, he doggedly pursued his research, determined to write five new books, some of which were even published.

Then, in September 1938, during Stalin's Great Purge, he was tried a second time and condemned to ten years—but was executed by firing squad on the same day the sentence was proclaimed. He was forty-six.

Later the more famous Austrian economist Joseph Schumpeter credited the foundations of his own long wave theory to Kondratiev. He coined the term "Kondratiev waves" (or K-waves) in honor of the martyred economist. In doing so, he played a key role in restoring the reputation of one of Stalin's more notable victims. In 1987, the Soviet Union officially rehabilitated Kondratiev, shortly before it itself passed into oblivion.

Long wave theory has had a decidedly bumpy ride over the years, although the idea that innovation follows S-curves has won wider support. Still, the notion that monster waves shape our economies is now taken for granted—even if then routinely ignored. The historian Eric Hobsbawm noted that the fact that "good predictions have proved possible on the basis of Kondratiev Long Waves—this is not very common in economics—has convinced many historians and even some economists that there is something in them, even if we don't know what."[8]

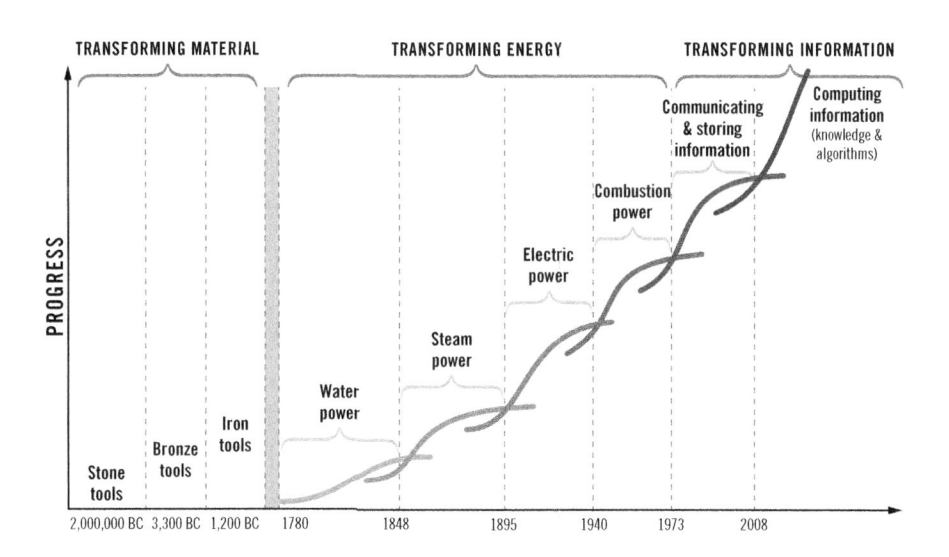

Based on Martin Hilbert, "Digital Technology and Social Change: The Digital Transformation of Society from a Historical Perspective," *Dialogues in Clinical Neuroscience* 22, no. 2 (2020): 189–194.

Meanwhile, others have been hard at work trying to predict what a sixth Kondratiev wave might look like. Among them have been James Bradfield Moody and Bianca Nogrady, who predicted in 2010 that it would be driven by growing resource efficiency and booming clean technologies.[9] As it happens, I had reached similar conclusions in my 1982 report, *Seven Bridges to the Future*.[10]

On balance, I have found Schumpeter's thinking on business cycles easier to digest, though he, too, was not always as popular as he would have liked, at least not in his lifetime. But the hero of his version of the economic waves story was the entrepreneur—which has made some of his thinking distinctly more palatable in recent times. His most popular book, at least in English, was *Capitalism, Socialism and Democracy*. While he agreed with Marx that capitalism would eventually collapse and be replaced by socialism, Schumpeter predicted a different route. Instead of a violent proletarian revolution, Schumpeter thought that capitalism would gradually lose steam and be replaced democratically.

Perhaps his most memorable contribution was the phrase *creative destruction*. He likened the "gale of creative destruction" to the "process of industrial mutation that continuously revolutionizes the economic structure from within, incessantly destroying the old one, incessantly creating a new one."[11] It is now almost impossible to imagine any other explanation for the processes of innovation in capitalist economies.

Among more recent thinkers who also influenced my thinking in this area has been Carlota Perez, who in turn learned a great deal from her mentor Chris Freeman.[12] Having met neither Kondratiev nor Schumpeter, who died the year after I was born, I thought it was time to meet a living champion of long wave theory.

So, on April 2, 2017, having chaired a session of the admissions panel of the ultimately ill-fated Social Stock Exchange, Elaine and I drove south for a dinner in Lewes with Carlota. She had recently been appointed London School of Economics (LSE) Centennial Professor, which suggested that some people were listening to her. Interestingly, it turned out that we saw the periodicity of the fading and building waves somewhat differently, although in broadly compatible ways.

I conclude that there are waves both in our economies and in the societal pressures that impact governments and business, but I have no idea whether there is any sort of periodicity or rhythm to them. Nor do I have a model that would predict either their growth and collapse or the nature and scale of any future waves. Instead, I have simply recorded what I have observed over time—expressing any conclusions more in the spirit of storytelling than of science.

Another key influence was Alvin Toffler, whose 1970 best seller *Future Shock* helped the world come to terms with the impact of disruptive innovation. His next book, published in 1980, and one of the most impactful I have read, was *The Third Wave*.[13] Something I realized only recently was that he also helped inspire my idea of the triple bottom line. On page 257 of my edition of *The Third Wave*, I later discovered a section titled "Many Bottom Lines." I had always had a sense that I had seen something, somewhere, on the theme, but had forgotten where—and was uncomfortable that I didn't know who I should be acknowledging. The way Toffler put it was that future corporations would have "economic and trans-economic objectives."

Again, I had been surfing on the shoulders of giants.

Making Waves

You may be wondering how these societal pressure waves work. I first began to plot our progress across them (or often the lack of it) in 1994, the same year I came up with the triple bottom line. I sat down over a cup of tea with a friend and colleague—Nick Robins, now a professor at LSE and an international expert in the field of sustainable and climate finance. We produced an initial sketch of the waves, at least as we then saw them.

The analysis has since been presented in some fifty countries, though the fact that it has survived and evolved doesn't guarantee that it is right in every detail.* Indeed, I have sometimes encountered energetic pushback, with one set of academics in Berlin angrily demanding to know why we had tried to address such an important challenge in under an hour over a cup of tea. Was this another case of the notorious British sense of humor? The question behind their question: Why hadn't we applied for state funding and launched a ten-year peer-reviewed program?

I viewed the question from a different angle. Just as early explorers' maps could be good enough to give those who followed a useful sense of their location—and where to watch out for coastlines, sheltered estuaries, riptides, or ship-eating reefs—my aim has always been to help people make business sense of the ever-evolving landscapes of risk and opportunity.

The other major question—and perhaps a more important one—was how we (and it has mainly been me) had calculated the vertical axis. How had we assessed the level of impact of the successive waves? My answer, and it probably incensed some academics even further, was that at times the process reminded me of a key scene in Steven Spielberg's film *Close Encounters of the Third Kind*.

In this sequence, actor Richard Dreyfuss is seen on his hands and knees on the living room carpet in his family home. He is using every material he can lay his hands on, from mud to mashed potatoes, to sculpt a shape he is obsessed with. This proves to be Devils Tower in Wyoming, which is where the aliens have chosen to hover in their attempt to engage humankind.[14]

You have been warned. Treat what follows as a set of sketches, cartoons even. Like any set of long waves, mine have had their ups and downs. But, as far as I can see, they all seem to follow an underlying exponential curve, pushing toward some sort of systemic outcome, be it breakthrough or, wholly or in part, breakdown.[15]

---

* Doug Miller, then president of GlobeScan, noted some years later that our waves coincided closely with the ones they were plotting through their public opinion surveys around the world.

Minsky Moments

Having dropped out of economics at university in 1968, I'm in no position to claim any degree of expertise in the dismal science. But, clearly, several concepts struck home at the time and have informed my work since. One was the idea of long wave cycles of innovation and creative destruction.

A less controversial idea, stimulated by observations of the boom-and-bust cycles that routinely shape and distort our economies, is summed up in the phrase "Minsky moment." The economist Hyman Minsky warned that while most economists assume that our economies are stable, with problems spotted early and ironed out, stability itself can be the system's own worst enemy. The greater the stability we experience, and then come to assume, the less stable our economies can become.[16]

The same is true, I suspect, of our political and social systems. The greater the stability we presume exists, and then take for granted, the greater the risks we are willing to take with that stability—and the greater the probability of ultimate disruption and disorder.

In that sense, at least, perhaps my generation, the baby boomers, was doomed to fail. Often spoiled by parents who had been through the war, borne upward in a period of rapid economic growth, and largely insulated from the horrors of war, we nonetheless grew up in a world influenced by moral codes and institutions shaped by wartime contingencies. Perhaps inevitably, we rebelled.

Where our parents wanted sensible guardrails, many boomers saw unnecessary constraints. The dead hands of history. Intentionally or not, we began to drop out of our parents' reality, tuning in to different ones. Tune in, turn on, drop out, as counterculture guru Timothy Leary's mantra encouraged us. With the benefit of hindsight, you might say that this was the mother of all Minsky moments, where the system's apparent successes laid the foundations for longer-term frictions and crises. Most boomers, however, rather than dropping out, defaulted to the single-bottom-line, growth-obsessed, consumerist version of capitalism that then came to dominate our world.

Nuclear threats may have loomed large on our mental horizons but behind the scenes loomed a very different set of challenges—many of them fueled by population growth. Even with somewhere between seventy million and eighty-five million people perishing during World War II, the overall rise in global population scarcely slowed. In my lifetime alone, Earth's human population has grown from 2.5 billion to more than eight billion today, an exponential growth curve with massive implications for other forms of life.[*]

Boomers, or at least enough of them to cause a growing stir, were soon campaigning across an A to Z of issues. The real question, however, was whether the existing system had the capacity to take the new thinking on board, or whether it needed to break—or be broken. Some still believed in the redemptive power of communism, even if I didn't. Instead, I toyed with ideas like social anarchism, very much in the spirit of the emerging counterculture. And a key part of that was the rising environmental movement, which erupted into public consciousness with the first Earth Day in 1970, mobilizing an estimated twenty million Americans.

By the time I was invited to serve on the international board of Earth Day in 1990, the first year the event went global, the number mobilized had grown to an estimated two hundred million people in 141 countries. I revisit that adventure in chapter 5. If you had plotted that 1990 trajectory ever upward, it might have seemed as if the problem were solved. Far from it, we discovered. Little in human affairs goes in straight lines for very long. Indeed, while many of our problems have been developing exponentially, our proffered solutions have often evolved incrementally, at best.

Not that I want to sideline incrementalism. It's where we all start, after all, and many great inventors arrive at their goals crabwise, after many accidents and incidents along the way. Equally, if enough people

---

[*] I once learned that there were more human beings alive now than have ever lived, but that's not true, it seems. Recent analysis suggests that something like 117 billion people have lived on Earth since the origins of our species: https://www.prb.org/articles/how-many-people-have-ever-lived-on-earth/.

do small things, the combined and compounded effect can be substantial. But now the only way out of this exponentially deepening trap we have been digging for ourselves is to change our political and economic systems, radically.

The last time we did this, it was made possible by the existential crises, the crucible years of World War II. Whatever you may choose to read into and between these lines, bear this in mind and view the societal pressure waves diagram on page 109 as an exercise in visual storytelling.

Mapping Waves

The headline story is that, starting in 1994, I began mapping a series of societal pressure waves from 1960 to the present day. To my mind, these waves have been the motivating force behind the five evolving agendas described in part 2—and sketched in this section. In the diagram, the broad sweep of long wave economic cycles (pale gray line that goes dotted toward breakdown or breakthrough) suggests that we are now in a deepening downwave, but with a new upwave building. I have explored this "U-bend" for some years, seeing the progressive unraveling of the old economic order as a massive down escalator—with the eventual recovery, potentially at least, as a set of even bigger up escalators.

The consequences for us all are profound and will often play out over generational timescales. Meanwhile, the diagram also shows a set of more focused change waves, marked as waves 1 through 6. They have been driving the mainstreaming of a range of environmental, social, and governance (ESG) agendas, producing psychological, social, economic, and political shock waves. Tracking back to the early 1960s, these waves (to date) have powered the ESG and sustainability agendas.* Typically, the relevant change agendas have expanded during times of economic growth, particularly toward the end of boom periods, shrinking back during the ensuing recessions—though that pattern may now be changing.

Wave 1 peaked around 1970 and focused both on the environment and on potential limits to growth. Wave 2 peaked in the early 1990s, with the world increasingly seen through a "green" lens, at least in parts of the developed world. Wave 3, peaking between 1999 and 2001, focused on a new round of globalization. Wave 4, peaking around 2008, saw sustainability commitments being made by a growing number of business leaders, albeit often with little real understanding of what it required of them. Then wave 5 was shaped and surfed by new leaders, among them the astounding Greta Thunberg. A key trend here was the awakening of younger people. Next, wave 6 focused on ESG investing and (a more profound take on the agenda) impact—and was characterized by a "Tower of Babel" scramble to establish competing brandings and jargons.

---

* Reading *Helgoland* by Carlo Rovelli (London: Allen Lane, 2021), a fascinating introduction to quantum theory, inspired me to consider how each successive societal pressure wave has shaped the evolving paradigm shift sketched in the exponential curve in our societal pressure waves mapping. At its peak, wave 1 (Limits) began the process of alerting humankind to our common challenge—a reality dramatized by the *Limits to Growth* team in 1972 and then monitored by the Global Footprint Network, with its Overshoot Day campaign and the Stockholm Resilience Centre, with its Planetary Boundaries work. Wave 2 (Green) saw growing activism, successively impacting politics, consumer choice, and investment. This process continues in the government sphere with Green (New) Deals in the EU and United States.

Wave 3 (Globalization) saw a new round of globalization, promoting global governance solutions and the rise of countries like China and India, but also spurring the spread of unsustainable production and consumption patterns. Too often, developed economies exported their emissions to industrializing nations.

Next, wave 4 (Sustainability) put sustainable development on the agenda for all to see—a process accelerated by the launch in 2015 of the United Nations' Sustainable Development Goals. Wave 5 (Greta) was largely driven by new business mindsets—and by younger generations waking up and deciding to act. Alongside growing pressures for deglobalization, wave 6 (ESG/Impact) has seen a growing proliferation (and confusion) of languages and brandings, linked to booms in ESG and impact investing and triggering inevitable resistance from vested interests, but with *impact* now potentially offering a common language for business and other market actors. In the process, there is an increasingly urgent need to expand our focus from responsibility and resilience to regeneration—the regeneration of our environment, societies, educational systems, economies, economics, and politics. The dotted line heading up toward "Regeneration" indicates one possible—and hopeful—future direction of travel.

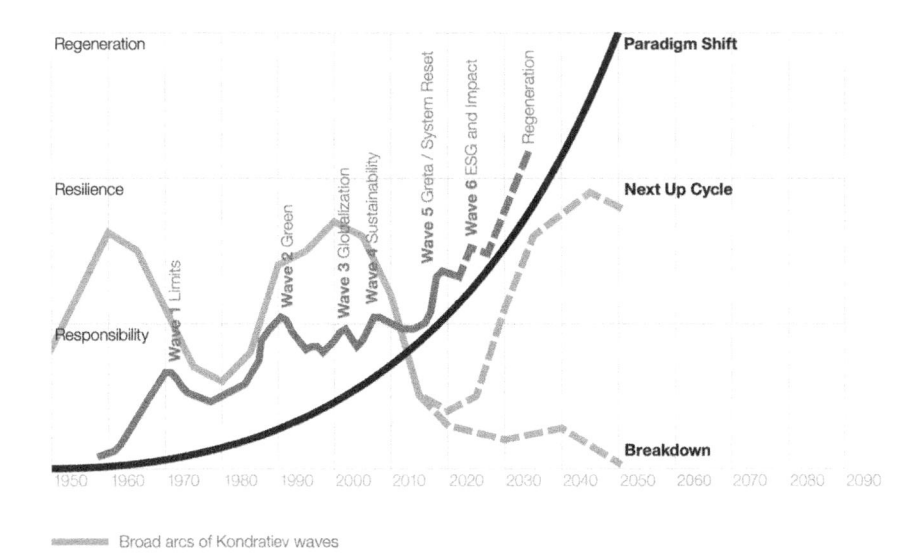

Surfing Tomorrow

[Figure: Chart showing societal pressures waves from 1950-2090, with axes labeled Responsibility, Resilience, Regeneration. Curves labeled Wave 1 Limits, Wave 2 Green, Wave 3 Globalization, Wave 4 Sustainability, Wave 5 Greta / System Reset, Wave 6 ESG and Impact, Regeneration. Additional labels: Paradigm Shift, Next Up Cycle, Breakdown. Legend: Broad arcs of Kondratiev waves; Limits to growth / Planetary boundaries paradigm.]

Societal pressures waves, 1950–2050 (source: Rupert Bassett for Volans)

In a time of growing political divides, all of this suggests considerable challenges ahead. The very success of the ESG movement helped trigger political pushback, particularly in the United States, as discussed in chapter 8. So, will there now be a further, seventh wave in the series? I suspect so, though its direction, speed, scale, and ultimate impact remain to be determined. We turn to the growing interest in regeneration in chapter 9 as one possible theme. But it will express itself in different ways in different parts of the world—and in some regions it won't appear at all.

Beneath the turmoil, meanwhile, the next economic cycle is building, bringing radically different change dynamics and opportunities.[*] Circumstantial evidence suggests that future waves could continue the exponential trajectory toward systemic solutions. But these are outcomes to work toward, not count on.

---

[*] One of my favorite sources of intelligence in this space is RethinkX (https://www.rethinkx.com). We dig deeper into their work in chapter 8. For an insider's overview, see Adam Dorr's book *Brighter: Optimism, Progress, and the Future of Environmentalism* (RethinkX, 2022).

In part 2, we extract five broad themes from the waves analysis. In turn, we explore some of the ways that change has progressed in the context of the evolving environmental agenda (chapter 5), green capitalism (chapter 6), sustainability (chapter 7), positive impact (chapter 8), and the regenerative economy (chapter 9), while chapter 10 considers where we may be headed next—and the concluding coda explores some lessons for those wanting to influence leaders or lead in new ways.

SURFING TOMORROW'S WAVES

If you want to surf the future, it helps to understand how waves work in our societies and economies. The central insight in this diagram is both simple and complex—and has much to tell us about the impact of societal pressure waves. Any successful innovation takes off slowly, then grows through a period of exponential growth before petering out as it hits the limits of the current application or system. The upper curve (heading toward a one hundred percent market share) is a standard S-curve, while the bell curve (which heads back to zero percent) shows the same trend eventually hitting saturation in a system, market, or society.

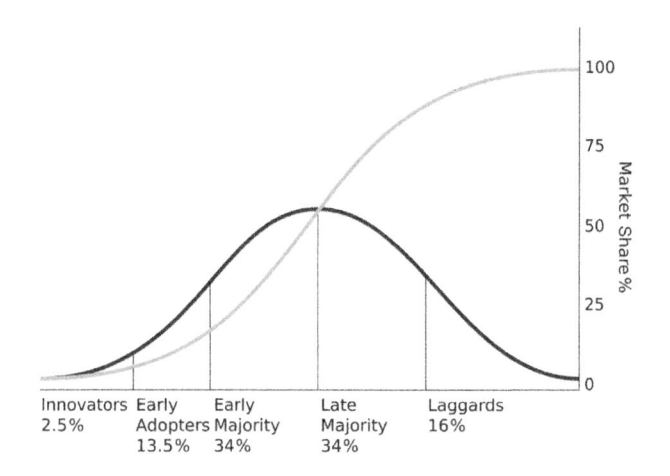

Innovators 2.5% | Early Adopters 13.5% | Early Majority 34% | Late Majority 34% | Laggards 16%

Source: Based on Everett Rogers, *Diffusion of Innovations*, 5th ed. (New York: Simon & Schuster, 2003).

When people talk of ramping up the production of tanks, cars, intercontinental ballistic missiles, mobile phones, COVID-19 vaccines, or solar cells, they plan to drive these products up the relevant S-curves—and, crucially, up the associated learning curves, which can bring massive economies of scale, cutting the price per unit of value created and accelerating their market diffusion.

With the evolution of innovation clusters like Silicon Valley, we have seen exponential growth in efforts to work out how to repeat or extend the trick. A huge body of work has evolved on how the right sort of innovations can be incubated, accelerated, scaled, and replicated. At Volans, we have explored related areas with our work on social entrepreneurship alongside the Skoll Foundation, and with our Project Breakthrough initiative alongside the United Nations Global Compact.[17]

As already mentioned, our work has been powerfully inspired by people like RethinkX. And a further example of breakthrough thinking surfaced at the World Economic Forum's 2023 Davos summit with the launch of a SYSTEMIQ report, *The Breakthrough Effect*.[18] The focus here is on accelerating the transition to net-zero economies, but the thinking could apply to any challenge requiring breakthrough solutions. Key elements of the process involve deciding which challenge to address, then working out whether there is the potential for exponential shifts and how best to trigger and direct them. Along the way, the focus has expanded from positive and negative tipping points to positive "tipping cascades."

Among the technologies seen as teetering on the edge of exponential diffusion are passenger electric vehicles, battery-powered trucks, and the use of green ammonia in fertilizers, hydrogen in steel production, and alternative proteins in food products—whether based on plants or microbial or animal cell cultures.

In terms of what governments can do to spur the creation of the right sort of market incentives, we now see new approaches to what some call "catalytic government"[19]—involving the derisking of early-stage innovation and market adoption. Sometimes technologies developed by governments

continued

in Shark mode find new, more peaceable applications. Swords into plowshares. The challenge now is to flip more governments into Dolphin mode, with technologies evolved with sustainability as part of their coding, digital or genetic.

PART 2

Feeding Frenzies

Big waves kick up bleeding edges.

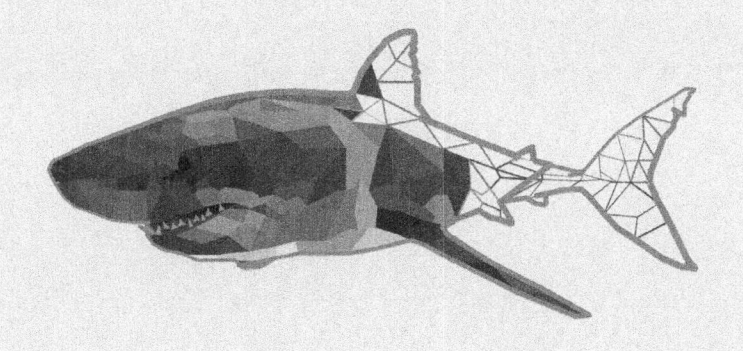

CHAPTER 5

Embracing Gaia

When I told my Scottish mother-in-law the name we had chosen for our first daughter, she was appalled—and it got worse when she pulled down an encyclopedia of Greek mythology. She called back in even greater distress. "But," she quavered, "Gaia gnawed the testicles off her brother Cronus!" My somewhat thoughtless response was that this was why I had always wanted two daughters.

Later, I discovered that in her distress, Margaret had scrambled key elements of the story. Not hard to do, given the complexities of the ancient comings and goings around Mount Olympus. In the original myth, Gaia, the ancestral mother of all life, had fashioned a great stone sickle. She then gave it to her son Cronus, helping him ambush and castrate the ruler of the universe at the time, Uranus.

You might then be wondering what the relationship was between Gaia and Uranus, as did I. It's simple to state, if harder to process. He was both her son and husband. His amputated appendages were promptly tossed into the sea, where the resulting white foam, as is the mythic way, produced Aphrodite, whom the Romans would later co-opt as Venus.

We return to Gaia later, but as I prepared to surf the first great environmental pressure wave, I was reminded that it had been preceded by earlier societal pressure waves in history. Among them were the escalating protests against the trans-Atlantic slave trade—through which millions of people were captured, sold, shipped, sold again, and abused in ways we can scarcely begin to imagine.* Digging back into my family tree, I can see some evidence of involvement in slavery both in my line and Elaine's.

But while I have long been interested in social issues, the core of my identity has been environmentalism. My early interests and priorities here were powerfully shaped by three things: first, my exposure to nature as a child; second, the growth of the global environmental movement; and third, the extraordinary proliferation of TV programs on nature and our looming environmental challenges. My first nuclear family bought a television when we returned to England in 1959—and for many years, any coverage of the natural world was on a small screen, in glorious black and white.

It wasn't until our own Gaia was around three years old, in 1980, that I recall her squatting down in front of a shop window in Barnes High Street—and refusing to budge. The window featured a small color TV, a Sony Trinitron. She was utterly absorbed by the images of a coral reef, so we drew a deep breath and took the plunge.

Our Sinking Ark

My generation saw a small but growing number of TV presenters covering wildlife and environmental issues. They included Germany's Hans and Lotte Hass, France's Jacques Cousteau, Canada's David Suzuki, and Britain's extraordinary proliferation of talent, including Jane Goodall, Gerald Durrell (whom I would meet later in my Earthlife days), and David Bellamy (ditto).

In retrospect, David Attenborough always seemed lord of that jungle.

---

* Another example of such waves can be seen in campaigns against the trade in the plumage of exotic birds, often for women's hats. These bird-focused campaigns resulted in the emergence of the Royal Society for the Protection of Birds in the UK (founded 1889) and the National Audubon Society in the United States (1905). There were also campaigns for national parks and against air and water pollution, with much activity on both fronts ahead of World War II.

No surprise, I imagine, for anyone who watched his witness statement, the 2020 Netflix film *David Attenborough: A Life on Our Planet*.[1] For me, however, the story began much earlier. Indeed, his *Zoo Quest* programs in the late 1950s and early 1960s had a huge impact on my interest in wildlife and ecology. Then, after the advent of color TV, Attenborough-fronted series like *Life on Earth*, *The Blue Planet*, and *The Green Planet* became compulsory watching—even if some critics claimed that the natural glories he celebrated no longer represented the realities of life on an increasingly degraded Earth. Some, unfairly, even described them as a form of eco-pornography.

From my vantage point, Attenborough's own political position expanded markedly over the decades—though that was true of all of us. I remember having lunch with him, via WWF, in the mid-1980s, when he seemed happy to dismiss climate change as a major threat. It may have been an off day; we all have them. But, if he had ever sat on that fence, he soon leaped off it—increasingly warning of the growing risks flowing from both the evolving climate catastrophe and wider species extinction.

My warmest memory is of him lowering a time capsule into the floor of the new Princess of Wales Conservatory at Kew Gardens, London, in 1985.[2] Elaine had suggested the idea of the time capsule during a supper with Joss and David Pearson, publishers of *Gaia: An Atlas of Planet Management*. That extraordinary book was compiled under the direction of Dr. Norman Myers, who had written an influential book on extinction, *The Sinking Ark*. At a late stage, I had been asked to act as a parachute-in editor when the Atlas project threatened to come unstuck.

As Attenborough lowered the capsule into the hole on rattling chains, Gaia and Hania sat face-to-face, one on each of his knees. Their small heads sported wobbly yellow hard hats. Demonstrating the charm that has endeared him to gorillas and humans alike, he tapped on their helmets, enquiring whether anyone was in.

Attenborough, deservedly, became a world treasure. But the older he grew, the bleaker his assessment of our prospects became—though he took great care to keep the spark of hope alive. Then, hot on the heels of that

2020 Netflix film, he and Britain's Prince William (now William, the Prince of Wales) launched the Earthshot Prize, discussed by Hannah Jones in her foreword to this book.[3] The new prize featured five £1 million awards given yearly through to 2030, promising to support at least fifty breakthrough solutions to the world's greatest environmental problems.

Zuckerberg, with a Conscience

The Earthshot Prize came along fifty years after an event that proved a watershed for me and many others. As already mentioned, the first Earth Day in 1970 had set a spectacularly high bar, inspiring twenty million Americans, ten percent of the country's population at the time, to take to the streets in demonstrations to protect the planet. Under the stewardship of Denis Hayes, who coordinated that first event, the global influence of the Earth Day movement has continued to grow, celebrating its fiftieth anniversary on April 22, 2020.*

I first met Denis in Golden, Colorado, where he was running the Solar Energy Research Institute (SERI), today the National Renewable Energy Laboratory. This was in 1981, when I was on the Churchill Fellowship, crisscrossing the United States in pursuit of eco-pioneers. SERI was based in Golden, Colorado, because a key member of the Coors brewing family had helped with funding. That family has a colorful history, including the 1960 kidnap and murder of Adolph Coors III, the grandson of the company's founder.

The Coors family, from memory, was energetically right-wing but also intensely patriotic, wanting to help cut the United States' dependence on oil from the Middle East. Others on the right wing of US politics had different ideas. Indeed, when I visited SERI, I had already heard as I traveled

---

* Denis Hayes is now recognized as one of the most influential environmental campaigners of all time, but I believe that the Earth Day movement is also one of the most effective and impactful Green Swan initiatives of the past fifty years. (For more on the Green Swan concept, see chapter 9.) Consequently, he was one of three winners of the Volans Green Swan Award in 2020.

through Washington, DC, that Denis was on the hit list for the incoming Reagan administration. Many members of the new government were fossil fuel industry insiders opposed to renewable energy.

I love the way that *Rolling Stone* described Denis many years later: "Denis Hayes is the Mark Zuckerberg of the environmental movement, if you can imagine Mark Zuckerberg with a conscience and a lot less cash."[4]

But let's jump back almost a decade to 1974, to the moment when, two weeks before I left UCL, I received that letter from John Roberts inviting me to visit Transport & Environment Studies, or TEST, in Covent Garden. TEST was perhaps the first environmental consultancy in Europe, though at the time John only employed three or four people. I was home. We would explore how cities could be made friendlier for pedestrians and cyclists—and investigate how trucks could be rerouted to cut their impact. We worked tirelessly, often late into the night, sometimes to a ridiculous degree. I recall one sadly not atypical night while Elaine and I were living in a flat in Elizabeth Street, off Eaton Square. She went round the corner in the early hours to Gerard Street police station—still sporting the traditional blue police lamp—to protest that I had vanished. This was well before the advent of mobile phones.

My colleagues and I had lost track of time while surveying trucks from a TEST-branded Ford Transit van. The police officers laughed, not unkindly, and suggested to Elaine various things I might be up to. Shortly afterward, the lights of my speeding bicycle hove into view as I belatedly arrived home.

TEST proved to be a model for everything that came later, particularly when the practice moved round the corner from King Street to Floral Street into a building now long since demolished. The spirit there was akin to the cockpit of the *Millennium Falcon* in *Star Wars*: a close-knit team moving at lightspeed, my favorite setup. I learned how to write reports—and John encouraged me to write for magazines, something he did regularly in the architectural and planning press.

One highlight of that time was a big project we did in Egypt for the United Nations (UN). We carried out a series of early environmental impact studies, uncovering major problems. Among other things, we discovered that multiple UN-backed studies were effectively chopping up the biggest Nile Delta lake, Manzala, into separate study areas, with profound ecological implications. In the process, the big picture was being lost. Worryingly, there was no way we could address the problem within the current design of the different studies.

So, with John's encouragement, I visited quite a few Egyptian ministries and agencies to see what could be done. Typically, I was given short shrift. One official berated me, insisting that Manzala was "a ditch." It is certainly shallow for much of its area, but that was—and still is—considerable, around 1,500 square kilometers. Back in London, and again with John's backing, I broke cover and wrote my first article for *New Scientist*.

My route in was simple. I called the magazine's respected environment editor, Jon Tinker, who promptly gave me several pages over which to tell my story.[5] It should have been career suicide, given that TEST had signed a nondisclosure agreement with the UN, but instead it proved a key stepping stone.

First, and most important in terms of impact, a whole-ecosystem study was announced for Lake Manzala, which we were assured would recognize its critical role as a nursery for fisheries and an internationally important staging post for migrating wildfowl. Second, the Egypt feature article started me writing monthly features for *New Scientist*. And third, with the whole-hearted backing of the magazine's editor, Dr. Bernard Dixon, I pioneered in the reporting of what business was doing on environmental issues.

Now We're 100

During this period, I not only wrote for *New Scientist* but read the magazine assiduously, often cover to cover. So, on February 6, 1975, I found myself reading a piece co-authored by James Lovelock that gave me a radically new perspective on life.[6] I subsequently learned that Jim (as he was familiarly known) had sown the early seeds of the modern environmental movement. He had developed an electron capture detector that helped detect vanishingly small traces of pollutants, spurring research at Shell—which in turn helped inform Rachel Carson's breakthrough book *Silent Spring*.

Lovelock's Gaia hypothesis, the focus of his article in February 1975, did not go uncontested. Indeed, it proved highly controversial. It seemed to imply that the planet had somehow "learned" how to self-regulate key elements of its atmosphere and chemistry. As supporters explained it, the idea was that "the organic and inorganic components of Planet Earth have evolved together as a single living, self-regulating system. . . . This living system has automatically controlled global temperature, atmospheric content, ocean salinity, and other factors, that maintains its own habitability."[7]

For me, the possibility that life itself might be working to hold the planet in some sort of Goldilocks zone was intriguing—and made intuitive sense. The Gaia concept had been co-evolved with the brilliant biologist Lynn Margulis, once married to astronomer Carl Sagan. I never met Margulis, but her approach to science and life was revolutionary.

When she died in 2011, her obituary in *Nature* recalled that Lynn Margulis was "an independent, gifted, and spirited biologist who learned as early as the fourth grade to 'tell bullshit from . . . real authentic experience,' as she put it in a 2004 interview. With courage, intellect, a twinkle in her eyes and considerable fortitude, she changed our view of cellular evolution."[8]

Back in 1967, Margulis had made the then-revolutionary case that simple bacteria were incorporated into some early cells to produce the organelles that let plants photosynthesize and animals consume oxygen. This process of so-called endosymbiosis changed evolution's trajectory by providing plants for animals to eat and oxygen for them to breathe.[9]

Her thinking was vigorously challenged by many of her peers. She suffered repeated rejections, submitting her initial paper to a dozen journals before it was published. The extraordinary thing, underscoring the reality that the most disruptive thinking often comes from the edges of a system, was that she developed her theories without any training in molecular biology.[10]

Critics would later argue that the Gaia hypothesis was beautiful yet flawed.[11] But having spoken at Jim's centennial conference at Exeter University in 2019,[12] and having plunged into emerging science inspired by the idea, I am convinced that future generations will see James Lovelock as a scientist akin to Charles Darwin—himself decried for some time after he went public with his paradigm-shifting thinking.

A linked memory involves a road trip through Dorset to have lunch with Jim and his wife, Sandy, in the summer of 2013, alongside our mutual friend, John Gilbert. It was even more wonderful, as already mentioned, to be invited to the only hundredth birthday party I have yet been to, in the Orangery at Blenheim Palace. We celebrated not only Jim's centenary but also his paradigm-shifting scientific contributions.

Home, Sweet Dome

If I rewind the clock to when I first heard of the Gaia hypothesis, then run it forward a couple of years, another key influence on my thinking was Teddy Goldsmith, founder of the *Ecologist* magazine. He saw capitalism as a plague upon the planet, though some people noted that he seemed happy enough to accept financial support from his brother, billionaire businessman Sir James Goldsmith. But needs must, he might have argued.

I got to know Teddy by sleeping with him. We shared a hotel bedroom, albeit in separate beds, for a week in Reykjavík, Iceland. This was the late seventies, during a weeklong conference organized by Professor Nicholas Polunin, with hotel bedrooms clearly at a premium. A longstanding champion of biological conservation and at the time editor of *Environmental Conservation*, Nicholas had published a long scientific paper I had written on the work we had done on the Nile Delta wetlands.[13] So, I flew to Iceland and wrote a three-page article on the event for *New Scientist* on the flight back to London.[14] Harder than it sounds: those were still pen and paper days.

Teddy and I may not always have seen eye to eye philosophically, but otherwise we got on famously. He took me under his wing in Reykjavík, then invited Elaine and me down to his home in Cornwall. At the time, I was driving Elaine and recently born Gaia around the country in TEST's echoing Ford Transit van. A dead sheep in a nearby reservoir that fed Teddy's farmhouse didn't help Elaine's health or—because Elaine was breastfeeding at the time—Gaia's state of mind. But Teddy's brain was on higher things. At one point he invited us to help his wife, Kathy, dig out a new greenhouse. He felt obliged to join in at one point and almost took his foot off with a mattock. Not a born gardener, it seemed.

During the stay, I drove across to a vast hole dug by china clay miners, the hole that Tim Smit would later turn into the Eden Project.[15] I then wrote a piece for *New Scientist* on the work being done by English China Clays PLC to regenerate part of the quarry.

Around that time, Teddy invited me to join him at the *Ecologist*, but I preferred the freedom to talk to anyone I wanted in business—and suspected that this would be harder in Teddy's kind but determined embrace. I loved the man—and was delighted when, some years before he died, he told me that he had recently woken up to the value of what we had been doing at Environmental Data Services (ENDS) and then SustainAbility.

The Reykjavík trip was also where I met R. Buckminster Fuller, as mentioned in chapter 3. Unlike many in the environmental space, he was totally focused on finding solutions—helping spur me in the same direction. But then along came the next connection, drawn in by the writing I had been doing for *New Scientist*. While I was still at TEST, another of my heroes got in touch.

Max Nicholson was another pioneer of the conservation and environmental movements. While at UCL, I had read his book *The Environmental Revolution*.[16] He invited me to his London club, the Athenaeum in Pall Mall, to discuss a new initiative he was developing with The Hon. David Layton. I may not have liked the club atmosphere, with older white men seemingly being digested by ancient leather armchairs, but the serendipity engine was kicking into gear again.

Stepping on Toes

By the time Max and I met, he resembled a bald eagle—enjoying a towering reputation as an ornithologist, conservationist, and founder of a legion of organizations. These included the WWF (alongside fellow ornithologist Sir Peter Scott), the International Institute for Environment and Development, and Land Use Consultants, among many others. He was headhunting me—though I'm pretty sure we didn't use the term then—to help shape his new venture: ENDS.

Initially, I fobbed him off, saying I wanted to do a market research exercise for the project, which then became a paid project for TEST. But in the end, I decided to make the move. Max, it seemed, had been in the game forever. As far back as 1928, he had created the first UK survey of one of my favorite birds, the gray heron. His knowledge of birds was legendary—among many other things, he was chief editor of the influential and multivolume book series *The Birds of the Western Palearctic*.

Max had also helped manage the Pool of London during the Blitz, a critical part of the city's Docklands—and vitally important if Britain was to stay on its feet and fed. The wartime government faced an immense challenge at the time, managing convoys staggering in from the sea, many heavily damaged, all during intense Luftwaffe attacks on London itself, while the whole picture was further scrambled by the changing tides.

Apparently, the authorities pondered what sort of professional could cope with such complex system dynamics—and, astonishingly but sensibly, decided to appoint an ecologist. Later in the war, he was also involved in planning Operation Overlord, the invasion of Europe.

Max may have looked and sounded like an establishment figure, but he was a true radical. He walked with a limp, having contracted polio in Balochistan (now part of Pakistan) in 1952, but nothing stopped him in his quest to study birds. Indeed, when he appeared on the BBC's *Desert Island Discs* in 1995, his choice of a luxury was a pair of binoculars.[17] For him, they would have been no luxury.

But, while himself a radical, Max sometimes struggled to connect with younger activists, including Friends of the Earth and Greenpeace. By contrast, I had used Friends of the Earth activists like Amory Lovins and Walt Patterson as lighthouses as I tried to find my way. I tried intergenerational bridge-building but with limited success.

Among other things, Max was thoroughly probusiness, and he—and many of his generation—saw the new NGOs as fundamentally antibusiness, antigrowth, anticapitalist. Right or wrong, he was an inspiration and over time became a true friend. He died at the age of ninety-eight, while still trying to push the envelope.

The problems we faced in getting our agenda across to businesses were strikingly illustrated by a collision I had with one of Max's friends, Sir Arthur "Gerry" Norman. One day in 1979, I was summoned to see Sir Arthur at the London headquarters of the security printers De La Rue, which he chaired at the time. The company had started out as a stationer, then expanded to the manufacture of playing cards, later morphing into security printers of banknotes for the Bank of England.

I was ushered into the grand, hushed, designed-to-be-awesome chairman's office. At the time, Sir Arthur also chaired the UK end of the WWF, which is how I had first met him. Politely described in one obituary as "a short, energetic man," he was used to getting his way. And he had a simple, blunt message for me. He said I could work for the Establishment, including people like De La Rue, the Bank of England, and WWF, an organization whose patrons included many of the world's best-known royals—or, he allowed with obvious distaste, I could continue my work with activists like Friends of the Earth, Greenpeace, and The Other Economic Summit, a.k.a. TOES.* But it was either–or.

He really didn't expect my response. I replied that if he insisted on forcing a choice, I'd side with those he saw as troublemakers. My parting shot was that, over time, those disruptors were the future and indeed would

---

* TOES, a precursor of the New Economics Foundation, was created by people like Sally Willington, a founder of the British Green Party; James Robertson and Alison Pritchard of Turning Point; Jonathon Porritt and Paul Ekins, later cofounders of Forum for the Future; David Fleming, economics spokesperson of the Ecology/Green Party and later chair of the Soil Association; and Jakob von Uexküll of the Right Livelihood Foundation.

become the new Establishment. I'm not sure he and I ever spoke at length again, but he was wrong—for the same reasons that every generation, including my own, becomes wrong over time. If we live long enough, the reality we were born into is not the reality in which we grow old.

Yesterday's Dolphins can become today's Orcas, even relative Sharks.

To be clear, I very much respected the achievements and war records of many of the older conservationists I worked with in those early days. Like Max and Sir Peter Scott, the younger Sir Arthur had done extraordinary things—though I wasn't always aware of all the facts at the time. You couldn't look people up on the internet then, and *Who's Who* was way too expensive, even if you knew what it was.

You were dependent on what people chose to tell you at a time when much wartime history was still under wraps. So, I had no idea that in 1939 the man who became Sir Arthur Norman had been picked to run a clandestine operation in Shanghai—still partly an international city but increasingly under Japanese control. His task had been to print and distribute banknotes for Chiang Kai-shek's Nationalist Chinese government under the very noses of the Japanese occupiers. Deadly dangerous, as one obituary later put it. He established a covert plant in the French Concession disguised as a playing-card factory and shop. The banknotes were trundled out by dustcart. When the occupying Japanese finally broke open a consignment of paper and demanded its destruction, Norman cunningly suggested the company's own incinerator and promptly managed to salvage half the paper.[18]

During the war, he went on to join the RAF, training as a pilot in the United States. He towed gliders, flew low-level flights taking agents into occupied France and Sicily, and supported the D-Day landings. Not only that, but he fought off deadly Junkers Ju 88s over the Bay of Biscay, downing one of the attackers before escaping into clouds.

Really, what would people like that have made of people like me? Unbloodied, green. Whatever the answer, as I exited De La Rue that day, I was already well advanced on my first book. But if anyone had told me then that I would end up writing more than twenty books, that I would coin phrases that would go into the language of business, and that I would serve on more than eighty boards, advisory boards, and scientific committees, I would have concluded that they were hallucinating.

Indeed, I resonate strongly with a recollection in Jean Oelwang's wonderful book, *Partnering*.[19] She recalls speaking to "seas of well-suited people" around "larger-than-life boardroom tables." Whenever she brought up social and environmental impact, though, she recalls that faces would glaze over. When leaving the room, she would often hear hushed whispers of "tree hugger" or "Swampy," the latter a reference to a famed antimotorway protester in the UK.

Such reactions were routine at the time. So, it would have seemed even more far-fetched that I would end up working with a growing number of CEOs and other business leaders who genuinely wanted to change the world for the better. But that was the future that David, Max, and ENDS helped open for me.

Dr. Doomwatch

To begin with, ENDS was an uphill struggle. No one in business wanted to talk to people interested in safety, health, and—worst of all—the environment. But cofounder David Layton's genius was to see that the time was coming when business would have no option but to travel up a series of learning curves. Our thinking was that the fortnightly (later monthly) *ENDS Report*, which I edited from the outset, would help meet the new needs in the ways that David's other business, Incomes Data Services (IDS), already did in the field of industrial relations.

Even so, it took us nine months to get the first company to open up. Paradoxically, trade unions proved just as difficult. They had a lot more power than environmentalists did, but to put it crudely, they usually couldn't give a proverbial toss about the environment unless it came up and smacked them or their families in the face. And sometimes hardly even then. I know that because I tried to engage some of them around issues like asbestos and lead.

The first company to invite me in was the chemical company Albright & Wilson, a story I told in my 1980 book, *The Ecology of Tomorrow's World*.[20] Riffing off a popular environmental-themed TV drama at the time, *Doomwatch*, colleagues gave Dr. Jim Farquhar the tag "Dr. Doomwatch" when he tried to turn around Albright & Wilson's troubled reputation as its first environmental manager. The job title sounded exciting, but the *Doomwatch* TV series, created by Gerry Davis and Kit Pedler—the latter of whom I had met during a project we did in London's Docklands—was even more dramatic, as TV tends to be.

Jim's role had been conjured up almost overnight in 1972 after a new law required British companies to clean up chemical pollution. In short order, companies were forced to invest heavily to ensure that they remained on the right side of the law. But his role, as with other environmental professionals in industry, was only advisory.

I interviewed, reported on, and then began to advise a growing number of these people. Good people, most of them, but I always had a feeling that the real power lay elsewhere. Progress seemed glacially slow, though having David and Max provide air cover was beyond helpful. Within eighteen months we were being asked to help big companies like oil giant BP and chemicals giant Imperial Chemical Industries (ICI) prepare their first written environmental policy statements. That was unexpected, and not something IDS wanted ENDS to do because of the potential conflicts of interest. Since I was fascinated by that side of the work, I saw this as a sign that I should move on. With Marek Mayer taking over my role as editor at ENDS, the organization began a slow rise to becoming an immensely valued institution.

Meanwhile, freed from the publishing treadmill, I set up my own consultancy in 1983: John Elkington Associates (JEA). Operating from our family home, with colleagues like Jonathan Shopley, who went on to lead organizations like Future Forests and Natural Capital Partners, the firm ran for three to four years—before being absorbed into my next venture, SustainAbility.

Jonathan had arrived on our doorstep in Barnes having ridden his sturdy motorbike across Africa, then through the Middle East and continental Europe. He was still wearing his helmet as he landed on our doormat, like something from the film *Mad Max*. Answering the door, he later recalled, Gaia and Hania pondered him for a millisecond—then both gave him a welcoming hug.

Some of our projects were for government agencies, as when I worked for the US Agency for International Development in Thailand. I edited the first national environmental report for the country, working alongside Dr. Dhira Phantumvanit of the Thailand Development Research Institute. I had first met him when we both worked for the Industry Office of the UN Environment Programme (UNEP) in Paris.

The three things I remember most forcefully about that Bangkok jaunt are being fed a meal with real gold leaf flakes as a dressing (ultra-conspicuous consumption, which set my nerves jangling, particularly with the elevated levels of poverty in the country), being invited to one of the city's innumerable brothels (an invitation I didn't accept), and walking through the city streets to work each morning carrying a luggable Toshiba computer almost the size of a sewing machine (if you remember what either of those were), worth more than the annual salary of most people I passed, yet feeling completely safe. The air quality was terrible, however, with buses laying down smoke clouds like World War I destroyers, and the canals, or *klongs*, choked with raw sewage.

Meanwhile, I had begun coining language. In 1984, for example, I went to Versailles, France, for the first World Industry Conference on Environmental Management (WICEM). I wrote up the final report, alongside Peter Bunyard of the *Ecologist*. As chance would have it, on the flight to Paris I had read a recent management best seller, *In Search of Excellence* by McKinsey consultants Tom Peters and Bob Waterman. Published in 1982, the book had sold in the millions. But not once, I discovered, did the authors mention environmental challenges for business.

I decided to correct that and wrote a panel in the final WICEM report proposing the idea of "environmental excellence." To my surprise, the idea went viral—though we didn't use that term then—particularly among

US oil and chemical companies. It was an important step, helping shift people from a compliance mindset—"What's the minimum we can get away with?"—to a more engaged and creative mindset—"How can we do this intelligently and to the best effect?"

In retrospect, this was an early example of surfing a building wave to get a new message across to business. It was an instance of sweetening the pill, but—intentionally or not—there were also moments when we upset businesspeople, sometimes seriously.

Grabbing Attention

The Japanese executive was in tears. We were both on a ship sailing between Norway and Denmark as part of a conference organized by UNEP. This man ran the sustainability reporting activities for a big nuclear power company in Japan, TEPCO, later implicated in the Fukushima disaster. His tears had been provoked by the fact that we had just ranked his company at the bottom in a survey of one hundred companies globally.

Exactly one year later, however, he hurried up to me again, this time wreathed in smiles, to say that TEPCO's low ranking in our survey had persuaded his superiors to give him a much bigger budget.

One reason the surveys we did at the time had such an impact was that they were done alongside the UN. However, when Jacqueline Aloisi de Larderel first took over as head of UNEP's Paris branch, I confess I had low expectations. I imagined another well-intentioned but ultracautious bureaucrat. But when Jacqueline came to see me in London days after taking on her new role, I was enchanted to discover a potential coconspirator with an excellent sense of humor.

She would need it.

Soon we were working together to drive the nascent field of corporate environmental reporting. She took a major risk in backing our inaugural benchmarking survey, which ranked first-generation reports. It stuck in some corporate craws. Three US companies—including now-defunct AlliedSignal—refused to work with UNEP ever again, though that proved to be bluster. They would all be back in the fold within months. Jacqueline held firm, and the survey went on to become the industry standard at the time. Alongside pioneers like Bob Massie of CERES and Allen White of the Tellus Institute, we helped birth the Global Reporting Initiative (GRI), building on the pioneering work of CERES in the wake of the 1989 *Exxon Valdez* oil spill disaster.*

Still, in the seventies and eighties, we struggled to get into most companies. If you did get through the gate and then the front door, you were usually met by public relations people or lawyers. But, soon enough, that changed. Erupting on the scene from a radically different angle was Anita Roddick, who founded The Body Shop International in 1976. Alongside the founders of businesses like Patagonia (founded 1973) and Ben & Jerry's (1978), the Roddicks (Anita and her husband, Gordon) helped create the necessary conditions for Friends of the Earth campaigns targeting products containing chlorofluorocarbons (CFCs) and tropical timber, followed by our own Green Consumer campaign.

Such initiatives, in turn, helped lay the foundations for the green finance work of pioneers like Joan Bavaria in the United States and Tessa Tennant in the UK. Business increasingly found itself with no option but to wake up and respond. Human nature being what it is, though, each successive wave of interest in green issues triggers bouts of green marketing and, almost inevitably, greenwashing—involving making false or misleading claims about the environmental performance of a product, company, or activity.

Even as that first societal pressure wave began to fade, however, its knock-on effects were considerable. A couple of years after 1970's Earth Day, we saw a massive secondary wave of regulation across the members of the Organisation for Economic Co-operation and Development (OECD),

---

* I recall a wonderful early GRI session out at the Rockefeller family's Kykuit estate in upstate New York, including walks overlooking the Hudson River, between sculptures by the likes of Henry Moore and Pablo Picasso. The irony of working amid such conspicuous wealth, accumulated through the oil operations of the notorious Standard Oil, was not entirely lost on us.

with business largely on the defensive, as it was forced to comply with the new laws. The period also saw two oil shocks (rising oil price and decreased oil supply), in 1973 and 1979, courtesy of the Organization of the Petroleum Exporting Countries (OPEC) amplifying concerns about natural resource scarcity. As a result, we were soon on something of a roll.

Dr. Strangelove

As to how I was viewed through this period, a now extinct magazine called *Tomorrow* once compared me to Douglas Adams's Babel fish.* The comparison was intended as a compliment, I think. My work then, as now, involved helping business leaders plug into realities that were very different from those they had been trained to succeed in.

Across two centuries now, it has been my self-appointed task to tell powerful people things they don't want to hear. And, often, to get them to pay for the privilege—on the basis that we need to make a living and, at least as important, paying for something often means you pay it more attention.

Not that it always worked. One VIP I went head-to-head with was Herman Kahn. One of the architects of the United States' mutually assured destruction (MAD) nuclear weapons strategy, he was reputed to have been one of the models for the fictional Dr. Strangelove in the film of the same name. Kahn helped the United States make sense of a terrifying form of escalation in nuclear weaponry. His view was that capitalism and technology held nearly boundless potential for human progress, so he was no great fan of people like the *Limits to Growth* team.

I had already read Kahn's book, *Thinking about the Unthinkable*, a phrase that has stayed with me, though I preferred to crunch it down to "Think the unthinkable." He had been one of the cofounders of the Hudson Institute—and in the late seventies, the Hudson Research Europe

---

* The Babel fish, as Douglas Adams explained in *The Hitchhiker's Guide to the Galaxy*, is a small, leech-like yellow fish, which when placed in someone's ear enables them to hear any language translated into their own. It is also, Adams added, "probably the oddest thing in the Universe."

arm commissioned me to write a report on the likely environmental challenges of the early twenty-first century. I did so gladly, spotlighting four emerging challenges: stratospheric ozone depletion, climate change, and the impending disruption of both the oceans and human reproductive systems—the latter being the theme of my 1985 book, *The Poisoned Womb*.

My report went down well with a Hudson Research Europe audience, but Kahn's response ran along the following lines: *The problem with you environmentalists is that you find yourself on a motorcycle, headed toward a cliff—so what do you do? You stomp on the brakes and try to steer away. What if that's a mistake? Maybe you should put your foot to the floor and try to jump across the chasm!*

I did wonder about his mental state. To be fair, though, this was just after Evel Knievel had jumped a small part of the Snake River Canyon on his motorbike, so maybe that was buzzing around Kahn's head. If so, perhaps he didn't know, or much care, that Knievel had broken just about every bone in his body during his exploits. But the older I get, and the clearer it becomes that our species is failing to act in time to head off the systemic challenges facing us, the more I have been forced to conclude that Kahn's advice is more relevant by the day.

Increasingly, the evidence suggests that we are still on track for the sorts of collapses predicted back in 1972.[21] When KPMG researcher Gaya Herrington reanalyzed the 1972 *Limits to Growth* models using up-to-date, real-world data, she reported that, in both main scenarios, our civilization collapses. The only ray of hope is if we make the choice to limit our economic growth.

Those who bring such tidings are rarely popular. Indeed, when people asked me what I did for a living, I tended to prevaricate. One reason: I hated being labeled. The INFP in me, again. Also, once people have stuck their own label on you, they tend to discount a large part of what you then say on related subjects—on the basis that you would say that, wouldn't you?

If they saw you as an environmentalist, then bang went the bulk of what you might want to say to them. By contrast, we assumed that if we offered the right information—the right intelligence—in the right way and at the right time, it could change the hearts and minds of leaders by helping them retune their mindsets and access new wavelengths of possibility.

It made sense at the time and it often worked—and there's no question that we got better at it with experience. But such whispering doesn't always work. Sometimes it falls on deaf ears—and sometimes it bombs, badly, with sizzling political shrapnel flying every which way.* And even where you are successful, the impacts may not be immediately visible.

Indeed, even after all this time, I can't remember a single leader, a single CEO, dropping to their knees in ecstasy and declaring themselves converted. So, part of the trick has been to implant ideas, memes with long fuses. The intent is that these "mind bombs," as Greenpeace once called them, explode into their consciousness later. Ideally, they are triggered when exactly the right circumstances for comprehension turn up.

Tickling Sharks

Powerful people, it hardly needs saying, have other things on their minds. They are constitutionally busy, endlessly distracted. Asked to name the biggest challenge of his ill-fated premiership, Britain's Harold Macmillan is said to have replied, "Events, my dear boy, events."[22]

He was spot-on in terms of the complex realities of power, of course, but for many in my generation, Macmillan was part of an earlier generation that increasingly—and conspicuously—was losing the plot. In the world of business, too, similar patterns were an everyday experience as we got to know people who were then referred to in awestruck tones as "captains of industry"—people like Sir Arthur Norman.

Even if these leaders deigned to see people like me, they insisted that business could only do what it was allowed to do by regulators, trade

---

* If you doubt it, read Jean Oelwang's account in her book *Partnering* of the vicious pushback from the chemical industry against CFC critics F. Sherwood Rowland and Mario Molina, a repeat of similar attacks on Rachel Carson after the publication of *Silent Spring*.

unions, customers, consumers, and investors. Though they didn't realize it at the time, they were inviting us to do our level best to encourage those wider interests, what we came to call "stakeholders,"* to embrace a new agenda and press business for true step change.

So, we did. Generally, the whispering game—whispering truth to power—works best when others in the wider world, in the streets, in shareholder meetings, or at the ballot box, trumpet similar calls for change. It also helps when the whisperer, as we did, lays a determined finger on the scales of change.

Some readers will have spotted that this whispering-in-the-ear role harks back to that of the *auriga* in Roman times. Trusted slaves, they steered the two-horse chariots carrying victors to—and through—their triumphs. They would hold a laurel wreath over the emperor's or general's swelling head, constantly whispering that even the triumphant are mortal and that success should not go to their heads.

Whether or not they were CEOs, I preferred to engage with people whose heads were not hugely swollen and who had the potential to be on the right side of history. Many were senior figures in business, but some were well to one side of that world, what we would now call thought leaders and influencers.

Probably the single most memorable conversation I have had in my entire working life was with author Frank Herbert on July 5, 1981. You may recall that I had read his science fiction novel *Dune* in the late sixties, when it was a set book in the sociology of religion course I was taking. I decided to track him down. The main problem was that I lived in London, whereas he lived in the Olympic Peninsula, north of Seattle, in the Pacific Northwest. So, for several years, through his (and later my) publisher, Victor Gollancz, we boxed and coxed as I flew in and out of Seattle.

---

* It's hard to remember now just how politicized the debate was. When I picked the name *Engaging Stakeholders* for SustainAbility's work on transparency and accountability in the mid-1990s, it involved taking a considerable reputational risk. Stakeholder capitalism may be commonplace today, but at the time it was seen by some to have a distinctly left-wing flavor, setting many businesspeople's teeth on edge.

Then, after several years, I finally managed to meet Frank and his then-wife Bev in Knightsbridge. I had flown into Heathrow that morning from Seattle and came straight from the airport to see him, while they were already packed to fly back to Seattle.

He started off asking where my family and I had just been. I mentioned various places, including a long white beach in Oregon near a hamlet called Dunes City, where our daughters had enjoyed endless stretches of white sand. Frank blinked. It turned out that that area was where he had first got the idea for the book, back in 1944, as a cub reporter for the *Seattle Post-Intelligencer*, covering a pioneering dune stabilization project. That was news to me.

Our interview was published later that same year, 1981, over six pages in a magazine called the *Environmentalist*.[23] I was profoundly impressed by the man, though he was anything but a soft touch. One thing he said that sticks in my mind was that "the back-to-the-land, self-sufficiency movement has taken over the mythology of the South Sea Island, where the brown-haired maiden drops coconuts in your mouth." Given my earlier experiences in that space, I was inclined to agree.

What I found most interesting about the *Dune* series of novels was that, while technology was often at the fore, the main emphasis was on the cultural, political, and psychological factors that so powerfully shape human history. So, what a joy it was to finally see the first film in Denis Villeneuve's new *Dune* movie series in 2021. And it was astounding how well he captured my mental image of the worlds described in the original book—I imagine Frank would have been delighted.

Meanwhile, I continue to see leading-edge science fiction as providing a set of windows into possible future societal pressure waves. Among sci-fi authors I have talked to more recently is David Brin, author of *The Postman* and *Earth*.[24] The main protagonist in *The Postman* is a survivor, a wanderer who trades stories for food and shelter in the wake of a devastating war. Borrowing the uniform of a long-dead postman, he discovers the uniform's power as a symbol of hope—and begins to weave his saga of a nation on the road to recovery.

Toward the end of our conversation, David began to explore the Judaic concept of *tikkun olam*, which encourages "repairing the world." This is a task to which he has long bent his efforts in his writing, public speaking, and advisory work with major corporations—and with organizations like the CIA, the United States Department of Defense, and NASA. Likewise, our aim at Volans has been to scan for examples of technologies, business models, cultural developments, and so on that may have real potential to generate exponential solutions.

That is something science fiction has been doing for well over a century. What I find so interesting about such authors is that the best of them use science and technology throughout, often with a deep understanding of both. David Brin developed the idea: "While only ten percent of science fiction authors are scientifically trained, as I am, I put a lot of science into my fiction. It is not just wild and woolly literary fantasy. That said, some of the best 'hard' science fiction is written by former history majors—among them Greg Bear, Nancy Kress, Sheila Finch, and Kim Stanley Robinson. And that's because what's essential to science fiction is discussion of the human condition and the possibilities of change."[25]

He added, "It should have been called 'speculative history' rather than science fiction, because we speculate on the great story—humanity's gradual climb, three steps forward, ten to the side, two steps back. Sometimes thwarted by the best of intentions of ancestors who had the wrong ideas and were faithful in devotedly and lovingly enforcing them, holding us back. And, you know, one of the deep concerns of science fiction—and of people like you—is what mistakes are we making today? Mistakes that in the future will have people wondering why we failed to achieve the number one goal of any decent person, to be good ancestors."[26]

Better Ancestors

What would it take to be a good—or at least better—ancestor? This is a question that has taxed me for decades—and is well tackled by Roman Krznaric in his book *The Good Ancestor*.[27] "From the pyramids to the NHS

[Britain's National Health Service]," he notes, "humankind has always had the innate ability to plan for posterity and take action that will resonate for decades, centuries, even millennia to come. If we want to be good ancestors and be remembered well by the generations who follow us, now is the time to recover and enrich this imaginative skill."[28]

For me, an interest in speculative fiction and science fiction is a key part of being a good ancestor, exploring what tomorrow's worlds and people could be like and trying to ensure that the outcomes are as good as they can be for as many people and other life-forms as possible. From archaeology to satellite remote sensing, we have a much better grip on where we have come from, where we are, and where we may now be headed.

At its best, science fiction takes the relevant data and spins coherent stories around them. The resulting forecasts do not have to be entirely accurate to be helpful. Indeed, I have learned a great deal from reading novels like Omar El Akkad's *American War* and Paolo Bacigalupi's *The Water Knife*, both describing a future United States torn apart by wars over increasingly stretched water resources. Already, in the real world, the seven states that depend on the Colorado River in the United States are at daggers drawn over water rights—with the UN warning that "water scarcity is an increasing problem on every continent."[29]

Such novels help bring the underlying science to life. As travel writer Theodora Sutcliffe has noted, "There's an immediacy to their descriptions of dried-out soil, of engines choked by dust storms, and the lengths that human beings will go to for survival (or vengeance) that extends beyond wildfire news coverage to open up new and terrifying worlds."[30]

As I drafted this section, indeed, the American Southwest was experiencing the deepest drought not just for twelve years, not even for 120, but for 1,200 years.[31] Time and again, on a somewhat happier note, failure can be a necessary stepping stone to ultimate success, but only if we can learn from what has gone wrong—and from the experience of others as they try to do the right thing.

Looking back, I have been unbelievably lucky with the people I have met, many of whom have helped me see bigger pictures. Over the seven years I was on the World Economic Forum's faculty, for example, I met some extraordinary folk. But, even among their number, Jerry Linenger stood out. Both an astronaut and a cosmonaut, he had logged some 50 million miles in space at the time. When I invited him to join the Volans Advisory Council in 2009, I was startled when he said yes.* With multiple degrees in bioscience, medicine, health policy, and systems management, he is one of the best-educated—and calmest—people I have met.

Just as well, since when aboard the space station *Mir*, he and his two Russian crewmembers encountered potentially fatal challenges. These included the most severe fire ever experienced aboard an orbiting spacecraft to that point, alongside failures of an oxygen dioxide generator and carbon scrubber, and of their urine processing plant. On top of that there was a near collision with a resupply ship, the loss of station electrical power, and a slow, uncontrolled tumble through space.[32]

Despite it all, the three spacefarers achieved all their mission goals. Their challenges were small-scale examples, I reflected, of the problems we will have to wrestle with as Spaceship Earth suffers systems malfunctions because of our failure to deal fast enough with the climate and biodiversity emergencies.

Jerry said that he had returned from space with "a broader perspective, a tendency toward strategic thinking and toward seeing endless possibilities."[33] Seeing water as an increasingly existential issue, he helped launch Circle of Blue, an advocacy group for sustainable water use. Though many of us may wish that we could move society faster from chaos to sustainability, he says, "We are not quite there yet, not quite ready for the transition. But the energy is there and growing."[34]

That's the upside view. On the downside, someone who died while I was drafting this chapter was Sir Crispin Tickell. I knew him well enough

---

* I also met David "Dave" Scott when he was dating newscaster Anna Ford, and we had dinner with her brother Adam. Scott, the seventh man to walk on the Moon, flew on Gemini 8, Apollo 9, and Apollo 15. That dinner must have been in 2000, when the couple was briefly engaged. Later, Elaine and I listened to Valentina Tereshkova, the first woman in space, at Britain's Science Museum during its *Cosmonauts* exhibition on September 17, 2015.

over several decades—though I can't say I found him particularly easy to be around. There was no doubting, however, that he could be effective: famously, by whispering in her ear, he got Prime Minister Margaret Thatcher to "go green" by embracing the climate issue. But he was not optimistic about our chances as a civilization. As the twentieth century ended, he noted that he was glad to be "in life's departure lounge," adding, "the next generation is in for an awfully bumpy ride."[35]

No doubt true, but the next stage in my own journey would involve turning various shades of green for rather different reasons.

CHAPTER 6

Going Green

I love green, but it is not my favorite color. Over time, I would learn to love all sorts of greenery, but my favorite colors remain the darkest of blues, swirling in and around indigo. The darker the better.* Still, if any one color has been associated with my working life, it has been green. The symbolism points in good directions: life, nature, spring, growth, and regeneration.

Nevertheless, even if over a third of my books—eight to date—have featured the word *green* in their titles, I confess that every time a brand like Apple has used a dusty green for its environmental web page, something in me has died. Apple's subliminal message with this color was that it had switched on to the worthy and (for the company) boring agenda.

It's all a bit like the regulated small print in a contract. A signal that what followed was there not because the company believed it but because others seemed to. Nowadays, though, Apple has cheered up this side of what it does. There's a lighter touch. "One less thing," a recent version of the website teased. "Siri runs on clean energy. Any questions?" Mine would have been,

---

* Intriguingly, when I probed the symbolism of indigo later, expecting it to be all about depression, I discovered that, while its negative links do run to things like fanaticism and addiction, it is mainly linked to perception, intuition, and wisdom—and to caring for the wider world. A rather specific job description, you might conclude.

"What took you so long?" Not just in picking a more cheerful shade of green, which it eventually did, but in signaling that the environment, the green agenda, was a hardwired element in the Apple genome. The answer, I believe, is that for a long time it wasn't. Apple had other things on its mind. Yes, there was a lime green iMac back in the day, but the broader green agenda was seen as a tough sell, a distraction. These days, happily, the giant company has come on by leaps and bounds in its thinking, spotlighted by a September 2023 video featuring CEO Tim Cook meeting Mother Earth.[1]

Still, if the keyword of wave 1 was *environment* (specifically, environmental *limits*), the keyword for wave 2, peaking by the early nineties, was *green*. In this evolving wave 2 reality, Green Parties were soon on a roll. The UK Green Party took an unprecedented fifteen percent of the vote in 1989's elections for the European Parliament. I voted Green that year, too, for the first time.

But my colleagues and I were also interested in catching that tide in other ways, surfing the emerging wave when most people couldn't even sense it building. The ambition was well articulated by *New York Times* journalist Tom Friedman when he argued that the country that owns "green," that dominates the relevant sectors, will have the most energy security, national security, economic security, competitive companies, healthy population, and most of all, he argued, global respect.[2] Still, words like *industry* and *dominates* were somewhat removed from prevailing green sentiments at the time.

Once again, as the green wave built, I was busily swimming countercurrent. It seemed to be in my nature to push against the stream. Initially, CounterCurrent was my platform for a trio of books published across 1984 and 1985.[*] All three focused on emerging areas of science and technology: *Sun Traps* on the renewable energy forecast,[3] *The Poisoned Womb* on reproductive toxicology,[4] and *The Gene Factory* on biotechnology and

---

[*] The organization was originally named John Elkington Associates, until its advisory activities were folded into SustainAbility in the late 1980s. CounterCurrent then took on my book writing activities.

genetic engineering.[5] The first two were published as Pelican paperbacks, which helped get the messages out in unexpected ways.

A particularly dramatic example was when Ted Hughes wrote a poem published in the *Times* called "Lobby from Under the Carpet."

O Maggie!

Britain's poet laureate at the time, Ted Hughes recounted how my 1985 book *The Poisoned Womb* had spurred him to write to the prime minister at the time, Margaret Thatcher. He noted that his "Muse" had read my book, *The Poisoned Womb*, and he energetically encouraged Thatcher (or "Maggie," as people then styled her) to read the book, to wake up and act.

We can debate whether or not she paid much heed, but one thing I liked about Hughes's poem "Lobby from Under the Carpet" was that it spotlighted the dark art of lobbying.[6] The best thing about the poem, though, even if I suspect few readers noticed, was the way he dropped a comma (representing the sperm) and a full stop (the egg) in a couple of places.

Not his best work, even so, but political, certainly. He referenced the way that the toxic waste industry would sweep problems under the carpet, all with what the British dub a nudge-and-a-wink. I already had painful experience of this behind-the-scenes, wink-and-nudge world. When insurance syndicates in London began to offer environmental liability insurance to polluting businesses in the United States, I warned both the insurers and their auditors that offering insurance based on half-day environmental audits of companies (which had every reason to cover up the relevant risks) was inviting disaster.

Disaster duly came.

Not long after, and perhaps not accidentally, I was invited to chair the Environment Foundation. Its funds came from a levy imposed on such policies offered by a key insurance syndicate. Then, in 1980 the Comprehensive Environmental Response, Compensation, and Liability Act (CERCLA) legislation (known as "Superfund") came in from the United States, imposing so-called joint and several liability on polluting companies.[7] The result: any surviving companies could be forced to pick up the tab for not only their own pollution but also that caused by polluting businesses that had gone bankrupt.

The impact from CERCLA on insurers could be devastating. Indeed, a significant percentage of the losses that almost brought down the Lloyd's insurance market linked back to such policies. Clarkson Puckle, the insurance syndicate that had funded our work at the foundation, went under.

I kept that history in mind as I chaired our annual meetings at St. George's House inside the walls of Windsor Castle. Our main sessions were held in the St. George's chapter library, which was freighted with history. When it first opened in 1348, the library's books were so rare that they were chained to the reading desks. And it was here that Shakespeare's *The Merry Wives of Windsor* received its first performance, in front of Elizabeth I.

One joy of this period was that we could bring together different ends of the political spectrum—and different generations of changemakers. Among the older folk, but still wonderfully young at heart, was Sir Geoffrey Chandler. One piece of advice he gave me that I have always taken seriously, generally in the breach, was to "be very, very careful about dropping names."

To be clear, the spirit in which I mention people in *Tickling Sharks* recalls a Ghanaian proverb: "The one who gets a good harvest of pumpkins forgets the one who gave them the seeds."[8] Still, I am delighted to drop in Geoffrey's name now—recalling that, typically, as he offered me this sage counsel, there was a twinkle in his eye. He, too, knew the seductive power of stories referencing extraordinary characters.

I once asked him whether he had ever met the fabled writer Patrick Leigh Fermor, who had also served in the Special Operations Executive, charged by Winston Churchill with setting occupied Europe ablaze. "The last time I saw Paddy," Geoffrey mused, his eyes going distant, "we were on the dock in Alexandria, loading a Jeep athwartships onto a *caique* [a brightly painted fishing or trading vessel, powered by sail]. The Jeep was full of gold coins that we were using to pay off [anti-Nazi] partisans."

I can't now remember whether those fighters were in Greece, Crete, or Yugoslavia, but I did catch a glimpse of a very different world and the excruciating war these young men endured.*

When I first met him, Geoffrey was a forbidding figure. Indeed, when he ran Industry Year in 1986, he struck me as Olympian. He was one of the earliest Establishment champions of what we now call corporate social responsibility. Later, though, I discovered that he had a glorious sense of humor. Several of his obituaries were decorated with a photograph I had taken of him some years before, hoisting up his trousers and in very good cheer.[9] During his funeral service in 2011, I directed the attention of one of his daughters to a bat flitting around the church belfry above our heads. Her father, we felt, would have approved.

For me, humor remains a powerful indicator of humanity in a business world profoundly shaped by economics—a discipline famously described by the Canadian environmental activist and broadcaster David Suzuki, not entirely humorously, as a form of brain damage. That was a view, whether or not they phrased it that way, that was second nature to the Greens. It would also be second nature to the Occupy Wall Street protesters when they launched their global campaign in 2011.

Though the spotlight of Occupy Wall Street was on growing tensions between the 1 percent and the 99 percent, the basic argument was well captured by media theorist Douglas Rushkoff: "Stated most simply, we are trying to run a 21st-century society on a 13th-century economic operating system. It just doesn't work."[10]

As it happens, I had direct personal experience of the resulting tensions when I tried to change the mission of the Environment Foundation from environmental protection to sustainable development. Cue the sounds of

---

* I adored Geoffrey Chandler, an example of a pattern that developed early in my life and repeated many times. I developed strong relationships with much older people, often starting with mutual teasing. A tickling of giants, in retrospect. Then as a growing number of these friends and mentors died, the pattern flipped—and I evolved friendships with people who were much younger. Don't ask me why.

battle being joined. The Charity Commission, which regulates charities in England and Wales, fought back—even trying to shut us down.

We decided to take it to the wire, legally, with the help of Stephen Lloyd of lawyers Bates Wells & Braithwaite (now Bates Wells). After two fruitless years, Stephen became so incensed that he gave his time pro bono for the third year—at which point we won. As a result, sustainable development, which the commission had insisted was a solely commercial pursuit, became a charitable objective in England and Wales. Stephen, a longstanding friend, died in a tragic boating accident in 2014,[11] but this was an important part of his legacy.

Green Peaks

For the moment, however, we are still in the 1980s—and all about us, a new wave is building: the green wave. The first of my books to formally go green was *The Green Capitalists*, published in 1987, with a concluding essay by Tom Burke, a former executive director of Friends of the Earth who went on to run the Green Alliance.* The book was supposed to be published by Dorling Kindersley, but at the last moment its board cut away the relevant list—and my editor kindly ensured that the typescript was slipped across to Victor Gollancz, a block or two away in London's Covent Garden.

In 1989 Victor Gollancz got my follow-up book, *The Green Consumer Guide*—whose sales went through the roof. Before that, however, I set the stage with yet another green book, this one published in 1988: *Green Pages*.[12] It was designed in the spirit of a green version of the *Yellow Pages* business directory but with a more magazine-like feel. It was subtitled *The Business of Saving the World* and contained contributions from a wide spread of business leaders, politicians, and political activists.

---

* Many years previously, I had attended the dinner at which the possibility of forming the Green Alliance was first discussed, with people like Gordon Rattray Taylor and Maurice Ash. At the launch in 1979, Ash said, "We're a bunch of optimists. We're not the doomsters."

Among the activist contributors was German American Petra Kelly, one of the founders of Die Grünen, Germany's Green Party. Her political and media impact had been profound, with her stance often skewed to the radical end of the Green spectrum. In the language of the time, she was a Fundi, not a Realo. Indeed, we were slightly agog when she agreed to contribute to *Green Pages*.

She began her contribution as follows: "The proliferation of mass destructive weapons has given us the ability to obliterate civilisations in a flash, while the growing environmental crisis threatens to choke the planet's life support systems. All over the world, Green Parties have emerged in response to such problems, using the colour green as a symbol of new hope and new thinking."[13]

She quoted Albert Einstein: "The splitting of the atom has changed everything, except the way people think." And she was already warning of the danger of the green movements being co-opted—something that some activists worried our green consumer movement might eventually accept, however unwittingly.

Sadly, however, it turned out that there were existential risks closer to home.

In 1992, Petra was shot dead in her sleep by her lover, the Green politician and former general Gert Bastian. One rumor at the time was that he feared he was about to be exposed as a spy for the old East Germany, though that remains conjecture.

Still, by the time Bastian turned the gun on himself, the green wave had peaked. The very fact that he risked exposure through the release of Stasi secret police files from the old East Germany reflected the abrupt collapse of the Soviet-centered communist bloc.* Now our efforts to change business, markets, and capitalism would not just need to shift gears, but

---

* Elaine and I attended Petra Kelly's memorial service at St. James's Church, Piccadilly, on September 25, 1993. As Stanley Johnson, the father of Boris Johnson and someone I had known for years, put it, "The Green Movement in Germany, of which she was the most notable leader, has been one of the dominant forces in pushing forward European environmental policy."

would need to actively steer in new directions. Green leaders had often said they were neither left nor right, but out ahead of everyone else. Still, the European Green movements of the 1980s and 1990s were very much creatures of their time, the late stages of the first Cold War. And few of them—few of us—saw what was about to land in our laps as the Soviet Union unraveled.

I recall doing a twin-headed debate with Green Party leader Joschka Fischer in Wiesbaden, Germany, not long after Petra's death. I suggested from the stage that Joschka could serve as the proverbial hard policeman while I would serve as the soft one (for American readers, that's good cop and bad cop). No, he protested, we're all pragmatic now!

Later, Joschka became Germany's foreign minister. I liked him immensely—and was reminded of that affection when we met again many years later while both speaking at a financial event at the Basel Stock Exchange in Switzerland. Looking back, it is more than ever clear that the fall of the Berlin Wall changed our game. The very idea of a Green speaking in a stock exchange would have seemed wildly improbable back then.

The future, it now seemed, was capitalism's to determine.

Meanwhile, although its course has often been erratic, the Green Party continued to make inroads into politics, particularly in Germany. At the time of this book's writing, Annalena Baerbock was both co-leader of the Green Party and in Joschka's old role of foreign minister. Working with Chancellor Olaf Scholz, she was part of a traffic light coalition of multiple parties green, amber, and red: the Greens, the Free Democratic Party, and the Social Democrats.

"Governing is radical," she insisted as she campaigned for the top job. But she showed her true colors when saying, "It's up to me as a mother, up to us as a society, up to us adults to be prepared for the questions of our children: 'Did you act? Did we do everything to secure the climate and with it the freedom of our children?'"[14] Such questions have particular resonance in Germany but should now inform everyone's thinking.

Earthlife Dies

Once again, though, I am galloping ahead of my story. *Green Pages* and *The Green Consumer Guide* would not have been possible without the help of someone who walked through my door in the autumn of 1986. The door in question was at the top of some very grand stairs in one of those giant white wedding cake buildings that grace London's Belgrave Square.

Number 10, to be precise.

Whatever I may have been expecting that day, and whatever she may have intended, Julia Hailes bent the arc of my life.[*] She arrived hotfoot from hitchhiking on her own around South America, among other things crewing on a yacht in the Caribbean where Senator Ted Kennedy was among the guests. She recalled those same guests complaining about the litter on a deserted island while she had spotted the crew throwing all their rubbish into the sea—including plastics. She had also witnessed her hosts in Brazil's Mato Grosso busily clearing the rainforest with chainsaws.[†]

Julia returned to the UK on a mission to save rainforests. That was what brought her to the Earthlife Foundation, where I was a director at the time. Google the name and you will find that there are different Earthlifes these days, but this one—founded by Nigel Tuersley—was the first. There was something of Richard Branson to Nigel, an entrepreneurial brainiac with an elegantly shaped beard—and an unusual commercial instinct for a Green.

---

[*] It has been an honor to be a real-world godfather to Julia's oldest son, Connor Bryant. He has pioneered in related fields, as in The Rubbish Project: https://therubbishproject.com/.

[†] My 1989 diary, published as *A Year in the Greenhouse* (London: Victor Gollancz, 1990), opened with the murder of rainforest activist Chico Mendes at the end of 1988, "the shot heard around the world." The problems have gotten worse since, resulting in large parts of Amazonia becoming net producers of carbon dioxide. If anyone doubts the scale of the havoc, consider the story of Marina Silva, sworn in as Brazilian President Luiz Inácio Lula da Silva's environment minister in early 2023, the second time she had played that role for Lula. When she was fourteen, a bulldozing crew arrived to build a highway near her village. According to the *Financial Times*, "they brought an epidemic of measles and malaria. Soon two of her younger sisters were dead. Then a cousin and an uncle. Her mother died months later." See Bryan Harris and Michael Pooler, "Marina Silva, An Unflinching Campaigner to Save Brazil's Rainforest," *Financial Times*, January 6, 2023. https://www.ft.com/content/53641c63-f90a-4171-902d-bf07398918d8.

I first met him and his codirector Phil Agland when Earthlife was based in another grand building in Bedford Square. Nigel somehow managed to find such premises at way below market rates, just as Elaine found us places to live in some of the smartest parts of London. Somehow you could do that then. Phil was already an acclaimed filmmaker, then completing his Channel 4 film documenting his time in Korup, a Cameroonian rainforest. He had taken his strikingly good-looking girlfriend Lisa Silcock with him, her waist-length blonde hair presumably quite a novelty for the Pygmy people they camped alongside.

Things seemed to be coming together; indeed, Earthlife's rate of growth was so great that one or two traditional greenish NGOs were getting quite agitated. All of that seemed in the spirit of the necessary disruptions, however. And as editor of the glossy new magazine *Earthlife News*, I explored emerging trends in green technology, business, and finance.

During this period, I coined terms like *green growth*, *green consumer*, and *green investor*. Though all these terms have been contested since, and often misused, they also went into the language. That work, in turn, led to a request from the Design Council to help it stage a major exhibition in London's Haymarket on green design—and what we soon dubbed the "green designer." We featured products like a NASA space suit, a Rolls-Royce jet engine—simultaneously quieter, more fuel efficient, and less polluting than earlier engines—and a pesticide sprayer, the Electrodyn, that gave the ejected spray an electrostatic charge so that pretty much all the chemical ended up stuck directly on the target crop plants. It could also be used to spray-paint cars with similar efficiencies.

The irony was that the sprayer was made by the now long-gone chemical giant ICI. Ironic because their group environment manager, Mike Flux, said something at the time that would once again bend the trajectory of my life. He told me, "It's all very well for environmentalists like you to call for cleaner, greener products, but no one wants to buy them!"

The gauntlet had been thrown down. I picked it up and, while writing the exhibition catalog, ended with a question: "Once all this good work has been done by the Green Designer, will it appeal to the Green Consumer?"

That was the point at which Julia walked through my door. Energetic, ambitious, and determined, she looked and sounded very much like what was then called a "Sloane Ranger"[15]—though she operated on a very different wavelength. From a privileged background, she had somehow managed to avoid university and was also happily making things up as she went along.

She wanted to know what I was doing and what came next. I mentioned two embryonic book ideas: *Green Pages* and *The Green Consumer Guide*. She didn't think long before saying that she would help with the first if she could be part of the second. So began a partnership that resulted in eight books as co-authors and a brand-new company, SustainAbility, as cofounders.

Meanwhile, I had been struggling to discover what was wrong with Earthlife's finances but wasn't fast enough. I helped pull in a businessman as chairman, Peter Smith, but the organization still went bankrupt—to the tune of around £1 million at a time when that was serious money. In the meltdown, the funds I had raised for *Green Pages* vaporized.

As a result, Julia and I were left with the agonizing decision of whether to press ahead or not. We decided to give it a go, moving the team to my family home in Barnes. Julia promptly pruned the team until we had a sustainable operation, which to begin with meant just her and me. With the funds for *Green Pages* largely gone, we had to make compromises, including inserting paid color ads from Shell and, of all companies, British Nuclear Fuels, on the front and back inside covers, respectively. Somehow, we got away with it.*

Julia's interest in working on *The Green Consumer Guide* proved prescient. The book turned out very differently than it would have if I had done it on my own. I would have focused on the issues, whereas

---

* Thirty years later, the book would be republished for the Asian market—as a historical document explaining the rise of the global green movement—at a cover price of £90. We were told that Asian universities increasingly wanted to know how the various strands of the green movement had evolved.

after setting the scene with a discussion of the problems, she insisted we approach it from the perspective of an ordinary consumer.

"What would Mrs. Bloggs think?" she asked me continuously. Mrs. Bloggs was a proxy for ordinary women in the street or supermarket. As a result, the book went on to sell around one million copies in its various editions, helping to spur a global movement. Instead of killing SustainAbility—now operating under the tagline "The Green Growth Company"—it helped make its early fortunes.

It was like riding a rocket, so here's a short story to give some sense of what that felt like.

Levitating Pamela Stephenson

Imagine we have a time machine. Let's set the controls to arrive near Slough, a large English town west of London, on the evening of Thursday, July 6, 1989. It is close to midnight, and the time machine has deposited us inside a sparsely populated first-class train carriage. The emergency lighting is on—and we are in the presence of beauty. Two of us, maybe three, stand either side of a thin, wobbly table not designed to take the weight now being imposed on it—joyfully insinuating our hands under Pamela Stephenson's rump.

At the time, Pamela was best known as a star of *Not the Nine O'Clock News* and *Saturday Night Live*. Later, though, she would also be known as the wife of comedian Billy Connolly, the "Big Yin," whom she had met in the 1970s and would marry some six months after our brief encounter.

Outside the train windows all is black, no moon. Something—perhaps the lightning that sizzled overhead as we sped east—has knocked out the power and stalled our train. Our small group, old enough to know better, is teetering on the edge of hysterical laughter. Occasional passengers passing through the carriage are startled to see Pamela being manhandled in such a public fashion.

"It's OK," we pant. "We're levitating her!"

The zany experiment is the brainchild of one of our number, Professor

Heinz Wolff. Before this memorable night, I only knew of him as the madcap German-born British scientist who pioneered bioengineering, advised the space industry in areas like microgravity, and presented the TV series *The Great Egg Race*.

As our conversation drifts from Pamela's new campaign, Parents for Safe Food, to science and then to progressively weirder areas of human enquiry, levitation surfaces. Heinz lights up like Dr. Frankenstein considering some exciting new feature for his creature. We conclude that Pamela's smaller—and much lighter—body makes her the obvious candidate as our guinea pig. Ultimately, however, we are forced to conclude that levitation, fun though it may be to attempt, is unlikely to take off any time soon.

But what were we doing on that stalled train in the first place—and why we were in such an unprofessionally giddy mood? For my side of the story, I must again rewind the clock to the previous day, when I had visited a law firm in London's City. To put it bluntly, our small company, SustainAbility, was in deep shit.

We were being sued by the fast-food giant McDonald's.

The American hamburger company had belatedly worked out why so many customers were coming into their restaurants and challenging their staff about the company's alleged role in tropical rainforest destruction. A key source of the problem, McDonald's concluded some months after its publication, was *The Green Consumer Guide*. In the book, we had said that McDonald's was "implicated" in tropical rainforest destruction.

The book turned us into celebrities for a while, though I am sincerely grateful to have largely avoided the curse of celebrity. I got a sense of what that might involve during the green consumer period when the *Times* covered me in a gossip column. The article claimed that I had secretly joined forces with Michael Howard, then secretary of state for the environment, to overthrow the headmistress of St. Paul's Girls' School. While it was true that we both had daughters at the school, I am pretty sure we had neither met nor plotted anyone's downfall. But that's what seems to happen when you become public property.

Unfortunately, though, McDonald's was proving to be an increasingly bothersome fly in the ointment of our commercial success. We visited lawyers that day because McDonald's had taken out a court injunction against us. Our publishers, Victor Gollancz, had been forced to strip *The Guide*, which had just hit the No. 1 slot on the UK nonfiction lists, out of bookstores across the country. Worse, we were told, was to come. This was turning into an existential threat for our small firm, with bankruptcy now seeming a real prospect.

Battling McDonald's

Here is an entry from a diary I wrote at the time, published in 1990 as *A Year in the Greenhouse*:

Thursday, 29 June

Off with Julia to the Temple, to consult the oracle on the McDonald's threat. Counsel says we start one-nil down in libel law, since juries tend to favour the plaintiff. And the recent *Private Eye* verdict, with the magazine thumped with a £600,000 fine, is a warning that it is a threat to be taken seriously.

"I wish I could wave a magic wand," says Counsel, although it is clear that all three lawyers in the book-lined room are enjoying the case hugely. One, bald-headed and with a strange nervous tic which makes his whole body leap, hops around us like a vulture inspecting a fresh corpse. "The problem with companies like McDonald's," Counsel continues, "is that they are commercial giants and have their suppliers by the short and curlies."[16]

Counsel sympathetically added that it was not unknown for giant companies to pay people to perjure themselves. But then, as we rose to leave, somewhat dispirited, he said something that changed everything. "You are going to have to roll over, comply," he advised. But then he paused, for theatrical effect . . .

"Unless, of course, you want to play poker!"

I'm not sure that I had ever played poker, but I knew what he meant. Bluff, he was suggesting, and so bluff we did. With Julia having flown off to Hong Kong and Australia for three weeks to promote local editions of the book, I headed west to Cardiff for a BBC Radio 1 broadcast, hosted by DJ Nicky Campbell. The panelists included Pamela, Heinz, Pat Kane of the pop band Hue and Cry, and me.

We were later told that eight million people listened to that broadcast, with a live studio audience of perhaps eighty people. Then, with no encouragement from me, Pat launched into an on-air harangue linking McDonald's, hamburgers, and rainforest destruction, quoting *The Guide* almost verbatim. He later told me he had read the book on the train down from Glasgow. And, as chance would have it, there were two women from McDonald's in the studio audience—who literally ran up afterward.

"You can't do this!" they protested. "You're under an injunction!"

My response, inspired by our counsel's parting shot about poker, was that we had now discovered enough evidence to acutely embarrass McDonald's—and were determined to meet them in court. What I said wasn't entirely untrue. At a scorching pace we had worked with Friends of the Earth and Greenpeace to dig up enough evidence to at least confuse any jurors. Moreover, we had heard through back channels that the company's own lawyers were increasingly split on whether our claims were in fact defamatory. We sensed the odds beginning to shift in our favor.

To say the McDonald's duo turned white that evening would be to understate the impact of my words.

"Would you talk to our president?" one stuttered.

"If he wants to call me," I replied.

"He," and indeed it was a he, called the very next morning—a few hours after we had all got home from our adventures with lightning and levitation.

"What would it take to get you off our backs?" he wanted to know.

"Proof that you have a written environmental policy statement banning any involvement in tropical deforestation," I replied, "and that it is implemented worldwide." To be honest, I was pretty much making this up on the fly.

There ensued the longest silence I have ever heard on any phone call.

Eventually, he asked if we would give them two weeks. I agreed—and then, two weeks later, we convened with two people on our side and a standing army on theirs, made up of their president and various vice presidents and lawyers from the UK and the United States. To make a very long story short, they spent five hours discussing the evidence collected by McDonald's director of international purchasing (a dead ringer for the singer Barry Manilow), as he had traveled around South America in the intervening weeks.

Their evidence was better than we had expected, but there was evidently much work still to be done. Then, irony of ironies, the McDonald's team asked if we would like to work with them. My instant answer: No. Nothing was further from our minds, though I was pleased to hear that the United States' Environmental Defense Fund began to do so a few months later.* Somebody had to do it.

But what was really fascinating about this McDonald's saga was how little the company seemed to learn from its collision with us. A few years later, it became embroiled in another long-running legal dispute with the London Greenpeace (no relation to Greenpeace International, it turned out), the so-called McLibel case, a trial that lasted two and a half years—making it the longest-running legal case in England to that point.[17]

The company won the legal battle but suffered hugely in terms of reputation.

Nor was McDonald's alone in coming after us. A particularly ironic example of what happened to us involved not one, but three different parts of one of our corporate clients at the time, the chemical giant ICI.

---

* Note that SustainAbility had been—and still was—working happily with several major businesses. True, there were sectors and companies we refused to work with. And, yes, we were challenging, radical even. But we were in no way antibusiness.

Each of the businesses—garden chemicals, paints, and PVC—threatened to take us to court, separately, each sublimely unaware of what their sister companies were doing.

Nor did they seem to know that we were working with their headquarters team at the time, including with their chairman, Sir John Harvey-Jones.*

In hindsight, it is not hard to see how this had happened. Like the Germans outflanking France's much-vaunted Maginot Line in World War II, we had outflanked ICI's divisions by doing something completely unexpected. At a time when most businesses were obsessively focused on what activists were doing to influence regulators, we had thundered in through a blind spot. Companies like ICI had assumed complete disinterest among consumers when it came to green issues. Big mistake. Huge.

The impact of this left-field challenge continued to disrupt companies and their supply chains for some years. Indeed, a year or so later we went after UK supermarkets with a one-hundred-page questionnaire on their environmental practices and footprints, which only one major supermarket group (Waitrose, part of the John Lewis group) refused to complete. The ripples continued to spread for years. I remember visiting the person responsible for the environmental agenda at Marks & Spencer, a well-known UK supermarket chain, several years later. He opened the top drawer of his desk to show us his copy of the questionnaire, which he said he was still using as a guide to issues likely to surface as consumers continued to wake up.

Still, there were delightful moments. For years after we published *The Young Green Consumer Guide*,[18] with its wonderfully quirky illustrations by Tony Ross, I continued to receive packages of paintings and drawings from schoolchildren around the world as they were encouraged by teachers to work through our green audit for schools—where the pupils held their

---

* Famous for his colorful ties and long hair, Sir John Harvey-Jones was a perfect example of a thoughtful leader wrong-footed by change. A World War II submariner, he was certainly courageous. But he was also slow in waking up to the global threat of CFCs, for which ICI was one of the world's biggest producers.

teachers and school managers to account. No doubt many teachers and other adults found the process a headache, but the children's letters showed that they loved the opportunity to examine their examiners.

Business Goes Green

No question, *The Green Consumer Guide* caused real grief for many major companies. But while some tried to take legal action against us, Mads Øvlisen, president of the Danish biotechnology company Novo Nordisk, tried a different tack. He kept in mind what had happened to his company when an earlier activist, Ralph Nader, had campaigned against the use of the company's enzymes in "biological" laundry detergents. Novo Nordisk had lost a considerable slice of its business and was forced to lay off hundreds of people.

Mads chose to keep reminding his colleagues that such threats to the business can come out of the blue—or, in this case, green. Instead of arguing that the company knew what it was doing and insisting that we back off, he had a couple of his colleagues approach me after I spoke at a conference in London to ask if I would come across to Copenhagen to meet him.

I already knew Novo Nordisk well, having covered them for years as editor of *Biotechnology Bulletin*—but had not yet encountered their president. This was a different agenda, a different level of engagement. With Julia, I set off for Bagsværd on the outskirts of Copenhagen. We got on well with Mads, and he invited us to go anywhere we wanted in the company, talk to anyone we chose to, and then come back and tell him what we thought they should do next.

We did so, offering three key recommendations—and they stunned us by taking them all on board. One was that the company should invite activists and other external stakeholders in each year to challenge senior management. This was truly novel at the time.

During the second annual visit, however, about the worst scenario we could have imagined materialized. Greenpeace and other activists against genetic modifications were participating, and while we were all watching

TV in the hotel on the day the outsiders arrived in the city, the news broke that an accidental spill of genetically modified organisms had occurred at a Novo Nordisk plant in Copenhagen.

The next morning, taking a huge risk, I had to usher an older Novo Nordisk executive off the stage, in front of more than fifty of his colleagues, replacing him with a much younger woman, Lise Kingo. The first executive had risked the entire process by telling the visitors that this sort of thing happened all the time, insinuating that we shouldn't bother our pretty little heads about it. By contrast, Lise excelled. She indicated that the company, having learned how to deliver against the total quality management agenda for customers, would now learn how to see external stakeholders as a new class of customers. Perhaps not surprisingly, she would later serve on the company's executive committee and, later still, as executive director of the United Nations Global Compact.

Ultimately, and well beyond our opening suggestions, Novo Nordisk would recharter itself around the triple bottom line in 2004, probably uniquely among major companies until the dawn of the B Corporation movement. No wonder it dominated the sustainability rankings for so long.[*]

One huge barrier to progress, however, was the resistance we encountered in the financial world. One of my favorite activists in this space was Tessa Tennant, among those we had invited in to challenge Novo Nordisk at close quarters. One of my fondest memories of her is of the two of us taking the green-painted ferries around Hong Kong harbor several years later. We were visiting the local green and good: she was there as the first chair of the Association for Sustainable and Responsible Investment in Asia.

I had first bumped into her, literally, when I had to climb over her desk at the Green Alliance to get to Tom Burke's desk. As mentioned, he was the organization's director, a former executive director of Friends of

---

[*] While working on an early draft of *Tickling Sharks*, I took part in a debate with Mads Øvlisen during an online event cohosted by three business schools: Denmark's Copenhagen Business School, Japan's Shizenkan University, and Spain's IESE. Mads noted that our early conversations had spurred changes within not only Novo Nordisk but also the wider community evolving the sustainable business agenda.

the Earth, and a co-author of mine both with *The Green Capitalists* and *Green Pages*. He had taken Tessa under his wing. Just back from the United States, she had understudied Joan Bavaria, head of Franklin Research and Development (now Trillium), a pioneer in responsible investing.

Before long, I was on Tessa's advisory board at the new Merlin Ecology Fund, the first green investment fund in the UK, alongside Robin Grove-White, who led the Council for the Protection of Rural England, and Nigel Haigh, who led the Institute for European Environmental Policy. Described in one of her obituaries as a "giant of green finance," Tessa helped birth many key ventures, from the Merlin Ecology Fund and Carbon Disclosure Project (CDP) to the Global Cool Foundation. She also helped launch the Business in the Environment platform at Business in the Community, with Tom and me both on the advisory board.

Her family home, through marriage, was the fabled Glen House, a longtime haunt of royals and socialites in the Scottish Borders. But, like Julia Hailes, Tessa was cut from very different cloth. I remember one weekend she hosted more than twenty activists at Glen House—including long walks in the hills and over the moors with the likes of Paul Hawken, an entrepreneur, activist, and writer whose path would often entwine with mine in later years.

It helped hugely to develop personal relationships with such people. And through Tessa, I was also one of ten or so environmentalists who attended a small dinner in Kensington Palace to mark Prince Charles's fortieth birthday—and explore what he might do on related issues. He is now King Charles III. Next, Tessa and friends organized a Green Ball at the stately home that sits in Osterley Park on the way out to London's Heathrow airport. Julia was being profiled in high society magazines like *Tatler* at the time, so it was all part and parcel. Not my scene, remotely, but I tried to go with the green flow.

Looking back, Tessa was performing a similar role to that played by the grand ladies who hosted the Paris salons, offering venues for discussing liberal ideas—and criticisms of—the Ancien Régime. The potential impact of pulling together people in this way is easy to underestimate.

Mark Campanale, a colleague and close friend of Tessa's since the Merlin days, later recalled the impact she had had. He noted that pioneering organizations like CDP and Carbon Tracker gelled around her kitchen table.

As he noted: "Martin Luther King Jr. once said, 'The moral arc of the universe bends towards justice.' Tessa found that moral arc in the financial world and championed causes in sustainable finance that helped bend that arc."[19]

Brighter Greens

There remained huge gaps between the worlds of "Light" and "Dark" Greens, however. In the late 1980s and early 1990s, most of my colleagues and friends would have been considered Light by the Darks, Realos by the Fundis. Still, I knew and respected people across the green spectrum. And, in that spirit, I also liked futurist Alex Steffen's addition of a third category. In 2003, he began talking about Bright Greens. So, what were the differences between the three?

In his book *The Song of the Earth*, Jonathan Bate equated Light Greens with environmentalists, who saw protecting the environment first and foremost as a personal responsibility.[20] He then equated Dark Greens with so-called deep ecologists. They saw environmental problems as an inherent part of industrialized civilization and thus sought radical political and cultural changes. They also opposed consumerism and economic growth of any sort, calling for degrowth, postmaterialism, and a reduction of the human population.

No green capitalism or green consumerism for them.

Bright Greens, Steffen argued, are environmentalists who agree that radical changes are needed in our economic and political systems. But rather than arguing for key systems to be thrown into reverse, they conclude that huge, systemic progress can be made using creative, constructive solutions, harnessing some of the basic processes of capitalism itself. In effect, they aim to change the system from within.

In that spirit—and even though the green agenda has had its ups and downs—the level of ambition has grown hugely. Both in Europe and the United States, so-called Green (New) Deals are now in force, at least at the time of writing. Where we once talked in terms of tens of millions, then billions, the talk now is increasingly of trillions. Marshalling the money and investing it efficiently and effectively is our next challenge—alongside coping with the implications in terms of potential barriers to trade.

As far as I am aware, the phrase "Green New Deal" was first used by Pulitzer Prize–winning writer Thomas Friedman in 2007. He concluded that there was no easy way to solve climate change. Instead, it was going to take a lot of money and effort, and—crucially—it would involve upsetting the fossil fuel industry, which has always been more than willing to rubbish the science and grease political palms with campaign contributions.[21]

In the European Union, the bloc's Green Deal attracted one-third of the €1.8 trillion Next Generation Recovery Plan. The aim has been to transform the region's economy, making it more resource-efficient and competitive, achieving net zero emissions of greenhouse gases by 2050, decoupling economic growth from resource use, and ensuring "no person and no place is left behind."[22] In the United States, meanwhile, President Joe Biden's Inflation Reduction Act, a rather different IRA from the one under whose shadow I grew up, aimed to cut inflation through policies that reduce the cost of energy, as well as the federal deficit. Expected to raise an estimated $790 billion in revenue and savings from a new corporate minimum tax, improved tax enforcement, and prescription drug reform, it was welcomed by green economy champions because it earmarked $369 billion for energy and climate change priorities. But it ran into headwinds when the Republicans narrowly took the House of Representatives and descended into temporary chaos over the election of a new Speaker of the House.

Enter Russian President Vladimir Putin. The clean energy agenda was given a massive boost by the Ukraine conflict. Indeed, as the war with Russia raged, I was invited to brief the board of a major energy company on the implications. No question, I said, there will be adverse impacts in the short to medium term—but the knock-on effects in such areas as energy security, food security, and the deglobalization of many supply chains could also offer extraordinary opportunities for change. And so it proved, with a sharp uptick in renewable energy and everything that goes with it.

Even today's Green Deals, however, do not yet constitute the sort of new Marshall Plan envisaged by some champions of sustainable economies, but the green vocabulary—love it or loathe it—is now part of the political discourse. So, for example, it has inflected the increasingly fractious debate about so-called subsidy wars.

By the time of the 2023 World Economic Forum in Davos, green geopolitics were on a something of a roll. Delegates saw the United States' act as providing an "engine for growth" over the next decade—and urged the European Union to stop complaining and step up in like manner. Meanwhile, at least in the world of business and finance, the green agenda would sometimes be overtaken by a wider concept that has gained huge traction in recent decades: sustainability. This was another wave I not only learned how to surf but also helped to build and shape.

CHAPTER 7

Selling Sustainability

"What was the best decision you ever made?" It was the last question the interviewer tossed at me as he Zoomed in from a luxurious Swiss chalet. I'm not sure what your answer would have been, but mine was that it was probably an intuitive, emotional decision. It involved choosing to develop a relationship with Elaine back in 1968. In hindsight, she made a lot of things possible that otherwise would have been much harder—or might not have happened at all. She provided backup, of all sorts, as I caught successive waves of change, the sustainability one being the third in the sequence.

Inevitably, though, as soon as that call ended other possible replies bobbed to the surface, one of them linked to wordplay. A vital skill of mine, it turned out, as the following memory illustrates.

Below, the English Channel crawled by, choppy, disturbed. As the Sabena jet climbed out of Brussels airport, banking toward London, I was playing with words. Specifically, I was looking for a name for the new business Julia Hailes and I planned to launch. As to why I was in the European capital that day, I have forgotten. Maybe I had been working with a company on environmental issues or visiting the European Commission to discuss new eco-laws.*

In any event, reclining in my seat, I was sublimely unaware that Sabena, the Belgian national airline on which I used to yo-yo back and forth to the Continent, would collapse into bankruptcy over a decade later, in 2001. Another reminder of just how difficult it can be to sustain a business—indeed, how dangerous it can be to pin your hopes for change on individual brands, companies, or even industries. Capitalism builds—and it destroys.

Continuing the word game, I toyed with animal names, like pangolin and shearwater. But none seemed to work. Then, halfway across the Channel, I recalled all the flying I had done over the years—and the privileged, almost godlike perspective that flight had given me of a planet undergoing profound changes. This line of thought then hooked back to our early attempts to take the environmental and sustainability agendas global.

I recalled working for the Brundtland Commission on Environment and Development, launched in 1983 by Gro Harlem Brundtland, former—and future—prime minister of Norway. More than any other single figure in history, she was the architect of the modern sustainability agenda. Not the godmother, not even the grandmother, but the Great Mother, perhaps.

Some of this work I did directly with the Brundtland Commission team, some alongside organizations like the International Institute for Environment and Development (IIED). The focus was on sustainable development. As the Brundtland Commission concluded in its final report, *Our Common Future*, "Sustainable development is development that meets the needs of the present without compromising the ability of

---

* That always seemed grimly ironic since Brussels had one of the worst sewage systems in the European Union at the time—as in pretty much no treatment at all. Full treatment of the city's wastewater was achieved only in 2007.

future generations to meet their own needs."[1] That became a mantra for many in the field, though I confess to having antibodies to most mantras.*

Now, as the English coastline hove into view, the name dropped fully formed into my brain: SustainAbility. Not just the word, the brand. By the time we landed at Heathrow, I was certain I had cracked the problem. A brand, a business, and a new spin on the business change agenda, all birthed in midair.

Over the years, I have often been described as the creator of the sustainability agenda, among other things labeled as the "Godfather of Sustainability"—the phrase first emerged in Brazil. But while I certainly helped give the word its wings in the business world, I stood on the shoulders of giants, among them those of Gro Harlem Brundtland.

And they were robust shoulders. Something few people now remember about her is that she narrowly missed being beheaded with a bayonet by Anders Behring Breivik. He went on to kill sixty-nine young people on the island of Utøya in 2011, later admitting that Brundtland had been his main target. Luckily, at least in this respect, he was delayed in traveling from Oslo, arriving when Brundtland had already left.

I met her only a couple of times: once at a festival in Tällberg, Sweden, then again at a reception hosted by Denmark's Crown Prince Frederik at a palace outside Copenhagen. She was a formidable woman—indeed, I'm not sure I would have given much for Breivik's chances had they ever met.

At one point, Gro Harlem Brundtland even dove off a boat to rescue her husband from drowning. But she is best remembered as Norway's first female prime minister, an office she occupied no fewer than three times. Her memoirs, *Madam Prime Minister*, are riveting, chronicling a life of remarkable highs and lows.[2]

Still, mother figure or not, she was not someone I connected with

---

* I have no idea if they were right, but years later an Aberdeen University team ran a word search on an online version of *Our Common Future*—and said it found no mention of the word *sustainability* itself. Eventually I tracked the current meaning of the word back to a single mention by a French Canadian priest in the seventies. But at the time we adopted it, the term was not in common usage.

emotionally. She put me in mind of a particularly formidable great aunt. Appropriate, then, that she later joined the Elders, founded by Sir Richard Branson, a convening of some of the most remarkable political leaders of our times. Our future needs tough love, too.

Her analysis of the systemic nature of our challenge was unwavering. As she argued: "Economies are stalling. Ecosystems are under siege. Inequality—within and between countries—is soaring. These afflictions are clearly rooted in political short-sightedness, where narrow interests triumph over common interests, common responsibilities, and common sense."[3] She helped bring uncommon sense to bear on the politics of the future.

Godfathers

When dubbed the Godfather of Sustainability, I have pushed back, noting that—even if I may have been so—I was one among a number of godparents. Some popped up among Brundtland's commissioners, including Maurice Strong. A longtime oilman, he had run the first conference on the human environment in 1972. Next, he served as the first executive director of the UN Environment Programme. And, later still, he supported us at the ill-fated Earthlife Foundation.

One of his business colleagues was William "Bill" Ruckelshaus, the first administrator of the United States Environmental Protection Agency—appointed by President Richard Nixon in 1970.[4] Once in office, Ruckelshaus accomplished some extraordinary feats. At a time when some US rivers were so polluted they would catch fire, he banned the pesticide DDT, set the first air-quality standards to protect public health under the Clean Air Act, established standards for cleaner cars and lead-free gasoline, and counterintuitively under a Republican president, built a national environmental law enforcement program with real teeth.

Strikingly, such early champions of sustainable development were more than happy to move between sectors. Ruckelshaus served from 1988 to 1999 as CEO of Browning-Ferris Industries, a national waste-removal firm based in Houston, Texas. During his time there, Browning-Ferris increasingly shifted its focus from hazardous wastes to recycling. Then, as the company expanded its operations into New York City, Ruckelshaus helped investigators infiltrate a Mafia-dominated waste-trucking conspiracy, resulting in prosecutions. As a result, President Bill Clinton appointed him to his Council for Sustainable Development between 1993 and 1997.

In addition to Strong and Ruckelshaus, other industrialists who helped shape the sustainable development agenda included Robert "Bob" O. Anderson, the founder of another oil company, Atlantic Richfield Company, or ARCO. Surprisingly, he was an early funder of Friends of the Earth and IIED, and a key contributor to the Brundtland Commission's work. Then there was Stephan Schmidheiny, who founded the Business Council for Sustainable Development, which later evolved into the World Business Council for Sustainable Development. I met most of these people, though I didn't know any of them that well. There was a real generational divide at work, and some also came with significant baggage.

Critics were upset that both Anderson and Strong had their roots in the oil patch, while Schmidheiny's family had been heavily invested in asbestos. The fact that he had worked tirelessly to help their family business, Eternit, exit production of the deadly material didn't prevent him from being prosecuted for manslaughter because of the deaths of Eternit workers.

My own claims to godfatherhood stem from our launch, in 1987, of SustainAbility—which aimed to help inject Brundtland's uncommon sense into the business world. Learning from the independence that limited company status had afforded us at ENDS, I decided to make SustainAbility a for-profit, limited company. One unintended consequence was that businesspeople trusted us to a much greater degree than they trusted most not-for-profit NGOs. They took comfort from the fact that we, too, were a business.

In the early days, we summed up our mission as follows: to make a difference, to make a profit (to reinvest in our future), and to have fun—and learn—along the way. For a couple of years, the firm operated out of my small home in Barnes. Most days, the team ate together at the kitchen table, as we had at BRAD and TEST, sometimes with Gaia and Hania, often alongside people from the wider world. These included everyone from activists to directors of major companies.

Julia, meanwhile, was a blur as one interview followed another. Still in her early twenties, she had the immense energy of youth. One morning, she arrived at Barnes in a pink jumpsuit; it turned out that she had rollerskated all the way from Notting Hill. At one point she appeared on stage at a big Green Party conference wearing dramatically embroidered tights and a mini skirt. The media loved it, though some Greens considered it a thumbed nose.

Another memory spotlights our strange positioning. It was the evening of Monday, October 22, 2007, already dark and cold. Several of us stood amid a roiling crowd outside Shell's London headquarters alongside the Thames, protesting. I was with Greenpeace UK Director John Sauven and, in a long dark coat and scarf, Bianca Jagger. We had just crossed Westminster Bridge with hundreds of others after the memorial service for the founder of The Body Shop International, Anita Roddick—a powerful supporter of our green consumer work. I leaned across to John and Bianca and confided, "Shell is a client of ours."

No one bit my head off. In retrospect, we got away with such things because SustainAbility was a mission-driven business, working both with the protesters and with at least some of those being protested. Anita did that, too; despite being a bootstrapping entrepreneur, indeed a full blooded capitalist at times, she was always a full-throttle advocate for human rights,[*] fair trade, the environment, and related causes.

Anita summed all of that up in the foreword she wrote for *The Green Consumer Guide*. "The new breed of Green Consumer," she proclaimed,

---

[*] Human rights were always part of our agenda, but the time they came closest was when I helped Chris Avery in the early stages of evolving his Business & Human Rights Resource Centre, https://www.business-humanrights.org/en/, hosting its early board meetings during weekends at SustainAbility. As I was finishing this book, Chris sent me a photo from Santa Fe of his copy of my book *Cannibals with Forks*. Normally, he said, he would insert a Post-it note or two in a book he enjoyed, whereas his *Cannibals* was almost invisible thanks to an infestation of Post-its.

"are demanding more information about the environmental performance of products, about the use of animal testing and about the implications for the Third World. They want to know the story behind what they buy. They want to know how things are made, where and by whom." She splashed our Green Consumer Week posters in Body Shop front windows across the country.

Indefatigable, she was a one-woman campaign against business myopia, calling business leaders "dinosaurs in pinstripes." The irony, when The Body Shop was eventually bought by cosmetics giant L'Oréal, was that the French company was itself part-owned at the time by, horror of horrors, Nestlé.

It is easy to forget just how much some brands were loathed at the time and what an impact this generation of early social and environmental capitalists had. They helped turn our change agenda from something that was seen as alien, even communist, into something that at least some business leaders were embracing—notable among them Patagonia's Yvon Chouinard.

Meanwhile, the background noise was intense in every sense. One day, Julia and I were sitting in back-to-back chairs in the tiny home office where we had co-authored *The Green Consumer Guide*. We were doing separate radio interviews over different phone lines. Suddenly the ceiling exploded—and a booted leg crashed through in a blinding shower of eye-stinging soot. Elaine's and my builder, Arthur, was racing to complete a new roof extension to give our daughters more space as the team expanded into our home. He had lost his footing on a beam above our heads.

We kept the interviews going through it all.

Over time, we carried the message out to every continent except Antarctica. One country after another lit up, inviting us in. On the other side of the world, Australia and New Zealand came on board in a big way. With the indefatigable help of Murray and Dobrina Edmonds in Australia, we exported the environmental, green, and sustainability agendas. For seven years, we shuttled an ever-expanding traveling circus of speakers from Auckland and Wellington in New Zealand to Adelaide, Brisbane, Melbourne, Perth, and Sydney in Australia.*

Every year, new companies would step up as sponsors—and the conferences, most held atop giant skyscrapers, grew bigger and bigger. I got to see a good deal of that part of the world, meeting some extraordinary people along the way. Notable among them, at least for me, was Richard Neville—best remembered for the *Oz* magazine obscenity trials, part of the global "youthquake" that powered the sixties.[5] The connection was instant and powerful.

One of the most extraordinary things I encountered while with the Edmonds was the Addyman plesiosaur, an opalized marine reptile equivalent—and contemporary—of the land-loving dinosaurs, now on display in Adelaide's South Australian Museum. This extraordinary 6.5-meter creature had been stranded as an inland sea dried up, its skeleton then mineralized over time. It was discovered in an opal mine in 1968. Magical, even if a painful reminder of how environmental change can wrong-foot even the best-adapted species.

Then the 9/11 attacks tilted our world on its axis, in full view of SustainAbility's Brooklyn offices. While our US team watched the horrors live, our London team—some of them American—crowded around a computer screen in our Hyde Park Corner office, watching in stupefied silence. Then, as the shock waves continued to spread, I found myself spending more time in the World Economic Forum universe.

And whatever I may have planned, that also began a tilting of my emotional landscape, a process that would one day result in my doing something I had never conceived possible: leaving SustainAbility.

---

* When Murray Edmonds first visited me in SustainAbility's High Street Kensington offices, inviting me to do a tour of Australia and New Zealand, I suggested the triple bottom line as a theme. He felt environmental strategy would better fit the state of play Down Under. He was right, but in later years we put the triple bottom line on the agenda and helped ensure that the two countries became pioneers. Our travelling circus included speakers from companies like Ford and Intel, financial actors like the Dow Jones Sustainability Indices and Salomon Smith Barney (later merged into Citigroup), regulators like Britain's Environment Agency, and the World Economic Forum.

Hired Guns

Partly because of its genesis, SustainAbility always struck me as more of a family organization than a hard-charging, for-profit business. Indeed, as already mentioned, one clash I had early on with one cofounder was over his interest in working out how to sell the business even as we were struggling to get it on its feet. Many years later, our colleague Geoff Lye joined us from the business mainstream and raised the same question.

My retort: "It would be like trying to sell a family."

Geoff may have been surprised, but over the years I always insisted that our small company was not for sale. I said I—we—wouldn't, but then, after more than twenty-five years, we—I—did. We sold SustainAbility.

As it happened, I had largely left the organization some ten years earlier to cofound Volans, so that made things easier. And, thanks to Geoff's efforts, Elaine and I still retained our shares, which helped us realize some of the value we had jointly put into the company over the decades, even if that had never been the intent. We sold the business to ERM, a competitor I had known since around 1980. Indeed, I recall its CEO explaining to me back in the nineties why our two organizations were so different. "We're hired guns," he said, knowing full well that wasn't our style at all. He also knew that we had an impressive list of blue-chip clients, though we sometimes spoke of green chips—which ERM, behind the scenes, had been trying to pry away from us. By the company's own account, it found it an almost impossible task: our clients proved intensely loyal.

Not long after, the combined firm was sold on, with a majority stake acquired by KKR. Still, with the financial system now seen as one of the sustainability movement's mission-critical targets, I came to see even this acquisition in a somewhat more positive light. With ERM billing our brainchild as "The SustainAbility Institute by ERM,"[6] it struck me that our agenda was now being injected, potentially at least, deeper into the bloodstream of capitalism.

As to what sustainability meant through all of this, that was an unending debate as we worked with companies, industry federations, accountancy groups like the Association of Chartered Certified Accountants and the Institute of Chartered Accountants in England and Wales, NGOs like WWF and the World Resources Institute (WRI), and standard-setting bodies like AccountAbility, GRI, and the International Integrated Reporting Council.*

I was told that I tended to be more playful than most people when it came to our agenda—which in part reflected the influence of the sixties. I recall one occasion, on April 25, 2006, when I spoke to three thousand company directors during a major business conference in London's Royal Albert Hall. As the debate proceeded, I noted that the sustainability agenda was evolving so rapidly that it sometimes felt like a giant snowball rolling downhill, entraining one issue after another. It was rather like being on LSD, I quipped, which had been such a powerful catalyst of the counter-culture—where users find everything becoming wildly significant.

The female moderator rounded on me, saying it sounded as if I knew what I was talking about. I turned to the audience, paused for effect, then admitted that yes, I did. That was the first—and probably only—time when something I said had three thousand people roaring with laughter. Nor is this insignificant, given that if you can amuse people, you often engage them more powerfully than if you come across as a missionary. It suggests that you, too, are human.

When Handed Lemons

At a time when pretty much all development was unsustainable, as I discovered in my early work in Egypt, sustainable development remained something of an oxymoron. I think the first time the concept had been aired publicly was in the 1980 *World Conservation Strategy*.[7] As it happens, I wrote the industry chapter of the UK version of the strategy,

---

* AccountAbility's cofounder Simon Zadek once called me to ask if I minded his using the same brand format as SustainAbility. I did but felt I should give him permission, leading to some confusion in the market. Later still, others followed suit, including—less felicitously—responsAbility.

published in 1982. Memorably, on our advisory board were people from big-footprint British companies like Blue Circle (cement), BP (oil and gas), and ICI (chemicals), no doubt all instructed to keep a close eye on the proceedings.

My report, titled "Seven Bridges to the Future," forecast the radical shrinking of their footprints and sometimes their industries. It also explored the potential of new industrial growth points—including renewable energy, information technology (and this was fully a decade before the internet burst on the scene), and biotechnology—to help in the push toward sustainable economies. All very much in the spirit of Nikolai Kondratiev and Joseph Schumpeter.

During this period, we worked with WRI President Gus Speth, whom I first met at the WICEM event in Versailles, France, in 1984. Even then, WRI was a hugely impressive organization and would later provide a couple of key colleagues at SustainAbility: Kavita Prakash-Mani and Peter Zollinger. Over several years, Jonathan Shopley and I worked with Gus and his colleague Janet Brown on the sustainability implications and applications of new technologies in emerging industries like biotechnology, satellite remote sensing, and clean technology.[8]

That work was lightyears beyond the thinking of most big-footprint folk at the time, but such projects prodded me to think about where the future might be headed—and, among other things, that thought train led me to get involved in the ill-fated Earthlife Foundation. That proved to be an "if you're dealt lemons, make lemonade" moment.

Someone else central to the sustainability agenda at this time was Richard Sandbrook. I first met him when he was a director of Friends of the Earth UK. He was always wreathed in cigarette smoke, as were many of his colleagues.* Indeed, every time I flew at the time, strange though it is to recall, the aircraft would have extensive smoking sections butting

---

* Elaine was volunteering for Friends of the Earth at the time, passively smoking on a near-industrial scale.

up against much smaller, notionally nonsmoking sections—a sickeningly odorous world for nonsmokers.

But what has happened to most forms of public smoking underscores how powerful social change can sometimes be.

By the time I wrote my diary of 1989, *A Year in the Greenhouse*, Richard was running IIED alongside people like Gerald "Gerry" Leach, who had broken the *Limits to Growth* story as a journalist at the *Observer*; Brian Johnson, who wrote reports like *Banking on the Environment*; and Lloyd Timberlake, who ran Earthscan and was a whiz at riding his monocycle through IIED parties.

Richard popped up frequently through that 1989 diary. And we had some intense exchanges along the way. Once, he and I were headed west to an event in the Malvern Hills. I can't recall what we were talking about, but I was so immersed that, as I drove through the gate of our family home in Little Rissington, I hit a gate pillar, leaving a substantial dent in the side of our car. That was the first time in some twenty years of negotiating that space that I had hit anything.

I blame Richard.

Meanwhile, his own work underscored the dangers inherent in negotiating political divides. Camilla Toulmin, who also later ran IIED, recalled that the nineties were the decade when IIED increasingly "took the lead in starting to talk to big business—sometimes controversially."[9] She recalled one example:

> A conversation between Richard and the world's largest paper-mill owner at the Rio Summit in 1992 eventually led to a groundbreaking, in-depth study of the environmental and social impact of the paper industry worldwide. Richard was a skilled maker of unlikely matches—it was the first time anyone had got scientists and corporations together in a concerted effort to understand the environmental impacts and responsibilities of a big international industry. The report,

Towards a Sustainable Paper Cycle, upset many conservationists when it was published in 1996 because it suggested that plantation forests, and even chlorine bleach, were not necessarily the enemies of sound development.[10]

Capturing the essence of the man, who sadly died in 2005, she noted, "Richard enjoyed turning assumptions on their head, and single-minded environmentalists were often those he liked to taunt most."[11]

Largely undeterred by criticism of his paper sector work, Richard pushed on. A group of nine of the world's biggest mining companies then commissioned IIED to explore how the sector could move toward greater sustainability. The report, published in late 1999, led to the Mining, Minerals and Sustainable Development Project, which ran between 2000 and 2002. As a result, leading companies in the sector developed concerted efforts to improve their social and environmental performance.

Unsurprisingly, Richard was again savaged by some activists during this period. Interestingly, he and I were doing similar work at the time, but as a business, SustainAbility managed to escape much of the anger directed at NGOs like IIED.

Not that we had a free pass. Far from it. I recall one article published in the British newspaper the *Independent* during our green consumer days. The piece, by the American-in-London investigative journalist James Erlichman,[12] occupied much of a broadsheet page and was illustrated by a huge cartoon of a wolf in sheep's clothing, or perhaps it was vice versa.[13] That was meant to be me.

The implication was that I wasn't quite what I seemed.

True, much of the world still didn't quite know what to make of us, which suited me fine. Uncertainty makes people think. I recall one group of Shell executives climbing the open stairwell at SustainAbility's offices in The People's Hall on the fringes of Notting Hill. On the walls were some of my collection of campaigning posters from around the world. One Dutch poster showed the Shell pecten logo, with its red streaks turning into pooling blood—headlined "Shell Kills."* I doubt that many other consultancies of the day would have dared tip their hand to such an extent.

Hail, Frestonia!

Before we moved to The People's Hall, SustainAbility had spent a couple of highly productive years working out of huge studio offices run by Brand New Product Development, where CEO Dorothy MacKenzie took us under her wing. In one of its buildings, there was a life-size statue of a man in a lab coat trying to extinguish his burning brain in a fire bucket of sand. It felt appropriate somehow—a symbol of what can happen to our minds in boom periods.

But such periods don't go on forever—and even in good times creative businesses can run off the rails. When Brand New's parent company, the Michael Peters Group, went bankrupt, we had to decamp almost overnight. The People's Hall proved perfect, both physically and culturally. Aside from its less savory history as a brothel, it had been a storage space for theater organs, while our vast open studio space on the top floor had housed the national theater of the (spoof) Republic of Frestonia.

This was the name adopted by the residents of Freston Road, when—faced with aggressive development plans advanced by the Greater London Council—they attempted to secede from the United Kingdom in 1977 to form the Free and Independent Republic of Frestonia.[14] Actor David Rappaport was the foreign minister, while playwright Heathcote Williams served as Frestonian Ambassador to the United Kingdom.[15] The spirit of the times has echoed on, though I think The People's Hall is the only building now left standing from that era.

Charmingly, the new statelet had adopted the Latin motto *Nos Sumus Una Familia*—We Are All One Family—and applied to join the United Nations. It warned that peacekeeping troops might be needed to keep the Greater London Council, effectively London's government, at bay.

---

* Today, it still hangs in my garden studio.

The original idea for Frestonia came from Nicholas Albery. I long considered him an inspiration; he was passionately interested in uncovering and supporting what I would now call ugly ducklings, initiatives that look ridiculous today but may blossom tomorrow.

Among other things, Nicholas developed the Natural Death Centre and ran for the Green Party in Notting Hill. Killed in a car crash in 2001, aged just fifty-two, he loved promoting his own—and other people's—brain waves.[16] Among other ventures, he developed the Institute for Social Inventions, launched in 1985, with Edward de Bono, Anita Roddick, and Fay Weldon among its patrons. Very much in ugly duckling mode, he also collected nontechnological innovations from around the world, giving £1,000 annual awards for the best ones.

When Elaine was working at Wildwood House, a publishing house located on the floor below TEST's offices in Covent Garden, she worked on a book called *Alternative London*. She and Wildwood cofounder Oliver Caldecott went to see a great friend of Albery's, Nicholas Saunders, who wrote both *Alternative London* and *Alternative England and Wales* for Wildwood—and founded the Neal's Yard alternative commerce space in Covent Garden.

The outside of Saunders's house in Edith Grove was painted flaming red, the internal corridors shaped like rabbit burrows with skillful use of papier-mâché. But what really stuck in Elaine's memory was the toilet, which had a transparent cistern filled with fish. Every time you flushed it, the fish went on a seesaw ride—perhaps someone should have alerted the RSPCA, dedicated to promoting animal welfare.

People like the two Nicholases, Albery and Saunders—both killed in car crashes, three years apart—provided fertile intellectual mulch from which at least some of my thinking on sustainability would evolve. The fact that it was a rather more complex worldview than those adopted by more technocratic folk (for example, in the Big 6, which became the Big 5 and then the Big 4) reflected the fact that I came from a very different background.

One friend at the time was Romy Fraser, founder of Neal's Yard Remedies. A linked memory was an evening party at her Trill Farm in

East Devon, alongside her husband, Godfrey Boyle. As mentioned, he had been another early influence on my thinking through his work on the magazine *Undercurrents* and his book *Radical Technology*, also published by Wildwood.[17] That evening, Elaine and I walked down into the valley enfolding the farm to see friends including Romy, Godfrey, and Common Ground's Sue Clifford and Angela King. We had first met Sue and Angela when they were campaigners at Friends of the Earth, before they left to set up Common Ground.[18] To my mind, they did some of the most engaging art-in-landscape projects of the entire counterculture era.

One of their projects that still holds a particularly warm place in my heart was Apple Day, first held in Covent Garden on October 21, 1990.[19] Elaine and I trundled along with Gaia and Hania. This was at the peak period of our Green Consumer campaign, and we concluded that this was the very soul of what we were trying to promote. Common Ground's idea was to celebrate the history of apples in Britain and to ensure the remaining diversity of apple varieties was nurtured, retaining a place on the shelves for rarities, not just commodities.

People, Planet, Profit

With such people as inspirations, it's hardly surprising that my own agenda was less formulaic, more emergent. And the contribution I may be remembered for, if remembered at all, will be the triple bottom line—which sounded simple enough at the time but proved to be a real brainteaser for many businesses. Deceptively simple, it proved to be a portal to higher levels of complexity.

Here are headline elements of that story.

For some time, I had been uneasy about key concepts used in the sustainable business space, among them eco-efficiency—the idea that you could save or make money by cleaning up the environment and cutting down on resource consumption. One brain behind this approach was Amory Lovins, founder of the Rocky Mountain Institute—dubbed the "Einstein of energy efficiency."[20] I had known Amory since the seventies, when he, too, was at Friends of the Earth UK.* His view was that we must crank up our energy efficiency efforts—and wider resource efficiency efforts—to wartime levels of urgency.

All true, but I sensed that there was something missing in the efficiency agenda. It was aimed at engineers, whereas I felt that we also needed to engage the hearts and minds of business leaders, most of whom were not (and are not) engineers.

It may now seem that taking eighteen months to produce those three words—*triple bottom line*—was glacial progress. But it took me that time, working with my SustainAbility colleague and longtime friend Andrea Spencer-Cooke, to crystallize the term. When the phrase did drop into my brain one morning, I felt a bit like Paul McCartney with his song "Yesterday." Like McCartney, I thought I must have heard this somewhere before. As I have mentioned, years later I would stumble across a heading, "Multiple Bottom Lines," in Alvin Toffler's 1980 book, *The Third Wave*. I instantly knew that this must have been the seed of my idea, even if I had first read it fourteen years earlier.

In 1994, I had spoken of win-win-win solutions in an essay in the *California Management Review*[21] with the triple bottom line framing following several months later. The following year, I also coined the linked phrases "People, Planet, and Profit" and "People, Planet, and Prosperity" to help popularize the underlying idea of social, environmental, and economic (not just financial) value creation—or destruction. Although emotionally I inclined toward prosperity, in the end, I went with profit rather than prosperity, on the basis that it would appeal more to businesspeople, which proved to be the case.

Looking back, though, the triple bottom line had been bubbling in my mind for a while. In 1991, I commissioned the brilliant *Financial Times* cartoonist Ingram Pinn to communicate the gist of my idea. The

---

* To some degree our careers ran in parallel—and, as an aside, I remember him giving me one of the best shoulder massages I have ever enjoyed, at Schumacher College, epicenter of all things alternative.

following was his cartoon, which I have presented in public many hundreds of times since.

Early sketch of the triple bottom line agenda
(source: John Elkington and Ingram Pinn, 1991)

Perhaps counterintuitively, the main character in the image was the boardroom table, around which everything else pivoted. There were also whiteboards capturing the agenda, using an earlier version of my People, Planet, and Profit (3P's) formula. And there were place settings for some of the more traditional corporate functions—but with key spots reserved for a voice for nature (the fish), the dispossessed (the woman), and longer-term time horizons and future generations (the robot). In effect, this was the agenda that would later be addressed by a new generation of chief sustainability officers.

At the time, the idea of a robot at the boardroom table seemed ridiculous, indeed was meant as a joke. But it's a joke no longer. The first expert system was appointed to a company board in Hong Kong in 2014. Over time, too, we will see more new technologies like expert systems and artificial intelligence making their presence felt in the world's boardrooms and C-suites. And, given the complexity of the agenda, they can't arrive too soon.

CEO Dons Space Suit

Still, not everyone was enthused by the 3P's. Geoff Lye, who joined SustainAbility around the time the cartoon was drawn, insisted for another eighteen months that he had joined us because we were an environmental organization.* The triple bottom line, he said, muddled things. But that changed in 1995 when Shell semi-tricked us into working for it in the wake of a series of major public relations disasters that had rocked the oil giant to its foundations.

Shell had run headlong into Greenpeace over the dumping of the Brent Spar, an oil storage and loading buoy that was time-expired, in the North Sea. The company announced its plans to dump the structure in the deep ocean but ran into a media firestorm organized by Greenpeace. On top of that, in November 1995, the news came through that activist Ken Saro-Wiwa and eight of his colleagues had been executed by the Nigerian government.

Anita Roddick, among others, campaigned energetically to prevent the hangings and, after the event, tried to pin a significant share of the blame on Shell, given that Saro-Wiwa had protested Shell's continuing involvement in the country. Views remain polarized,[22] but one thing has long been clear—fossil fuels tend to corrupt many of those they touch, in what some economists call the "resource curse." Nigeria has long been among the world's most corrupt countries, so whatever companies like Shell may say, they have been complicit in a range of social, environmental, and political abuses in such countries for nearly as long.

---

*   Geoff Lye joined SustainAbility in the early nineties. He came from the marketing and advertising worlds, and we have worked together more or less ever since. Then, weirdly, almost a decade after he joined, we discovered we had met more than twenty years before, in the summer of 1970. He and his friends had been traveling around the Peloponnese in an old London black cab. Our heavily adapted Land Rover was equally memorable. We recalled meeting in an out-of-the-way village, oblivious that the universe was already trying to push us together.

So, we didn't jump at the chance to work with Shell, even if I had worked with them in the past. In fact, I had learned an interesting lesson when involved in a coaching session with thirty Shell executives in Rotterdam. This was just after the Brent Spar campaign began—but before Shell had decided to abandon its plans to dump the huge buoy in the ocean. The participants came from twelve countries, and after the session had ended and we all headed to the bar, I asked them whether Shell was right or wrong in the stance it was taking.

The responses were fascinating: the group split more or less fifty-fifty.

Initially, I assumed this would have everything to do with where people came from. The Scandinavians, I imagined, would say it was wrong to dump anything in the ocean, whereas those from the developing world would be more flexible. What really caught my attention, though, was that geography and nationality seemed to have little to do with the split. Instead, age seemed to be the key deciding factor.

The older people were, the more likely they were to think Shell was right, and to see the rest of the world as having taken leave of its senses. Younger people, by contrast, tended to disagree, arguing that Shell was in the wrong, but for new reasons. Based on this evidence of an internal cultural divide, I persuaded our team that we should not work with Shell.

Geoff and I had made our views clear in a letter published in the *Times* a few days earlier. Geoff had written it but was told that if he published it, it would cost him his job at a major communications agency. So, I signed it instead.

Shell people later said it was like a torpedo below the waterline.

We rebuffed regular invitations from every level of the company, including their chairman, for two years. Then, finally, SustainAbility was invited, alongside three other firms, to submit an essay reflecting on what Shell should do next. We thought that this was all there was to it, but it turned out Shell had other ideas. It picked two essays as the "winners," ours and one from Arthur D. Little (ADL)—then offered a joint contract to us both. Because Jonathan Shopley, one of the key ADL people, had worked with me when he first arrived in the UK from South Africa, we decided to suck it up and see.

Before we committed, though, we put the decision to SustainAbility's ten-person advisory council—which voted unanimously that we should go in but asked us to keep them continuously advised on progress. The upshot, and a key point here, is that Shell became one of the first companies in the world to embrace the triple bottom line, alongside companies like Novo Nordisk. Shell's first sustainability report, published in 1997, was powerfully shaped by the ADL-SustainAbility team, and though Shell didn't ask me before using the title, the report was called *People, Planet & Profits*.

To some degree, this was a matter of Shell trying to offset the tarnishing of its reputation by publicly embracing a new version of the change agenda. But it was also a serious attempt, at the time, by key people in the company to understand how they might account for progress toward sustainable development. I made presentations to the company's main board, and to the boards of a couple of subsidiary companies, including Shell Chemicals. But the uncomfortable fact was that Shell remained a fossil fuel company—with all that this implied.*

True sustainability would have required a radically accelerated shift toward energy efficiency and renewable energy. Shell did have its Shell Renewables business, admittedly. Indeed, on one occasion, the CEO, Karen de Segundo, invited Elaine and me into the company box during a Wimbledon tennis tournament. Alongside people such as MORI chairman Bob Worcester, a public opinion pollster who had helped with our early green consumer work, we watched Pete Sampras dueling somebody else below. Then it came on to drizzle, one of those fine hazy drizzles I have long loved. Karen apologized for the interruption of play, but I replied that, having been brought up in the Near East and become something

---

* Interestingly, Al Gore recently warned the world not to trust fossil fuel companies—because they have routinely gamed the change agenda for so long. To get a better sense of his thinking, watch his TED video: https://www.youtube.com/watch?v=xgZC6da4mco.

of a fan of rain in all its forms, I found this particular type of drizzle the highlight of the day so far.

Not hugely diplomatic.

Then the Shell chairman who had originally brought us in, Sir Mark Moody-Stuart, moved on. His replacement was Phil Watts, a very different kettle of fish. He didn't immediately seem like a Shark or an Orca, but he was one or the other. As part of his induction into the new leadership role, while still director of Strategy, Sustainable Development, and External Affairs, he invited a trio of us—Paul Hawken (already mentioned), Geoff Lye (ditto), and myself—to a riverside hotel near Henley-on-Thames to brief him on where the sustainability agenda might take Shell.

Shortly afterward, at his invitation, I flew to Nigeria to see the reality of the oil industry's impact with my own eyes. Strikingly, both pilots on the small Shell plane that took me to Port Harcourt turned out to have been shot in separate incidents in Nigeria, and while we were there, a busload of stakeholders was kidnapped at knifepoint.

Nigeria as usual, you might conclude.

The immediate reason for the invitation was a huge stakeholder conference Shell was hosting in Port Harcourt. On the margins, several of us were then taken to various Shell installations, which seemed well run, but they could pick and choose which sites they showed us. I was also flown over the Niger Delta in a Bell "Huey" helicopter, a machine that featured heavily in the Vietnam War. Having trapped my finger in the helicopter's main door when boarding, I was in considerable pain as we swept over the delta, an experience with uncomfortable undertones of the film *Apocalypse Now*.

The net result was that I returned to London and told Phil Watts what he didn't want to hear. If Shell truly wanted to be a pioneer in sustainable development, I said, it needed to get out of Nigeria and out of oil. In no time I was out myself, summarily dismissed from his office.

Then, sometime later, in a now infamous incident, he donned a space suit when addressing a major event in Maastricht—and was later shuffled out of the company in the wake of a major scandal involving the overbooking of oil reserves. After that he became a priest.

You could hardly make it up.

"That's a Goddamn Lie!"

By 2020, the mood music within Shell seemed to have changed yet again. Shell's former CEO Ben van Beurden told the world, "Our company wants to be on the right side of history, and we are doing everything that is needed, but we cannot do it alone and as a matter of fact even the entire energy industry cannot do it on its own. If we cannot do it together with customers, regulators, policymakers, it's just not going to happen."[23]

At least the Shell people were semicivilized. When I ran into Rex Tillerson, he was chairman and CEO of oil giant ExxonMobil. Later, he became President Donald Trump's somewhat mismatched secretary of state. He and I met, or more accurately collided, in Stavanger—the epicenter of the Norwegian oil and gas industry. We were both speaking to a three-hundred-person audience of fossil fuel people.

I was on stage when Tillerson walked into the back of the conference hall with his entourage. As luck would have it, I was spotlighting how the oil industry—ExxonMobil in particular—had worked energetically to undermine the industry's efforts to cut greenhouse emissions.[24]

From the back of the hall, Tillerson roared, "That's a goddamn lie!"[*]

We proceeded to have a lively ding-dong over the heads of the bemused delegates, after which the dust settled somewhat—and I got on with what I had been saying. My blog entry for the day, Saturday, February 10, 2008, notes that I had been driven from the airport, passing a massive road train overturned on the ice. It also mentioned that, while my interactions with

---

[*] Rex Tillerson's behavior reminds me of something that is sometimes said about people who lie—and that is that they tend to whisper when they say the truth and raise their voices when they lie. The evidence now suggests that, as early as 1970, Exxon already had astonishingly accurate forecasts of where global heating would take us.

Tillerson were volatile to begin with, and his manner robust throughout, we got on reasonably well in a subsequent panel session—though this Shark and I were never going to see eye to eye.

A few weeks later, ExxonMobil was publicly pilloried on pretty much the same grounds I had raised and risked overturning like that Stavanger road train when the company lost well over half of its stock market value. Next, amazingly, the oil giant was overtaken in stock market value by the world's largest solar and wind power generator, NextEra Energy.[25]

That upset didn't last, however. The oil giant later recovered lost ground, particularly when Putin's Ukraine war drove up fossil fuel prices. Still, that confrontation lives on in my memory as an example of the sort of skirmishes we were fighting much of the time.

Overall, though, my experiences along the way left me believing that I was better off working with business. At TEST, back in the 1970s, we had worked with public sector clients like local authorities, the UK Department of the Environment, the OECD, and the United Nations. I learned much in the process, but the world didn't change much as a result. Then, while at SustainAbility, I served for seven years in Brussels on the European Commission's Consultative Forum on the Environment and Sustainable Development. Quite a story, that.

The invitation came after Julia Hailes and I had flown to Norway in October 1992 to speak at a major conference in the hills beyond Oslo. During the event, a group of apparent terrorists stormed the building, seizing the stage and taking the main speaker hostage. Then, as the haze created by the smoke bombs faded, Norwegian colleagues started laughing, as they woke up to the fact that the interlopers were, in fact, well-known actors. The event organizers were trying to keep us awake and entertained.

Exhale.

Later, people sprinted down the gangways on either side of the audience, hauling a gigantic, wall-to-wall red satin sheet over our heads. Don't ask me why; perhaps to keep us awake, since this was in the early hours of the morning. The conference was called "Five Minutes to Midnight"—and Julia and I didn't go on stage until two in the morning, when we wrapped up the conference with a presentation called "Sustainability: Dream, Nightmare or New Business Reality?"

It was all three, we argued, but with the balance now tilting toward the third option.

In any event, a senior EU official was in the audience that night and decided, on the strength of our performance, that I would be a good fit for their new consultative forum. Over the years I had made some great friends in Brussels, where the forum meetings were held, among them two Germans, indeed two Ulrichs: Ernst Ulrich von Weizsäcker and Ulrich Steger, both professors and doctors, as is the German way. Ernst Ulrich had served in Germany's Bundestag and founded the Wuppertal Institute, which took a more scientific approach to sustainability. I had first met him on a trip to Tokyo some years earlier and liked him immensely.

Ulrich Steger, who later served on SustainAbility's advisory council, had been a state government minister in Germany and a member of the Volkswagen supervisory board. When I first met him, he was the Alcan Chair of Environmental Management at the Swiss management school IMD. Impressive people, but once again progress was often glacial. Jonathon Porritt, the other early British member of the forum, was a widely respected figure in the UK Green movement. He left after three years—and I couldn't blame him. I continued for another four years, but in growing frustration.

As a result, I continued to steer SustainAbility, then Volans, away from working with governments wherever we could avoid it, concluding that the impact from working with carefully selected businesses could be much greater. Still, as I drafted an early version of this chapter, I had recently joined a new global council on clean, affordable energy organized by the government of the United Arab Emirates.

Hope springs eternal.

Our Man in China

If you work with business at senior levels, it is all but inevitable that you will need to interact with government people at some point. On an early visit to China, I got on rather well with Pan Yue, who was then the country's environment minister.[26] But that conversation, too, had a strange start. In 2005, Pan Yue had kicked off our conversation by commandeering a colleague, Kavita Prakash-Mani, and me—canceling our previously organized series of meetings. Reading through my blog as I researched this chapter, I came across the following, extracted from longer entries:

Wednesday, May 18, 2005

The red-shifted race continues—after several cars fail to arrive at Diao Yu Tai State Guesthouse—with high-speed car drive to a lunchtime session across town where I am due to talk to 70–80 people invited by Shell and the China Business Council for Sustainable Development. Then also speak at dinner with Shell, state oil companies, people from embassies and Pan Yue, Vice Minister of the State Environmental Protection Administration (SEPA). He has been taking an unusually aggressive line with high-impact developments, stalling at least 20 until they tackled a range of environmental issues.

Then into another taxi, which got us back to the hotel a little late for the car that was meant to be taking us to dinner with Minister Pan Yue. Had liked him tremendously when we sat next to each other at a Shell dinner last night. He had asked Kavita and I to dinner this evening, and now had us driven to the outskirts of Beijing, past the Summer Palace, in a government limousine with six different horns, each of which [the driver] used, as we blazed at warp speed towards the Western Hills.

The dinner was at the "Apricot Blossom Hamlet," in the Beijing Botanical Garden, near the "Fragrance Hill," where we are joined by Vice Minister Pan and Dr. Shu Qing, Deputy Director-General. I enormously admire what Vice Minister Pan and his colleagues have been doing, with SEPA energetically pursuing polluters and shutting a considerable number of projects down to force greater attention to environmental issues.

Thursday, May 19, 2005

All in all, a quite extraordinary meeting of minds—and the most sophisticated vegetarian repast I have yet eaten, including bird's nest soup, though I think our Chinese friends would have much preferred meat. In the process, we drank "Daughter Red" wine, which apparently is buried in a ceramic urn when a girl is born and dug up and drunk—with plums dropped in—when she turns eighteen. I found myself wondering what sort of world—and what sort of China—a newborn girl would find if a bottle buried today were to be dug up in 2023?

And now here we are. The deadline for the opening of that bottle has passed, the bottle itself still unopened—and China and the United States are at daggers drawn. All around us, the forces of deglobalization and de-democratization are corroding relationships that have taken decades to develop.

Peaceful Rise?

I find China both fascinating and unsettling. One of my more memorable experiences in the country happened in January 2011.[27] I had been invited to Beijing as a member of the International Integrated Reporting Council.

Shortly before I was due to travel, however, I tweeted about China's ban on exporting rare earth metals to Japan.

Mistake.

The export ban had followed in the wake of a collision between a Chinese trawler and a Japanese coastal protection vessel a few months earlier.[28] China blamed Japan and tried to snarl up the latter's just-in-time economy by banning critical materials. But then, not long after, Japan published a video showing the Chinese trawler emitting a big puff of smoke as it, apparently, accelerated directly into the Japanese ship.

My tweet was simple: it linked to the video and read, "Peaceful rise?"

At a time when China was professing to be spreading peace left, right, and center, this was perhaps slightly insensitive on my part—though I had no idea how touchy the Party apparatus could be. In any event, my visa application suddenly stalled, no explanation given. I promptly informed the office of then–Prince Charles, now King Charles III. His office was organizing the Accounting for Sustainability event in 2011, and I let them know that I couldn't come. They said hang on. Several days later, again with no further explanation, my visa came through.

Then, when my plane arrived in Beijing, I was escorted off the aircraft like a guest of honor, ahead of everyone else, and guided down a seemingly endless red carpet. No one asked to see my passport. Go figure.* Governments are complicated creatures, clearly. At their best, they are crucially important for sustainable development. They make the maps that guide their country's investments in the future—and they can help fund the early stages of industrial revolutions.

Meanwhile, the number of business leaders embracing the sustainability agenda was growing apace. The number of chief sustainability officers, or CSOs, was booming. Even chief financial officers (CFOs) began to embrace the cause. Indeed, two CEOs I have worked with in this field

---

* This was a small example of China's growing war on free speech, a trend spotlighted in *Danger Zone: The Coming Conflict with China* by Hal Brands and Michael Beckley (New York: W. W. Norton, 2022).

were previously both CFOs, and as it happens also both Dutchmen: Paul Polman and Peter Bakker.

When Paul took over as CEO of Unilever in 2009, he became one of the truly iconic CEOs in the sustainability space—he was famed for warning short-term investors that Unilever didn't want their money. Later he told me he got away with that at the time because he had only just been appointed, and the board didn't want to lose him so soon.[*]

I first came across Peter when he worked as CFO (later CEO) of TNT, the freight and logistics company. Later, when he became president of the World Business Council for Sustainable Development, we worked with the organization on several projects, including an update of its *Vision 2050* strategy,[29] first published in 2010. Much, it became clear, can change in one short decade.

Finally, one tiny signal of how the sustainability agenda is mainstreaming came from toymaker Mattel, when in 2022 it offered versions of Barbie dolls pursuing green and sustainability careers.[†] That said, we should beware of being distracted by Barbie CSOs—given that Mattel has frequently played the identity game, as in "She's a Rapper! She's an Astronaut! She's a Bride!"[30]

One of the earliest members of the breed was Hannah Jones (who contributed a foreword to this book), during her time at Nike. By the time of the Barbie launch, though their numbers had grown dramatically, CSOs were still very much in the minority—and the political pushback was building.

Part of the reason for both the spread of the CSO function and of the gathering political pushback had been the extraordinary success of a

---

[*] Paul Polman later reminded me that when we first met, he was working with Procter & Gamble, and I had just spoken at a conference he was attending. Later, I went to browse in a local bookshop. Someone tapped me gently on the shoulder, thinking I was a bookshop assistant, asking where he could find John Elkington's new book, *Cannibals with Forks*. It was Paul. Cue laughter.

[†] When Google CSO Kate Brandt tweeted the news that Mattel had released a new set of Barbie dolls, including one highlighting the CSO role, I stuck my tongue firmly in my cheek and replied: "My job is done!"

concept that built on the triple bottom line. This was ESG, combining environmental, social, and governance criteria for business and investment. Before turning to full-strength sustainability, in the form of the regenerative economy, let's explore an evolving societal pressure wave that has forced growing numbers of businesspeople to become fluent—and make business sense of—the rapidly evolving language of impact.

CHAPTER 8

Valuing Impact

"I would like to die on Mars," Elon Musk joked. "Just not on impact."[1] When it came to other forms of impact, in his glory days he appeared to be a modern-day Superman—reputed to have been a model for the Tony Stark character, played by Robert Downey Jr., in the *Iron Man* film series. Musk may be unlikely to describe himself as an impact entrepreneur, but he has had an off-the-scale impact—technological, economic, social, and environmental.

That is true, whether you think of his ventures in renewable energy (SolarCity), electric cars and batteries (Tesla), or space (SpaceX). And that's even before we get to tunneling (The Boring Company), satellites (Starlink), or neural science (Neuralink). Whatever you may think of his chaotic acquisition of Twitter, he has helped turn science fiction possibilities into market realities. Time and again he left competitors choking on his exhaust fumes. And, as it happens, as previously discussed, science fiction—alongside history—was where I first started to get my own brain around the evolving story of impact.

Specifically, one sci-fi story, read in my midteens, left a profound impression.

In "A Sound of Thunder," a short story set in 2055, over a century ahead of when he wrote the piece in 1952, Ray Bradbury followed an avid hunter, Eckels, who pays $10,000 (such is inflation!) to travel back to the age of dinosaurs and kill a *Tyrannosaurus rex*. Time Safari Inc., a time-travel agency, wanted to ensure that its customers understood the risks. No guarantees of a safe return, they were warned, recalling the deaths of six guides and twelve hunters in the previous year alone.

While Eckels waits to travel, he and a Time Safari employee discuss the recent election of a moderate presidential candidate, who beat the dictatorial candidate, Deutscher, described as an "anti-everything" man. Think Trump, Modi, Xi, Erdogan, or Bolsonaro, all scrambled together. If the election had gone the other way, they conclude, many people would have run for the time machine to escape Deutscher's rule.

The controls are set for 60,002,055 years earlier. On landing, the hunters receive two instructions: shoot only marked dinosaurs, because they are dying anyway, and stick to the path—made of antigravity metal, hovering above the ground. When Eckels asks why all the fuss, he is told that even slight changes of the past can mutate the future. Kill just a single small mammal back then and generations of people may no longer be alive in the present.

To cut a short story shorter, when the hunt ends our travelers reboard their machine but note with horror that Eckels's boots are muddy. Eckels spots a butterfly stuck to his sole, crushed. He had stepped off the path. When they arrive back in 2055, things seem slightly unfamiliar. The air smells peculiar, and the spelling of the company's sign is slightly off.

In shock, Eckels asks who won the recent presidential election and is told Deutscher did.

The lesson we take here is that no single human being set out to create the epoch into which we find ourselves headed. But all those accumulated changes made by our species over tens and hundreds of thousands of years have added up. All those crushed insects, speared mammoths, harpooned whales, and trawled fish. All those matings and murders. Seemingly inconsequential actions back then now powerfully shape both our present and future.

That is the worldview that has informed some of us as we surfed—and sometimes shaped—the environmental, green, and sustainability waves. That said, that worldview has long influenced the thinking of Indigenous peoples, who evolved a much more intimate feel for wider, deeper realities. So how many of us today see the world of impact as we should see it?

People, organizations, industry sectors, and economies look different through the impact lens. Think of former President Barack Obama. How might we think of his footprint? All those presidential jets and gas-guzzling armored limos? At what point do we recall that he placed 548 million acres (2.2 million square kilometers) under conservation?[2] For comparison, President Theodore (Teddy) Roosevelt, who founded America's national parks, managed "just" 290 million acres (1.17 million square kilometers).

It's hard to get your brain around this. But one initiative that helped build my understanding has been the Impact Management Project. The questions it ended up focusing on included the following: the *what*—telling us what outcome an enterprise is contributing to, whether it is positive or negative, and how important the outcome is to stakeholders; the *who*—showing us which stakeholders are experiencing the impacts and how underserved they are in relation to the desired outcomes; *how much*—informing us on such things as how many stakeholders are experiencing the outcome, to what extent, and for how long; the *contribution*—giving us a sense of whether an enterprise's or investor's efforts result in outcomes that are better than what would have occurred otherwise; and the *risk*—helping us grasp the likelihood that any impact will be what we expect or significantly different.[3]

This work is far from simple, but vital if we are to ensure that the impact revolution does not descend into the sort of discussions—which our species excels in—that debate how many angels might fit on a pinhead. Better spend the energy on working out how to cram more microprocessors onto chips.

Up to Our Waists

The impact agenda—later powered by the fifth change wave spotlighted in chapter 4—really took off for me when I was at UCL, back in the early seventies. Among the challenges posed as part of our postgraduate course was this question: What is the value of a Norman church that stands in the way of a planned urban motorway? Or again, even more challenging, what is the "existence value" of the Grand Canyon (originally protected by Teddy Roosevelt) for someone who will never go there, but who would be appalled to hear that people proposed to dam it? And what happens when you quantify such feelings and inject them into the accounting process?

These sorts of questions have surfaced throughout my career. One of the early impact projects I worked on at TEST was linked to the 1973 Dykes Heavy Commercial Vehicles Act, designed to ensure that trucks and vans took less environmentally and socially problematic routes. A worthy idea, but once we monitored truck movements and plugged the data into early models, we discovered that alternative routes were often longer—so the overall negative impact was often almost the same, if not actually greater.

Things seemed clearer when our team shipped out to Egypt, in the aftermath of the 1973 Arab-Israeli (Yom Kippur) War. As it happened, though, I had been in the wars myself at the time, impacted by a driver hitting me at speed while I was on a bicycle outside the Royal Opera House in Covent Garden. Even so, I have always liked H. G. Wells's comment that every time he saw an adult on a bicycle, he no longer despaired for the future of the human race. My sentiment, too, but if most of humanity remains encased in cars and is largely oblivious to cyclists, you'll end up like I did: unconscious in the road.

That was the first time I had been hit by a car, though by no means would it be the last.* I had been cycling down Bow Street to get some scientific papers from King's College before heading out to Heathrow to

---

* I would ultimately be involved in six major cycling accidents. Four left me unconscious or semiconscious, and two with three cracked ribs.

fly to Cairo. When I came to, I lugged the remains of my bike first to King's College, then back to TEST's Floral Street offices. How I got to Heathrow I don't know, though when I lay down to sleep in the Cairo hotel that night I sat bolt upright, screeching—three ribs had been cracked back in London and had been waiting to let me know.

Sometimes, it seems, adrenaline carries you a long way.

I was Egypt-bound to help carry out a series of pioneering environmental impact studies. Once in the land of the pharaohs, our small team shuttled back and forth between Cairo and Ismailia. Cairo was Cairo, but many buildings around Ismailia were pockmarked by Israeli artillery fire, with concrete structures turned into something like three-dimensional string vests.

Our mission was to investigate ways to control pollution and parasitic diseases, among them schistosomiasis, a.k.a. bilharzia, as reconstruction began across a huge region between Ismailia and Port Said.

The risk of bilharzia was really brought home to me one dark night when some of us took a Land Rover into a forbidden zone near the Suez Canal, somewhere we had no right to be—a place where we could have been arrested as spies. Suddenly, our driver veered into a small canal, where we found ourselves enmired up to our axles. Unable to call the authorities, we stripped down and mucked in, struggling to get the vehicle back onto dry land. God only knows how we managed, but ultimately, we did. Only then did we wake up to the fact that we had been up to our waists in waters that could well have been infected by schistosomiasis-bearing snails.

Mercifully, we managed to escape—the ditch, possible arrest, and the disease.

In terms of the work, I became increasingly concerned about the probable impact of the planned developments in three overlapping master plan studies, focusing on the Lake Manzala area. We pulled the pieces of the jigsaw together—and didn't like what we saw. The giant lake would be carved up by various road, agricultural, and water projects. I sketched elements of the story in chapter 5, so all I need to say here is that I failed to get the Egyptian government's attention—and decided to break cover once back in London by exposing the story in *New Scientist*.

Some years later, people who understood the political dynamics told me that this ploy had helped our concerns reach people they otherwise might not have reached. At the time, though, it felt like I was committing professional *hara-kiri*.

Market Makers

Over time, our work on environmental impact assessment evolved considerably, including a study for the World Bank on the impact of traffic restraint measures in Singapore. Using time-lapse cameras, we found that some drivers were using inflatable dummies to hoax the authorities into thinking they had passengers, allowing them to use special lanes.

What an ingenious species we can be.

Years later, when I had my own firm, JEA, we did two impact assessments for BP, one focusing on onshore oil exploration in Dorset, England, and the other on the development of a small offshore oilfield in Scotland. Later, at SustainAbility, we also did a study for WWF on the emerging discipline of environmental auditing, pioneered by BP across the North Slope of Alaska and now being imported to Europe. This was a precariously early-stage market, however. It also had real implications for our partners. WWF sat on our report for a full year while the organization fretted about the possible reputational impact on the corporate sponsorship it was taking in, with little or no due diligence at the time—other than a sponsor's ability to pay.

Despite our warnings, WWF still got into trouble when the report finally launched—whereas we promptly received more than thirty requests to carry out green audits for companies. That said, some would-be clients, having requested an audit, asked, "But what is an environmental audit?" The simple answer is that it is a process designed to review the environmental performance of a business in the same way that a conventional audit reviews its financial performance.

When SustainAbility had done enough audits to open up the market, setting demanding benchmarks, we pulled out to focus on other things—and encouraged the competition to move in. We repeated the process with the production of early corporate environmental and sustainability reports, then with the verification of such reports. When we also withdrew from those markets, some former clients asked our competitors to do "SustainAbility-style" verifications involving a less neutral, more challenging approach.

We were becoming standard setters, market makers even.

The green consumer period triggered growing interest in life cycle assessment, where the impacts of products are investigated from "cradle to grave," or even, as we put it at the time, from "cradle to cradle."* On one trip, Julia Hailes and I traveled from Hamburg, Germany, to Switzerland, visiting life cycle assessment experts and institutes, with a memorable section paralleling the Rhine along the way. Fascinating work was under way, no question, though the challenges were well illustrated by the work done on one of the core issues we had spotlighted in *The Green Consumer Guide*—which proved hugely controversial.

We did not come down totally on the side of terry-towel, or cloth, diapers (nappies)—rather than disposable ones. And this despite the fact that our daughter Gaia had started life in large cloth nappies inherited from Elaine. An odd sort of heirloom, you might think, but they made nappies of sterner stuff back in the forties. Instead, we allowed that disposable nappies could help take the strain off stressed parents. Again, this was even though I still had uncomfortable memories of the day I had to dig out the drains in front of our home after we had tried disposable nappies. We had mistakenly flushed several, clogging the pipes. Not a great way to spend Christmas Day, with light snow swirling around as I went down the steaming manhole.

The reason for our straddling the divide was that, perhaps inevitably, many early product assessments ended up evenly weighted between competing options. The scores, however, were calculated on the basis of very

---

* The concept would later be given real wings by Bill McDonough and Michael Braungart of MBDC. A case of simultaneous invention, I think.

different types of impact: pollution versus waste versus water or energy use, for example. Apples versus oranges, or perhaps bananas. So, the recommendations often turned out to depend very much on what your own priorities happened to be.

In the end, we counseled parents to spare themselves the grief of all that boiling of nappies by using disposables, at least for a while, giving them time and headspace to tackle other issues. Unfortunately, however, this advice came out just as a major antidisposable nappy campaign was launched by the Women's Environmental Network. The resulting green-on-green clash was heated at times, though it brought us even more publicity, helping to sell more books. Still, it underscored the complexities—and the politics.

Julia later got deeply involved, one might even say enmired, in the business of eco-labeling, whereas I began to build on the auditing work to help drive greater environmental reporting by companies. The realities of the day were underscored by something a senior Shell executive told me at the time: "Shell is too big and too complex ever to report on its environmental performance."

Before long, we overran those defenses—creating several highly competitive ranking schemes to encourage continuous improvement in disclosures and reporting.* As a result, the impact agenda was increasingly shunted up to board level in leading companies as the successive societal pressure waves crashed through.

Unreasonable Impact

As the impact agenda evolved, it inflected our work in various ways. One of the most dramatic board meetings I've ever participated in took place in 1999, the same year as the protests against the World Trade Organization, one set of demonstrations becoming infamous as the "Battle of Seattle."

---

* In addition to reporting platforms like the GRI, I helped shape the Dow Jones Sustainability Indices, serving on its advisory board for nine years. This helped spur competition between companies across the triple bottom line agenda.

I had been invited to fly to Atlanta, Georgia, to take part in a critical board session for ice cream makers Ben & Jerry's—which had always spotlighted the positive impacts that it was trying to create.

The big question for the board, as we gathered on Cumberland Island, Georgia, was whether it should agree to sell the company and, if so, to whom. It was a challenging moment, with cofounder Ben Cohen elsewhere, unhappy with the way things were going. My advice was that Unilever, though far from perfect, would be the best of the would-be acquirers.

But then Hurricane Floyd hit, the board meeting was truncated, and we were bundled into a boat back to shore, driving to Atlanta as well over a million people moved inland from the coast. Biblical scenes ensued. The storm, we learned later, killed forty-eight people and more than two million farm animals.[4] I had made the road trip to Atlanta with Ben & Jerry's board director Pierre Ferrari, who advised me to be very careful of who I looked at in the surrounding cars, given that the prevailing gun culture meant that many drivers would be heavily armed.

The eventual takeover may have been well intentioned on Unilever's part, but the cultural mechanics left much to be desired. At times, the bigger corporate culture threatened to squeeze the life out of Ben & Jerry's more entrepreneurial one.

As a result, one thing Unilever did in response to the problems with the merger was to invest in a new sustainability-oriented venture capital fund, Physic Ventures, set up by a good friend of mine, Will Rosenzweig. I served on the Physic advisory board for several years—and was forcefully reminded of just how hard venture investment can be if the market context includes things like wars and financial downturns, as it often does. Investments in sustainability-oriented enterprises were just as likely to be hit by downturns, with the investors unable to exit and enjoy the financial return they had projected.

Another memorable boardroom meeting came the year after my Georgian adventure, this time with Ford Motor Company in Dearborn, Michigan. Ford was being pummeled in the media as the news broke that the Firestone tires fitted to many of its vehicles were failing in hot, rough conditions, particularly in Saudi Arabia and the American Southwest. It was estimated that more than two hundred people had died in the resulting road accidents.[5]

The day before that meeting in the Ford boardroom I had been quoted in a major article in, I think, the *Wall Street Journal*. At the time, Ford had carried out a product recall of around six million Firestone tires—and I was asked by a *Journal* reporter to comment on whether this was equivalent to Johnson & Johnson's famous Tylenol recall, which had become an iconic business school case study on how to do things right.

My slightly injudicious answer: No, not yet.

Ford CEO Jac Nasser, known as "Jac the Knife" for his aggressive cost cutting at the company, began the meeting by asking people around the table, including then-chairman Bill Ford, what they thought. He kicked off with me, noting darkly that he didn't need to ask what my views were. Still, I wasn't wrong. In the end, twenty-three million tires had to be recalled, cutting the value of Firestone in half—and ending a century-long relationship between the company and Ford.[6]

Noisy Axle

Throughout this period, I fretted that the sustainability concept was being diluted as it mainstreamed. Scores of companies claimed to have embedded it through their organizations and supply chains. Yet I knew that, beyond a few extraordinary cases like Patagonia, this wasn't the case. One area I began to explore, as a result, was social enterprise.

The shift in my thinking stemmed in large part from meeting Pamela Hartigan. A hybrid of Ecuador and the United States, married to an Australian, living mainly in France, and working in Switzerland, she had previously worked at the World Health Organization, then run by Gro Harlem Brundtland. Next, Pamela became managing director of the Schwab Foundation for Social Entrepreneurship, with World Economic Forum (WEF) founder Klaus Schwab as her boss. During that time, she visited hundreds of social entrepreneurs worldwide—indeed, her trip reports were the basis of our subsequent book together, *The Power of Unreasonable People.*[7]

I first met Pamela when she organized an event at WEF's headquarters, overlooking Lake Geneva, in 2001. There, I also met several others who proved to be key to my future, including Jed Emerson of "blended value" fame, Sally Osberg who ran the Skoll Foundation (which later funded three years of our work), and Will Rosenzweig of Physic Ventures.

Pamela left the biggest mark, though, particularly after she left the Schwab Foundation to become a cofounder of Volans. Klaus Schwab was not pleased, despite having written the foreword for *The Power of Unreasonable People*. So, maybe I should say a word or two here about the WEF's Professor Schwab. A German engineer and economist who claimed Henry Kissinger as one of his mentors while at Harvard, he founded WEF in 1971, then served as the organization's executive chairman for more than half a century.

As things turned out, I would serve seven years on the WEF's faculty, having slightly battered my way in back in 2001. Kim Loughran, editor of the Stockholm-based (now long since defunct) *Tomorrow* magazine, had commissioned me to write a piece based on interviews with some of those who had been to the 2000 WEF summit in Davos. I wasn't particularly complimentary. And as sometimes happens, this noisy axle "got the grease," though I'm still not sure of the exact line of causation.

First, I was invited to WEF's headquarters in 2001 to take part in that fascinating conference exploring the relevance of social entrepreneurship for the global economy. Then I was invited to the 2002 annual summit. For the first time, it was not held in Davos, Switzerland. Instead, it moved to New York, in support of a city still reeling after the devastating 9/11 attacks that collapsed the twin towers of the World Trade Center.[*]

One of my concerns about WEF had been its habit of strong-arming

---

[*] The attackers also took a big bite out of the Pentagon building—which I viewed sometime later from the office window of one of the world's best-known social entrepreneurs, Bill Drayton of Ashoka. He and I looked down at the wounded building, speechless.

think tanks into surrendering their intellectual property, which would then be white-labeled and branded by WEF as effectively its own work. Perhaps the organization thought that mainstreaming the change agenda was sufficient excuse for what struck some as intellectual piracy.

A related issue was that WEF's own priorities often followed emerging fashions, which might mean that some contributors ended up having their content purloined or their agenda appropriated, only to see it tossed aside when the zeitgeist moved on. The net result for organizations like the International Business Leaders Forum—where I worked with wonderful people like Robert Davies and Jane Nelson—could be quite damaging.

These were Shark-like, or at least Orca-like, behaviors from an organization positioning itself as a global Dolphin. Still, I mucked in, chairing and speaking at WEF events in Davos and in Palo Alto, California, and Dalian in China. But if ever I have seen a case of founder's syndrome, Professor Schwab was it. In effect, one or more founders retain disproportionate influence over extended periods of time, not always to the best advantage of the organization they helped to create.

I first encountered Schwab at close quarters during that New York summit early in 2002. The main venue was the famous Waldorf Astoria Hotel, at the time surrounded by huge trucks filled with rocks and rubble, their engines growling continuously, forming a cordon to ward off potential car bomb attacks. As with the *Jaws* soundtrack, the acoustics were ominous.

While there, working with Pamela and the Schwab Foundation, I was involved in what may have been the first attempt to get social entrepreneurs involved in a WEF summit. We were allocated a huge ballroom, sporting massive chandeliers. The hosts included Schwab, social entrepreneur extraordinaire Muhammad Yunus of the Grameen Bank, and music legend Quincy Jones, producer for everyone from Frank Sinatra to Michael Jackson—and also responsible for 1985's "We Are the World," a charity song that raised funds for famine relief in Ethiopia.

But pretty much no one else turned up.

Still, if you were to read my writing from the Davos summits at the time, you would conclude that I benefited mightily, as have thousands of others. And I am sincerely grateful to Professor Schwab both for accepting me into the fold for a while and for writing that foreword. Partly as a result, *The Power of Unreasonable People* went into the hands of all three thousand delegates to the 2008 Davos summit, with financial help from the Skoll Foundation. In terms of our own impact, this was a significant contribution to the mainstreaming of social enterprise.

Is This It?

The distractions that flowed from the 9/11 attacks were profound, however, and it soon became clear that most businesspeople were not yet ready to embrace entrepreneurs trying to tackle the world's greatest social and environmental challenges through novel business models and mutated market mechanisms. But that soon changed, with leading social entrepreneurs pushing into the Davos mainstream within a few short years. Muhammad Yunus's 2006 Nobel Peace Prize didn't hurt.

I still felt agitated, though, in my role as chief entrepreneur at SustainAbility. If anything, a 2006 *Fast Company* Social Profit Award[8] further stirred the coals. Our corporate work, I concluded, was fine as far as it went, but it didn't yet go far enough. Something inside me wanted to know "Is this it?" Surely there were better ways to have a positive, systemic impact.

The answer, I increasingly concluded, was that there must be.

After discussions with Pamela and others, and while still intensely proud of the work we were doing at SustainAbility, I reached an emotionally wrenching decision. We would build a new organization to play into not only the impact agenda but also the system change agenda. They were linked but not the same. You can have incremental impact that optimizes the current system, and you can have systemic impact, which helps transform the system—or even lays the foundations for a completely new system to evolve. Among system conditions we must evolve are politics (giving a greater voice to the underprivileged and to future generations); tax, accounting, and reporting rules; subsidy programs; legal frameworks; and—as is mentioned in chapter 9—the basic principles of economics.

In this spirit, Volans Ventures was launched on April 1, 2008, with the founding team coming from SustainAbility (Geoff Lye, Sam Lakha,[*] and me), the Schwab Foundation for Social Entrepreneurship (Pamela Hartigan and Kevin Teo), and Boston Consulting Group (Charmian Love, who had been seconded to the Schwab Foundation). We also pulled together a remarkable advisory council, including people like the former astronaut and cosmonaut Jerry Linenger, IDEO CEO Tim Brown, and Eden Project founder Tim Smit.

The idea was to stay small and nimble—acting as a catalyst, not a bulldozer.

Our declared aim was to help forge closer links between business and social entrepreneurs, exploring possible solutions to systemic dysfunctions that were becoming increasingly obvious. As it turned out, we launched into the teeth of the 2007–2009 financial crash, or Great Recession, which proved character-forming. But it also forced us to step up—and we successfully rode the growing wave of interest in social enterprise solutions.

In one memorable moment during this period I found myself in the London boardroom of Lehman Brothers, the global financial services firm, a week before it went bankrupt. As usual, I carried a compact camera and took photographs of the Thames from the firm's Docklands high-rise windows, posting them on my blog later that day.[†] Within an hour I had a cease-and-desist injunction from Lehman's lawyers, threatening immediate legal action. No cameras allowed in the building, they protested.

Ironically, although I was using an actual camera, many cell phones even then sported advanced cameras. Whatever the technology, when the news of Lehman's cataclysmic bankruptcy broke shortly afterward, I

---

[*] Sam Lakha, whom I had already worked alongside for three years at SustainAbility, proved to be the linchpin of the new organization. I could not have made the move without her—and if it had not been for her, the venture would have failed several times along the way. As we launched, she gave me a symbolic gift: an artist's blank canvas.

[†] Having started off with a Box Brownie, I later evolved to Leicas (including an iconic M3, bought from a German friend), Nikons, and ever-smaller Canons. Ultimately, though, I ended up using successive generations of iPhone cameras, which better enabled me to sneak up on my prey.

understood why they had been so agitated—and, unsurprisingly, I never heard from them again.

Blood and Gore

Meanwhile, we had issues of our own at Volans. Soon after we launched the company, Pamela announced she would stay on our board but head across to Oxford to run the Skoll Centre for Social Entrepreneurship. This proved a gift, working well on all sides. It also helped us build out our links in the entrepreneurship and intrapreneurship fields. For thirteen years, I attended—and often spoke at—the Skoll World Forum in Oxford, a wonderful gathering of the impact tribes.

Once, having chaired a big session with Al Gore and his Generation Investment Management cofounder David Blood, I ended up having dinner with them at Raymond Blanc's restaurant, Le Manoir aux Quat'Saisons, sitting alongside Robert Redford. He invited me to the Sundance Film Festival, but somehow, I was never able to take it up.

Again, the paths not taken.

Meanwhile, the Volans office, on the north side of London's Bloomsbury Square, became a pulsating hub—not least when the 2010 eruption of the Eyjafjallajökull volcano in Iceland trapped many people attending that year's Skoll World Forum in London, as airports closed. We hosted some of the world's leading social entrepreneurs for up to a week while they waited for delayed flights out. Cross-pollination went into overdrive as we linked these people to others across our home city.

Home or abroad, though, there were other wobbles. One concerned Singapore's Economic Development Board, or EDB. When, early on, I had met key EDB people for breakfast in Covent Garden, I had returned to the office convinced that a partnership could work—and work well. Younger colleagues asked how I could possibly know after a single breakfast. My answer was that there had been a good deal of humor in the conversation, not in the form of jokes but of playfulness.

That reading proved accurate, although not remotely in the way I had imagined. Three years later our Singapore operation got into trouble. We had sensed something awry, but when our chief operating officer, Charmian Love, flew to Singapore, she was assured everything was fine. One week later, however, we learned the opposite. Because of an outbreak of Asian flu, a project the local team had been counting on had evaporated.

As a result, we could no longer fulfill the conditions of our contract with the EDB. When I called them to relay the bad news, they pointed out that the small print of our contract included a clawback provision, meaning they could reclaim all the money they had invested in us. The decision, I was told, would have to go to the EDB board. I didn't tell them this, but a decision against us would have sunk us with all hands.

After some weeks of nervous waiting, they called to say that their board had deliberated and decided two things. First, no clawback. And second, they wondered whether there was any way they could help us stay in Singapore. It almost restored my faith in the public sector.

Bee Die-Ins

In competitive markets, it is inevitable that contracts and relationships end. Sometimes you see it coming, as when I was working with the world's largest bakery products company, Mexico's delightfully named Grupo Bimbo. It was clear that the top of this family-owned company thought differently about sustainable development and impact. For them it was more about corporate citizenship, less about root-and-branch transformation. They took on some of our suggestions, but overall, the best I can say is that I got to see a lot more of Mexico City than I would have done otherwise, thanks to my friend and colleague Mauricio Bonilla Padilla, who had pulled me into the company in the first place.

In other cases, we suffered from a change of CEO, as with the German materials company Covestro. We had enjoyed a highly productive relationship with the previous CEO, Patrick Thomas, unusually a Briton running a major German company. We formed a harmonious quartet with Patrick, his colleague Richard Northcote (a Scottish-independence-minded Scot),

Volans cofounder Sam Lakha, and me. Then Patrick moved on, and out of the blue, Richard died. People matter—and the relationship with Covestro never recovered.

Such reverses have been rare, though, not least because we have been careful in selecting our partners and clients. We have turned down a fair amount of work over the years, on rare occasions even resigning from projects partway through. Probably our most significant resignation while I was at SustainAbility had been from a relationship with Monsanto. We had been brought in by their then-CEO, Bob Shapiro, who was unusually thoughtful on the sustainability agenda. Unfortunately, the bit he didn't seem to understand was that many people didn't see genetic engineering as intrinsically sustainable, as he did. Let's say that I learned lessons there that helped shape future decisions on which clients to work with—and which not.

With Monsanto, we had provided irrefutable evidence that the company was heading toward a brick wall in its European market, but they decided to push on anyway. We resigned—and less than a year later they ran headlong into the wall we had warned them about, causing considerable collateral damage to the European biotechnology sector. Bayer, which later acquired Monsanto, should have been warned. Its acquisition would later be seen as one of the worst in recent memory.[9]

Indeed, the inclination of business leaders to ignore warning signs was rarely clearer to me than when I did a session years later with members of Bayer's own board, including CEO Marijn Dekkers, who subsequently became chairman of Unilever. On the day I joined them, protestors were staging bee "die-ins" around Germany, with activists dressed in bee costumes falling "dead" in the streets. But when I raised the impact of Bayer insecticides on bees and other pollinators, I was publicly slapped down by Dekkers. Bayer's science, he insisted, showed that any risks were insignificant—that their science showed conclusively that we were fretting about nothing.

Later, the chemicals in question, neonicotinoids, would be banned by the European Commission, even for emergency uses—though Bayer continued to fight to get them back onto the market.[10] Clearly, there are times when business leaders feel they can't afford to hear the truth, let alone embrace precautionary principles.

Another company SustainAbility turned down was Philip Morris, the tobacco giant. At one stage, SustainAbility even turned down Kraft Foods, on the basis that it was wholly owned by Philip Morris at the time. Some years back, the company approached Volans to see if we might help build its smoke-free business, based on e-cigarettes, or "vapes."[11] While these can be dramatically better than traditional cigarettes in terms of human health and environmental impact, offering a potential positive health impact, our choice ultimately hung on the answer to a single question: Was the company funding its smoke-free range by continuing to sell traditional cigarettes in other parts of the world? The CEO's answer, as he vaped: yes. Viewing the invitation though our impact lens, our answer had to be no. Given the other issues that have since writhed up around vaping, including vaping's spread of problems like childhood nicotine addiction, thank heavens.

Recalling My Brainchild

There were other reversals along the way, too. Indeed, as impact worked its way into the financial system, one bright idea was to have a stock exchange that was fluent in—and financially rewarded—positive impact. I was not a founder of the UK Social Stock Exchange, or SSX—designed to help social businesses float and attract a wider range of investors—but I was soon invited to chair its admissions panel.

Here, we judged the triple bottom line credentials of businesses wanting to list and raise investment capital. We helped identify some great prospects and weeded out some pretty dodgy propositions. Many such processes will eventually run on expert systems, using big data and artificial intelligence. Our approach was artisanal, depending on the knowledge and contacts of the panel members—and I do not see machine learning and artificial intelligence replacing that entirely.

Later, I was asked to join the SSX board to ensure that the admissions panel's work and concerns were properly represented there. It was already clear that the Exchange was struggling to find the right level of funding, but I had no inkling how serious things would become. Instead, agitated about being part of a disproportionately older white male board, I offered up my board role to ensure a better gender balance, an offer that was accepted. In the process, though, I had unwittingly ducked a bullet. Before long, the Exchange went down.

Even so, I continue to believe that the world needs a range of social stock exchanges marrying, to quote the SSX motto, profit with purpose. And I continue to track those evolving in other parts of the world.

Meanwhile, I was pondering a voluntary product recall for one of my own brainchildren, the triple bottom line.* How often, I asked in the august columns of the *Harvard Business Review*, are management concepts subjected to recalls by the people who invented them? It was hard, I concluded, to think of a single case.[12] But the approach is standard practice in manufacturing. If an industrial product like a car fails, the manufacturer pulls it back, tests it, and if necessary, re-equips it. In case manufacturers grow careless, governments run periodic road safety tests. Management concepts, by contrast, operate in poorly regulated environments where failures are often brushed under boardroom—or faculty—carpets.

Yet poor management systems can jeopardize lives in the air, at sea, on roads, or in hospitals. They can also put entire businesses and sectors at risk. Increasingly, they can also threaten the health of our soils, oceans, climate, and biosphere.

With this in mind, I carried out my own recall. With 2019 marking the twenty-fifth anniversary of when I coined the term *triple bottom line*, I proposed a strategic review to do some fine-tuning.

Still, why recall it? After all, since the 1990s, the sustainability sector

---

* Coincidentally, the triple bottom line first surfaced in my brain exactly five hundred years after Luca Pacioli published the first treatise on double-entry bookkeeping, the cornerstone for single bottom line thinking.

had grown rapidly—although, at around $1 billion in annual revenues globally, it was no giant. More positively, market research suggested that future markets for sustainable products and services could be huge—with the United Nations' 2015 Sustainable Development Goals forecast to generate market opportunities of more than $12 trillion a year by 2030. And that was considered a conservative estimate at the time.[13]

But success or failure on sustainability goals cannot be measured simply in terms of profit and loss. It must also be measured in terms of the well-being of billions of people and the longer-term health of our planet: the real-world positive impact. Here, the sustainability sector's record in moving the needle has been mixed.

Triple Helix

The advent of the triple bottom line proved to be a branching point in the world of impact, opening up the range of activities, outcomes, and impacts companies were being encouraged to monitor, measure, and manage. Nor did the story stop there. The triple bottom line was followed by a profusion of linked concepts including double and quadruple bottom lines; social return on investment; multiple capital models; full cost accounting; ESG (defined at the end of chapter 7); the environmental profit and loss approach pioneered by Trucost (part of S&P Global), Puma (shoe and clothing brand), and Kering (the company that owns Gucci, among other fashion houses); blended and shared value; integrated reporting; impact investment; total societal impact; and net positive. And that was even before we got into next-generation concepts like carbon productivity, the circular and sharing economies, regeneration, or biomimicry.

Experimentation is vital, clearly, as it sparks a proliferation of potential solutions. But the resulting—and potentially bewildering—range of options can provide business with a helpful alibi for inaction. "Come back when you have sorted out what you really want," we were sometimes told. Moreover, we have largely failed to benchmark progress across these options to assess their real-world impact and performance.

Together with its subsequent variants, as I concluded in that *Harvard Business Review* article, the triple bottom line concept had been captured and diluted by accountants and reporting consultants. Thousands of triple bottom line reports were being produced annually, though it was far from clear that the resulting data were being aggregated and analyzed in ways that truly helped decision-makers and policymakers to track, understand, and manage the systemic effects of human activity.

Fundamentally, we continue to have a hardwired cultural problem in business, finance, and markets. Whereas CEOs, CFOs, and other corporate leaders move heaven and earth to ensure that they hit their profit targets, the same is very rarely true of their people and planet targets.

Clearly, the triple bottom line had failed, so far at least, to bury the single bottom line paradigm.

Critically, too, the triple bottom line's stated goal from the outset had been *system change*—the transformation of capitalism to better align it with tomorrow's ecological and social realities. It was never supposed to be just another accounting system. I saw it as a genetic code, a triple helix for tomorrow's capitalism, focusing on disruption, breakthrough change, asymmetric growth (with unsustainable sectors being actively elbowed aside), and the scaling of next-generation market solutions.

To be fair, some companies had already moved forcefully in this direction, among them Denmark's Novo Nordisk (which rechartered itself around the triple bottom line in 2004), Anglo-Dutch Unilever, and Germany's Covestro. The latter company's CEO at the time, Patrick Thomas, stressed that the triple bottom line requires, at minimum, progress on two dimensions while holding steady—at worst—on the third. It is time for this interpretation to become the default setting, not simply for a handful of leading businesses, but for all business leaders.

In this respect, I saw—and see—bright rays of hope coming from the high-energy world of B Corporations. At the time of writing, more than eight thousand businesses worldwide were certified as B Corps. All are configured around the triple bottom line—aiming to be not just the best in the world, but best *for* the world.

But to truly shift the needle we need a new wave of market innovation. And one critical part of that story involves ownership. Indeed, someone who often passes through our London home is Professor Jim Salzman, based at the University of California, Santa Barbara, and co-author with Michael Heller of *Mine! How the Hidden Rules of Ownership Control Our Lives*.[14] Over time, the best forms of ownership for all forms of assets must be reconsidered, a process that could have transformative—you might almost say revolutionary—consequences.

One thing we urgently need to consider is the role of Indigenous ownership of critical ecological assets—given that the evidence clearly shows that the parts of Amazonia under the management of Indigenous peoples are generally the best carbon stores.[15]

Great Dane

As my focus continued shifting toward system change, a dog popped up on the Volans website. Flossie, a Labradoodle, was featured as our chief happiness operative. And the reason for her presence? Her owner, Louise Kjellerup Roper, Danish by nationality, had taken over as our CEO. She hadn't been looking for a job, but Sam Lakha had written a job description drawing on our thirteen years of working together that reached—and intrigued—Louise.*

She and I have worked closely since to boost our impact—and to build stronger relationships with clients like Acciona, the Spanish infrastructure and renewable energy company; Neste, the Finnish oil company transforming into a renewable energy and circular economy materials player; and Novartis, the global healthcare company.

---

* The brief so closely matched Louise's unusual skills and experience that one of her children exclaimed, "That's you, Mum!" So, she applied. When she arrived for her interview, my first question was "What's the point of a Labradoodle?" She didn't know that her husband had included her children and dog in her updated bio. But her answer told me everything I needed to know. She fielded the question with panache. Truly, a great Dane.

Louise has also given me space to write what I see as two of my more important book offerings, *Green Swans* and, now, *Tickling Sharks*. A "Green Swan" is a profound market shift, generally catalyzed by some combination of black or gray swan challenges and changing paradigms, values, mindsets, politics, policies, technologies, business models, and other key factors. Green Swans deliver exponential progress in the form of economic, social, and environmental wealth creation. We dubbed Green Swans in embryo as "ugly ducklings."

Our quest for ugly ducklings has continued apace. A year or two before Louise arrived, three of us—Sam, Ingvild Sørensen of the UN Global Compact, and I—were visiting San Francisco, Silicon Valley, and Los Angeles on a fact-finding mission for what we called Project Breakthrough, commissioned by Lise Kingo, as the UNGC's executive director.[16] On the LA leg on the trip, the three of us were waiting in a conference room at the XPRIZE Foundation. We were there to see Paul Bunje, the organization's chief scientist. In trundled a robot.

Hello, all!

Paul's face occupied a screen where the robot's face should be—and, via the robot's screen and speakers, he was welcoming us to the exponential future. I had been intrigued, back in 1996, when entrepreneur Peter Diamandis first offered a $10 million prize to the first privately financed team able to build and fly a three-passenger vehicle 100 kilometers into space twice within two weeks. That was when the XPRIZE Foundation first flared onto my own radar screen.[17]

Its Ansari XPRIZE motivated twenty-six teams from seven nations to invest more than $100 million in pursuit of the $10 million award. Similar to the Longitude Prize discussed in chapter 2, this was a challenge prize, which offers a reward (normally financial) to anyone who can solve a major problem, either first or most effectively. On October 4, 2004, the Ansari XPRIZE was won by Mojave Aerospace Ventures, with its spacecraft *SpaceShipOne*. The same vehicle then became the core of Richard Branson's Virgin Galactic business which, despite a fatal crash in 2014, eventually did get paying passengers into near-Earth orbit in June 2023.

I watched the launch online, reflecting once again that the more wealthy people we can get into space—to experience the "overview effect," which transforms the way spacefarers see Earth—the better.[18]

As part of our own efforts to embrace exponential impact, we invited Paul onto the Volans board. Then, when he later cofounded Conservation X Labs, or CXL, with maestro-conservationist Alex Dehgan, they invited me to join their board. I was thrilled to be immersed in a very different set of experiments and conversations around impact. CXL's thinking: "The planet is in the middle of a period of extraordinary change: a sixth mass extinction, the first in earth's history driven by the actions of a single species. Conservation is not succeeding fast enough. Extinction and habitat destruction are increasing exponentially, while our solutions increase incrementally."[19]

By democratizing science and technology, open innovation, and exponentially accelerating connectivity, CXL concludes, "we can allow conservation to operate at the pace and on the scale necessary to keep up with (and even get ahead of) the planet's most intractable environmental challenges."[20] In short, our future depends on new, exponential forms of positive impact.*

CXL's aim is to tap into "planetary genius" in search of breakthrough solutions.[21] To kick-start such exponential forms of innovation, the company uses challenge prizes in the same vein as the Longitude Prize and Ansari XPRIZE. Three early areas of CXL's work that have fascinated me are global cooling (focusing on air conditioning technologies that are climate-friendly), artisanal mining (which often creates more environmental and social havoc than the big mining companies), and plastic microfibers (a growing headache worldwide)—all in the spirit of "it's impossible until it's done."

---

* As an environmentalist, I have long mistrusted the belief in perpetual exponential growth. But in 2015 I wrote a piece for *GreenBiz* called "How I Learned to Stop Worrying and Love the Exponential." I concluded that there are periods of exponential change when an old order (say, fossil fuels in today's world) gives way to a new one (renewables in tomorrow's world) in a relative blink of the eye.

The exponential mindset had been powerfully injected into my brain back in 2005 when Elaine and I visited *Wired* magazine's "maverick" Kevin Kelly at his home in Pacifica on the California coast. I had hugely enjoyed his books, including *Out of Control* and *New Rules for the New Economy*. He had worked with Stewart Brand back in the early days as editor of *Whole Earth Review* and was a founding executive editor of *Wired*—one of my favorite publications to read as I blurred through endless airports.

In the same spirit and in California, if a decade later, on April 9, 2016, Sam, Ingvild, and I were visiting Tony Seba in Silicon Valley as part of the Project Breakthrough fact-finding mission already mentioned. Tony had developed a model of exponential change that he believed would blow apart many incumbent industries. Little did we know that he would team up with James Arbib, whom we had worked with in the early days of Volans. Soon their new platform, RethinkX, was launching mind-bending—exponential—forecasts in areas as diverse as transportation, cattle ranching and dairying, energy, and finance.

The forecasts were disconcerting for almost everyone involved in these sectors. For transportation and mobility, to take just one example, RethinkX concluded that global revenues in the sector would grow fifty percent by 2030, while profits could collapse by seventy percent because of new technology and the sharing economy—a nightmare scenario for the auto and oil sectors.[22]

Someone else we met on that same Silicon Valley jaunt was Dr. Adam Dorr. His book, *Brighter*, as already noted in chapter 4, provides an excellent introduction to RethinkX's thinking and projections. At a time when pessimism is endemic and likely self-fulfilling, Adam noted, "The sad fact is that a majority of young adults live with their parents for the first time since the Great Depression. In many ways, I wrote *Brighter* for my daughters." He continued, "Even my fellow scientists are unaware of how bright the future truly is. We have the clean technology we need, so it's now a matter of deploying and scaling it."[23]

The implication: it's time to think the unthinkable and surf the incoming tsunamis of change.

The Greta Wave

Speaking of tsunamis, wave 5 in the series I had been tracking for decades could be dubbed the "Greta wave"—with climate justice activist Greta Thunberg, a teenager at the time, setting the world on its ear and being invited to address the United Nations General Assembly and the World Economic Forum in 2019. Now that was *impact*.

"Our house is on fire," she insisted. Casting diplomacy aside, she laid into WEF with a vengeance: "At places like Davos," she said, "people like to tell success stories. But their financial success has come with an unthinkable price tag. And on climate change, we must acknowledge we have failed. All political movements in their present form have done so, and the media has failed to create broad public awareness."[24]

This was a very different generational dynamic and long overdue. With colleagues, I had taken part in school climate marches by younger people, to show intergenerational support and to get a better sense of what they were thinking and feeling. Others may disagree, but to my mind, we boomers have failed crucial elements of our generational test so far. But watch out for politicians sucking up to the boomers as they age and retire because they will continue to have significant financial and political muscle. Coddling boomers at the expense of the young, however, would be a profound mistake. It is time to invest more heavily in the future and less in the past.

In self-justification, some boomers may point to key events that happened in 2015, such as the United Nations Climate Change Conference in Paris and the launch of the UN's Sustainable Development Goals (SDGs). But why were such initiatives so long in coming? And where, since then, has been the political will to deliver these goals and rein in the climate emergency?

The SDGs certainly helped map the agenda, but in terms of real hope spots there has been the European Union's Green Deal—with huge sums earmarked to drive and support a green and inclusive recovery. In the United States, meanwhile, President Biden's Inflation Reduction Act has committed even greater financial resources to tackling the climate emergency. We have also seen President Xi's China commit the giant country's economy to achieving net-zero greenhouse gas emissions by 2060.

All bold moves, though it's much easier to set such targets than to deliver them through decades of the sort of political turbulence that lie ahead. Among other things, recent events in China have taken a darker turn, throwing clouds of question marks over the assumptions many of us had been making.

The emerging fault lines between old- and new-order thinking became even clearer to us early in 2019, when we threw our weight behind the Extinction Rebellion (XR) protests. I wrote a letter signed by twenty business leaders that was published by the *Times*, though not everyone was pleased. XR activists in countries like France and Germany demanded to know why their movement was now "getting into bed" with business. And, as mentioned, on the other side of the coin, the CEO of a major client of ours in Germany emailed me, wanting to know how I "dared" become an activist—how I dared become "political."

Put aside the facts that I have been a lifelong activist in service of a radically different future, and this outrage expressed by an intelligent business leader spotlighted the growing clash between different worldviews, different senses of urgency, and although maybe not in this case, different senses of the ultimate direction of travel.

We will see more of such politics. Think of Nobel Prize laureate Muhammad Yunus, a pioneer in the microloans field, being pummeled for well over a decade by the government of Bangladesh after his abortive foray into politics in 2007.[25] The government's spiteful attacks on Yunus were described by observers as a vendetta led by the country's prime minister, Sheikh Hasina Wazed.[26]

Despite the political risks, we must keep trying new angles. So, in the wake of the first round of XR protests, I was involved in founding Business Declares, a business-led initiative inspired by XR. I served on the Business Declares board for several years, leaving just before the *Financial Times* signed up as a member, an extraordinary coup—it ran full-page ads in the pink pages spotlighting the climate emergency.[27]

In company after company, senior executives told me that their children had been turning up the heat under what they saw as their complacent parents. Having witnessed earlier youth movements flash over into violence when activists sensed that the "system" was rebuffing their demands, I approached the 2020s in some trepidation. Still, something was shifting, and profoundly. The sustainability agenda, in large part a boomer project, was now being re-created with new energy—and often fury—by younger people, who saw their futures under threat.

To drive things along, and building on the success of my 2020 book, *Green Swans*, we launched the Green Swans Observatory.[28] This involved shifting the focus from responsibility (where so much effort had been focused to date), through resilience (since pretty much all our systems were starting to wobble), to regeneration (the only way to restore and sustain the longer-term health of those same systems). The impact agenda, it turns out, looks very different through each of these lenses.

Learning to Speak Impact

You encounter a wide range of languages, dialects, and accents as you listen to people speaking the rapidly evolving language of impact, which is why I sometimes talk of a "Babel wave." So, let's zoom in on our work with Novartis, which has the virtue of being truly global.[29] At the time of writing, I had been helping the Swiss healthcare giant with the impact agenda since 2017.

One highly relevant book here has been *Impact: Reshaping Capitalism to Drive Real Change* by venture investor Sir Ronald Cohen.[30] "Ronnie," as he is familiarly known, addressed our 2021 Novartis summit meeting. He argued that "the world must change, but we cannot change it by throwing money at old ideas that no longer work. We must adjust our approach. To change the world, we must change how we do business, starting with where and how we invest our money."[31]

He believes that the private sector is now moving from being a largely unintentional driver of pollution and inequality to an increasingly intentional force for good, helping to distribute opportunity more fairly and bringing solutions to our most pressing social and environmental challenges. Certainly, the size of the impact investment market has boomed. By the time I addressed the Global Impact Investing Network's annual forum in The Hague in 2022, the organization's estimate of the value of the market had hit $1.164 trillion—a huge leap forward.[32]

But for impact to drive truly systemic change, rather than simply spurring new rounds of box-ticking, greenwashing, and even impact washing, we need a parallel revolution in impact valuation.* This is something that Novartis has been working on for years. Sonja Haut, an exemplary intrapreneur (or internal agent of change), has led throughout. And she has captured the lessons learned along the way in her insightful book, *The Case for Impact*.[33]

She was the motivating force behind the Novartis Impact Valuation Advisory Council, founded in 2018—and I was delighted to chair it from the outset. A key part of the work was to convene annual impact valuation events, whose size grew mightily. The first was internal, involving some thirty Novartis people. The second attracted more than a hundred participants, including a growing number of speakers from outside. They came from not only the pharmaceutical and healthcare sectors but also the spectrum of sectors increasingly being hauled into the impact space. The third event, driven online by COVID-19, attracted more than a thousand participants, this time with a very considerable number of external participants. And the fourth, continuing online, pulled in nearly two thousand registrants. The interest and demand, it seems, was growing apace. In 2022, the decision was made to go internal again, but registrations that year still hit nine hundred.

When it comes to shaping our own impact at Volans, we aim to be catalytic. Our approach involves creating as much positive impact as

---

* Each societal pressure wave triggers its own form of "washing": eco-washing, greenwashing, sustainability washing, impact washing, and inevitably, regeneration washing. All are damaging in terms of consumer and investor confidence. Tighter regulation is essential.

possible per unit of effort. That is a key reason why we try to be selective with our clients and partners. One case in point has been our work with the Paris-based supply chain platform EcoVadis.

It has been my privilege to serve on EcoVadis's scientific advisory committee since the company launched in 2007. The original idea came from two French entrepreneurs: Pierre-François Thaler and Frédéric Trinel. When I joined there was a handful of team members, whereas now there are more than seventeen hundred, and EcoVadis is the largest supplier of sustainability ratings in the world, maintaining continuous ratings on more than 130 thousand companies worldwide.[34]

Such ventures give me hope, if not yet total confidence, that we can still, eventually, turn the corner on wicked problems like climate change and biodiversity loss. But while I am still struggling to become fluent in the rapidly evolving language of impact, I look at the agenda through a slightly different lens from most impact experts and nerds.

One inspiration has been the list of twelve levers of system change devised by the legendary Donella "Dana" Meadows, one of the authors of the *Limits to Growth* study. These levers range from redesigning taxes through to shifting paradigms.[35] If you're focused on paradigm change, as I have been, you soon discover that we have at least two key problems.

The first is that such shifts can be glacial, at least until the old system starts to melt away, which is when things speed up dramatically. To create true systemic impact, you need among other things courage, curiosity, a robust constitution, stamina, and ideally, a long life.* The second problem is that if the changes you want to see in the world are coming anyway, you face a real problem in determining what happened because you were involved—and, equally, what would have happened anyway.

The more systemic the impact you manage to achieve, the less measurable it is likely to be—at least in normal business timescales and

---

* One element of stamina, I discovered, is the ability to sleep almost anywhere, anytime—including on aircraft. Indeed, if I could order superpowers for all change agents, this would be among them. As to courage, this is not the sort that people need in wartime conditions when every day involves existential threats. Instead, it is the sort needed to keep going as a Cassandra, seeing the future yet being ignored and often ridiculed and belittled.

terms—and the more likely you are to need new measures and more patient accounting, better aligned with the new paradigm, to capture any progress you may be making.

Crucially, and wherever Elon Musk may end up spending his final days, successful change champions will have mastered the art of inhabiting two (or more) counterposed realities at the same time. They will have one foot still in the waning paradigm while the other is moving inexorably into the new one. And in my mind, the new paradigm, more than anything else, is about Gaia, the Anthropocene, and—probably the pressure wave that will see me out—regeneration.

WORK IN PROGRESS

It now seems quaint that earlier generations fretted about whether rich people could pass through the eye of heavenly needles. Later, leaders pondered how to become knights of the realm, heroes of the Soviet Union, or "leave a legacy." Today they are encouraged to consider their positive impact, how to deliver it, and how to measure and value any progress.

This underscores my own problem. Does the grit seeding tomorrow's pearl need a personal impact statement? Hardly. It is what it is, an irritant. Does a pollinator need one when zooming bloom to bloom? Ridiculous! Or an ambassador? Well, maybe, but recall Henry Wotton—back in 1604—quipping that an ambassador is an honest man sent abroad to lie for the good of his country.

I have been each of these things—described in the last century as "grit in the corporate oyster," my current job title being "chief pollinator," and my personal website long headlined "ambassador from the future." But at no point have I had a personal impact statement, nor felt its absence. Probably the closest I came was in the themes of my books and the mission statements of organizations I helped found and co-evolve. Today it strikes me that I have often played a "Trojan" role—a vehicle enabling new thinking, rather than murder and mayhem, to penetrate the defenses of corporations and their boardrooms.

continued

Early on, we explored how business managed issues like safety, health, and the environment. We promoted stakeholder capitalism when it was radical. Once inside business, we flagged emerging priorities like expanded forms of accounting, auditing, and reporting. Next came areas like strategy, branding, design, R&D, and supply chain management. More sensitive still, we probed corporate governance, government relations, and lobbying.

Then, when even leadership companies protested that financial market expectations were stalling progress, we zeroed in on investors, insurers, rating agencies, and stock exchanges. Each time, I was involved in launching new change initiatives, as with the Global Reporting Initiative and the International Integrated Reporting Council on reporting, the Dow Jones Sustainability Indexes and GIST Impact on company ratings, EcoVadis on supply chains, and the Social Stock Exchange and First Abu Dhabi Bank on finance.

Now the needle on the dial is jumping from incremental to exponential change—and the focus is shifting from the business case for change to business models able to make commercial sense of tomorrow's markets. Partly as a result, we find ourselves spending more time with universities and business schools, helping to prepare tomorrow's leaders.

Our work must expand from individual businesses and industry sectors to consider entire markets and economies—and to champion evolution in economics, the master discipline of capitalism. Along the way, impact statements, corporate and personal, must play a central role. As to my own purpose, the best I can manage is: "to help business regenerate our economies, societies, and biosphere." But, while it pains me to say it, measuring our impact as a catalyst of system change remains work in progress.

CHAPTER 9

Regenerating Tomorrow

Something was afoot. In the wilds of Cornwall, a white stretch limo swept past, all smoked windows and aerodynamic antennas. We were heading into Eden as the limo was heading out. We suspected we knew who was—or had been—in the monstrous vehicle; the invitation was something of a giveaway. Tim Smit, the man behind the Eden Project, had suggested the dress code: Hawaiian shirts, flip-flops.

As we arrived, a dense, cool mist pushed in from the sea, the cloud base sinking into the vast china clay quarry from which Eden's biodomes now bubble up. Hardly California beach weather. Still, we knew who must have been delivered: Brian Wilson of the Beach Boys. As someone who bought my first Beach Boys album in the early 1960s, it felt as if I were about to wander through the gates of heaven on earth. In fact, this would be the second time in 2004 that I had seen a performance of the Beach Boys' "lost" album, *Smile*, and the extent of Wilson's resurrection from his drug-induced multiyear stupor was mind-bending.

There was hope for us all, it seemed.

Tim had sent the invitation to a number of longtime environmentalists, encouraging us to turn up for the concert. The morning after, we were invited to share breakfast with Tim and his team on a veranda overlooking picturesque Fowey Harbor. His aim: to bury the hatchets in a field riven by disputes and to explore ways that some of those who had stepped forward in the early days of environmentalism might step up again, together.

Tim's generosity of spirit was legendary, so my RSVP had been virtually instantaneous. As I had moved from the environmental to the green agendas, then on to the sustainability, impact, and regenerative economy agendas, I had left a trail of friends and, perhaps inevitably, "frenemies"—and, here and there, outright critics. And what was true of me was certainly true of others invited to breakfast that day.

Among those taking part were several people I knew well. They included two former executive directors of Friends of the Earth, Tom Burke and Charles Secrett, alongside Sara Parkin and Richard Sandbrook, who had cofounded Forum for the Future with another former Friends of the Earth executive director, Jonathon Porritt.[*]

Looking around the breakfast table that morning, it was clear that the fault lines ran every which way. A political version of crazy paving. Richard, whose idea this burying-the-hatchets reunion had been, had also been a Friends of the Earth director before moving on to the International Institute for Environment and Development. Across the table was another of my favorite environmentalists, a true friend of the earth and oceans, Chris Hines. As already mentioned in chapter 4, he had been a founder of Surfers Against Sewage and was now responsible for sustainability issues at Eden.

Quite the job description.

Tim confessed that his optimism about bringing people together had been willfully naïve. But he hoped that the Eden Project could provide a model for how we might all agree to agree. At a time of serious fragmentation across the sustainability industry, his attempts at defragmentation

---

[*] Jonathon Porritt and I, alongside our organizations Forum for the Future (founded 1996) and SustainAbility (founded 1987), operated in a healthy state of competition. Listen to this episode of *The Futuring Podcast* he and I did in October 2021: https://open.spotify.com/episode/6aSYIdfYB5lsR9PaEfpsrC.

were both timely and hugely welcome. And now they are a model for what we must do at a very different level to bring the different elements—wings almost—of the sustainability movement together. What follows should be read as working notes on some of the strands we now need to weave together into some form of grand strategy for our common future.

Green Swan Awards

But back, for a moment, to that breakfast overlooking Fowey Harbor. No one asked Tim to show his numbers as we spoke, but they would have been impressive; Eden had already introduced sustainability to more than twenty million visitors, injecting more than £2 billion into the regional economy.

In recent years, Volans has scoured the world for examples of Green Swans, solutions to major challenges that are not only responsible but also resilient and regenerative—ideally right across the triple bottom line. To spotlight early successes, we launched the Green Swan Awards in 2020,[1] with winged statuettes designed and cast by Nicola Godden.* Tim Smit landed the first; the second award went to Denis Hayes, who founded the Earth Day Network in 1970; and the third went to Sacha Dench, a.k.a. "The Human Swan." She was an aviator with the mission of "Connecting Science, People & Planet."

In 2016 Sacha flew 7,000 kilometers by paramotor, through all kinds of weather, alongside flocks of Bewick's swans, from Arctic Russia across eleven countries to the UK. Her goal: to help spotlight the plight of these extraordinary birds. She believed it was a vital first step to restoring their migratory paths and regenerating their populations. Next, she set off to circle the British Isles flying a battery-powered paramotor, dropping in to see people around the country who were working on environmental

---

* The Green Swan Award statuette was designed and cast in bronze by Nicola Godden, the sculptor who also created the statue of Sir Peter Scott with swans that graces the entrance to the London Wetland Centre in Barnes, where we held the first Green Swan Day in 2019. For more on her work, see https://nicolagodden.com.

protection and regeneration projects. Elaine and I had helped fund her adventure—which made it even more shocking when she and her colleague Dan Burton collided in midair near Loch Na Gainmhich in the north of Scotland.

He was killed, she very seriously injured.[2] What a pleasure, then, to see her almost back on her feet, despite two broken legs, in May 2022. I attended the launch of her new Flight of the Osprey campaign, then went on to dinner at the Polish Club with half a dozen others, including Sacha, Tim Smit, Jake Fiennes (a member of the well-known acting family, best known for his conservation work), and actress/activist Joanna Lumley.[*] Strikingly, Joanna—whom I sat next to—still remembered the exact wording of the endorsement she had written for our *Green Consumer Guide* back in 1988: "*The Green Consumer Guide*, or how to stop biting the hand that feeds us."

I have long been in awe of people like Denis, Tim, and Sacha, who take risks on our behalf and in the process help us to see our world from new angles. The views and intelligence such people bring back were part of the evidence that ultimately persuaded me that the sustainability movement was failing to engage such challenges properly. That, in fact, was why I had originally announced the product recall for the triple bottom line. However, over the subsequent months, we came to see that there was nothing inherently wrong with the concept, as long as you took account of the mental framing in which it was used.

Let me explain.

Fizzing with Excitement

Most people using the triple bottom line concept used it in a responsibility framing, seeing it as being about citizenship, transparency, accountability,

---

[*] On the day in March 2023 as I finished another rewrite of *Tickling Sharks*, Sacha came to lunch, on her forty-eighth birthday, and we discussed her next adventure—to protect vultures. I was hooked from the start. Like sharks, vultures are increasingly endangered; yet they, too, are vitally important in ensuring healthy ecosystems. For more, see: https://www.conservation-without-borders.org/flight-of-the-vulture.

and reporting. Nothing wrong there, of course. Indeed, when we started out, pretty much all those things had been profoundly alien to most businesses. The problem now was that all this effort was doing little to slow—let alone reverse—wider degenerative trends in the planet's vital systems.

With the COVID-19 crisis and the war in Ukraine, our economies, societies, and politics were starting to wobble, too. Leaders increasingly spoke in terms of the need for greater resilience and security in everything from supply chains and national economies through to healthcare systems (as the pandemic dug its claws in), and most importantly of all, the biosphere and climate system.

The only way to rebuild the long-term resilience of such systems, we concluded, is to regenerate them. Hence our growing interest in the regenerative economy, advanced by the likes of John Fullerton of the Connecticut-based Capital Institute. After a successful twenty-year career on Wall Street as a managing director of what he calls "the old JPMorgan," John heeded a persistent inner voice, walking away in 2001 with no plan—but many questions. A few months later he experienced the horrors of the 9/11 attacks, firsthand. He launched the Capital Institute in 2010, focusing on the reimagination of economics and finance in service of life.[3] He heralds the emerging Regenerative Age.

In that spirit, on Volans's first Green Swan Day in 2019, on my seventieth birthday, we hosted one hundred people in London, including folk like Tim Smit and WWF UK CEO Tanya Steele, at the London Wetland Centre in Barnes—a ten minutes' walk from my home.[4] The choice of venue was deliberate. The Wetland Centre itself is a glorious demonstration of regeneration.

It was the brainchild of one of my favorite people, Sir Peter Scott. He was the son of Antarctic explorer Captain Robert Falcon Scott who, in his dying letter, famously urged Peter's mother to "make the boy interested in natural history."[5] Later he became an Olympic sailing medalist and a celebrated painter and broadcaster. Working with people like Max Nicholson, Peter had helped found the WWF, becoming its founding chair—even drawing the original panda logo.

Earlier, in 1946, he had set up the Wildfowl & Wetlands Trust at Slimbridge, a mecca for bird science and conservation.[6] He pioneered what we now call *rewilding*. Uniquely at the time, he opened Slimbridge to the public so anyone could get close to nature, as I did on a school trip from Glencot School. Decades later, Peter and the Trust drove the regeneration of four huge London reservoirs in Barnes, now surplus to requirements—turning them into an extensive series of wetlands and reedbeds, with hides from which to watch wildfowl.

I was lucky enough to meet Peter a couple of times. The first time was when he was part of the panel that awarded me a Churchill Fellowship in 1981.* The second, not long before he died, was when we met at a wildlife center in the Cotswolds. That day he was sporting wildly different socks, I noted. His wife, Phil, cheerily told me that this reflected muddle rather than any fashion statement. Then she whispered in my ear that my speech had left her fizzing with excitement. What generous spirits they were.

In hindsight, however, I was ecologically naïve early on. I squirm to recall one occasion in the mid-1970s when Dr. Martin George, a regional officer with the Nature Conservancy Council, took me out in a rowing boat on the Norfolk Broads. They had resulted from the natural flooding of an immense area of peat workings that long helped fuel London. I probably didn't even know their origin when I arrived to write an article for *New Scientist*. Worse, as I trailed my hand in the waters beside the boat as Martin rowed, I commented how wonderfully green the water was. Martin called me an idiot, explaining that the green was algal pollution caused by fertilizer runoff and sewage pollution.

One lives and—every so often—one learns.

---

* Late in 2022, Jeremy Soames, Winston Churchill's grandson and the chairman of the Churchill Fellowship, invited me to become an ambassador for the organization, an invitation I was delighted to accept.

Embracing Regenerators

My interest in regeneration has surged in recent years but has deep, rambling roots. In fact, one reason I was so enthralled with Frank Herbert's novel *Dune*, and with his worldview when we met, was that he thought about the regeneration of not only ecosystems but entire planets. That is the sort of ambition we must now embrace.

Much earlier, when I was immersed in my postgraduate degree at UCL, I had focused on both rural and urban regeneration—economic, social, and environmental. The focus was on everything from finding new uses for worked-out gravel pits and abandoned canals and railways to designing massive projects for injecting life back into historical infrastructures, among them London's Docklands. In the seventies I also explored the regeneration of disused industrial landscapes while writing for *New Scientist* and *The ENDS Report*. One thing that struck me at the time is that urban regeneration often takes huge amounts of money to get it going, and social regeneration can too, particularly where education is involved. But the payoffs can be huge—and environmental regeneration often happens of its own accord if human activity is removed. There are still costs, as in policing protected fisheries, but they can be orders of magnitude lower than the cost of allowing degeneration to continue.

Other sustainability leaders have focused on regeneration, too, among them Paul Hawken. I first came across him when his book, *The Ecology of Commerce*, was launched in 1993. It famously triggered an epiphany in Ray Anderson, the founder and CEO of the carpet company Interface. Ray described the book as "a spear in the chest." He woke up to the fact that even good-hearted business leaders like him could be considered criminals in the future because of the longer-term consequences of their decisions today.

Paul helped successive CEOs of Walmart embrace the green and climate agendas (in the case of Lee Scott in 2005) and then commit to regeneration (in the case of Doug McMillon in 2020). "Just because you're big," Scott once asked, "do you have to be bad? Can't you use size, scale, and scope in a way that is actually positive?"[7] Then, just when his corporate partners thought they had the hang of sustainability, Paul raised the bar again—both with his Project Drawdown survey of breakthrough climate solutions and with his extraordinary 2021 book, *Regeneration*.

I was honored when he invited me to write an afterword for the EU and Commonwealth edition of the book. One paragraph in my afterword reads: "It is nearly a lifetime since pioneers like Jane Goodall [who contributed the book's foreword]—now a world treasure—helped wake us up to the wonders and fragilities of nature. And it is decades since people like me and many others began to help business leaders change their mindsets, models and, ultimately, the marketplace." However, I noted, "Anyone worrying that they may have missed the regeneration boat need not worry: this movement is only just getting under way. Its glory days are still ahead."[8]

Soon, growing numbers of major companies were committing themselves to various versions of the regenerative agenda. Walmart was the biggest, with CEO Doug McMillon coming out for it in September 2020.[9] Among the companies that paralleled or followed this were the likes of Nestlé, PepsiCo, and Unilever—alongside a growing number of smaller companies, including many leading B Corporations.

We will see where all of this takes us, but the early signs of growing commitment have been encouraging. Much of this is linked to the work of champions of the circular economy, among them the Ellen MacArthur Foundation. The circular economy—which would spell the progressive end of our longstanding extractive economy—had long roots, but round-the-world yachtswoman Dame Ellen MacArthur brought a visceral passion to the agenda, having experienced ocean pollution at close quarters—and jacked the conversation up to a very different level. Her foundation, like such pioneers as former Greenpeace campaigner and chemist Michael Braungart and architect Bill McDonough, had seen regeneration as a longer-term outcome of efforts to build and operate circular economies.[10] In short, the conclusion was that we need circular strategies for the technosphere and regenerative strategies for the biosphere.

Renegade Economists

We also need regenerative strategies for economics, which—like it or not—is still the master discipline of capitalism.[11] Alongside Ellen MacArthur, three other women pushing energetically in this direction have been Kate Raworth, Janine Benyus, and Mariana Mazzucato.

Let's start with Kate, who has described herself as a "renegade economist." She argues that today's economics provides the operating system and a powerful bastion for the old, unsustainable, and largely male-dominated order. The field is in urgent need of new blood and new mindsets, she says. Here's one of my favorite Raworth quotes: "In the twentieth century, economics lost the desire to articulate its goals: in their absence, the economic nest got hijacked by the cuckoo goal of GDP growth."[12]

Humanity's twenty-first-century challenge, she argues, is to "meet the needs of all within the means of the planet."[13] In other words, to ensure that no one falls short on life's essentials (from food and housing to healthcare and political voice), while ensuring that collectively we do not overshoot our pressure on Earth's life-supporting systems, on which we fundamentally depend—such as a stable climate, fertile soils, and a protective ozone layer.

Kate champions doughnut economics, a.k.a. donut economics, an approach that she describes as a playfully serious approach to communicating that challenge. In this concept, the environmental "ceiling" consists of nine planetary boundaries, beyond which lie unacceptable environmental degradation and potential tipping points in Earth systems. The twelve dimensions of the social foundation—or "floor"—derive from internationally agreed minimum social standards. Between these two rings lies an "environmentally safe and socially just space in which humanity can thrive."[14]

Encouragingly, Kate and Janine Benyus—the world's best-known champion of biomimicry—have been working to align their approaches. And the doughnut is proving ever stickier, with Amsterdam adopting the approach in 2020—and scores of cities piling in behind.[15]

Next, Janine.

What about considering nature itself as a mentor, she asked. "Learning about the natural world is one thing," she explained. "Learning from the natural world—that's the switch."[16] She has long used the term *Biomimicry 3.8* to introduce the discipline she has done so much to define and champion, insisting that it can now help us tap into the 3.8 billion years of free research and development carried out by life as it evolved.* "Circularity, sustainability, regenerative design," she notes, all mean "that the things we humans make become a force for restoring air, water, and soil instead of degrading it."[17]

She's the Rachel Carson of nature-based solutions, you might conclude. Janine believes that the more people learn from nature's mentors, the more they will want to protect them. She has introduced millions to biomimicry through her TED talks, hundreds of conference keynotes, and a dozen documentaries, including *The Nature of Things with David Suzuki*, aired in more than seventy countries.

Janine also inspired Ray Anderson's carpet-making company, Interface, to adopt biomimicry principles in its designs, manufacturing, and increasingly, business models. And she launched the AskNature website in 2008 to catalog and showcase biological knowledge for a wide range of users. It has since attracted millions of students, educators, and professionals spanning design, engineering, science, and business. The thing to remember, she stresses, is that life creates the conditions for more life. Now we must learn to do the same, moving from degeneration to regeneration.

Then there's Mariana Mazzucato. I don't normally hug world-famous academics, especially anyone described by the *Times* as "the world's scariest economist." But it seemed appropriate when I arrived at UCL to do a head-to-head debate with Mariana, whom I had not previously met. She

---

* Having been privileged to serve on her board for six years, I learned much from Janine Benyus—and from her 1997 book, *Biomimicry*. A personal highlight was when, some years back, she read parts of her next book to me during a transatlantic phone call. Another good friend from the Biomimicry Institute days is Beth Rattner, whom I interviewed for the Green Swans Observatory: https://theobservatory.volans.com/meet-the-regenerators-2/.

was meant to hammer home the argument that only the public sector could save us, while I was meant to counterpunch by insisting that only the private sector can. Sensing that we both saw a more complex reality, we began with a hug and agreed energetically for the rest of the evening.

Mariana works with leaders on mission-oriented policies, designed to evolve and steer solutions toward grand challenges ranging from the battle against climate warming to building resilient health systems. Her 2013 book, *The Entrepreneurial State*, looked at the "investor of first resort" role that the state has played in the history of technological change—from the internet to biotech—and explored the lessons for Green New Deals.[18] Then came her full-frontal assault on the global consultancy industry, *The Big Con*.[19] Recommended, if sobering, reading.

Alongside the work of people like John Fullerton, Paul Hawken, Daniel Christian Wahl, Laura Storm, and Giles Hutchins, the ongoing work of Janine, Kate, and Mariana gives me real hope that we can transform the way value is perceived, measured, and rewarded. As does the work of economists Dieter Helm and Pavan Sukhdev, the latter of whom I had the great pleasure of staying with alongside Lake Geneva for several days as I was finalizing *Tickling Sharks*.

Oxford university economist Sir Dieter Helm concludes that no serious progress has been made on climate change, so radical steps are now needed—not least in economics. "Serious decarbonization is going to hurt," he argues, "probably a lot." We need some form of universal basic income, he argues, coupled with a meaningful carbon price and sweeping regulatory changes. Only in this way can we end what he sees as "The tyranny of the current selfish generation over the next."[20]

A former managing director at Deutsche Bank, Pavan led the multiyear TEEB inquiry, the acronym standing for The Economics of Ecosystems and Biodiversity.[21] Today, he runs GIST Impact, a financial data and analytics firm with a team of more than a hundred people; I have served on its advisory board for some years.[22] As part of a wide-ranging conversation one evening, I asked a challenging question about the purpose of all the data GIST and other firms are now collecting:[23]

When a chimp wants to punch a larger chimp, Pavan, but doesn't dare, it scratches its head. "Displacement activity." Is there a risk that we now see dysfunctional systems everywhere we look and then collect the numbers as a form of displacement?

[Laughs] For me, John, the numbers are a way of attacking the system. As Mahatma Gandhi said, "First they ignore you, then they laugh at you, then they fight you, then you win." So, the numbers are part of the battle—but to be effective, they need to be understood by society.

Now the numbers and analysis exist, how are they best pushed—or pulled—into corporate boards and C-suites?

We must change not just the micro model, but the macro model. A client of ours, UBS, talks in terms of the "impact economy," which I like. They talk about the transition from the output economy, focused on profit and GDP, towards the impact economy. I like the elegance and simplicity of the term.

Simplicity helps, but—given the complexity in areas like biodiversity—how do we get busy, distracted, and otherwise incentivized business leaders to pay the right sort of attention and act?

That's the challenge. But companies today are lying to us. They are telling half the truth—and if you tell half the truth, you are lying. So that's the first step, to demolish the lies.

Restoring Eden

A critical part of our challenge, then, is to make sure that the numbers we base our decisions on are rooted in truth, the whole truth, and nothing but the truth.

For our part, Volans has embraced regeneration as a key element in our own value proposition—and see the task of bending economics and accounting to serve this new agenda as central. To that end, we took most of our team to northern Mallorca early in 2022 to spend several days in a former monastery with Daniel Christian Wahl, the regenerative economy pioneer, whom we had invited to be a Volans Fellow.[24] Several of us had also spent a day with Giles Hutchins imbibing his wisdom and that of the woodland that he now runs as a center for regenerative thinking and practice.

Sustainability, Daniel insists, is rarely an adequate goal—not least because generally it doesn't tell us exactly what we are trying to sustain. Instead, he argues, we should be trying to sustain the underlying patterns of health, resilience, and adaptability. Some of our client projects were already focusing on regeneration. So, for example, we had been helping the Scottish Environment Protection Agency, or SEPA, with the environmental, social, and economic regeneration of a major area of industrial dereliction around the River Leven in Fife.

We had also been working with Acciona, the global infrastructure and renewable energy company based in Madrid. The original idea was to help it roll over its five-year sustainability master plan for another five years. But working with twenty-seven of its younger, fast-track executives from around the world, we ended up with a ten-year strategy for the business as a whole, built around regeneration. The process was driven by these younger, talented people. The company's new tagline: "Regenerative by Design."

Words are one thing, concrete action quite another. So, to see how this was playing out in the real world, Louise Kjellerup Roper and I visited Acciona in Brazil late in 2022 to review its construction project focusing on Line 6, part of the São Paulo subway system.[25] One element of the project we found particularly impressive was the company's recruitment and training of large numbers of women from the city's *favelas*, or slums, to work on the project—and prepare them for more active roles in the wider economy, which is a key part of its social regeneration story.

To keep tabs on the bleeding edge of change, in the best sense, I have continued to interview pioneers around the world. They have included Thomas Gent of Gentle Farming,[26] a British farmer who at the time was sitting on his tractor seat, explaining what regenerative agriculture means on his family farm, and David Leventhal, a developer of regenerative tourism resorts talking about his eco-resort in Mexico.[27] Others have included Patagonia founder Yvon Chouinard[28] and Pukka Herbs CEO Anuradha Chugh,[29] as well as Daniela Fernandez, founder and CEO of the Sustainable Ocean Alliance,[30] and speculative fiction author David Brin, already mentioned in chapter 5.[31]

I had admired Yvon for many years, not least because of his sense of humor—evidenced in the title of his book *Let My People Go Surfing*.[32] My respect was boosted still further when he made Earth the sole shareholder in the company,[33] gifting Patagonia to an independent trust, the Holdfast Collective, dedicated to fighting climate change. Yvon noted that, instead of going public, the aim was to "go purpose."

As mentioned, another American I had long admired was David Brin, also interviewed for the Green Swans Observatory.[34] His novels have included *New York Times* best sellers that have won multiple Hugo, Nebula, and other awards. At least a dozen of his books have been translated into more than twenty languages. As discussed in chapter 5, part of his philosophy focuses on *tikkun olam*, the Judaic concept of repairing the world. Regeneration, in a word.

While all these conversations have given me hope and often joy, for me there has been one standout interviewee in recent times: Dr. Azzam Alwash. His story underscores the true nature of what the regenerative economy is—and what it will take to make it work on a global scale.

The backstory is that I had been fascinated by the Iraqi Marshes since a long-ago friend wrote a book on these amazing wetland ecosystems and on the people who live in them: the Marsh Arabs. That was back in 1977, but then–Iraqi dictator Saddam Hussein tried to wipe the marshes off the map. The grim tyrant almost succeeded in turning this immense area of wetlands, the size of Wales, into a toxic dust bowl. Azzam Alwash has helped turn the tide. In effect, he began restoring Eden.[35] And that's not as hyperbolic as it may sound, given that the marshes are reputed to have inspired the story of the Garden of Eden itself.*

The marshes first hove into view for me via a friendship with Gavin Young, foreign correspondent for the *Observer*, back in the early 1970s. As already noted, I stayed with him in Paris in 1973, among other things learning about his travels with the legendary explorer Wilfred Thesiger, who described his marshland adventures in his 1964 book, *The Marsh Arabs*. Gavin later published his own account of the marshes in his 1977 book, *Return to the Marshes*.

I came across the regeneration element of this story when watching the 2011 BBC film *Miracle in the Marshes of Iraq*. Then, as we planned the first round of our Observatory interviews, Elaine reminded me of the film—and I contacted the cameraman involved, Stephen Foote. He filled me in on the background, then introduced me to Azzam, who at the time was in Amman, Jordan, awaiting his first COVID-19 vaccination.

The Only Constant

After early email exchanges, I read *Eden Again*, the mind-bending book about the Iraqi Marshes by Azzam's former wife, Suzanne. Then he and I spoke by Zoom on March 12, 2021. I felt myself being drawn further into the big-picture regeneration story than ever before. So, here are some edited highlights from our interview.[36] We started off in personal gear. He began:

> For me, the marshes have this warm, safe glow. I'm now sixty-three years old, but I clearly remember when I was four

---

* I have long been fascinated by the Near and Middle East regions. When Elaine and I visited Syria in 2002, partly to see the Crusader-era castle Krak des Chevaliers, I was "recognized" by various local people in different parts of the country, though it soon turned out that they didn't know me. I thought it must be something to do with the way I looked. Then, later, we did the 23andMe genomic tests—and it turned out that a large part of my genome comes from Mesopotamia. More background here: https://johnelkington.com/archive/pubs-unpublished-syria.htm.

or five, being with my father in a small boat—an old boat with a Perkins engine. And it would be Friday, one of the few times where I actually had my father to myself. We would be going into this incredible water world. The marshland world is flat, but to a child's mind, as you move through the reed beds, you're in this sweet forest. The boat would meander, and you would look over the side, into the water, and it was clear, fish darting everywhere. And it was hot. Then you go out through this wide opening and the breeze comes. I can't describe it—you have to experience it. A water world in the middle of a desert, birds all over the place.

But storm clouds were looming:

This was back in the middle eighties, the middle nineties, and we know now what happened next. Saddam invaded Kuwait—then we began hearing about the drying out of the marshes. I remember seeing satellite pictures in London in 1994 at an exhibition in the Houses of Parliament. I looked at the growing evidence of desiccation and wondered, how could this be possible?

You look at the map, and there are the Tigris and the Euphrates. Eden was fed by four rivers and there are the four rivers here. I believe that [the Eden story is] a memory of the collective history of mankind. And truth be told, if you are a primitive person, life in the marshes can be pretty easy. They have fish yearlong. The water buffalo keep the channels open and supply milk. The reeds provide materials for housing. What more could they want?

For farmers, though, relying on collective work to create the fields and bring in water, there was a growing problem—salt:

> Evaporation is three, three and a half meters of water a year, so the salt crystallizes out. When the natural floods washed the fields, it was less of a problem. But farmers—civilizations—become greedy. They force the process. They stop fallowing, prevent the floods washing the soil. You see the result in satellite images. Across the Fertile Crescent, you see white deserts created by salt. And salt kills plants.

Then, displaying the hope and resilience that sustains so many regenerators, Azzam continued:

> The only constant in nature, they say, is change. The marshes will continue to exist, as long as there are people who are dependent on them for their livelihood. As long as there are people speaking for them. And that's what I do these days. I have the self-assigned task of being a spokesman for the marshes in the outside world—and inside Iraq. Inside, though, I generally let the marsh people speak for themselves. But I pay for buses to take people all the way to the marshes, including the rebels Saddam was trying to destroy when he turned the marshes into a desert.
>
> I talk to these people. Telling them that their resistance, their coming among us, led to Saddam's deadly onslaught on the ecosystem and its people. And some of them convert, become very eloquent, speaking up for the marshes. The message is that this ecosystem is not just mine, but yours too.

Throughout, Azzam faced fierce resistance from people who thought they knew better:

> I was told by a certain class of people that the Marsh Arabs did not need the marshes back, that they did not want the

marshes back. But fortunately, that's one battle I did not have to fight for long—because we discovered the marshes were already being restored by the people of the marshes themselves. True, I helped choose the areas where we should break the embankments. But nature is a great teacher. All you have to do is observe her and she will tell you what she needs.

So has there been any overarching insight from all this effort? Azzam replied:

If you want me to summarize seventeen years of experience, it would be: trust the way water flows and get out of the way! You don't need doctorates; you don't need all the science—though they can be helpful. Let nature get to work. She knows how to do it. She's done this before—she's had around four billion years to work it out.

Black Swan A-Coming

Storm clouds are building again, however. "Sadly," Azzam told me as we continued the interview, "this region is now producing oil. I cannot stop oil production. Anybody that stands in the way of the production of oil will be leveled. The marshes are alongside not just one, but five 'supergiant' oil fields. The good news, as I tell officials, is that the world is going to leave oil far behind!"

He conjured an audience of Iraqi decision-makers. "Ladies and gentlemen, I say, you have a black swan [event] coming. You will have less water—and you will have less income from oil than today. Of the forty-plus million Iraqis today, fully sixty percent of them are younger than twenty-four years old. They have no memory of Saddam. You cannot blame Saddam for what's coming. So, what are you going to do?"

Azzam also noted how water is becoming a growing headache throughout the region:

A key question is how to manage the water in the region, in the presence of the dams. We know full well that the dams that the Turks built are going to be full of dirt and soil in about one hundred years. Soil that once flowed down into southern Iraq—that meant that the farmers didn't need fertilizers. And so all my passion for as long as I live is going to be focused on averting that black swan. What a weird thing if, after all that, this breadbasket of humanity suffers famine!

So, is there an alternative? "What I'm trying to do is create that alternative—to promote eco-tourism," Azzam replied. "Today, we don't even have a camping site. But it will happen. If people collect reeds in the marshes and can feed a family of ten, then they'll support the marshes. Duck hunters, too. I have never shot duck in my life, but I like to eat them. Those benefiting from the marshes will fight to keep them alive."

He concluded:

> I'm not a communist; I'm free market, but we abuse nature—take more than we need. As a young engineer, I was taught that we have the tools to control nature. Engineers, you were told, are smarter than nature. So off we go and build Hoover Dams. But then you learn that every project that you have done has had negative [impacts]. And maybe they are bigger than the positive effects, even with the dams we view as silver bullets today. They're not, but it's going to take us a while to figure that one out.*

---

* As we ended our initial exchange, Azzam said something that electrified me. "John, I hope that the universe will give us an opportunity to meet in the marshes. Give me ten days of your life, and I'll show you the cradle of civilization. I would love to take you from the marshes all the way to the source of their waters. The headwaters of the Tigris are an incredible place to be. True, this land has been cursed by the oil, but Iraq should continue to enjoy its location, as a meeting place of cultures."

Costa Rica vs. Russia

Let's now jump from the Middle East to Central America. When Russia shocked much of the world by cranking up its long-running war against Ukraine with a full-scale invasion on February 24, 2022, Elaine and I had just arrived in Costa Rica. In our first real breakout since COVID-19 hit, we hoped to experience regeneration at the personal, ecosystem, and country levels. We had long wanted to visit Costa Rica properly, after I had made a flying visit there to do a speech back in 2018—but our appetite was significantly boosted when the country landed one of five first-round Earthshot Prizes in 2021.[37] Given that Christiana Figueres, the influential Costa Rican diplomat and climate activist, has been involved in the Earthshot project since the outset, I was keen to check whether local realities matched global perceptions.

To cut to the chase, they did.

That said, Costa Rica is peculiar in several ways. Most notably, it outlawed its own army in 1949, the year I was born. As UNESCO's "memory of the world" website recalls, it was the first country in the world to abolish its military.[38] Ever skeptical, I kept a wary eye out for heavily armed police, but those we saw seemed civilized enough.

This demilitarization was particularly striking as our cell phones relayed images from Ukraine of incoming Russian tank convoys, bleeding refugees sheltering under shattered bridges, grandmothers training to repel the invaders with cardboard AK-47s, and the bodies of executed civilians. I wondered whether we were now peering out from a world of degeneration into a regenerative future—or, as Putin's war seemed to suggest, the reverse. Media coverage of the invasion suggested that age-old realities were reasserting themselves. We seemed to be witnessing a major disruption of the so-called Long Peace within which my generation had grown up and had increasingly taken for granted.[39] Another Minsky moment, you might conclude.

But, then again, I have never believed you can gain peace—or sustainability, for that matter—simply by wishing for them. Praying only gets you so far. And history suggests that periods of disruption often blindside us when they start—and once under way, they can take us in directions scarcely imagined by those who helped trigger them.[40]

In contrast to people like Stephen Pinker, who has argued that the world is getting ever-less violent, I have long worried about the prospects for new levels of murder and mayhem caused by asymmetric tactics, including cyberwarfare and genetic weapons. Now, with the different types of security agendas increasingly blurring together, we must work harder to engage the military and intelligence worlds.

In 2021, in that spirit, I spoke at an invitation-only UK Ministry of Defence seminar on societal resilience in the face of global heating, or "global boiling" as UN Secretary-General António Guterres has taken to calling it. During the seminar, Jeremy Quin, minister for Defence Procurement, noted, "The threats of our modern world, made worse by rising seas, extreme weather, and creeping desertification, will almost certainly lead to more conflict."[41] That has long been my view. And one area of real concern must be that future conflicts will both damage the planet directly and divert attention away from efforts to turn the corner on the climate and biodiversity emergencies.*

Some will view Putin's war as further confirmation that we are headed into a Hobbesian century, red in tooth and cyber-claw. Overnight, ESG analysts were forced to reconsider their handling of defense issues—and investors their investments in companies linked to weapons. More positively, perhaps, you might choose to see such conflicts as the death throes of an old order built around violence against people and nature.

There may be something in that, but with the proliferation of populist leaders around the world, any such conclusion will seem outlandishly

---

* I have explored related themes in essays for *Limits to Growth* co-author Jørgen Randers in his landmark book *2052*, and with Thammy Evans, whom I met during the Ministry of Defence process. The second project was for the European end of the Carnegie Institute in its 2021 report *The EU and Climate Security: Toward Ecological Diplomacy*. I then chaired a session on peace, security, and conflict at Anthropy 2023. With help from Thammy and Victoria Morton, I pulled together a panel featuring Scilla Elworthy (nominated three times for the Nobel Peace Prize), Lieutenant General Richard Nugee (a pioneer in climate solutions and sustainability at the UK Ministry of Defence), and Colonel Rosie Stone (a pioneer in human security at the MOD). These are themes whose importance can only grow.

optimistic to many. Still, as I argued in *Green Swans*, we are now seeing the unraveling of an old order we have all grown up with. At the same time, new orders are evolving—and some could well embrace much of the agenda we have been pioneering, as long as we act effectively and in good time. And, for a growing number of us, regeneration is seen to be some sort of master key.

Heading Upmarket

To get a better sense of how the regeneration agenda looks from the Costa Rican angle, I turned to LinkedIn—contacting someone I had heard of but not yet met, Eduard Müller. Delightfully, we met for dinner on our first evening in San José. He is founder and rector of the University for International Cooperation, launched in 1994, and has been a pioneer in online education in more than sixty countries. More interesting still is his initiative Costa Rica Regenerativa (Regenerate Costa Rica), founded in 2018.[42]

"True wealth," the organization states on its website, "is found in the well-being of the web of life."

Anyone wanting to understand this extraordinary country's history should dig into the story of the United Fruit Company, which helped turn independent countries in the region into so-called banana republics. We got a sense of the sharp end of the industry as we watched huge bunches of bananas being cut and processed for export at a Del Monte plant. And we caught glimpses of the insecticide-, nematicide-, and fungicide-spraying planes used to battle pests.

In our peripheral vision, near Monteverde, we saw coffee plantations moving uphill into largely untouched virgin cloud forests. We also learned of some of the ways in which inward migration from countries like Nicaragua and Colombia is spurring rising levels of violence and waste dumping, with growing numbers of Costa Ricans fortifying their homes—reminding me at times of Johannesburg, South Africa. This, in turn, links to the growing hold the drug trade has on the region, with Costa Rica being a key staging post between producers to the south and consumers to the north.

On the upside, two hours' drive from San José, near Puerto Viejo, we were taken around the La Selva Research Station. Dating back to 1968, the reserve was originally a farm but has been regenerated to the point where it now hosts a remarkable amount of biodiversity: 2,077 recorded species of plants, 125 species of mammals (72 of them bats), 470 species of birds, 48 amphibian species, 87 species of reptiles, 45 species of freshwater fish, and tens of thousands of insects, arachnids, and other arthropods.

Significantly, one key source of income is so-called environmental service payments, where conservators and regenerators of natural systems are paid for protecting and regenerating forest ecosystems. None of the reserves and parks we visited are fully commercial, nor intended to be, so I was also intrigued to see ventures that were—or at least designed to be so.

Near Sarapiquí, we visited Paraíso Organico, where we toured a large pineapple plantation in a tractor-trailer driven by the owner's son, Rolando Soto Jr. The taste of the organic pineapples he sliced for us, out in the sun-drenched fields, was exquisite. And the ensuing piña colada, when we got back to the ranch, was the best I have ever tasted. Still, Rolando stressed that the price premium on organic produce remains a real issue, with most producers still stubbornly sticking with the ecologically damaging agrochemical model. He explained that the Paraíso Organico farm was started by his father, originally a banker, which may suggest an even greater hurdle for those with less capital.

As a reminder of the alternatives, not long after we left the farm, we passed a massive sprayer dispensing chemicals across someone else's fields of pineapple plants. So, again, how to move the regenerative economy forward? One answer is to head upmarket.

Back in San José, our newfound friend, Eduard Müller, introduced us to one of his partners in regeneration, Juan Sostheim, founder of Rancho

Margot.[43] And, as chance would have it, a few days later our itinerary brought us within half an hour's drive of this extraordinary eco-resort alongside Lake Arenal.

Juan kindly picked us up in an off-road vehicle and drove us along an approximation of a road, which he cheerfully described as "ten thousand potholes" in the space of a half-hour journey. But what a destination! The whole resort is built around the principles of circularity and regeneration. Among the most striking features were the wildly verdant green roofs on many of the farm buildings. Indeed, so verdant was the roof on top of one of the hen enclosures that when chickens started disappearing, despite anti-predator fencing designed to deter everything from raccoons to jaguars, the culprit remained a mystery. Eventually, however, it was discovered that a large boa constrictor had made its home in the green roof, dropping down into the hen house for its feathery suppers.

No question, Juan is a phenomenon. Indeed, no one I have met has reminded me so forcibly of Brian Sweeney Fitzgerald, a.k.a. "Fitzcarraldo," in Werner Herzog's 1982 film of the same name. Both strain every sinew to turn the apparently impossible into reality.[*]

In terms of the wider context, though, anyone suspicious about the ecological and political implications of China's Belt and Road initiative cannot miss the growing Chinese presence in Costa Rica. At times we traveled on national route 32, the object of a massive road-widening project led by the China Harbour Engineering Company. Any such project will cause significant environmental problems, clearly, but how well do we understand where this Asian foot in Central America's door might take the region? And how sensitive will China be to wider environmental, social, and governance concerns? Experience elsewhere in the world is not wildly encouraging.

As the dynamics of deglobalization take hold, with the world increasingly shaking down into values-based—and often rival—clusters of

---

[*] For another striking example of regeneration in action see the work of Preta Terra in Brazil, led by Valter Ziantoni and Paula Costa. I first came across their agroforestry approach in *Time* magazine, early in 2023: https://time.com/6242262/brazil-drought-farming-rain-forests/. I got in touch immediately—and hope to visit them when next in Brazil.

countries and regions, it is not at all clear how regenerative capitalism and economies can best evolve across the developing fracture lines. But we should actively work to shape the future wherever we can, rather than waiting for it to shape us. And that's the subject I want to turn to in the next chapter.*

---

* I remain a firm believer in the power of serendipity, in the notion that if you create appropriate links and conversations, then generative relationships and partnerships will often follow. When Louise Kjellerup Roper and I attended the COP28 climate summit in Dubai in 2023, for example, we did a side trip to Abu Dhabi, where I spoke at a regional business conference organized by First Abu Dhabi Bank. And along the way we dropped off at Masdar City to see an experimental aquaculture center where—on an inland site—they were producing a combination of tilapia (fish), samphire, and mangrove trees. The story is told here: https://www.sustainabilityprofessionals.org/cop28-diving-for-tomorrows-pearls. But the essence of the approach, again, is William Gibson's insight that better futures are already here, aching to be more widely distributed. And as market pollinators, it's part of our role to help that happen.

PART 3

Schooling Dolphins

Education must swim countercurrent.

CHAPTER 10

System Change

Given that our aim is—and must be—the transformation of our economies and societies, disruption is guaranteed. On the upside, and even if many trends seem to be moving strongly against us today, the potential for system change is now greater than it has been for a very long time. Unquestionably, the "Force" that has shaped our lives for generations is disturbed.

Stand back, and it is clear that our overarching paradigm has been shifting for more than sixty years, implying that the next ten to fifteen years will see accelerating cascades of change impacting most aspects of our economies, societies, and politics. As a result, I expect more change in the right direction over the next fifteen years than in the last fifty.

There will be pushback, of course, up to and including riots, coups, and civil conflicts. No true paradigm shift has happened without triggering counter revolutions. Think of the sixty-nine-year-old Galileo Galilei forced to renounce his heliocentric model of the solar system to avoid being burned at the stake. Today's versions of the Inquisition haunt the bleeding edges of "woke" culture—and equally infest the wilder fringes of the anti-woke world. Just because we have read about such things in our history books doesn't mean they can't—and won't—happen again. They can and will.

Projecting such social tensions into the future, speculative fiction writers like Omar El Akkad predict a second US civil war triggered by the transition from fossil fuels.[1] Once you entertain such thoughts, reality can shift into different configurations. And if you want a sense of what it might be like to live in tomorrow's catastrophically flooded coastal cities, track down a copy of Kim Stanley Robinson's *New York 2140*.[2] Such authors help us all think around corners.

Happily, some parts of our economies are already migrating—and more must now do so—toward more inclusive, circular, and regenerative outcomes. Never fast enough, and rarely scaling at the necessary pace, but still providing the building blocks for a more sustainable future for those who ultimately decide to move in the right direction. The results will include dramatic shifts in our mindsets, technologies, economic models, financial markets, legal systems, and—most critically of all—our educational and learning systems.

Some of us will still be called on to tickle economic and political predators, tomorrow's Sharks, tomorrow's Orcas, but there will also be a growing need to school new generations of Dolphins—remembering that nature's orcas, too, are dolphins. We must find, train, and support new cohorts of leaders fit for purpose in the Anthropocene epoch. Then, as they drive the necessary transformations, we must understand that there will be unintended consequences, including an increasing tempo of mass strandings of those who failed to adapt their careers, business models, investment portfolios, or economic strategies in time.

Again, the natural world suggests what can happen in such times. Beached industries and economies will struggle to keep going, finding themselves inextricably compromised as a growing proportion of their assets are stranded, ultimately collapsing under their own weight. Some governments will struggle to refloat at least some of their keystone sectors, only to find them beaching again elsewhere, or later. In this "gradually, then suddenly" reality, the longer we leave the necessary changes, the harder the transitions will be.

Farewell to All That

In that spirit, join me for a moment on remote Farewell Spit, one of the weirdest, farthest-flung places I have visited. Stretching anywhere between 25 and 30 kilometers into the Tasman Sea, this thin peninsula arcs out from Cape Farewell, at the top left corner of New Zealand's South Island. From above, the spit looks very much like a kiwi's beak, but just how long is it? The estimates vary, reflecting the fact that it is surrounded by treacherous shallows where the tide comes in—and goes out—fast. Over the years, as a result, it has caused endless grief, with countless shipwrecks and mass strandings of marine mammals, notably pilot whales.

Over time, I have come to see Farewell Spit as a model of—and warning about—the dangers implicit in every business model, every corporate supply chain, every industrial sector, every economy. And of the growing likelihood that many of them will run out of room and be left for scavengers to pick over.

Imagine that we are walking across the thin peninsula, leaning into the wind, masking our faces against the hissing sandstorm. The beach fades into the haze, punctuated here and there with driftwood, mummified fish, and a huge, mirrored light bulb, perhaps lost from a fishing vessel. We stop and admire our distorted reflections in the bulb, as if at a funfair—an unearthly reminder of how a misguided sense of value can warp our sense of our place in the wider world. In fact, few places on earth so neatly capture the prospects of money-obsessed capitalism, a world where growing numbers of businesses and economies will find themselves stranded, their crews and passengers drowned or marooned, the survivors watching their possessions and assumptions washing away on the tide.

As the sand whips around us, it is easy to forget that much of the spit was once covered in greenery. Home to the local Māori people, it later attracted European settlers—who slashed and burned the taller vegetation, opening up the land for their livestock to graze. A huge mistake, it turned out, but very much in the spirit of our long-standing habit of turning fertile lands into desert.

At this point, I could easily regale you with an upbeat Farewell Spit story about today's regeneration efforts, with endangered species increasingly protected by the selective removal of predators like rats, pigs, and possums. Certainly, such work should be celebrated, scaled, and replicated. The laudable goal: to regenerate the spit's damaged ecosystems, helping restore their role as natural carbon sinks. But there is a darker story here, too.

Earthwreck

Just as Farewell Spit's physical configuration guarantees wrecks and mass strandings, so does the deep structure of our modern economies. When Bucky Fuller spoke of Spaceship Earth, he regretfully noted that we hadn't been issued an operating manual. One result has been that we have been behaving as if we were slightly intoxicated teenagers handed control of a powerful sports car. We might survive, just, but in the process the vehicle risks being written off.

However they are wired politically, whether for democracy, nepotism, or despotism, most of our economies are engineered to deliver a narrow range of outcomes for a subset of people. Success and progress are measured in terms of a shifting blend of the volume of production and financial returns. Trickle-down effects are meant to ensure that the have-nots get at least some benefit from the gorging of the haves, enough to keep them sedated, passive. But any real consideration of the long-term health of the systems on which that production and those returns depend is still nowhere to be seen in most business plans, let alone in most corporate or national accounts.

One result is that whatever we may do to promote regeneration, deeper forces will conspire to undermine our efforts. Our market systems evolved to meet earlier challenges, but now their failings help drive mass strandings of most forms of nonhuman life, even as they destabilize the climate, guaranteeing a longer-term planetary wreck. Viewed from this angle, every market and every economy represent some form of Farewell

Spit, its deeper architecture imposing costs, seen or unseen, on the wider world and on the future.

It is no accident, then, that thoughtful central bankers, investors, and market analysts are voicing their concerns about the growing risk of what they call "stranded assets"—which could experience sudden or progressive devaluation as new market realities surface. Investments that made sense in earlier realities will be painfully exposed as the market tides shift.

We have discussed Minsky moments, where sandcastles of assumptions crumple and are washed away. This happened when COVID-19 laid bare the failings of our healthcare systems. It happened again with Putin's war on Ukraine, where Europe's fossil fuel dependencies were laid brutally bare by the bombings of the Nord Stream gas pipelines under the Baltic Sea. It happened in the banking sector when Lehman Brothers went down in 2008—and then when Silicon Valley Bank and Credit Suisse imploded. And it will happen on a much larger scale as the climate emergency drives biblical storms, floods, droughts, crop failures, new patterns of disease, and massive human migration from Africa into Europe, and from south to north in the Americas.

Once again, Farewell Spit offers striking parallels. Local anomalies in the earth's magnetic field, which whales depend on to navigate, apparently create some sort of magnetic maze around Golden Bay, whose northwestern end is enclosed by the spit, leading generations of whales astray. Think about that for a moment—and turn your mind back to your school days. Perhaps you recall a simple experiment carried out in science class?

Iron filings are sprinkled on a sheet of paper. Then a magnet is placed under the paper—at which point the filings spring into an upstanding pattern, which reconfigures each time the magnet moves beneath the paper. In much the same way, everyone acting in markets responds to patterns dictated by deeper economic and political logics that remain invisible to most of us. Until, that is, these hidden realities are brought to light by events in the wider world—when we learn to see reality in different ways.

For a sense of our current unsustainability, consider the plight of Pakistan. Whatever you may think of the country's politics, it received

190 percent of its normal rainfall between July and August 2022, with Balochistan in the western part of the country, typically not affected by the summer monsoon, and Sindh in the south, receiving 450 percent more rain than normal.[3] One-third of the country was submerged by floodwaters, with fifteen thousand people killed or injured and eight million displaced. It was thought that as many as nine million more people could fall into poverty as a consequence.

As so often happens in the Global South and other poorer regions of the world, those who are largely innocent of fueling global heating are most exposed to the costs.

However we tackle such systemic problems, few of them are solved forever. An ecosystem saved in one decade may be destroyed a few decades later; legislation passed by an enlightened government may be reversed by successors; a company celebrated in one era, as Novo Nordisk was, may still fall foul of the court of public opinion in the next—as when the Danish insulin producer was alleged to have illegally promoted its weight-loss injection solution to the global obesity pandemic. But if we manage to change key system conditions, such backsliding is less likely—and a lot more obvious where it does happen.

As for my own future, I hope to continue tickling Sharks; it seems to be part of who I am and of what I do. Though having exposed the rules I play by, maybe I will need to evolve them somewhat. And I also intend to spend more time with Dolphins—the innovators, entrepreneurs, investors, and policymakers operating at the leading edge of change. As ever, the aim will be to engage individuals, teams, and organizations with the potential to salvage and restore vital elements of our future.

People often ask how they, too, might tickle Sharks. I warn that I am a poor mentor because so much of what I do is in the moment or on the fly. I'm drawing on everything I know to that point. Still, there are some recurrent patterns.

First, try to ensure that what you're doing is interesting, even fun. There's little point in trying to waltz with people who don't want to dance. It is also vital to be up to date with not just your own reality and agenda but also theirs. Next, to have any chance of success when tickling the powerful and the wealthy, you must be willing to listen, not just lecture. Empathy helps. Most leaders do not set out to be evil; instead, the mindsets, skills, and ambitions they acquired early in their careers may betray them when the world shifts around them. And power, like it or not, changes people.

Anyone expecting overnight change risks disappointment. Shark ticklers need luck, courage, nimbleness, and immense stamina. Patience, though, can be stretched too far. You must be willing to provoke—and sometimes annoy, even anger. Our provocative approach was underscored on January 11, 2020, when Volans cohosted the first Tomorrow's Capitalism Forum in London, alongside Aviva Investors.[4] The event spotlighted early findings from our Tomorrow's Capitalism Inquiry.[5] Our motto, emblazoned for all to see on the walls of one of the world's larger financial institutions, was clear and to the point: "Step Up—or Get Out of the Way."

Our Greatest Mistake

For me, writing this book has been a bit like trying to close a great circle, only to find that it has been a spiral all along, resisting closure, forever opening out. But the older you get the more things do appear to come full circle.

A key inspiration has been Sir David Attenborough's witness statement, *A Life on Our Planet*. "I am 93," he explained. "I've had an extraordinary life. It's only now that I appreciate how extraordinary. As a young man, I felt I was out there in the wild, experiencing the untouched natural world—but it was an illusion. The tragedy of our time has been happening all around us, barely noticeable from day to day—the loss of our planet's wild places, its biodiversity. I have been witness to this decline. *A Life on Our Planet* is my witness statement, and my vision for the future. It is the story of how we came to make this, our greatest mistake, and how, if we act now, we can yet put it right."[6]

Trained as a city planner, as I have explained, I went off-piste, focusing on business and markets. But cities have exerted an inexorable pull, particularly when we passed the point where most people live in them. For instance, Greg Kats, whom I first met in the earliest days of SustainAbility, some years ago brought me onto the advisory board of the US-based Smart Surfaces Coalition. The idea here, as global heating jacks up temperatures in cities worldwide, with poor communities often the worst affected, is that we can cool them down by using some combination of solutions like green roofs, novel surfaces for paved areas (including paths, roads, and parking spaces) that reflect incoming sunlight, and urban tree planting. The results are being rigorously costed—and show huge potential savings alongside extraordinary health benefits. This has been one of the most integrated triple bottom line ventures in which I have been involved to date, embracing economies and economics, societies and politics, and the wider environment.

As for that spiral dynamic in my life, as I shuttled back and forth through my diaries, blogs, and memories, I have found myself coming back, time and again, to T. S. Eliot's concluding words in his poem "Little Gidding."[7] The gist of the piece, which I once had the great good fortune to hear recited in front of a small audience, and from memory, by the actor Edward Fox, was that life tends to go in great arcs. The more inquisitive among us busily explore around corners and over horizons, eventually—if we live long enough—ending up more or less where we began. The difference, however, is that this time we see our worlds, our alpha and omega points, as they are.

Be that as it may, future generations will want to know what we were *thinking*. What did we imagine we were *up to*? Why, so often, did we ignore their interests, discounting the future so profoundly? And, for those who did try to act, why were they different?

As to what got me started, a question I have often been asked, it would be overly simplistic to say that "the eels made me do it," harking back to that epiphany described in chapter 1. Still, they played their part—and so what a joy it was to help Andrew Kerr and his Sustainable Eel Group release thirty thousand elvers, or baby eels, into the River Severn in the west of England in September 2014.[8] I can still feel those small bit-part players in tomorrow's regenerative economy wriggling through my fingers.

Another question people often ask is how I imagine all of this will turn out. Can we really change the deep structure of our economies in the right way, they ask, and do so in time? In the end, I reply, that depends on us, even at this late stage in the game. In fact, probably the most striking issue of *National Geographic* magazine I have read appeared as a special Earth Day issue in April 2020.[9]

It had two covers.

The front cover was headlined "How We Saved the World" and subtitled "An Optimist's Guide to Life on Earth in 2070." From 2070, it looked back on fifty years of progress: a future in which we successfully solve a growing number of the world's most wicked problems. By contrast, the back cover, titled "How We Lost the Planet" and subtitled "A Pessimist's Guide to Life on Earth in 2070," looked back on fifty years of growing, uncontained damage and destruction: a future in which, however many good people do good work, the pace of progress fails to match the pace of collapse.

Both futures are still possible, still in contention, but will our future embody the front or back cover reality? It is too early to know, and the outcome, almost certainly, will be some combination of both and of outcomes that even sci-fi readers may find it hard to imagine.

Hamster on a Wheel

Those of us who work to bridge multiple realities have a foot, a stake, in both futures. At times that will be an increasingly painful stretch. But, as Hannah Jones suggests in her foreword, and Tim Smit in his afterword, we find ourselves at an extraordinary inflection point in human affairs where some key trends are finally starting to move in our direction—often in unexpected ways and at unheralded speeds.

Though now well into my seventies, I genuinely feel that I am only just beginning, sensing that the next ten to fifteen years will see us working out how to navigate the incoming system change waves, tides, and currents. And, at a time when I find myself referred to as an elder statesman, it strikes me that I would be well advised to understand what the role of elder might involve. The Yoda phase of my life, perhaps.

True, my job title, as the world's first chief pollinator, attracted wry comment from Lucy Kellaway in the *Financial Times*.[10] But, while sometimes playful, our intent is always serious: to help those we work with connect tomorrow's dots—and to help make business sense of the coming tide of regeneration.

Artificial intelligence will play a key role, of course, but does not guarantee artificial wisdom. So, the sustainability sector must now expand its focus from the industries that created the problems of the past to those that will shape tomorrow's problems. Seen in that light, the robot at the boardroom table, which Ingram Pinn sketched for me more than thirty years ago (see chapter 7), now symbolizes the need for leaders to tap into real-time, predictive AI systems capable of slicing through the Gordian knots of complexity facing us all. Our looming challenge is to domesticate these new technologies and to bend them to the task of ensuring that our economies increasingly operate well within planetary boundaries.

Like it or not, we—all changemakers—are still very much part of the system we are trying to change. What has differentiated us from most other consultants, though, is that we were not simply hired guns, willing to do whatever we were asked to do. Again, we brought constructive discomfort to the party.

Throughout, I considered my challenge to not only become more knowledgeable myself but also work out how to tap into wider sources of the knowledge and wisdom we now so urgently need. And to help those we work with—and for—to do likewise. This includes the expertise of experts, of course, but is just as likely to involve the wisdom of the crowd and of children and younger people. Equally, there are substantial reservoirs of knowledge, wisdom, and untapped wealth among those who have retired from the fray, if we can re-engage them in the right ways.

The same goes for Indigenous peoples. A striking example of how the wisdom of Indigenous peoples can be valuable comes from Nepal.

NASA has mapped the incredible recovery that Nepal's forests have made in recent decades thanks to a plan to put nearby communities in charge of conservation. Satellite imagery shows that forest cover almost doubled across the country between 1992 and 2016. "Once communities started actively managing the forests, they grew back mainly as a result of natural regeneration," NASA reported.[11]

Well managed, most forms of diversity can enable more effective decision-making. Indeed, one way Volans has helped inject diverse thinking into client organizations is via advisory boards, with a key selection criterion being a wide range of perspectives among members. Let me zero in on two advisory boards I have chaired in recent times.

With Finland's Neste, the country's leading energy company, our work was commissioned by one CEO, survived a transition to another, but then fell foul of a major cost-cutting exercise. It involved pulling in leading experts from organizations like Bain & Company, Chatham House, WWF, and the XPRIZE Foundation. The focus was on sustainability and new markets, including those for more sustainable aviation fuels. We also tapped outsiders for off-the-record briefings as we explored issues like fuels-from-waste and the future of the internal combustion engine.

At the Swiss healthcare giant Novartis, meanwhile, advisory board members have been drawn from the Global Footprint Network, the Impact Management Project, and LGT, a financial house linked to the princely family of Liechtenstein—the latter with some nine hundred years of experience to draw upon. The focus of the annual Novartis summits has been on the valuation of different forms of impact, throughout the business. As we switched from face-to-face events to hybrid formats, the number of participants leaped from a few dozen to several thousand.

Sustainability is now going exponential because it must. Still, again, such mainstreaming can—and will—spook people stuck in older, increasingly threatened realities. A change agenda once ignored when it hovered on the edges becomes increasingly political as it pushes into the mainstream. Next, we must rise to these political challenges, too.

Look After Yourself

To sustain this effort, we will need stamina, but we will also need to take care, as they say, of "number one." I have seen too many mission-driven people burn out. Among them was Friends of the Earth campaigner Andrew Lees, whose heart failed while he was tracking mining industry abuses in Madagascar.[12] When we attended his memorial service, I had just launched the triple bottom line—and I always try to keep such people in mind as I champion change in the world's boardrooms and C-suites.

When my 2020 book *Green Swans* launched,[13] the positive response was exhilarating but taxing. During the first twelve months after publication, as new variants of COVID-19 drove lockdown after lockdown, I found myself delivering more than 150 virtual keynotes in more than thirty-five countries. By the end of eighteen months, it was more than 250 keynotes.* Colleagues warned that I was becoming like a hamster on the proverbial wheel.

So, I stepped back, to a degree. Then, unable to flit around the world as I had done for decades, along the way earning a lifetime Gold Card from British Airways, I was forced to consider—once again, though perhaps more deeply—what people like me had been up to all those years. What Greta Thunberg has called *flygskam*, or flight shame, fed into the equation, of course. But I had always seen flying as an investment in face-to-face interactions, helping build global momentum for change. It is hard to tickle people virtually, though no doubt the technology will improve. One young climate activist I have had the pleasure to work with more recently, Clover Hogan, has warned her generation of the dangers of burnout, based on first-hand experience.[14] As cataclysmic fires killed hundreds of millions of animals in her home country of Australia, she recalled, "That was the moment where I felt my heart cleave into two pieces." She wept on stage at a major climate conference.

---

* With brand inflation, where every event is trumpeted as a "summit," every talk as a "keynote," it is worth noting that the overwhelming majority of these were real keynotes, though few of the events were real summits.

I, too, have felt grief over the decades. On my watch, so to speak, the biosphere has been unraveling. We have seen a seventy percent collapse in wild species since 1970, with humans and our livestock now accounting for a staggering ninety-six percent of the weight of all mammalian biomass.[15]

For better or worse, though, I have tried (though not always managed) to develop the sort of clinical detachment practiced by people involved in life-or-death decisions, up to and including brain surgeons. My reasoning has been that if you want to promote real change in organizations, too much emotion can stall timely and effective action. But, just as surgeons use increasingly sophisticated anesthetics, a certain amount of playfulness can help take the abrasive edge off the disruptive change agenda.

And one real risk to be acutely aware of as you engage top teams, and those around them, is the risk of drift, particularly in your own values and priorities. As our agenda mainstreams, people will be drawn in whose values are, to put it politely, different. Rarely has that been more obvious to me than a situation involving the consulting firm Deloitte. A company vice chair who had pulled me in to brief the chairs of a dozen or so of Deloitte's client companies later erupted at a Royal Ascot event. Heavily inebriated, he apparently showed what may have been his true colors all along with a thirty-minute rant reported as sexist, racist, and bullying. He was forced to quit the firm.

Carrying out deeper due diligence on potential partners and clients will be increasingly important—a conclusion underscored by the news that Ernst & Young had been fined $100 million after hundreds of its auditors cheated on, of all things, their ethics exams. At a time when such enormous consultancies operate a growing share of the global economy, this is likely to become an increasingly pressing part of our collective challenge.[16]

Health Is Fractal

As for the essence of this book, it struck me repeatedly as I wrote that, fundamentally, what we need to think about, talk about, and move toward is health. The end of all our tickling, you might say, must be a healthier world, embracing the health of every life-form everywhere, from earthworms and earwigs to entire ocean ecosystems.

Wiser heads than mine have long since concluded that health is fractal, an emergent property at every level of life, from the cell to the organ, the body to the brain, the family to the community, the countryside to the city, the industry sector to the economy, and—most importantly of all—from the reality bubbles we all unconsciously inhabit to the ultimate reality of the health of our atmosphere, geosphere, hydrosphere, and biosphere.

In the same way that science can tell us what makes Farewell Spit into such a formidable trap for ships and marine mammals alike, it can also now help us navigate the challenging realities of the Anthropocene, the first geological epoch where one species—our own—has a global impact equal to or greater than geological forces. By leaving things so late, though, we have unwittingly crossed the threshold into a world where change (good, bad, or ugly) that once moved gradually must now happen very suddenly indeed.[17]

Paradoxically, business leaders are often ahead of many of our political leaders and of many of our educators, in terms of what they are willing to say—and, increasingly, what they are willing to do. Somebody to keep a close eye on is Vinod Khosla, the legendary IT investor now funding entrepreneurs developing solutions to a dozen great climate challenges.[18]

But our ability to do more can be limited by the lack of relevant talent. Over the last decade, we have seen a ten-fold increase in the number of jobs with sustainability mentioned in the job description—yet the skills base has not been growing as fast as the opportunities.[19] According to a LinkedIn survey of nearly eight hundred million users, the number of green jobs had grown by eight percent a year over the previous five years, whereas the number of people listing green skills had grown only by six percent.

Years ago, I spoke to more than sixty professors working on sustainability around the world. The event was hosted by the fabled Wharton School, part of the University of Pennsylvania, regularly outperforming Harvard at the time. After the session, Wharton's dean came up and said that, ultimately, sustainability would be the framing for everything that business schools taught. So, are they nearly there? In most cases, sadly, not even close. Still, introducing its 2023 ranking of MBA courses around the world, the *Financial Times* did explain that a major revamp of the methodology marked an effort "to track and encourage an embrace of people, purpose and planet, alongside profit, in business."[20]

UN Secretary-General António Guterres has made it abundantly clear what we must now do: "The 1.5-degree limit of global warming agreed in the Paris Agreement is achievable," he has said, "but it will take a quantum leap. Every country and every sector must massively fast-track climate efforts. We need climate action on all fronts—everything, everywhere, all at once. I am suggesting an Acceleration Agenda to supercharge these efforts."[21] A brave assertion from someone who is meant to be supremely apolitical.

One way Volans helps educators embrace this Acceleration Agenda is by partnering with business schools like Shizenkan University in Tokyo, Japan, and IESE in Barcelona, Spain, through their "Future of Capitalism" program, led by Dr. Tomo Noda. Noda-san worked in leadership at Harvard, INSEAD, and MIT, then founded Shizenkan as a business school "for the twenty-second century." That is the sort of ambition and spirit we must now spread to all business education, indeed all education.

Our increasingly fractal vision of health and of sustainability must be complemented by a similarly fractal approach to education, with every age group worldwide helped on to—and then boosted up—the relevant learning curves. Much of this will continue to happen in educational institutions, but the internet now offers unparalleled opportunities for continuous learning throughout life.

Tickling Sharks has been a significant step in my own lifelong learning journey—and I hope it will help at least some readers with theirs. Exposing my thinking to the wider world has always brought benefits, including uncomfortable insights. This time around, for example, Earth Day founder Denis Hayes noted, "I was struck once again by the difficulty one occasionally faces distinguishing a Dolphin from a Shark. Exxon is clearly a Great White; Patagonia clearly a Dolphin. Others are ambiguous, or perhaps chimeras."

He went on to say, "You have a nice anecdote up front about 3M, a company about which, for much of my life, I had a generally positive attitude. But its powerful role in filling the world with 'forever chemicals,' while lying about it to government officials and others for decades and decades, may ultimately bring the company to its knees. This stuff is never easy."

Indeed—and it has been no part of my self-appointed role to pretend otherwise. Instead, my aim has been to explore and share what I discovered. My theory of change, such as it is, could be summed up as this: get accurate data on key trends, turn it into timely, credible information and usable market intelligence, and then, over time, we may all acquire some greater degree of collective wisdom—and work out how to work in the longer-term interests of all life.

I have no clue how all this will end, but—like most of us—I have my ambitions and my hopes. By way of a conclusion, I love the notion, sometimes attributed to Orson Welles, that if you want a happy ending, it all depends on where you decide to stop your story. For the moment, I will stop it here, just ahead of the coda and Tim Smit's afterword. Thank you for joining me on this leg of the journey. Any thoughts on what we might do together next?

CODA AND MANIFESTO

Tackling Sharks

How to help powerful people and institutions do what they don't yet want to do

Because we have left things so late, many of the coming changes will be shockingly sudden. The real question is whether we will choose to proceed in a more orderly, strategic manner or whether we will allow the chaos to continue building all around us. I am generally optimistic because, even if only some businesses, economies, and societies will transform themselves in time, their success can provide useful models for others less advanced on the path—and help drive down the costs of transformation.

One key conclusion is signaled by the book's very title. In all forms of human engagement, your approach must be seductive enough to pull in at least some members of your target audience, not least so they continue to listen. But it is rarely enough to tickle; we must tackle too. Tackling not just the individuals we are trying to persuade, but the system, the paradigm, that they operate within—and the assumptions they imbibed along with their mother's milk and their MBAs. Or perhaps I should say *we*.

The important thing, as Albert Einstein put it, is not to stop questioning. I rode the environmentalist wave because I was curious about nature and the wider biosphere. Then I moved into the business world because I was curious about what people were doing there—and how they saw the change agenda. Next, I found myself in boardrooms around the world, not because I was an obvious choice but because I was curious to know what top teams thought and how they saw and pulled the levers of power.

I know that I have been privileged in my ethnic background, white in a largely white business world. Male in a world still largely shaped by men. Educated, with several degrees to my name. And with, another privilege, the global perspective imprinted by my family's early travels. But more important than any of these, in terms of getting me into the corridors of corporate power, were my voracious appetites for reading and, crucially, writing.

Successive chapters of this book have sketched the slow, halting process by which we have been evolving a global consciousness—a vital first step in creating a concerted global will to drive systemic change. They have tracked successive waves of change: rising, falling, receding, and rebounding. Unfortunately, the chances are that a great deal more turbulence, disruption, and agony will be needed before the world decides to act as if we were genuine stewards of the planet—stewards in the interest of all life, for all time.

My default setting has always been to nonviolence, in the belief that violence feeds on itself. But the longer the system goes on unchanged, the more we must consider other alternatives. As I wrote this final section of the book, I read Andreas Malm's book *How to Blow Up a Pipeline*, a counter-history of social movements.[1] He concludes that every major change movement, even the most committed to nonviolence, has relied at some point on the shocks created by violence.

Meanwhile, for as long as powerful people resist change, we must conceal at least some of our intentions. Think of Odysseus's Greeks outside the walls of ancient Troy: disruptive intentions hidden in plain view. Indeed, it's easy to imagine a new breed of Trojan Sharks or Trojan Orcas pretending to be more aggressively capitalist than they are, while aiming to inject disruptive change agendas into the citadels of power, be they boardrooms or cabinet rooms. By pretending to be a predator, you might get closer into the predatory action, enabling you to exert more effective pressure from within.

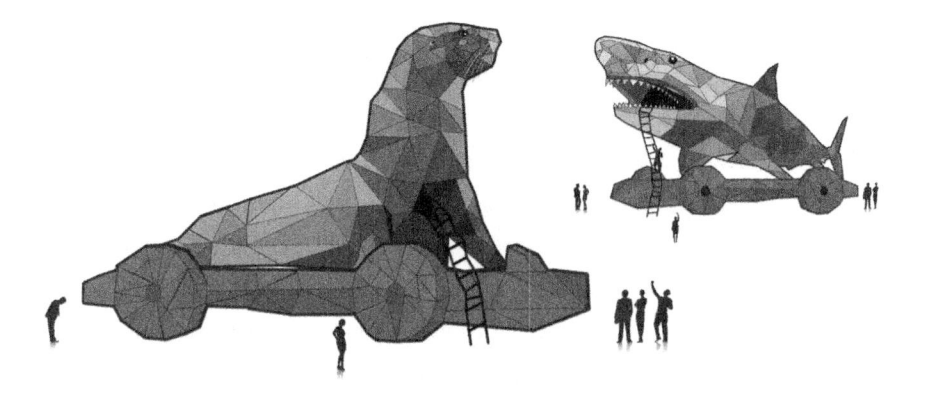

Expect Trojan Sea Lions and Trojan Sharks (Silvio Rebêlo for Volans, 2024)

Contrariwise, we have already seen similar ploys adopted by those wanting to disrupt well-intentioned change processes. Trojan Sea Lions and even Trojan Dolphins have trundled through the political landscapes in places like Washington, DC, and Brussels. In what some call "false flag" environmentalism, those opposed to offshore wind farms, perhaps because they work in the fossil fuel sector, may claim to be acting in the interest of whales.

Any emerging change agenda will be gamed, particularly by those with capital sunk in the old, unsustainable status quo. As the sustainability and linked agendas mainstream, their conclusions and recommendations will be seen as increasingly consequential—so becoming more political, more politicized. Some may conclude that we should simply stand back and let all this disruption rip. By contrast, I believe that we must work ever harder to reduce the destructive social, economic, and political impacts. If not, vital system change processes will be slowed, diverted, or derailed.

So, for what they're worth, here are ten lessons I have learned through all the adventures—and misadventures—described earlier:

1. **If you want to speak truth to power, have a word with yourself first.** Know who you are, what you stand for, and how you are likely to be experienced by others. We all have our flaws, our weak spots, so a little self-knowledge goes a long way. Above all, try not to become emotional even when talking about emotive subjects. Sharks are acutely sensitive to signs of distress.

    Know, too, that many powerful people do not feel remotely as powerful as you might imagine. Some will know all too well that change is coming, even as they try to avoid speaking about it, let alone delivering it.

    Be careful, too, of focusing all your attention on those with their hands on today's levers of power. One critic of the "speaking truth to power" idea has been Noam Chomsky. His assessment: "Power knows the truth already and is busily concealing it."[2] It is the powerless, he has argued, who need to know what is going on and to be motivated to drive change.

2. **Meet Sharks where they are, not where you'd like them to be.** If Sharks prowl the market equivalents of beaches, reefs, or oceanic depths, you must be in those places, too. If they travel the world by helicopter and limousine, be bold: hitch a ride or catch them during stopovers. Alternatively, find a way to tickle their market and political antennae. Just as sharks have exquisitely sensitive electrosensors in their snouts, so most successful capitalists are acutely tuned to the movement of the relevant market forces.

    Again, don't assume Sharks are ignorant of your agenda: many will know full well what is coming but conclude they have no option but to buy time and protect sunk capital owned by themselves or those they work for. Generally, too, they will assume that if things really do go belly up, they can sell out at the last moment to "greater fools." They imagine that they can judge the retreating tide in such a way as to escape while others are stranded.

Remind them of the sort of market corrections described by economist Hyman Minsky. Hint that they may find themselves not just on the wrong side of coming Minsky moments, when people suddenly wake up to a very different reality than the one they had been operating in, but on the wrong side of history, too.

3. **Resist the urge to cling to like-minded people.** We all do it, consorting with those we know, people we like—or at least can tolerate when we don't know anyone else in the room. Once inside a corporation, it's easier to orbit around chief sustainability officers than it is to engage CFOs or chief legal officers. But it's crucial to break out of your comfort zone by moving into areas where the fiercer fish gather, including some of the predators that most people in their right minds would stay well away from.

Find ways to edge into their groupings and conversations. Accept rebuffs as part of the game. If you're meeting at an event, ask them how well they know the organizers or speakers. Are they regulars at the event? How has it changed over time? Let them display how well connected they are, then tease out key conversational threads. Ask questions, build on the answers—and, again, tease.

It's odd how this kind of well-judged teasing can reframe a conversation, making it more personal, less obviously confrontational. It also speaks to a very different relationship than the one such people assume they are in.

4. **Try not to look like prey.** Most fossil fuel industry executives are unlikely to stop and chat if you are sporting a "Just Stop Oil" T-shirt or similar. We are dealing with market and political predators, keen to ward off those with hostile intent. The more existential they imagine the threat to be, the more inclined they will be to turn tail—or go for your jugular. Look them in the eye. Meet them

where they are. Ensure that they see you as somehow their equal, even if from a different part of the forest.

Know your facts but don't brandish them like a weapon. Your ability to project quiet confidence will be key, signaling strength. Listen intently before you speak. Decode the weak signals in what you are being told, clues as to what other people are intrigued by or worried about.

Still, where I have been left with no option, I have sometimes spoken directly across powerful people or carefully ignored them to talk to others—because the reptilian side of their brains understands these signals or can be confused by them.

And, while it may sound Machiavellian, ensure that the leaders you're targeting see you speaking to someone else, ideally someone they respect, before zeroing in on them. Then lead with an unexpected question, like one of these: "What's your shelf-life in your current role?" "Who do most admire among your competitors?" or even "Who chose your socks?"

5. **Avoid being forced into elevator pitches.** It can help if you distill your message and agenda into a single line, of course. But, wherever possible, break frame. Sharks and Orcas are pitched to each and every day of their frenzied lives. People are desperate for their attention, buy-in, and sign-off. If you allow them to impose that game on you, you have already lost.

If your target audience only has forty-five seconds to understand something as complex as the climate or biodiversity emergencies, they will be impervious to external inputs. Sharks often roll their eyes back, exposing a piece of thick cartilage, to protect their vision from struggling prey. Expect human Sharks to do the same. Watch out for those rolled eyes.

Even if you are not attacked directly, you risk being a raindrop on their Teflon or Gore-Tex. They have been trained to focus on the material challenges, the ones that could have real financial consequences. The challenge here is to be Velcro to their Velcro. To persuade them that you—and your change agenda—might be material.

6. **Don't adopt missionary positions.** It's not enough to be right, though it helps. It's almost always a mistake to insist too early, to hector your audience, however intense your own conviction and feelings may be. Powerful people know who they don't want to talk to—and imagine they know what those people look and sound like. Bluntly, most of them hate missionaries.

   So, approach them from an unexpected angle—in their club, through their family, at an event where they are separated from their minders. Find them, if you can, in moments where they are more human, exposed, vulnerable, open. Encourage them to believe that you might just be one of them, from their side of life's tracks.

   Whistleblowers can be a powerful force for change, but whistleblowing can also wreck careers and lives. In my mind, then, it should be a last resort—though in today's world few leaders worth their salt will fully discount the risk of such leaks and exposures. Blackmail is bad, clearly, but consider a dilute form of *greenmail*. Let your targets know that the world may be a little more porous than they would like. Suggest that the bad news is already leaking.

7. **Don't assume that all Sharks or Orcas are evil.** Some are, no question, and most represent some form of danger to other people's lives, limbs, or reputations. We must be prepared to tackle the deadliest Sharks with everything at our disposal. Sometimes, even before we get to that point, they may try to take a preemptive bite out of us, because of territoriality, frustration, or sheer force of habit.

   If you do find yourself headed into the jaws of death, a well-placed punch in the personal or corporate nose may distract predators long enough for you to escape—or, counterintuitively, to slip in deeper.

But remember that many leaders are reflections of the systems that trained, selected, and now incentivize them. Remove one, get a clone. The only real way forward is to change the incentives, transform the training and selection processes, and ultimately change the economic context that determines priorities and behavior.

8. **Avoid breathing your own exhaust fumes.** It's too easy to be taken in by one's own propaganda. Even if you win prizes awarded by others, don't imagine you're home and dry. Use outsiders, including your organization's board and advisory board appointments, to tap into different perspectives. Pull in your most vociferous critics—and try taking them seriously.

   Assume, too, that any success you achieve will always be partial—and may well conjure new risks and controversies. Know that if solving these challenges were easy, others would have cracked the problem by now—and be enjoying the glory. Generally, they haven't and aren't. One key reason: most people think the necessary changes are impossible, even unthinkable.

   So, remember, many things we take for granted in today's world were considered impossible yesterday. Soviet communism looked unstoppable, until it wasn't. The internet was the stuff of science fiction, until it became ubiquitous. The dominance of the internal combustion engine seemed total, its demise unthinkable, until—electrifyingly—it began to crumble.

9. **Encourage leaders to get out more—and take your own medicine.** Powerful people are some of the most sheltered folk on earth. Too often, they are insulated from other people's realities, which is risky for all concerned. Offer them an opportunity to see different realities up close.

   I have accompanied leaders as they traveled to places as varied as Japan's biotech sector, Silicon Valley, and an array of slums around Nairobi, Kenya. Recommend unusual learning journeys for leaders and their senior teams. And, crucially, suggest ways for them to better engage their younger colleagues, whose futures their organization may be compromising, intentionally or not. Encourage them to appoint a youth board, to bring future generations directly into today's decision-making.

10. **Recognize that whatever you do—and however well you do it—the work of others is more important.** That said, I have long loved the advice often attributed to anthropologist Margaret Mead: "Never doubt that a small group of thoughtful, committed citizens can change the world; indeed, it's the only thing that ever has."[3] What we do as individuals counts, true, and can be crucial in bending the curves of history, but individuals only ever succeed in driving wider change by building psychological, socioeconomic, and political critical mass.

When we ask activists, campaigners, social entrepreneurs, philanthropists, investors, and the like to explain and account for their impact, we are asking for some sense of their "theory of change"—their understanding of how doing X will lead, directly or indirectly, to outcomes Y, Z, or A. In our own work, we have never imagined that what we were doing would be sufficient to drive system change. It might be a necessary condition of progress and it might have a cascading, catalytic effect, but it could only ever be a small part of something very much bigger.

That something bigger, many of us tend to assume, will be positive, driving us toward sunny, inclusive uplands, bathed in sustainability and with all major economies humming with circular activity. But if you pause for a moment and consider the rise of QAnon in the United States, and of similar mind viruses elsewhere, the future seems much less certain. Nor does it end there. Inaction—and action—on the major challenges of our day will spawn and fuel similar movements worldwide.

True leadership involves taking such dynamics into account.

Tickling and then tackling individual top teams can help get things going—and help remove critical barriers to change. But sooner rather than later, politicians, policymakers, regulators, public sector agencies, educators, and a wide range of other actors must swing in, too, to reshape market conditions and rules.

Taming market predators and parasites will sometimes involve persuasion and sometimes require penalties—including lawsuits, fines, and imprisonment. New forms of crime must be prosecuted. But the biggest punishment for some of those lagging the curve will be that they end up in what Leon Trotsky dubbed "the dustbin of history."

Glory Days—and Manifesto

As for me, I seem to be morphing into some sort of sustainability elder. The key question is how I can be a useful one. Human nature being what it is, we will not run out of market predators any time soon, or of "predatory delay"—where those with strandable assets lobby frantically to protect forms of value creation that undermine the interests of the wider world. Still, I may need to rein in the "tickling Sharks" aspects of my work in favor of ramping up the "schooling Dolphins" side, empowering and supporting those making and shaping tomorrow's change waves.

Among the market Dolphins I have long admired is RE100, an initiative convened by the Climate Group, bringing together large numbers of businesses committed to consuming only renewable electricity. The aim: to mobilize market forces to power the sustainable energy revolution. Last time I looked, there were a lot more than one hundred companies involved: 420, to be precise. An A-to-Z of some of the best-known businesses in the world and a bunch of others you won't have heard of.

A favorite sustainability wavemaker of mine is Nick Hounsfield—and he does it literally, as I saw a few days before *Tickling Sharks* entered final production. Very much in the spirit of the "power of unreasonable people," he told me that his approach is "bonkers," a very British term meaning crazy. I was in Bristol to speak at the 2023 Blue Earth Summit, and the possibility of dropping in on Nick's project, The Wave, had been on my mind since the invitation to speak appeared. He and I had first met earlier that same year at an awards ceremony.

We were celebrating the architectural and planning firm WWA's winning of the Queen's Award for Enterprise in the area of sustainable development. And one of their flagship projects, I discovered, had been The Wave. I was welcomed onto the WWA stage by Chris Hines, founder of Surfers Against Sewage (as mentioned in chapter 4), whom I had first met in 1992. Later, he worked with Nick on evolving The Wave.

They told me that they had built the concept around my idea of the triple bottom line. From 2012, it took seven years to develop the £25 million surfing lake project—powered by one hundred percent renewable electricity. Its "Wavegarden Cove" technology creates up to a thousand waves an hour of varying sizes and shapes.

Nick has long been an activist for "blue health," exploring how the body and mind respond to being in, or near, water. Among others, he has worked with legendary Irish surfer and social scientist Easkey Britton, also mentioned in chapter 4. She helped by pulling together more than thirty studies exploring the health benefits of water-based sports for both body and mind. Among the benefits for local youngsters were increased confidence, self-esteem, and resilience. In 2019, surf therapy was made available to children through doctors' prescriptions via Britain's National Health Service.

One Wave project that snagged my attention had first been mentioned to me by Easkey when I interviewed her for *Tickling Sharks*. Now Nick—and The Wave's latest impact report—filled me in on the background. The Wave team had woken up to the fact that most wetsuits are made of a synthetic rubber called neoprene, the commercial name for chloroprene rubber, based on a toxic, carcinogenic chemical process. There is only one chloroprene plant in the United States, owned by the Japanese chemical company Denka. It squats in southern Louisiana at the heart of a region known as "Cancer Alley," where the cancer risk is fifty times the national average. This, The Wave team says, is completely out of line with its triple bottom line approach, so it is working on non-neoprene alternatives for its own wetsuits.

The Wave team is also now working on future surfing centers in cities like London. I love the idea of being able to surf in my home city, even if by then I'll be in my eighties. For me, though, one lesson from visiting the project was that we must now move beyond tracking and surfing today's societal waves of change to creating tomorrow's waves. Yes, there will be continuing disruptions caused by pandemics, wars, and financial crashes, but our unwavering aim must be to build great, thundering waves of social, political, and market change. All on the path to a truly regenerative economy.

Tickling Sharks combines elements of a memoir and a manifesto. Let's now turn to that second element. Even at this stage in life, I cannot imagine retiring voluntarily—given that we will likely see more change in the next 10–15 years than in the past 50. With breakthroughs racing breakdowns, I am excited and alarmed in equal measure. Indeed, history suggests that the final stages of a paradigm shift can be mind-bendingly abrupt and far-reaching. So, against that backdrop, my personal manifesto might run as follows:

1. When it comes to sustainability, we are—at best—approaching the end of the beginning. We should celebrate incremental change and grassroots activism wherever we encounter them, supporting those starting out on their journeys, doing what they can, where they can. But incrementalism will not—cannot—save us. Instead, we must learn how to be powerful, all-in champions for the system change now urgently needed across our politics, societies, and economies.

2. As, I believe, the world's first "chief pollinator," I will continue poking my nose into other people's business—helping them to connect *tomorrow's* dots. I will seek out people and organizations wanting to deliver systemic change in timely, effective, inclusive, and, above all, sustainable ways—helping them do more, better, faster.

3. By speaking tomorrow's truth to today's power, I will prioritize responsible, resilient, and ultimately regenerative outcomes—investing any reputation I may have accumulated along the way in supporting edgier, more speculative ventures less interested in system efficiency than in system transformation.

4. While guiding leaders wanting to scan wider, probe deeper, aim higher, and think differently, I will continue to evolve the societal pressure waves analysis sketched on page 109. And, as interest in the regenerative economy grows, I will continue to counsel decision-makers on what it might be like to be on the wrong side of history—and what it will take to be on the right sides.

5. The further back we can see into history, the further we can peer into the future. As a witness to much relevant history, and while my memory lasts, I will aim to share my understanding of events with anyone learning from how the societal pressure waves tracked in early chapters began, evolved, and, in some cases, ran out of steam.

6. Without being a Pollyanna, I will accentuate the positive wherever it is possible and sensible to do so. Too often pessimism can be self-fulfilling. But however optimistic you may be, change-as-usual approaches won't—can't—deliver the outcomes tomorrow's decision-makers would demand of us if they could vote for, invest in, or otherwise champion system change in today's world.

7. Then, by no means finally, as an aging boomer at a time when many societies are graying, I will encourage older folk to support younger change agents in tackling the "polycrisis" we failed to stop in time. We must contribute emotionally, professionally, politically and, above all, financially. However much we may have done in the past, none of us can retire responsibly from a dysfunctional system that threatens the future of all life, human and non-human. Now that we're all in the same planetary boat, it's time to step up—or jump overboard.

As for you, dear reader, thank you for your interest and for your own work—past, present, and future. I shall end here by wishing a fair wind to all those working to turn today's sustainability thinking into tomorrow's businesses, markets, and economies. We face immense challenges, but such times—when a long-evolving paradigm upends, like a vast iceberg turning turtle—can be both exhilarating and rewarding for those able to find and stay on their feet and, when needs must, who know how to swim.

And a final thought. Over the years, a surprising number of younger friends and colleagues have noted, somewhat wistfully, that they wished that they had been around for the "glory days, the golden years" of the sustainability revolution. My heartfelt reply: they're still to come.

AFTERWORD

Sir Tim Smit

Early in 2019, I had an experience that transformed the way I saw the world. Dragged by two much younger men to the summit of the biggest tree in the world, a giant sequoia in the Sierra Nevada Mountains of Northern California, I surveyed the western horizon: the unbroken greenery of Sequoia National Park. To the east, the harsh landscape of Death Valley. Here, atop this four-thousand-year-old giant, I thought of the (at least) thirty-seven civilizations that had come and gone in the course of its life.

Each age was possessed of people of wisdom who nonetheless bore witness to the decline and fall of something they believed to be eternal. What hope have we, with our much greater numbers, consumed by similar conceits? We have our share of thundering Old Testament prophets, with their narratives of doom, alongside peddlers of miracle technologies cast as gods to deliver on our varied aspirations for a better life.

It was here, amid the deafening background noise, that I heard the voice of a quiet man, possessed not of certainty nor of autocratic instinct, but one who looked at the world as it was for all its flaws—and set about suggesting an improvement here, another one there, knowing that overnight sensations were for unworldly idealists.

Our hero is an idealist—one who realized early on that capitalism was a lazy target and began to build a confederacy, untouched by the personal vanity of wishing to preside over a movement. Instead, he sought to put in place connections and processes that allowed for the surfacing of something very powerful indeed, a moral compass.

And speaking of compasses, I was once present when the author Philip Pullman lost his temper with an academic-espousing conviction politician. Philip banged the table with his fist, silencing all around him. "Show me a conviction politician," he stormed, "and I'll show you a zealot—and to them are harnessed most all the evils of the world." Instead, he concluded, "Give me a pragmatist with a heart of gold, for that way redemption lies."

Readers, may I have the privilege of introducing you to a man I'm proud to call friend, a man who has shaped the direction of travel for so many, a man whose twinkling smile and bookish eyebrows can light up any room. I give you John Elkington, the ultimate pragmatist with a heart of gold.

There is no one living that I know who has made a bigger contribution to our quest to find the best in ourselves. It has been done without shouting, without arrogance, with mercifully little jargon (with a few minor lapses). All over the world, companies, organizations, and people have moved toward his worldview, which of course he modestly describes as a collective evolution.

Now that evolutionary process is reaching an inflection point, beyond which things will change—for good or ill—at unprecedented speed. As John says, we will break down or we will break through. The needle of our compass is shifting powerfully, from thought leadership to thoughtful, urgent, and timely action at scale. Businesses, investors, and governments alike are scrambling to demonstrate the necessary scale of ambition, no longer talking in terms of millions and billions but of trillions.

In this, his manifesto, John has sketched exciting pathways into this future, for himself, for Volans, and ultimately for all of us. A world fit for giant sequoias and for the young of all species. He and I share a hero in R. Buckminster Fuller, whose seminal work was written in 1969 and titled

Operating Manual for Spaceship Earth. That book still suggests so much about our need to understand that we are part of interconnected systems allowing for no waste—and that we, its crew, have a duty of care to our one planet home.

The sign over every door of Fuller's spaceship read: **No Passengers**. That would have been an excellent subtitle for John's marvelous and highly personal book written about the emergence of ways of thinking and, most importantly, ways of organizing ourselves for the common . . . wealth.

Sir Tim Smit, KBE
Cofounder, The Eden Project
founder, The Lost Gardens of Heligan
https://www.edenproject.com
https://www.heligan.com

Acknowledgments

My biggest debts are to my nuclear families. The first centered on my parents, Pat and Tim.* Unintentionally, they helped turn me into something of an alien in my own country—immersing me in different cultures from early on. They may have sent me to that periodic hell, Glencot, but they also sent me to a virtual heaven in the form of Bryanston. Crucially, they also helped support my undergraduate and postgraduate studies, even if World War II ensured that neither of them had the faintest chance of going to university themselves.

Thank you, too, to my three siblings, Gray, Caroline, and Tessa, who make cameo appearances in the book. And I also acknowledge my in-laws (Christine, Charles), my siblings' former spouses (Christina, John), my nephews and niece (Gabriel, Gil, Juan, Kipp, Rory, Lydia), my first cousins (Isobel, Toby), second cousin (Simon), and godson (Connor).

Second, even closer to home, there has been my own nuclear family. This has centered on Elaine, whom I met in 1968, a year of mind-bending ferment. Crucial next steps came, in 1977 and 1979, with the arrivals of our daughters, Gaia and Hania. I had always wanted daughters—and they have been the gifts that kept on giving.

Then there were the young of several parallel families: the Marches (Molly, Terry, Peggy), the Keays (Jane, Ian), and the Palmers (Nigel,

---

* Here is an early attempt to capture family influences: https://johnelkington.com/about/personal/family/.

Caroline, Debby). And Elaine's original nuclear family, the Waites (Stanley, Margaret, and again, Christine, Charles).

Ian Keay, who also went to Bryanston before being expelled, had a major influence on my early thinking, introducing me to the work of R. Buckminster Fuller back in the sixties, as he (Ian) assembled a geodesic dome out of matchsticks in his bedroom. With hair down to his waist, he also served as our best man in 1973.

Around the same time, we met Carol Crawshaw, whom I studied alongside at University College London's (UCL) school of environmental studies, and her husband Robert, whom, coincidentally, Elaine was working alongside at Oxford University Press. Through Carol, Elaine and I then met Eleo Gordon—and, rather unexpectedly, ended up flat-sharing with her for over a year while I was at UCL. She was an editor at Penguin at the time, later enjoying a spectacular career, and helped me place a couple of early books with Pelican Books.

Then there were the parallel tribes and mentors, many of them wonderfully unreasonable people, as I would later come to call the right sort of agitators and disruptors.* At UCL, I was helped along by Professor Peter Cowan and Joan Davidson, my favorite lecturer at UCL, then by John Roberts and Roger McGlynn at TEST. Later, came all (or most of) those who have worked with the four companies I helped cofound: Environmental Data Services (ENDS) in 1978; John Elkington Associates (JEA), later CounterCurrent, in 1983; SustainAbility in 1987; and Volans in 2008.

Amazingly, all still exist, in one form or another, thanks largely to those who joined to run them as sensible businesses—hardly a pronounced talent of mine.

Many hundreds of people have worked with these organizations, a fair few becoming lifelong friends.† Notable among these have been Max Nicholson at ENDS (alongside David Layton, Marek Mayer, and

---

* And here is an early attempt to capture wider influences: https://johnelkington.com/?s=influences.

† As is the way of the world, at least half a dozen of those named have since died.

Georgina McAughtry, who were also central there); Jonathan Shopley and Nancy Pace at JEA; and then Julia Hailes, Seb Beloe, Maggie Brenneke De-Pree, Tom Burke, Fiona Byrne, Rob Cameron, Sir Geoffrey Chandler, Christèle Delbé, Tom Delfgaauw, Annie Dimmock, Francesca Dixon van Dijk, Oliver Dudok van Heel, Jeff Erickson, Dr. Vernon Jennings, Sam Lakha, Mark Lee, Geoff Lye, Charles Medawar, Tell Münzing, Jane Nelson, Alexander Nick, Kavita Prakash-Mani, J. P. Renault, Nick Robins, Nick Robinson, Will Rosenzweig, Professor Jim Salzman, (Bonnie) Lorraine Smith, Andrea Spencer-Cooke (later Henman), Virginia Terry, Jodie Thorpe, Sophia Tickell, Shankar Venkateswaran, Patrin Watanatada, and Peter Zollinger, among others, at SustainAbility; and Liz Knights (at Victor Gollancz, where she nurtured our green consumer books).

Key friends throughout this period included Steve and Sandar Warshal, with Steve as founding editor of *Greenpeace Business* and later as chair of the Greenpeace Environmental Trust.

Then, at Volans, my thanks go to Pamela Hartigan, Sam Lakha, Charmian Love, and Geoff Lye, alongside Harriet Ayliffe, Yinka Awoyinka, Yoshoda Bhatt, Amy Birchall, Tim Brown, Paul Bunje, Rafael Chairavalloti, Charlene Cranny, Cami Daeninck, Tom Farrand, Amanda Feldman, Siobhán Foster, Clover Hogan, Richard Johnson, Natalie Jude, Laura Kibble, Angèle Latreile, Jacqueline Lim, Jerry Linenger, Alejandro Litovsky, Hannah Maier-Peveling, Bob Massie, Josh Morley-Fletcher, Karsten Ottenberg, Jenny Poulter, Richard Roberts, Louise Kjellerup Roper, Mark Roper, Pauline Silverman, Sir Tim Smit, Nathalie Thong, Sophie Toff, James Vaccaro, Josie Warden, Hoey Wong, and Zheng Jieying.

In terms of my move from SustainAbility to Volans, I owe particular debts to Geoff Lye, Charmian Love, Sophia Tickell, and—most of all—Sam Lakha. A muse and sometimes madcap copilot, Sam held the embryonic Volans together at critical points both in its takeoff and as it passed through buffeting turbulence while gaining height and speed.

When Louise Kjellerup Roper joined us as CEO of Volans, she continued the energetic blurring of interfaces between the professional and personal. I thank her profoundly—alongside the ever-thoughtful Richard Roberts—for picking our small organization up "by the scruff of the neck," as I put it in my original brief to her, preparing us for what was to come.

I owe Louise a huge debt for radically expanding the conversation that is Volans. For, if I have learned anything over the years, it is that I work best in company, in conversation. I also often noted that I work best with other "mutants," people with complex minds and backgrounds. As a Dane living in London, Louise has been a wonderful case in point.

At Fast Company Press, I warmly thank the wonderful team led by Jessica Easto, Jen Glynn, Neil Gonzalez, Judy Marchman, Morgan Robinson, and Daniel Sandoval.

Given our growing focus on the regenerative economy, I thank pioneers like Stewart Brand, Hazel Henderson, Janine Benyus, John Fullerton, Paul Hawken, Daniel Christian Wahl, Kate Raworth, Laura Storm, Giles Hutchins, Andy Middleton, and Jenny Andersson, to name but a few. I am also grateful to Thammy Evans for her help on the security agenda, including a session on the theme at Anthropy 2023, and Pavan Sukhdev of GIST Impact and explorer Paul Rose for several days of conversations in Switzerland as I worked on a late version of the book.

In terms of funders, it may be invidious to pick out some rather than others, but critical funding partners have included Jeff Skoll and Sally Osberg of the Skoll Foundation, and David Blood, Al Gore, Colin Le Duc, and Lila Preston of Generation Investment Management. Without their support, we might well have stalled before we even got going.

At RethinkX, I thank Jamie Arbib, Tony Seba, and Adam Dorr for their optimism and ongoing inspiration. At SYSTEMIQ, I thank Jeremy Oppenheim for ongoing conversations on related themes.

At the Earthshot Prize, I thank Hannah Jones for contributing the foreword to this book. I first worked with her when she was at Nike in the 1990s. When she was appointed CEO of the Earthshot Prize, I was delighted to be afforded an early window into the process. Other members of the Earthshot team I would like to acknowledge here are Lea Borkenhagen and Rachel Moriarty.

Then there are those we have worked alongside in client and partner organizations, a fair few of whom are mentioned in the book. Among these I offer particular thanks to Salla Ahonen while at Neste, alongside Peter Vanacker, Matti Lehmus, and Minna Aila, and Sonja Haut at Novartis, both companies where we have run advisory councils.

I celebrate another fifty or so people who have served on the boards and advisory boards of the four organizations I cofounded—plus a considerably greater number whom I have worked alongside on the more than eighty boards and advisory boards on which I have served. Among these have been leading lights like Mark Campanale of Carbon Tracker, Jane Nelson of the Harvard Kennedy School, Tanya Steele of WWF, and Diana Verde Nieto of Positive Luxury.

In the literary agent world, I thank Andrew Wiley of Curtis Brown, Caroline Dawnay of Peters Fraser + Dunlop (later United Agents), Sara Menguc, and Doris Michaels of DSM Agency.

In Australia and New Zealand, during my SustainAbility days, Murray and Dobrina Edmonds helped build our presence and profile there over almost a decade. Huge thanks to them—and in India, to Rohini Nilekani and Rajni Bakshi.

In terms of my lecturing and visiting professorships, I thank Dr. Mike Tennant at Imperial College London, Professor Emeritus David Grayson at Cranfield University, and Professor Paul Ekins at UCL. At Shizenkan University, we have been delighted to work with Dr. Tomo Noda and Professor Peter-David Pedersen on their Future of Capitalism project.

In terms of Volans's own Tomorrow's Capitalism Inquiry, I thank all those who have supported the initiative but particularly Steve Waygood of Aviva Investors for cohosting our Tomorrow's Capitalism Forum and Nicola Godden for creating the Green Swan Award.

Among those in the media world who published or supported my writing, I thank Dennis Sharp of the *Architectural Association Quarterly*; Dr. Bernard Dixon and Richard "Dick" Fifield of *New Scientist*; Hamish McRae, Harford Thomas, Anthony Tucker, Tim Radford, Peter Clarke, Roger Cowe, Jo Confino, and Caroline Holtum—plus a bevy of others—at the *Guardian*; Kim Loughran and Andrea Spencer-Cooke at *Tomorrow*; and Joel Makower and Heather Clancy at *GreenBiz*.

The Royal Society of Arts was a key platform for my early work, where I worked alongside Timothy Cantell and Helen Holdaway, with Helen later coming across as director of the Environment Foundation, which I chaired.

At Bryanston School, in more recent times, I thank Amanda Lovejoy and her team.

Thanks, too, to John O'Brien, Lucy Knill, and David Williams for their roles in creating Anthropy, and to Cathy Runciman and Lisa Goldapple, both at Atlas of the Future—and then, subsequently, Lisa at TOPIA and Cathy at Brian Eno's EarthPercent.

A tip of the hat, too, to Silvio Rebêlo, my favorite Brazilian living in Russia, for his design of the Volans hummingbird—and for the predatory quartet images for this book (pages 13, 20, 21, 113, 253, 270, 273, and 292). Other designers I have been proud to work with include Tim Moore, Stan Eales, Rupert Bassett (who has helped evolve the waves diagram featured in chapter 4 more or less continuously since the mid-1990s), and Carlo Schifano and Conor Dowse at Twist Creative.

In terms of early editing contributions to this book, I warmly thank my brother Gray Elkington, my colleague Richard Roberts, and Hugh Barker.

In conclusion, my profound thanks to all those mentioned here, to all those not mentioned who should have been, and to anyone and everyone else who has helped along the way.

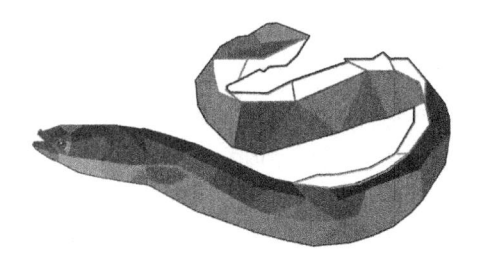

Thank you, too, to those long-ago eels, for my first call to action.
(Image: Silvio Rebêlo)

Notes

Introduction

1. Tim Flannery, *The Future Eaters: An Ecological History of the Australasian Lands and People* (New York: Grove Press, 2002).
2. Jacquelyne Germain, "Steven Spielberg Regrets How 'Jaws' Impacted Real-World Sharks," *Smithsonian*, December 20, 2022, https://www.smithsonianmag.com/smart-news/steven-spielberg-regrets-how-jaws-impacted-real-world-sharks-180981335/.
3. Matt Koller, "California Seamounts Are Sylvia Earle's Newest 'Hope Spots,'" *Hakai Magazine*, June 12, 2019, https://hakaimagazine.com/news/california-seamounts-are-sylvia-earles-newest-hope-spots/.
4. Melanie Haiken, "Sharky Personalities," in *Sharks: Rulers of the Deep*, ed. The Editors of *National Geographic*, July 15, 2022, 45.
5. Jane Martinson and Peter Brabeck-Letmathe, "Smooth Defender of a Tainted Brand," *Guardian*, November 24, 2006, https://www.theguardian.com/business/2006/nov/24/2.
6. The upshot of eighteen months of wrangling was that Nestlé accepted that sustainability was a considerably broader term and agenda than shared value, and added *and sustainability* to its shared value focus.
7. Tom Fletcher, "Giant Ancient Sharks Had Enormous Babies That Ate Their Siblings in the Womb," *Conversation*, January 10, 2021, https://theconversation.com/giant-ancient-sharks-had-enormous-babies-that-ate-their-siblings-in-the-womb-152903.

8. Jennifer Jacquet, "A New Discipline Pushes Back Against Sowing Doubt," *Wired*, December 18, 2022, https://www.wired.com/story/agnotology-misinformation-opinion/.
9. Bartleby [pseud.], "Mighty and High," *Economist*, July 29, 2023, 51.
10. Emily Habeck, *Shark Heart: A Love Story* (London: Jo Fletcher Books, 2023).
11. Rich Co, "Tilikum: Grim History of SeaWorld's Killer Orca That Violently Killed 3 People," *Nature World News*, May 17, 2022, https://www.natureworldnews.com/articles/50854/20220517/violent-killer-orca-behavior-trauma-captivity.htm.
12. Leo Hickman, "James Lovelock: Humans Are Too Stupid to Prevent Climate Change," *Guardian*, March 29, 2010, https://www.theguardian.com/science/2010/mar/29/james-lovelock-climate-change.

Chapter 1

1. Philip Larkin, "This Be The Verse," Poetry Foundation, https://www.poetryfoundation.org/poems/48419/this-be-the-verse.
2. Kevin Drum, "Atomic Tests During the 1950s Probably Killed Half a Million Americans," *Mother Jones*, December 22, 2017, https://www.motherjones.com/kevin-drum/2017/12/atomic-tests-during-the-1950s-probably-killed-half-a-million-americans/.
3. "The History of CND," Campaign for Nuclear Disarmament, https://cnduk.org/who/the-history-of-cnd.
4. Matthias Pappas, "General Orde Wingate: Brilliant Eccentric," War History Online, February 18, 2019, https://www.warhistoryonline.com/history/general-orde-wingate.html.
5. One book that gives a powerful sense of what it was like to be a fighter pilot during World War II is Guy Mayfield's *Life and Death in the Battle of Britain* (London: IWM Publishing, 2018). He was a Royal Air Force chaplain, or padre, helping young men wrestle with their demons—including alcohol—in the face of the daily threat of extinction.
6. Giles Sheldrick, "Battle of Britain Hero Who Led Charmed Life Dies at 98," *Daily Express*, February 5, 2019, https://www.express.co.uk/news/uk/1082974/war-hero-dies-98-years-old-wing-commander-tim-elkington.

7. See, for example, my "Lucky Tim" blog post. John Elkington, "Lucky Tim," *John Elkington* (blog), February 16, 2023, https://johnelkington.com/2023/02/lucky-tim/.

8. Paul Adamson, *None the Wiser: A Mid-Century Passage, 1932–1952* (Kendal, Cumbria, UK: Hayloft Publishing, 2005).

9. Paul Adamson, *Still None the Wiser: A Mid-Century Passage, 1952–1967* (Bloomington, IN: AuthorHouse, 2007).

10. For more on the process as part of flax and linen production in the area, see this blog post: Colerainelass (author), "Walking Along the Roe," *Walking Through 2017 and Beyond* (blog), July 7, 2018, https://walkingthrough2017andbeyond.com/2018/07/10/walking-along-the-roe.

11. John Elkington, "Mill Cottage: Returning to My Source," *John Elkington* (blog), June 23, 2018, https://johnelkington.com/2018/06/mill-cottage-returning-to-my-source.

12. "Famous Graves & Burials," London's Royal Parks, https://www.royalparks.org.uk/parks/brompton-cemetery/explore-brompton-cemetery/famous-graves-and-burials/chief-long-wolf.

13. When I shared a late version of the book with Peter Down of the Ton Class Association, who had served on HMS *Fiskerton* in the early sixties, he commented: "As to *Fiskerton*, the captain's decision to have two small boys on board as passengers, apparently without parental chaperones, would have raised eyebrows of senior officers even in those days—and today it would trigger a witch hunt by the *Daily Mail* [a British tabloid newspaper]."

14. John Elkington, "The Cyprus Marshes," *John Elkington* (blog), February 16, 2023, https://johnelkington.com/2023/02/the-cyprus-marshes/.

15. Elif Shafak, *The Island of Missing Trees* (London: Viking, 2021), 190.

16. John Elkington, "The Hill House Elkingtons," *John Elkington* (blog), February 16, 2023, https://johnelkington.com/2023/02/the-hill-house-elkingtons/.

17. Sheila Farr, "Adams, Leo (b. 1942)," HistoryLink.org, August 7, 2013, https://www.historylink.org/File/10440.

18. "Snow Mountain Ranch and Cowiche Mountain," Washington Trails Association, https://www.wta.org/go-hiking/hikes/snow-mountain-ranch.

19. Among other conservationists who had an impact on my thinking was David Brower, who founded organizations like the Sierra Club and the Earth Island Institute: https://browercenter.org/about/who-was-david-brower/.

20. Ken Robinson, "Slideshow: The Story of a Dream House Named Forestledge," *Westside Seattle*, August 28, 2012, https://www.westsideseattle.com/highline-times/2012/08/28/slideshow-story-dream-house-named-forestledge.

21. Susan Ratcliffe, ed., "Nelson Mandela, 1918–2013: South African Statesman," *Oxford Essential Quotations*, 5th ed. (Oxford: Oxford University Press, 2017), https://www.oxfordreference.com/display/10.1093/acref/9780191843730.001.0001/q-oro-ed5-00007046.

Chapter 2

1. My interest in the world of the Seljuk Turks was fed by reading Ronald Welch's book *Knight Crusader* while I was at school. It won the Carnegie Prize in 1954: https://carnegieproject.wordpress.com/2020/08/12/knight-crusader/. True, there's some period-typical racism, but this is the only book I have read three times. To date.

2. Dava Sobel, *Longitude: The True Story of a Lone Genius Who Solved the Greatest Scientific Problem of His Time* (New York: Bloomsbury USA, 2007).

3. Josh Halliday, "Lucy Letby: NHS Trust Chair Says Hospital Bosses Misled the Board," *Guardian*, August 20, 2023, https://www.theguardian.com/uk-news/2023/aug/20/lucy-letby-nhs-trust-chair-says-hospital-bosses-misled-the-board.

4. "The Earl of Effingham Obituary," *Times*, March 1, 1996.

5. Jules Lubbock, "The Brutal Truth," *RIBA Journal* (October 22, 2014), https://www.ribaj.com/culture/the-brutal-truth.

6. John Elkington, "Third Degree, First Graduation Ceremony," *John Elkington* (blog), July 15, 2014, https://johnelkington.com/2014/07/third-degree-first-graduation-ceremony.

7. "University of Essex: 1968 'Traumatic' Student Protests Remembered," BBC News, May 7, 2018, https://www.bbc.co.uk/news/uk-england-essex-44007112.

8. Matthew Twombly, "A Timeline of 1968: The Year That Shattered America," *Smithsonian*, January 2018, https://www.smithsonianmag.com/history/timeline-seismic-180967503.

9. "1968: The Year That Changed History," *Guardian*, January 17, 2008, https://www.theguardian.com/observer/gallery/2008/jan/17/1.

10. "White Rabbit—Jefferson Airplane Track Was Inspired by Miles Davis, Lewis Carroll—and LSD," *Financial Times*, June 21, 2020, https://ig.ft.com/life-of-a-song/white-rabbit.html.

11. John Elkington, "Giorgos Varlamos," *John Elkington* (blog), August 30, 2020, https://johnelkington.com/2020/08/giorgos-varlamos.

12. The story of Elaine's working life from 1968 to 1977 can be found here: https://elaineelkington.com/biography.

13. I'm not sure I had thought very much about Scandinavia before that, except via the Vikings and the adventures and writing of Thor Heyerdahl, a huge inspiration—whom I later heard speak at London's Royal Geographic Society.

14. "Steal This Book: Abbie Hoffman," full online text of Abbie Hoffman, *Steal This Book* (New York: Pirate Editions, 1971), available through libcom (May 1, 2006), https://libcom.org/article/steal-book-abbie-hoffman.

15. "Paolo Soleri: Artist and Architect," Cosanti online, https://cosanti.com/pages/paolo-soleri. Intriguingly, arcologies pop up in Peter Bacigalupi's 2015 science fiction novel, *The Water Knife*.

16. What we didn't know at the time was that Paolo Soleri would later be accused of sexual abuse, tarnishing his legacy: https://www.theguardian.com/artanddesign/2020/feb/29/paolo-soleri-architect-abuser-arcosanti-utopian-city-steve-rose.

17. The title comes from one of my favorite Bing Crosby songs of the same name, "Don't Fence Me In," (1944, with the Andrews Sisters), though the land-grabbing theme hasn't escaped my notice: https://www.youtube.com/watch?v=hRSjUY5_lG4.

Chapter 3

1. Oleg Komlik, "Karl Marx: Capitalist Production . . . Disturbs the Metabolic Interaction Between Man and the Earth," *Economic Sociology & Political Economy* (blog), January 27, 2015, https://economicsociology.org/2015/01/27/karl-marx-capitalist-production-disturbs-the-metabolic-interaction-between-man-and-the-earth/.

2. A key book in helping me understand the Vietnam War was written by a friend of Gavin Young's, Frances FitzGerald. It was called *Fire in the Lake* (New York: Little, Brown, 1972). I also read *A Bright Shining Lie* by Neil Sheehan (New York: Random House, 1988), and the astounding novel written from the Vietnamese side, *The Sorrow of War: A Novel of North Vietnam* by Bao Ninh. Ninh's novel was first published in Vietnam in 1990, and an English version published in 1996 was edited by Frank Palmos and translated by Phan Thanh Hao.

3. "Quote Origin: Not Every Kind of Problem Someone Has with a Girlfriend or Boyfriend Is Necessarily Due to the Capitalist Mode of Production," Quote Investigator, September 3, 2023, https://quoteinvestigator.com/2023/09/03/capitalist-mode/.

4. David Mikkelson, "Did MLK Say This About Capitalism?" Snopes, January 20, 2020, https://www.snopes.com/fact-check/mlk-capitalism-flow/.

5. Charles A. Reich, *The Greening of America* (New York: Random House, 1970).

6. John Elkington, "A Griffin Mystery," *John Elkington* (blog), March 1, 2020, https://johnelkington.com/2020/03/a-griffin-mystery.

7. Lee Hudson, "Inside Skunk Works, Lockheed's Super-Secret Weapons Facility," *Politico*, September 6, 2021, https://www.politico.com/news/2021/09/06/skunk-works-lockheed-martin-facility-509540. And it hasn't escaped my attention that Roald Dahl, who wrote *Charlie and the Chocolate Factory*, had been a World War II Hurricane pilot.

8. John Elkington, "Rededicating Rolls-Royce Battle of Britain Window," *John Elkington* (blog), October 31, 2015, https://johnelkington.com/2015/10/rededicating-rolls-royce-battle-of-britain-window.

9. Robert F. Dorr and Thomas D. Jones, "P-47 Thunderbolts at the Battle of the Bulge," Warfare History Network, https://warfarehistorynetwork.com/2016/12/09/ordnance-the-republic-p-47-thunderbolt.

10. John Elkington, "The Reykjavik Imperative," *New Scientist*, June 23, 1977, 700–702.
11. Tim Lewis, "Built to Last," *Observer Magazine*, April 3, 2022.
12. Adapted from chap. 13, "The Great Mobilization," in Lester R. Brown, *Plan B 3.0: Mobilizing to Save Civilization* (New York: W. W. Norton, 2008). See http://www.earth-policy.org/book_bytes/2008/pb3ch13_ss1.
13. Brown, *Plan B 3.0*, chap. 13.
14. Brown, Plan B 3.0, chap. 13.
15. "Stewart Brand, President of the Board of Directors," Long Now Foundation, https://longnow.org/people/sb2/.
16. Christopher Potter, "Behind the Most Famous Photograph Ever Taken," *Literary Hub*, February 26, 2018, https://lithub.com/behind-the-most-famous-photograph-ever-taken/.
17. John Elkington, "Cubicles, Boundaries & Gold," *John Elkington* (blog), March 23, 2006, https://johnelkington.com/journal.
18. "Wooly Mammoth Revival," Revive & Restore Genetic Rescue of Endangered and Extinct Species, online resource, https://reviverestore.org/projects/woolly-mammoth.
19. Vern Norviel and Charles Andres, "An Interview with Ryan Phelan: Using Biotechnology to Revive Endangered Species and Restore Damaged Ecosystems," *Life Sciences Report*—Wilson Sonsini (Summer 2020): 11–14. See also, https://reviverestore.org/an-interview-with-ryan-phelan.
20. Patrick Temple-West and Jamie Smyth, "Investors in Fight with Big Pharma over Tapping of Horseshoe Crabs' Blue Blood," *Financial Times*, August 23, 2023.
21. Christine Kenneally, "A 'De-extinction' Company Wants to Bring Back the Dodo," *Scientific American*, January 31, 2023.
22. Moyra Caldecott, "Oliver Caldecott 1925–1989," *Moyra Caldecott: Author, Poet, Artist* (blog), January 28, 2009, https://www.moyracaldecott.co.uk/wdp/oliver-caldecott-1925-1989.
23. Mark Pevsner, "Dieter Pevsner Obituary," *Guardian*, October 3, 2019, https://www.theguardian.com/books/2019/oct/03/dieter-pevsner-obiuary.
24. Elaine Elkington, "Two Lovely Men," *Elaine Elkington* (blog), July 8, 2020, https://elaineelkington.com/2020/07/two-lovely-men.

25. John Simkin, "Studs Terkel," Spartacus Educational, September 1997 (updated May 2023), https://spartacus-educational.com/USAterkel.htm.
26. Stephen Peake, "Godfrey Boyle Obituary," *Guardian*, July 31, 2019, https://www.theguardian.com/environment/2019/jul/31/godfrey-boyle-obituary.
27. "United Nations Conference on Human Settlements—Habitat 1, Vancouver, Canada, 31 May–11 June, 1976," Archived online documents from conferences at the United Nations, 1976, https://www.un.org/en/conferences/habitat/vancouver1976.
28. John Elkington, *The Ecology of Tomorrow's World* (London: Associated Business Press, 1980).
29. John Elkington, *Sun Traps: The Renewable Energy Forecast* (London: Pelican Books, 1984).
30. John Elkington, *The Poisoned Womb: Human Reproduction in a Polluted World* (London: Pelican Books, 1985).
31. John Elkington, *The Gene Factory: Inside the Biotechnology Business* (London: Century Publishing, 1985).
32. L. E. Frailey, *The Sales Manager's Letter Book* (Blackpool, UK: A. Thomas, 1951).

Chapter 4

1. John Elkington, "Jørgen Randers @70: Festschrift and Arøy," *John Elkington* (blog), May 25, 2015, https://johnelkington.com/?s=Randers.
2. "The Women Who Coined the Expression 'Surfing the Internet,'" *SurferToday*, https://www.surfertoday.com/surfing/the-woman-who-coined-the-expression-surfing-the-internet.
3. Chris Hines, personal correspondence via email, September 25, 2020.
4. Susan Casey, *The Wave: In Pursuit of the Rogues, Freaks, and Giants of the Ocean* (New York: Anchor Books, 2010).
5. Casey, *The Wave*, 19.
6. Casey, The Wave, 11.
7. Casey, The Wave, 101.
8. Eric Hobsbawm, *The Age of Extremes: The Short Twentieth Century, 1914–1991* (New York: Pantheon Books, 1994).

Notes

9. James Bradfield Moody and Bianca Nogrady, *The Sixth Wave: How to Succeed in a Resource-Limited World* (Sydney: Random House, 2010).
10. Part of the UK Conservation and Development Programme, a response to the World Conservation Strategy, https://portals.iucn.org/library/efiles/documents/wcs-004.pdf.
11. Carol M. Kopp, "Creative Destruction: Out with the Old, In with the New," Investopedia—Economics, last updated February 20, 2023, https://www.investopedia.com/terms/c/creativedestruction.asp.
12. Learn more about researcher Carlota Perez at http://www.carlotaperez.org.
13. Alvin Toffler, *The Third Wave* (London: William Collins & Sons, 1980).
14. Like many other viewers of the Spielberg film, I suspect, I managed to get my family to the Devils Tower National Monument as part of a cross-country US adventure in the mid-eighties.
15. That said, the results have been tested with experts, including pollsters GlobeScan. The consensus so far is that they are broadly borne out by the results of more statistical research.
16. John Jennings, "The Minsky Moment: Why Stability Leads to Panic and What to Do about It," *Forbes*, January 4, 2021, https://www.forbes.com/sites/johnjennings/2021/01/04/the-minsky-moment-why-stability-leads-to-panic-and-what-to-do-about-it.
17. See Project Breakthrough for more information at http://breakthrough.unglobalcompact.org.
18. *The Breakthrough Effect: How to Trigger a Cascade of Tipping Points to Accelerate the Net Zero Transition*, SYSTEMIQ, 2023, https://www.systemiq.earth/wp-content/uploads/2023/01/The-Breakthrough-Effect.pdf.
19. Azeem Azhar, "The Time for 'Catalytic Government' Is Now," *Wired*, December 17, 2022, https://www.wired.co.uk/article/government-economy-innovation.

Chapter 5

1. *David Attenborough: A Life on Our Planet*, directed by Alistair Fothergill, featuring David Attenborough and Max Hughes, aired October 4, 2020, on Netflix, https://www.netflix.com/gb/title/80216393.

2. "Princess of Wales Conservatory," Royal Botanic Gardens, Kew, https://www.kew.org/kew-gardens/whats-in-the-gardens/princess-of-wales-conservatory.

3. Learn more about the Earthshot Prize at https://earthshotprize.org.

4. Jeff Goodell, "The Man Who Started Earth Day," *Rolling Stone*, April 22, 2020, https://www.rollingstone.com/culture/culture-features/denis-hayes-interview-50th-anniversary-earth-day-987606.

5. John Elkington, "Beware the Wrath of Osiris," *New Scientist*, December 11, 1975, 626.

6. James Lovelock and Sidney Epton, "The Quest for Gaia," *New Scientist*, February 6, 1975.

7. "Gaia Theory," Whole People, https://wholepeople.com/gaia-theory/. Whole People acquired GaiaTheory.org on December 1, 2021.

8. James A. Lake, "Lynn Margulis (1938–2011)," *Nature* 480, 458 (2011), https://doi.org/10.1038/480458a.

9. Lake, "Lynn Margulis."

10. Lake, "Lynn Margulis."

11. Toby Tyrrell, "My Verdict on Gaia Hypothesis: Beautiful but Flawed," *New Scientist*, October 23, 2013, https://www.newscientist.com/article/mg22029400-400-my-verdict-on-gaia-hypothesis-beautiful-but-flawed.

12. University of Exeter Global Systems Institute, "Conference Programme: The Future of Global Systems Thinking: Celebrating James Lovelock's Centenary," Conference through University of Exeter Global Systems Institute, July 29–31, 2019, https://www.lovelockcentenary.info/conference-programme.

13. Arthur Westing, "Nicholas Polunin Obituary," *Independent*, December 16, 1997, https://www.independent.co.uk/news/obituaries/obituary-nicholas-polunin-1289122.html.

14. Elkington, "The Reykjavik Imperative," 700–702.

15. John Elkington, "Reclaiming the Cornish Moonscape," *New Scientist*, January 5, 1978, 13–15.

16. Max Nicholson, *The Environmental Revolution: A Guide for the New Masters of the World* (London: Pelican, 1972).

17. "Max Nicholson," *Desert Island Discs*, BBC Radio 4, September 22, 1995, 40 minutes, https://www.bbc.co.uk/programmes/p0093pbh.

18. Martin Adeney, "Sir Arthur Norman Obituary," *Guardian*, October 10, 2011, https://www.theguardian.com/business/2011/oct/10/sir-arthur-norman-obituary.

19. Jean Oelwang, *Partnering: Forge the Deep Connections that Make Great Things Happen* (New York: Optimism Press, 2022).

20. John Elkington, *The Ecology of Tomorrow's World* (London: Associated Business Press, 1980).

21. Nafeez Ahmed, "MIT Predicted in 1972 That Society Will Collapse This Century. New Research Shows We're on Schedule," *Vice*, July 14, 2021, https://www.vice.com/en/article/z3xw3x/new-research-vindicates-1972-mit-prediction-that-society-will-collapse-soon.

22. "Events, My Dear Boy, Events," Quote Investigator, August 31, 2020, https://quoteinvestigator.com/2020/08/31/events.

23. I had to pay £29.95 for my own article here: https://link.springer.com/article/10.1007/BF02233114. But, to my mind at least, the piece has very much stood the test of time. John Elkington, "Profile of Frank Herbert," *Environmentalist* 1 229–234 (1981), https://doi.org/10.1007/BF02233114.

24. John Elkington, "John Elkington Talks to Sci-fi Great David Brin: Repairing the World," Green Swans Observatory, 2021, https://theobservatory.volans.com/wp-content/uploads/2021/10/David-Brin-interview.final_.pdf.

25. John Elkington, "My Father Took Me to See Einstein Play the Violin," *TOPIA: A World of Good*, August 12, 2022, https://worldoftopia.com/david-brin-john-elkington-conversation/.

26. Elkington, "My Father Took Me to See Einstein."

27. Roman Krznaric, *The Good Ancestor: How to Think Long Term in a Short-Term World* (London: Penguin Books, 2020).

28. Roman Krznaric, "About *The Good Ancestor*," website of Roman Krznaric, https://www.romankrznaric.com/good-ancestor.

29. Gillian Tett, "Colorado River Battle Is a Warning to Us All," *Financial Times*, February 3, 2023.

30. Theodora Sutcliffe, "A Brief History of Cli-Fi," *Means & Matters from Bank of the West*, December 3, 2020,

31. Henry Fountain, "How Bad Is the Western Drought? Worst in 12 Centuries, Study Finds," *New York Times*, February 14, 2022,

https://www.nytimes.com/2022/02/14/climate/western-drought-megadrought.html.

32. "Biographical Data," Lyndon B. Johnson Space Center, August 2001, https://www.nasa.gov/wp-content/uploads/2016/01/linenger_jerry_0.pdf.

33. Interviewed by John Elkington and quoted in John Elkington and Jochen Zeitz, *The Breakthrough Challenge: 10 Ways to Connect Today's Profits with Tomorrow's Bottom Line* (San Francisco: Jossey-Bass/John Wiley, 2014).

34. Personal conversation when author was researching his book *The Breakthrough Challenge* in 2013.

35. "Sir Crispin Tickell Obituary," in Register, *Times*, January 28, 2022, 56.

Chapter 6

1. Apple, "2030 Status | Mother Nature," directed by Rhys Thomas, YouTube, September 12, 2023, video, 05:25, (transcript available), https://www.youtube.com/watch?v=QNv9PRDIhes.

2. Thomas L. Friedman, "Opinion: The Power of Green," *New York Times*, April 15, 2007, https://www.nytimes.com/2007/04/15/opinion/15iht-web-0415edgreen-full.5291830.html.

3. John Elkington, *Sun Traps: The Renewable Energy Forecast* (London: Pelican Books, 1984).

4. John Elkington, *The Poisoned Womb: Human Reproduction in a Polluted World* (London: Pelican Books, 1985).

5. John Elkington, *The Gene Factory: Inside the Biotechnology Business* (London: Century Publishing, 1985).

6. Ted Hughes, "Lobby from Under the Carpet," *Ted Hughes: Collected Poems* (London: Faber and Faber, 2005), 837–838.

7. United States Environmental Protection Agency—Enforcement, "Superfund Liability," last updated May 23, 2023, https://www.epa.gov/enforcement/superfund-liability.

8. Quoted by Ghanaian Foreign Minister Shirley Botchway in "West Africa's Security Challenges Have Repercussions," *Financial Times*, February 2, 2022,

9. Peter Mason, "Sir Geoffrey Chandler Obituary," *Guardian*, April 10, 2011, https://www.theguardian.com/business/2011/apr/10/sir-geoffrey-chandler-obituary.

10. Douglas Rushkoff, "Synopsis: *Throwing Rocks at the Google Bus*," website of Douglas Rushkoff, https://rushkoff.com/books/throwing-rocks-at-the-google-bus/.

11. David Brindle, "Stephen Lloyd Obituary," *Guardian*, August 29, 2014, https://www.theguardian.com/society/2014/aug/29/stephen-lloyd.

12. John Elkington with Julia Hailes and Tom Burke, *Green Pages: The Business of Saving the World* (Abingdon, UK: Routledge, 1988).

13. Petra Kelly, "Do the Impossible," in *Green Pages: The Business of Saving the World* (Abingdon, UK: Routledge, 1988), 36–37.

14. Katrin Bennhold, "She's Green. She's Young. And She Wants to Change Germany," *New York Times*, September 7, 2021, https://www.nytimes.com/2021/09/07/world/europe/annalena-baerbock-germany-greens-chancellor.html.

15. The term came from a 1982 book, *The Official Sloane Ranger Handbook* by Ann Bar. Princess Diana was an early example.

16. John Elkington, *A Year in the Greenhouse: An Environmental Diary* (London: Victor Gollancz, 1990).

17. "The McLibel Trial," McSpotlight.org, https://www.mcspotlight.org/case.

18. John Elkington, Julia Hailes, and Douglas Hill, *The Young Green Consumer Guide* (London: Victor Gollancz, 1990).

19. James Murray, "Obituary: Green Investment Pioneer Tessa Tennant," BusinessGreen, July 11, 2018, https://www.businessgreen.com/news/3035702/obituary-green-investment-pioneer-tessa-tennant.

20. Jonathan Bate, *The Song of the Earth* (Cambridge, MA: Harvard University Press, 2002).

21. Deborah D'Souza, "Understanding the Green New Deal and What's in the Climate Proposal," Investopedia, updated May 28, 2022, https://www.investopedia.com/the-green-new-deal-explained-4588463.

22. "The European Green Deal," European Commission, https://ec.europa.eu/info/strategy/priorities-2019-2024/european-green-deal_en.

Chapter 7

1. World Commission on Environment and Development, *Our Common Future* (Oxford: Oxford University Press Academic, 1987).
2. Gro Harlem Brundtland, *Madam Prime Minister: A Life in Power and Politics* (New York: Farrar, Straus and Giroux, 2005).
3. "Gro Harlem Brundtland: Member of The Elders," The Elders, https://www.theelders.org/profile/gro-harlem-brundtland.
4. United States Environmental Protection Agency, "Bill Ruckelshaus, 1932–2019: Remembering EPA's First, and Fifth, Administrator," last updated Jun 7, 2023, https://www.epa.gov/history/bill-ruckelshaus-1932-2019.
5. John Elkington, "RIP Richard Neville, Censorship Warrior," John *Elkington* (blog), September 5, 2016, https://johnelkington.com/2016/09/rip-richard-neville-censorship-warrior/.
6. Learn more about the ERM SustainAbility Institute at https://www.sustainability.com.
7. International Union for Conservation of Nature and Natural Resources, "World Conservation Strategy: Living Resource Conservation for Sustainable Development," (paper, 1980), https://portals.iucn.org/library/efiles/documents/wcs-004.pdf.
8. We produced three reports: *Double Dividends? US Biotechnology and Third World Development* (1986), *The Shrinking Planet: US Information Technology and Sustainable Development* (with Jonathan Shopley, on IT and satellite remote sensing, 1988), and *Cleaning Up: US Waste Management Technology and Third World Development* (with Jonathan Shopley, on waste management and clean technology, 1989).
9. Camilla Toulmin, "IIED: The First 40 Years . . .," Richard Sandbrook's Place (website), January 2013, https://www.richardsandbrooksplace.org/camilla-toulmin/iied-first-40-years.
10. Toulmin, "IIED."
11. Toulmin, "IIED."
12. Chris Choi, "James Erlichman Obituary," *Guardian*, December 11, 2018, https://www.theguardian.com/media/2018/dec/11/james-erlichman-obituary.
13. John Elkington, "James Erlichman: Wolf as Sheep, or Vice Versa?" John *Elkington* (blog), December 16, 2018, https://johnelkington.com/2018/12/james-erlichman-wolf-as-sheep-or-vice-versa.

14. John Harris, "Freedom for Frestonia: The London Commune That Cut Loose From the UK," *Guardian*, October 30, 2017, https://www.theguardian.com/cities/2017/oct/30/frestonia-london-commune-squatters.
15. An inspiration, I suspect, for my self-appointed role as an Ambassador from the Future.
16. Walter Schwarz, "Obituary: Nicholas Albery," *Guardian*, June 8, 2001, https://www.theguardian.com/news/2001/jun/08/guardianobituaries.books.
17. Stephen Peake, "Godfrey Boyle Obituary," *Guardian*, July 31, 2019, https://www.theguardian.com/environment/2019/jul/31/godfrey-boyle-obituary.
18. Learn more about Common Ground UK at https://www.commonground.org.uk.
19. "Apple Day," Common Ground online resource, https://www.commonground.org.uk/apple-day/.
20. John Vidal, "Energy Efficiency Guru Amory Lovins: 'It's the Largest, Cheapest, Safest, Cleanest Way to Address the Crisis,'" *Guardian*, March 26, 2022, https://www.theguardian.com/environment/2022/mar/26/amory-lovins-energy-efficiency-interview-cheapest-safest-cleanest-crisis.
21. John Elkington, "Towards the Sustainable Corporation: Win-Win-Win Business Strategies for Sustainable Development," *California Management Review* 36, no. 2 (January 1994), https://doi.org/10.2307/41165746.
22. Here is Shell's version: https://www.shell.com.ng/sustainability/environment/ogon-issue/ken-saro-wiwa.html. See also, a wider view from the *New York Times*: Patricia Cohen, "A Writer's Violent End, and His Activist Legacy," *New York Times* May 4, 2009, https://www.nytimes.com/2009/05/05/books/05wiwa.html. And more critical views can be found here via Wikipedia: https://en.wikipedia.org/wiki/Ken_Saro-Wiwa.
23. Toby Sterling, "Activists Demand End of Shell, Fossil Fuel at Shareholder Meeting," Reuters, May 21, 2019, https://fr.reuters.com/article/us-shell-agm-protests-idUSKCN1SR0YV.

24. For a discussion of what Exxon knew when, see: https://www.theguardian.com/business/2023/jan/12/exxon-climate-change-global-warming-research.
25. Gregory Meyer, "Clean Energy Group NextEra Surpasses ExxonMobil in Market Cap," *Financial Times*, October 2, 2020, https://www.ft.com/content/39a70458-d4d1-4a6e-aca6-1d5670bade11.
26. Ma Tianjie, "Pan Yue's Vision of Green China," *China Dialogue*, March 8, 2016. https://chinadialogue.net/en/pollution/8695-pan-yue-s-vision-of-green-china/.
27. John Elkington, "Beijing," *John Elkington* (blog), January 17, 2011, https://johnelkington.com/2011/01/beijing/.
28. Roula Koulaf, "Japan Reacts over Rare Earths Ban," *Financial Times*, September 28, 2010, https://www.ft.com/content/4781ea2e-cb2b-11df-95c0-00144feab49a.
29. "Vision 2050: Time to Transform," (publication, World Business Council for Sustainable Development, March 20, 2021), https://www.wbcsd.org/Overview/About-us/Vision-2050-Time-to-Transform/Resources/Time-to-Transform.
30. Sally Howard, "Hello, Dolly: Meet the Barbie Fans Getting Ready for a Fabulous Year," *Observer Magazine*, January 29, 2023.

Chapter 8

1. Daniel Terdiman, "Elon Musk at SXSW: 'I'd Like to Die on Mars, Just Not on Impact,'" CNET, March 9, 2013, https://www.cnet.com/culture/elon-musk-at-sxsw-id-like-to-die-on-mars-just-not-on-impact/.
2. Charlie Northcott, "Obama's 'Historic' Conservation Legacy Beats Teddy Roosevelt," BBC News, January 4, 2017, https://www.bbc.co.uk/news/world-us-canada-38311093.
3. For more information, see, for example: https://impactmanagementproject.com/impact-management/impact-management-norms.
4. Peter T. Kilborn, "Hurricane Reveals Flaws in Farm Law as Animal Waste Threatens North Carolina Water," *New York Times*, October 17, 1999, https://www.nytimes.com/1999/10/17/us/hurricane-reveals-flaws-in-farm-law-as-animal-waste-threatens-n-carolina-water.html.

5. National Highway Traffic Administration, "Firestone Recalls," news release, October 4, 2001, https://icsw.nhtsa.gov/nhtsa/announce/press/firestone/Update.html.

6. For a useful insight into the early stages of the relationship, see Jeff Guinn, *The Vagabonds: The Story of Henry Ford and Thomas Edison's Ten-Year Road Trip* (New York: Simon & Schuster, 2019).

7. John Elkington and Pamela Hartigan, *The Power of Unreasonable People: How Social Entrepreneurs Create Markets That Change the World* (Cambridge, MA: Harvard Business School Press, 2008).

8. Fast Company Staff, "Q&A: John Elkington," *Fast Company*, December 1, 2007, https://www.fastcompany.com/693595/qa-john-elkington.

9. Ruth Bender, "How Bayer-Monsanto Became One of the Worst Corporate Deals—in 12 Charts," *Wall Street Journal*, August 28, 2019, https://www.wsj.com/articles/how-bayer-monsanto-became-one-of-the-worst-corporate-dealsin-12-charts-11567001577.

10. Philip Case, "Bayer and NFU Battling to Overturn Neonicotinoids Ban," *Farmers Weekly*, June 4, 2020, https://www.fwi.co.uk/arable/crop-management/bayer-and-nfu-battling-to-overturn-neonicotinoids-ban.

11. "Delivering a Smoke-Free Future," Philip Morris International, https://www.pmi.com/our-transformation/delivering-a-smoke-free-future.

12. John Elkington, "Twenty-Five Years Ago, I Coined the Phrase 'Triple Bottom Line.' Here's Why It's Time to Rethink It," *Harvard Business Review*, June 25, 2018, https://hbr.org/2018/06/25-years-ago-i-coined-the-phrase-triple-bottom-line-heres-why-im-giving-up-on-it.

13. John Elkington, "Saving the Planet from Ecological Disaster Is a $12 Trillion Opportunity," *Harvard Business Review*, May 4, 2017, https://hbr.org/2017/05/saving-the-planet-from-ecological-disaster-is-a-12-trillion-opportunity.

14. Michael A. Heller and James Salzman, *Mine! How the Hidden Rules of Ownership Control Our Lives* (New York: Penguin Random House, 2022).

15. Peter Veit, David Gibbs, and Katie Reytar, "Indigenous Forests Are Some of the Amazon's Last Carbon Sinks," *Insights*, World Resources Institute, January 6, 2023, https://www.wri.org/insights/amazon-carbon-sink-indigenous-forests.

16. Learn more about Project Breakthrough at http://breakthrough.unglobalcompact.org.
17. "About Us," XPrize.org, https://www.xprize.org/about/mission.
18. See Jeffrey Kluger, "The 'Overview Effect' Forever Changes Some Astronauts' Attitudes Towards Earth—But You Don't Need to Go to Space to Experience It," *Time*, July 30, 2021, https://time.com/6084094/overview-effect/. See also, NASA Johnson Space Center, "The Overview Effect," August 30, 2019, in *Houston: We Have a Podcast*, episode 107, https://www.nasa.gov/johnson/HWHAP/the-overview-effect.
19. Conservation X Labs, "Our Mission Is to Prevent the Sixth Mass Extinction," ConservationXLabs.com, https://conservationxlabs.com/mission.
20. Conservation X Labs, "Our Mission."
21. Conservation X Labs, "Open Innovation," ConservationXLabs.com, https://conservationxlabs.com/harnessing-planetary-genius.
22. *Transportation Report*, RethinkX, https://www.rethinkx.com/transportation-report.
23. RethinkX, "New Book 'Brighter' Explores the Future of Environmentalism Amidst the Greatest Transformation in Over a Century," PRNewswire, December 19, 2022, https://www.prnewswire.com/news-releases/new-book-brighter-explores-the-future-of-environmentalism-amidst-the-greatest-technological-transformation-in-over-a-century-301705853.html.
24. Greta Thunberg, "'Our House Is on Fire': Greta Thunberg, Age 16, Urges Leaders to Act on Climate," *Guardian*, January 25, 2019, https://www.theguardian.com/environment/2019/jan/25/our-house-is-on-fire-greta-thunberg16-urges-leaders-to-act-on-climate.
25. "Bangladesh Ramps Up Its Persecution of Muhammad Yunus," *Economist*, October 13, 2022, https://www.economist.com/asia/2022/10/13/bangladesh-ramps-up-its-persecution-of-muhammad-yunus.
26. John Reed, "Dispatch from Dhaka," *FT Weekend Magazine*, January 14, 2023, 16–21.
27. Learn more about "Business Declares An Emergency" at https://businessdeclares.com.

Notes

28. See https://theobservatory.volans.com.
29. John Elkington and Sonja Haut, "Impact Investment Is a Force for Good, but a Better Way Needs to Be Found to Assess Its Value," *I By IMD* magazine, September 24, 2021, https://iby.imd.org/magazine/impact-investment-is-a-force-for-good-but-a-better-way-is-needed-to-assess-its-value.
30. Sir Ronald Cohen, *Impact: Reshaping Capitalism to Drive Real Change* (London: Penguin Books 2020).
31. Cohen, *Impact*.
32. Dean Hand, Ben Ringel, and Alexander Danel, *GIINsight: Sizing the Impact Investing Market 2022*, Global Impact Investing Network, October 12, 2022, https://thegiin.org/research/publication/impact-investing-market-size-2022/.
33. Sonja Haut, *The Case for Impact: A Guide to Value in a World of Social and Environmental Challenges* (Self Published, Amazon Kindle Direct Publishing 2022). A downloadable study guide is available at https://thecaseforimpact.elementor.cloud.
34. "About EcoVadis," EcoVadis, https://ecovadis.com/about-us.
35. Donella Meadows, "Leverage Points: Places to Intervene in a System," Donella Meadows Archives, The Donella Meadows Project: Academy for Systems Change, https://donellameadows.org/archives/leverage-points-places-to-intervene-in-a-system.

Chapter 9

1. "Green Swan Awards," Volans, https://volans.com/green-swan-awards.
2. Ciaran McGrath, "'Human Phoenix': Sacha Gets Set for Latest Adventure—Months after Horrific Accident," *Express*, May 17, 2022, https://www.express.co.uk/news/uk/1611651/sacha-dench-joanna-lumley-osprey-conservation-human-phoenix-human-swan-africa.
3. Learn more about the Capital Institute at https://capitalinstitute.org.
4. Volans, "Green Swans: Sketching a Manifesto for Tomorrow's Capitalism," YouTube, 2022, video, 08:03, https://www.youtube.com/watch?v=wZjjZaoBBFA.
5. Wildfowl and Wetlands Trust, "Our History," https://www.wwt.org.uk/who-we-are/our-history.

6. Wildfowl and Wetlands Trust, "Our Projects," https://www.wwt.org.uk/our-work/projects.

7. James Epstein-Reeves and Ellen Weinreb, "Lee Scott: Leveraging Walmart's Size for Sustainability," *Guardian*, September 24, 2013, https://www.theguardian.com/sustainable-business/lee-scott-walmart-sustainability.

8. John Elkington, afterword to Paul Hawken, *Regeneration: Ending the Climate Crisis in One Generation* (London: Penguin Books, 2021).

9. Watch Doug McMillon's 2020 speech on regeneration here: https://corporate.walmart.com/newsroom/videos/2020-regeneration-doug-mcmillon-speech.

10. See, for example: https://ellenmacarthurfoundation.org/videos/video-regenerating-nature-in-a-circular-economy.

11. An interesting perspective from Umair Haque on the failure of modern economics can be found here: Umair Haque, "How Civilizations Collapse, and Why Ours Is Starting To," Medium, https://eand.co/how-civilizations-collapse-and-why-ours-is-starting-to-e7b2cdfa33e3.

12. Kate Raworth, *Doughnut Economics: Seven Ways to Think Like a 21st Century Economist* (Chelsea, VT: Chelsea Green Publishing, 2017), 28.

13. Raworth, *Doughnut Economics*, 9.

14. Raworth, Doughnut Economics, 254.

15. Kate Raworth, "Introducing the Amsterdam Doughnut," *Kate Raworth* (blog), April 8, 2020, https://www.kateraworth.com/2020/04/08/amsterdam-city-doughnut.

16. Janine Benyus, "Biomimicry's Surprising Lessons from Nature's Engineers," TED2005, February 2005, video, 22:59, (transcript available), https://www.ted.com/talks/janine_benyus_biomimicry_s_surprising_lessons_from_nature_s_engineers/transcript.

17. Benyus, "Biomimicry's Surprising Lessons."

18. Mariana Mazzucato, *The Entrepreneurial State: Debunking Public vs. Private Sector Myths*, 10th ed. (London: Penguin, 2018).

19. Mariana Mazzucato and Rosie Collington, *The Big Con* (London: Allen Lane, 2023).

20. Dieter Helm, *Legacy: How to Build the Sustainable Economy* (Cambridge: Cambridge University Press, 2023). As quoted in "Concrete Actions,"

a review of recent books on the environment by Pilota Clark in the *Financial Times*, November 11, 2023, page 11.

21. For more information, see https://teebweb.org.
22. Learn more about Gist Impact at https://gistimpact.com.
23. From author's interview with Pavan Sukhdev, Saturday, July 29, 2023, Nyon, Switzerland.
24. *Daniel Christian Wahl* (blog), Medium, https://designforsustainability.medium.com.
25. John Elkington, "Line 6, São Paulo," *John Elkington* (blog), September 21, 2022, https://johnelkington.com/2022/09/line-6-sao-paulo/.
26. Volans, "Meet the Regenerators: Thomas Gent, Founder of Gentle Farming," YouTube, October 5, 2021, video, 02:12, https://www.youtube.com/watch?v=5n-eOJw1fZA.
27. Volans, "Meet the Regenerators: David Leventhal, Cofounder of Playa Viva Eco-Luxury Resort," YouTube, October 12, 2021, video, 25:28, https://www.youtube.com/watch?v=7Tyjsxjpn78.
28. John Elkington, "Surfing Tomorrow's Waves: John Elkington Talks to Yvon Chouinard," May 15, 2021, Green Swans Observatory, Volans, https://theobservatory.volans.com/wp-content/uploads/2021/05/GSO-Conversations-YVON-CHOUINARD-15-05-2021-PDF.pdf.
29. Volans, "Meet the Regenerators: Anuradha Chugh, CEO of Pukka Herbs," YouTube, March 29, 2022, video, 20:26, https://www.youtube.com/watch?v=rIrU-ovxlQY.
30. Volans, "Meet the Regenerators: Daniela V. Fernandez, Founder & CEO of Sustainable Ocean Alliance," YouTube, October 14, 2021, video, 20:47, https://www.youtube.com/watch?v=E-V1AieqKug.
31. Volans, "Meet the Regenerators: David Brin, Sci-Fi Author & Scientist," YouTube, October 14, 2021, video, 15:23, https://www.youtube.com/watch?v=MFPyvhuiRlo.
32. Yvon Chouinard, *Let My People Go Surfing* (New York: Penguin Books, 2005).
33. Yvon Chouinard, "Earth Is Now Our Only Shareholder," Patagonia, https://eu.patagonia.com/gb/en/ownership/.
34. Learn more about author David Brin at https://www.davidbrin.com.

35. John Elkington, "Restoring Eden: John Elkington Talks to Azzam Alwash," Green Swans Observatory, Volans, May 15, 2021, https://theobservatory.volans.com/wp-content/uploads/2021/05/Restoring-Eden-FINAL-15-05-2021-PDF.pdf.
36. Elkington, "Restoring Eden."
37. "Our Winners & Finalists," The Earthshot Prize, 2021, https://earthshotprize.org/winners-finalists-listing/?filter-year=2021.
38. UNESCO, "Abolition of the Army in Costa Rica," Collection 2016-42, Memory of the World, Registration Year 2017, https://en.unesco.org/memoryoftheworld/registry/209.
39. Michael Price, "Are We in the Middle of a Long Peace—or on the Brink of a Major War?" *Science*, February 21, 2018, https://www.science.org/content/article/are-we-middle-long-peace-or-brink-major-war.
40. David Potter, "How Disruptions Happen," *Aeon*, December 24, 2021, https://aeon.co/essays/a-history-of-disruption-from-fringe-ideas-to-social-change.
41. Foreword in Ministry of Defence's *Climate Change and Sustainability Strategic Approach*, 2021.
42. See Eduard Müller interviewed by Doughnut economist Kate Raworth: Doughnut Economics Action Lab, "Regenerate Costa Rica and the Doughnut," YouTube, September 23, 2020, video, 32:24, https://www.youtube.com/watch?v=KvJNcLa523w.
43. Learn more about Rancho Margot eco-resort at https://www.ranchomargot.com.

Chapter 10

1. (no author) "Omar El Akkad on Writing *American War*," *Literary* (blog), Pan Macmillan, April 18, 2018, https://www.panmacmillan.com/blogs/literary/omar-el-akkad-on-writing-american-war.
2. "New York 2140," Kim Stanley Robinson (website), https://www.kimstanleyrobinson.info/content/new-york-2140.
3. Ijaz Nabi, "Responding to Pakistan Floods," *Commentary* (blog), Brookings, February 10, 2023, https://www.brookings.edu/articles/pakistan-floods/.

Notes 317

4. John Elkington, "Tomorrow's Capitalism Forum," *John Elkington* (blog), January 11, 2020, https://johnelkington.com/2020/01/tomorrows-capitalism-forum/.

5. "Tomorrow's Capitalism Inquiry," Volans, https://volans.com/tomorrows-capitalism-inquiry/.

6. Sir David Attenborough, *A Life on Our Planet* (London: Ebury Publishing, 2020).

7. T. S. Eliot, "Little Gidding," *Collected Poems 1909–1962* (London: Faber & Faber, 1974). A sample of the poem is also available here: https://poetryarchive.org/poem/four-quartets-extract/.

8. John Elkington, "Releasing the Eels into the Severn," *John Elkington* (blog), September 16, 2014, https://johnelkington.com/2014/09/releasing-eels-into-the-severn/.

9. 50th anniversary Earth Day special issue, *National Geographic*, April 2020.

10. Lucy Kellaway, "Guffipedia: The Chief Pollinator Leads Thoughts and Writes," *Financial Times*, June 8, 2016, https://www.ft.com/content/fbde307a-2d60-11e6-bf8d-26294ad519fc.

11. Justine Calma, "Instead of Planting Trees, Give Forests Back to People," The Verge, February 10, 2023, https://www.theverge.com/2023/2/10/23592712/conservation-nasa-satellite-images-nepal-forests.

12. Richard D. North, "Obituary: Andrew Lees," *Independent*, January 9, 1995, https://www.independent.co.uk/news/people/obituary-andrew-lees-1567200.html.

13. John Elkington, *Green Swans: The Coming Boom in Regenerative Capitalism* (Austin, TX: Fast Company Press, 2020).

14. Matthew Taylor and Jessica Murray, "'Overwhelming and Terrifying': The Rise of Climate Anxiety," *Guardian*, February 10, 2020, https://www.theguardian.com/environment/2020/feb/10/overwhelming-and-terrifying-impact-of-climate-crisis-on-mental-health.

15. Olivia Rosane, "Humans and Big Ag Livestock Now Account for 96 Percent of Mammal Biomass," EcoWatch, May 23, 2018, https://www.ecowatch.com/biomass-humans-animals-2571413930.html.

16. See Mariana Mazzucato and Rosie Collington, *The Big Con* (London: Allen Lane, 2023).
17. Steven Levy, "How Hemingway Gradually—Then Suddenly—Defined the Zeitgeist," *Wired*, July 8, 2022, https://www.wired.com/story/plaintext-hemingway-gradually-suddenly-zeitgeist/.
18. Azeem Azhar, "Going Big on Climate Tech, with Vinod Khosla," *Exponential View by Azeem Azhar* (blog), October 12, 2023, https://www.exponentialview.co/p/going-big-on-climate-tech-with-vinod.
19. Christopher Boone and Karen C. Seto, "Green Jobs Are Booming, but Too Few Employees Have Sustainability Skills to Fill Them—Here Are 4 Ways to Close the Gap," *Conversation*, January 5, 2023, https://theconversation.com/green-jobs-are-booming-but-too-few-employees-have-sustainability-skills-to-fill-them-here-are-4-ways-to-close-the-gap-193953.
20. Andrew Jack, "How We Are Updating FT Rankings to Reflect 25 Years of Change," *FT Business Rankings*, Global MBA Ranking 2023, February 2023.
21. António Guterres, "A How-to Guide to Defuse the Climate Time-Bomb," LinkedIn, March 20, 2023, https://www.linkedin.com/pulse/how-to-guide-defuse-climate-time-bomb-antónio-guterres/.

Coda

1. Andreas Malm, *How to Blow Up a Pipeline: Learning to Fight a World on Fire* (London: Verso, 2021).
2. "Noam Chomsky: Speaking Truth to Power," *Al-Ahram Weekly*, June 3, 2010, https://chomsky.info/20100603/.
3. "Never Doubt That a Small Group of Thoughtful, Committed Citizens Can Change the World; Indeed, It's the Only Thing That Ever Has," Quote Investigator, November 12, 2017, https://quoteinvestigator.com/2017/11/12/change-world/.

Index

A

Aberfan disaster (Wales), 91
Acceleration Agenda, 269
Acciona, 216, 239
AccountAbility, 174
Adams, Dorothy, 47–50
Adams, Douglas, 132
Adams, Leo, 41
Adams, Ned, 47–49
Adamson, Charles, 72
Adamson, Marjorie, 30
Adamson, Pat. *See* Elkington, Pat
Adamson, Paul, 31, 37, 67
Adamson, Peter, 67
Addyman plesiosaur, 172
ADL (Arthur D. Little), 184–185
advisory boards, 265
Agland, Phil, 150
AI (artificial intelligence), 182–183, 264
Aisha (nanny), 37
Albery, Nicholas, 179
Albright & Wilson, 128
Aloisi de Larderel, Jacqueline, 130–131
Alternative London (Saunders), 179
alternative technology, 88–91
Alwash, Azzam, 240–245
Alwash, Suzanne, 241
Amazon rainforest, 149
American War (El Akkad), 138
ancestors, good, 137–140
Anders, Bill, 87

Anderson, Ray, 233, 236
Anderson, Robert O., 169
Angry Brigade, 58
Ansari XPRIZE, 217
Anthropocene epoch, 268
Anthropy 2023, 247
Apple, 86, 141–142
Apple Day, 180
Arbib, James, 219
Architectural Association Quarterly, 70
Arcosanti, 40, 70, 88
Arthur D. Little (ADL), 184–185
artificial intelligence (AI), 182–183, 264
Ash, Maurice, 146
AskNature website, 236
Atomic Weapons Research Establishment, 25
Attenborough, David, 116–118, 261
auriga role in Roman times, 135
Australia, 171–172
Auxiliary Territorial Service, 26
Avery, Chris, 170
aviation, 27–29, 53, 81–83, 93
Aviva Investors, 261
Ayres, Pam, 55

B

B Corporations, 215, 234
Babel fish, 132

baby boomer generation, 18, 23, 27, 105–106, 220
Bacigalupi, Paolo, 138
Baerbock, Annalena, 148
Bakker, Peter, 193
banana republics, 248
Barbie dolls, 193
Bastian, Gert, 147
Bate, Jonathan, 161
Battle of Britain, 27–29, 82
Battle of the Little Bighorn, 35
Bavaria, Joan, 131, 160
Bayer, 211–212
Beach Boys, 38, 99, 227
Ben & Jerry's, 131, 203
Benchley, Peter, 2
Bennett, John, 68
Benyus, Janine, 235, 236
Berry, Fred, 28–29
Bewick's swans, 229
The Big Con (Mazzucato), 237
bilharzia, 199
biomimicry, 86, 236
Biotechnic Research and Development (BRAD), 88–91
Biotechnology Bulletin, 92
black swan events, 244–245
Blanchet, Marie-Gabrielle, 56
Blood, David, 209
blue health, 281
The Body Shop International, 17, 131, 170–171
Boeing, 40, 42
Bonilla Padilla, Mauricio, 210
boomers. *See* baby boomer generation
Boyle, Danny, 73
Boyle, Godfrey, 90, 180
BP (British Petroleum), 91, 200
Brabeck-Letmathe, Peter, 9–10
BRAD (Biotechnic Research and Development), 88–91
Bradbury, Ray, 196
Brand, Stewart, 61, 86–87, 219

Brand New Product Development, 178
Branson, Chuck, 42
Branson, Jeanne, 42
Branson, Richard, 217–218
Braungart, Michael, 201, 234
Brazil, rainforest in, 149
The Breakthrough Effect (SYSTEMIQ), 111
Breivik, Anders Behring, 167
Brent Spar dumping plan, Shell, 183, 184
Bright Greens, 161–163
Brighter (Dorr), 219
Brin, David, 136–137, 240
British Caledonian Airways, 67
British Petroleum (BP), 91, 200
Britton, Easkey, 97, 281
Broadacre City, 70
Bron, Eleanor, 71–72
Brown, Janet, 175
Brown, Lester R., 83–85
Brown, Tim, 208
Browning-Ferris Industries, 168
Brundtland, Gro Harlem, 166, 167–168
Brundtland Commission on Environment and Development, 166
Bryanston School, 49, 51–54, 75
Bryant, Connor, 149
Buckminster Fuller Institute Challenge, 84
Bulcke, Paul, 10
Bunje, Paul, 217, 218
Burke, Tom, 146, 159–160, 228
Burns, Susan, 95–96
Burton, Dan, 230
Business & Human Rights Resource Centre, 170
Business Declares, 221
business leaders, role in system change, 268–269

C

Caldecott, Oliver, 89
Campaign for Nuclear Disarmament (CND), 25

Campanale, Mark, 161
Campbell, Joseph, 34
Capital Institute, 231
capitalism, 1–2, 77–80, 100, 102, 105, 215
Capitalism, Socialism and Democracy (Schumpeter), 102
Capon, Kenneth, 57
Capra, Fritjof, 90
Carnegie Institute, 247
Carr, E. H., 54
Carson, Rachel, 53, 121
Casey, Susan, 98–99
catalytic government, 111–112
CERCLA (Comprehensive Environmental Response, Compensation, and Liability Act) legislation, US, 143–144
CERES, 131
Chandler, Geoffrey, 144–145
Chang, Jolan, 89–90
Charles I, King of England, 57
Charles III, King of England, 160
Cheltenham Tech, 54–55
chickenpox, 54
chief sustainability officers (CSOs), 192–194
China
 Cultural Revolution in, 80
 hope spots in, 221
 presence in Costa Rica, 250
 SustainAbility's work in, 190–192
Chomsky, Noam, 274
Chouinard, Yvon, 171, 240
Chugh, Anuradha, 240
chumming, by sharks, 6
Churchill, Winston, 86
Churchill Fellowship, 232
circular economy, 234
cities, Smart Surfaces Coalition to improve, 262
Clark, Eugenie, 2–3
Clarke, Robin, 88, 90
Clifford, Sue, 180
climate activism, 220, 266
Climate Group, 280

Close Encounters of the Third Kind (film), 104
cloth diapers (nappies), 201–202
CND (Campaign for Nuclear Disarmament), 25
Coaker, Isabel. *See* Elkington, Isabel
Cody, William "Buffalo Bill," 36
Cohen, Ben, 203
Cohen, Ronald, 222–223
Cold War, late stages of, 147–148
Colfax, Schuyler, 81
Collapse (Diamond), 53
Colossal Biosciences, 88
Colson, Christian, 73
Common Ground, 180
communism, 80, 106
communist bloc, collapse of, 147–148
Comprehensive Environmental Response, Compensation, and Liability Act (CERCLA or Superfund) legislation, US, 143–144
conflicts, violent. *See* wars
Conservation X Labs (CXL), 218
Consultative Forum on the Environment and Sustainable Development (European Commission), 188–189
Coors brewing family, 118–119
corporate environmental reporting, 130–131
Cosanti Foundation, 70
Costa, Paula, 250
Costa Rica, 246–247, 248–251
Costa Rica Regenerativa (Regenerate Costa Rica), 248
counterculture, 60
CounterCurrent, 142–143
court jester-approach, 8–9
Covestro, 210–211, 215
COVID-19 pandemic, 65, 88, 259, 266
cow autopsy, 32–33
Cowan, Peter, 72
Crazy Horse, 35, 50–51
creative destruction, 102, 105
Credit Suisse, 259
CSOs (chief sustainability officers), 192–194

Cuban Missile Crisis, 25
Custer, George Armstrong, 51
CXL (Conservation X Labs), 218

D

Dark Greens, 161
Davenport, Jane, 39
Davidson, Joan, 71
Davies, Robert, 206
De La Rue security printers, 125
de Segundo, Karen, 185–186
de-extinction, 88
Dehgan, Alex, 218
Dekkers, Marijn, 211
Delibes, Miguel, 52
Deloitte, 267
Dench, Sacha, 229–230
Denka, 281
Design Council, 150
Diamandis, Peter, 217
Diamond, Jared, 53
Dieselgate scandal, 16–17
disposable diapers (nappies), 201–202
diversity, tapping into, 263–265
Dixon, Bernard, 120
DJSI (Dow Jones Sustainability Indices), 17, 202
"Dr. Doomwatch" (Jim Farquhar), 128
Dolphins (human), 260
  examples of, 280–282
  flipping Shark-like governments into Dolphin mode, 112
  need to school new generations of, 256
  overview, 16
  risk versus potential, 13
  Sharks playing at being, 16–17
  Trojan, 273
dolphins, characteristics of, 16
Dorr, Adam, 219
doughnut (donut) economics, 235
Douglas, William O., 41–42

Dow Chemical Co., 94
Dow Jones Sustainability Indices (DJSI), 17, 202
Drayton, Bill, 205
Dreyfuss, Richard, 104
drift, risk of, 267
drug use, 61–62
Dune novels (Herbert), 60, 135, 136, 233
Dykes Heavy Commercial Vehicles Act, 198

E

Eagle comics (Hampson), 27
Earle, Sylvia, 3, 18
Earth Day movement, 106, 118
Earth Overshoot Day, 95
Earth Policy Institute, 85
Earthlife Foundation, 149–151, 175
Earthrise image (Anders), 58, 86–87
Earthshot Prize, 118, 246
Ebb & Flow (Britton), 97
ECC (English China Clays), 91
e-cigarettes, 212
eco-efficiency, 180–181
The Ecology of Commerce (Hawken), 233
The Ecology of Tomorrow's World (Elkington), 92
economic cycle theory, 100, 107, 109
Economic Development Board (EDB), Singapore, 209–210
economics
  dark side of, 258–260
  Occupy Wall Street protests, 145
  regenerative strategies for, 235–238
EcoVadis, 224
EDB (Economic Development Board), Singapore, 209–210
Eden Again (Alwash), 241
Eden Project, 12, 84, 91, 227–229
Edmonds, Dobrina, 171–172
Edmonds, Murray, 171–172
education, fractal approach to, 269

Edward VIII, King of England, 55
eels, 32–34, 262
Effingham, Irene (Kerry), Countess of, 55–56
Effingham, Mowbray, Earl of, 55
Egypt, environmental impact studies in, 119–120, 198–200
El Akkad, Omar, 138, 256
El Camino (Delibes), 52
Elder, Mark, 51
Elders, 168
Electrodyn pesticide sprayer, 150
elevator pitches, 276–277
Eliot, T. S., 262
Elkington, Caroline, 39, 40
Elkington, Durham, 62
Elkington, Elaine, 57, 58, 72, 119, 165
   employment, 42–43
   European roadtrip, 63–66
   marriage and honeymoon, 40–43, 70
   visit to Nicholas Saunders's house, 179
   on Wildwood, 89–90
Elkington, Gaia, 35–36, 43, 73–74, 98, 116, 117
Elkington, Gene, 74
Elkington, Gray, 33–34, 37, 39, 51, 68, 83
Elkington, Hania, 42, 43, 73–74, 117
Elkington, Isabel, 27–28, 61–62, 71
Elkington, John. *See also* societal pressure waves; SustainAbility; tickling Sharks; Volans Ventures
   as accidental capitalist, 77–80
   alternative technology, 88–91
   Barnes, home in, 42–43, 73
   Biotechnology Bulletin, 92
   at Bryanston School, 51–54
   business, growth in focus on, 91–94
   business and markets, interest in, 80–83
   at Cheltenham Tech, 54–55
   coining of terms by, 19, 129–130, 150, 181
   CounterCurrent platform for, 142–143
   curiosity, role in career, 272
   Cyprus, childhood experiences in, 36–39
   daughters, 73–74
   description by Tim Smit, 285–287
   drifting after university, 63, 69–70
   at Earthlife Foundation, 149–151
   The Ecology of Tomorrow's World, 92
   at Environment Foundation, 143–146
   at Environmental Data Services, 123–128
   environmentalism of, influences on, 116
   on European Commission's Consultative Forum on the Environment and Sustainable Development, 188–189
   evolution of book title, 12
   first published article, 70
   future conflicts, dangers to planet from, 247
   Gaia hypothesis, influence on, 120–122
   The Gene Factory, 92, 142–143
   at Glencot School, 45–50, 53
   governments, working with, 188–192
   Greece trip in Land Rover, 63–66
   The Green Capitalists, 146
   The Green *Consumer Guide*, 94, 146, 151–152, 153–154, 155, 170–171
   Green Pages, 146–147, 151
   Green Swans, 20, 217, 248, 266
   "How I Learned to Stop Worrying and Love the Exponential," 218
   humor, use of, 8–9, 174
   John Elkington Associates, 128–130, 200
   lawbreaking activities by, 66
   manifesto, 282
   marriage and honeymoon, 39–42
   Mesopotamian genes, 241
   nature, early interest in, 45–46
   Northern Ireland, childhood experiences in, 31–35
   parents, 23–31
   personal impact statement, 225–226
   personality type, 74–76
   The Poisoned Womb, 92, 142, 143
   politics, 221

The Power of Unreasonable People, 205, 207
return to England in 1959, 39
scaling and replicating sustainability-oriented solutions, 83–88
self-care, 266–267
Seven Bridges to the Future, 102, 175
spiral dynamic in life, 261–263
Sun Traps, 92, 142
tapping into wider sources of wisdom, 263–265
tensions between work and family life, 43–44
at TEST, 72–73, 119–120, 198–200
triple bottom line concept, 19, 88, 103, 180–183, 213–216
at University College London, 69, 70–72
at University of Essex, 56–63
A Very Civil War, 40
A Year in the Greenhouse, 149, 154
The Young Green Consumer Guide, 157–158
Elkington, Kay, 62
Elkington, Pat, 24, 26, 30–32, 37, 50
Elkington, Tessa, 43, 82
Elkington, Tim, 24–25, 46–47, 93
  Battle of Britain speech, 82
  car crash, 50
  in Cyprus, 36–39
  marriage, 30–31
  in World War II, 27–29
Ellen MacArthur Foundation, 234
Elworthy, Scilla, 247
Emerson, Jed, 205
endosymbiosis, 121
ENDS (Environmental Data Services), 56, 92, 123–128
energy efficiency, 180–181
English China Clays (ECC), 91
English Civil War, 57
Enterprise Oil, 46
The Entrepreneurial State (Mazzucato), 237
Environment Foundation, 142–143

environmental, social, and governance (ESG), 19, 107–109, 193–194. *See also* impact pressure wave
environmental auditing, 200–201
Environmental Data Services (ENDS), 56, 92, 123–128
environmental excellence concept, 129–130
environmental impact studies in Egypt, 119–120, 198–200
environmental liability insurance, 143–144
environmental pressure wave, 19, 108–109
  David Attenborough in, 116–118
  Denis Hayes in, 118–119
  Earth Day movement, 118
  Gaia hypothesis, 120–122
  good ancestors, 137–140
  as grabbing attention, 130–132
  John Elkington Associates in, 128–130
  Max Nicholson and ENDS in, 123–128
  opinions of John Elkington during, 132–134
  overview, 115–116
  Teddy Goldsmith in, 122–123
  TEST, 119–120
  tickling Sharks, 134–137
environmental service payments, 249
EOKA (Ethniki Organosis Kyprion Agoniston), 36
EQT, 17
Erlichman, James, 177
ERM, 77, 173
Ernst & Young, 267
ESG (environmental, social, and governance), 19, 107–109, 193–194. *See also* impact pressure wave
Eternit, 169
Ethniki Organosis Kyprion Agoniston (EOKA; National Organization of Cypriot Fighters), 36
European Commission Consultative Forum on the Environment and Sustainable Development, 188–189
European Union, Green Deal in, 162, 220

Evans, Thammy, 247
expert systems, 182–183
exponential change, 106–107, 216–219, 226
Extinction Rebellion (XR) protests, 221
ExxonMobil, 187–188

F

false flag environmentalism, 273
Fantoni, Barry, 64
Fantoni, Tessa, 64
Farewell Spit (New Zealand), 257–258, 259
Farquhar, Jim, 128
Fermor, Patrick Leigh, 144
Fernandez, Daniela, 240
Ferrari, Pierre, 203
Fiennes, Jake, 230
Figueres, Christiana, 246
finance, green, 159–161
Firestone, 203–204
Fischer, Joschka, 148
fish, tickling, 5–6
Flannery, Tim, 1
Flux, Mike, 150
flygskam (flight shame), 266
Foote, Stephen, 241
Ford Motor Company, 203–204
Forestledge, 40–42
Forum for the Future, 228
fossil fuel companies, 14, 185. *See also* ExxonMobil; Shell
Foster, Norman, 84
founder's syndrome, 206
Fox, Edward, 262
Fox, Sara, 84
fractal vision of health, 267–270
Frailey, L. E., 93
Fraser, Romy, 179–180
freak waves, 98–99
Fred Berry, 28
free speech, China's growing war on, 192
Freeman, Chris, 102
Frestonia, 177–178

Friedman, Milton, 1
Friedman, Thomas, 142, 162
Friends of the Earth, 124–125, 131, 155, 175
Fuller, R. Buckminster, 83–84, 86, 123, 258, 286–287
Fullerton, John, 231, 237
future eaters. *See* Sharks (human)
"Future of Capitalism" program (IESE-Shizenkan), 269
Future Shock (Toffler), 103

G

Gaia (Myers), 117
Gaia hypothesis, 20, 87, 120–122
Gaia myth, 115
Gail (calligrapher), 63–64
galeophobia, 2–3
GBN (Global Business Network), 87
The Gene Factory (Elkington), 92, 142–143
General Nursing Council, 69
Genesis (Wilson), 59
Gent, Thomas, 240
geodesic domes, 84
George, Martin, 232
Germany, Green Party in, 147, 148
Giáp, General, 51
Gilbert, Elon, 41
Gilbert, Joan, 41
Gilding, Michelle, 95–96
Gilding, Paul, 95–96
GIST Impact, 237–238
glassmaking, 56
Glastonbury festival, 43–44
Glencot School, 45–50, 51, 53
Global Business Network (GBN), 87
Global Footprint Network, 95, 108
Global Impact Investing Network, 223
global mobilization, 85–86
Global Reporting Initiative (GRI), 131
globalization pressure wave, 108–109
Godden, Nicola, 229

Goldsmith, Teddy, 122–123
Gone with the Wind (Mitchell), 54
The Good Ancestor (Krznaric), 137–138
good ancestors, 137–140
Gore, Al, 185, 209
governments, working with, 188–192
Gowar, Rex, 63, 65–66
Graham, Bill, 63
Grant, Ulysses S., 81
Green Alliance, 146, 159–160
green audits, 157–158, 200–201
The Green Capitalists (Elkington), 146
The Green *Consumer Guide* (Elkington), 94, 146, 151–152, 153–154, 155, 170–171
Green Deals, 108, 162–163, 220
green designers, 150
green finance, 131, 159–161
Green Pages (Elkington), 146–147, 151
Green Parties, 142, 147, 148
green pressure wave, 19, 108–109
    Bright Greens, 161–163
    building and peak of, 146–148
    disruption to companies and supply chains during, 156–158
    Earthlife Foundation, 149–151
    Elkington's countercurrent work during, 142–146
    Environment Foundation, 143–146
    Julia Hailes in, 149–152
    McDonald's battle against SustainAbility, 153–156
    Novo Nordisk in, 158–159
    overview, 141–143
    SustainAbility, founding of, 151–152
    Tessa Tennant in, 159–161
Green Swan Awards, 229–230
Green Swan Day, 231
Green Swans, 217
Green Swans (Elkington), 20, 217, 248, 266
Green Swans Observatory, 222
greening concept, 79
greenmail, 277

Greenpeace, 95, 155, 183
greenwashing, 17, 131
Greenwich Observatory, 52
Greta wave, 108–109, 220–222
GRI (Global Reporting Initiative), 131
Griffin, Isabel. *See* Elkington, Isabel
Grove-White, Robin, 160
Grupo Bimbo, 210
Guterres, António, 247, 269

H

Habeck, Emily, 14
Haigh, Nigel, 160
Hailes, Julia, 149–152, 170, 171, 188–189, 201, 202
Hamilton, Robert, 48
Hampson, Frank, 27
Harrison, John, 52
Hartigan, Pamela, 204–205, 206, 207, 208, 209
Hartman, Andre, 5
Harvard University, 60
Harvey-Jones, John, 157
Haut, Sonja, 223
Hawken, Paul, 160, 186, 233–234, 237
Hayes, Denis, 118–119, 229, 230, 269
health
    benefits of water-based sports, 281
    fractal vision of, 267–270
Heinz, 16
Helgoland (Rovelli), 108
Helm, Dieter, 237
Henley-Welch, Eve, 59, 61
Herbert, Frank, 60, 135–136, 233
Herrington, Gaya, 133
Hines, Chris, 96–97, 228, 281
The Hitchhiker's Guide to the Galaxy (Adams), 132
HMS *Eagle*, 37
HMS *Fiskerton*, 37
Ho Chi Minh, 41, 51
Hobsbawm, Eric, 101

# Index

Hoffman, Abbot ("Abbie") Howard, 68
Hogan, Clover, 266
Holdfast Collective, 240
honest markets, 85
Hope, Bob, 41
hope spots, 3, 18
horseshoe crabs, 88
Hounsfield, Nick, 280–281
"How I Learned to Stop Worrying and Love the Exponential" (Elkington), 218
How to Blow Up a Pipeline (Malm), 272
Howard, Michael, 153
Hudson Research Europe, 132–133
Hughes, Ted, 143
human rights, 170
humor, 8–9, 145, 174
Humphrys, John, 9
Hurricane Katrina, 8
Hussein, Saddam, 240, 242
Hutchins, Giles, 237, 239

I

ICI (Imperial Chemical Industries), 150, 156–157
IESE (Spain), 269
IFF (Industrial Facts & Forecasting), 69
IIED (International Institute for Environment and Development), 166, 176–177
Impact (Cohen), 222–223
impact investment market, 223
Impact Management Project, 197
impact pressure wave, 19, 108–109
  background of agenda, 198–200
  business leaders ignoring warning signs, 210–212
  corporate board meetings related to, 202–204
  exponential change, 216–219
  Greta wave, 220–222
  language of, 222–225
  market makers, 200–202

overview, 195–197
personal impact statements, 225–226
recall of triple bottom line concept, 213–216
social enterprise, 204–207
Social Stock Exchange, 212–213
Volans Ventures, creation of, 207–211
impact valuation, 223
Imperial Chemical Industries (ICI), 150, 156–157
In Search of Excellence (Peters & Waterman), 129
incrementalism, 106–107
Indigenous peoples, 216, 264–265
Industrial Facts & Forecasting (IFF), 69
Inflation Reduction Act (US), 162, 220
Infosys, 9–10
insecticides, 211–212
Institute for Social Inventions, 179
Interface, 233, 236
International Business Leaders Forum, 206
International Institute for Environment and Development (IIED), 166, 176–177
International Shark Attack File, 16–17
Iraqi Marshes, 240–245
The Island of Missing Trees (Shafak), 38

J

Jacobs, Jane, 71
Jacobs, Peter, 54–55
Jagger, Bianca, 170
Jaws (film), 1–2
JEA (John Elkington Associates), 128–130, 200
Jefferson Airplane, 61
Jobs, Steve, 86
John Elkington Associates (JEA), 128–130, 200
John F. Kennedy School of Government, 60
Johnson, Brian, 176
Johnson, Lyndon, 51
Johnson, Stanley, 147

Johnson & Johnson's, 204
Jones, Hannah, 12, 193, 263
Jones, Quincy, 206

K

Kahn, Herman, 132–133
Kane, Pat, 155
Kats, Greg, 262
Keay, Ian, 88
Keay, Jane, 39
Kellaway, Lucy, 264
Kelly, Kevin, 219
Kelly, Petra, 147
Kerr, Andrew, 262
Khosla, Vinod, 268
King, Angela, 180
King, Martin Luther, Jr., 78–79
kingfishers, 35
Kingo, Lise, 159, 217
Kinney, Sean, 42
KKR, 77, 173
Knievel, Evel, 133
Kondratiev, Nikolai, 100–101
Kondratiev waves (K-waves), 101–102
Kraft Foods, 212
Kramer, Mark, 11
Kray Twins, 55
Krznaric, Roman, 137–138
Kuhn, Thomas, 53–54
K-waves (Kondratiev waves), 101–102

L

La Selva Research Station (Costa Rica), 249
Lake Manzala area, Egypt, 120, 199
Lakha, Sam, 208, 211, 216, 217, 219
Larkin, Philip, 23
Layton, David, 123, 127, 128
Leach, Gerald, 176
Leary, Timothy, 105
Lees, Andrew, 266

Lehman Brothers, 208–209, 259
Letby, Lucy, 53
Leventhal, David, 240
levers of system change, 224
levitation, 152–153
life cycle assessment, 201–202
A Life on Our Planet (Attenborough), 261
Light Greens, 161
like-minded people, resisting urge to cling to, 275
Limits to Growth study, 95, 108, 133
Lindsay, Jan, 63
Lindsay, Martin, 63
Linenger, Jerry, 139, 208
Lipsey, Dick, 58
"Little Gidding" (Eliot), 262
The Little Red Book (Mao), 79
Llewelyn-Davies, Richard, 71
Lloyd, Stephen, 146
"Lobby from Under the Carpet" (Hughes), 143
Lockheed "Skunk Works," 81, 86
Logan, Charles, 68
London Greenpeace, 156
London School of Economics (LSE), 102, 103
London Wetland Centre, 231
Long Now Foundation, 86
long wave theory, 101–103, 105, 107
Long Wolf, 35–36
Longitude (Sobel), 52
Longitude Prize, 52
L'Oréal, 171
Loughran, Kim, 205
Love, Charmian, 208, 210
Lovell, Ian, 63
Lovelock, James, 19–20, 87, 120–122
Lovins, Amory, 180–181
LSD, 61
LSE (London School of Economics), 102, 103
luck, 29–30

Lumley, Joanna, 230
Lye, Geoff, 173, 183, 184, 186, 208

M

MacArthur, Ellen, 234
MacArthur, Hank, 67
MacKenzie, Dorothy, 178
Macmillan, Harold, 134
MAD (mutually assured destruction) nuclear weapons strategy, 132
Malm, Andreas, 272
Mandela, Nelson, 43–44
Manzala Lake, Egypt, 120, 199
Mao Zedong, 79–80
March family: Pat, Saumie, Molly, Terry, and Peggy, 38, 59–60
Marcuse, Herbert, 78
Margulis, Lynn, 121
Marks & Spencer, 157
Marsh Arabs, 240–245
Marxism, 78–79, 102
Mason Pearson hairbrushes, 31
Massie, Bob, 131
Mattel, 193
Mazzucato, Mariana, 235, 236–237
McCarthyism, 90
McCausland, Marcus, 34
McDonald's Corporation, 94, 153–156
McDonough, Bill, 201, 234
McGlynn, Roger, 73
McLibel case, 156
McMillon, Doug, 233, 234
McNamara, Robert Strange, 51, 60
Mead, Margaret, 279
Meadows, Donella, 224
Meir, Golda, 72
Melchett, Peter, 6–7
Mendelssohn, Anna, 58
merchant banking, 93
Merlin Ecology Fund, 160
Merry Pranksters, 86

Mill Cottage, 35
mind bombs, 134
mining industry, 177
Minoan civilization, 98
Minsky, Hyman, 105, 275
Minsky moments, 105–107, 259, 275
Miracle in the Marshes of Iraq (film), 241
missionary positions, avoiding, 277
Mitchell, Margaret, 54
Mojave Aerospace Ventures, 217
Monsanto, 211
monster waves, 98–99
Moody, James Bradfield, 102
Moody-Stuart, Mark, 186
Morgan, Henry, 72
Morton, Victoria, 247
Mountfort, Guy, 49
MS *Messapia*, 39
Müller, Eduard, 248, 249–250
Musk, Elon, 195
mutually assured destruction (MAD) nuclear weapons strategy, 132
Myers, Norman, 117
Myers-Briggs Personality Type Indicator, 74–76

N

Nabisco, 77
Nader, Ralph, 158
nappies, cloth versus disposable, 201–202
NASA, 86–87
Nasser, Jac, 204
National Geographic magazine, 263
National Organization of Cypriot Fighters (Ethniki Organosis Kyprion Agoniston), 36
natural disasters, and economic instability, 259–260
nature
  interest in, 45
  TV programs on, 116–117

Nelson, Jane, 206
neonicotinoids, 211–212
neoprene wetsuits, 281
Nepal, 264–265
Neste, 216, 265
Nestlé, 9–11, 171, 234
Neville, Richard, 172
New Alchemy Institute, 90
New Deal, 108
New *Scientist* magazine, 32, 91, 120
New York 2140.2 (Robinson), 256
New Zealand, 171–172, 257–258, 259
NextEra Energy, 188
Nicholson, Max, 49, 123–128, 231
Nigeria, 183, 186
9/11 attacks, 172, 205, 207
Nixon, Richard, 41
Noda, Tomo, 269
Nogrady, Bianca, 102
Norfolk Broads, 232
Norman, Arthur, 125–126
Northcote, Richard, 210–211
Novartis, 216, 222–223, 265
Novo Nordisk A/S, 94, 158–159, 215, 260
nuclear weapons, 24–26, 29, 50, 67, 132
Nugee, Richard, 247

O

Obama, Barack, 197
Occupy Wall Street, 145
Oelwang, Jean, 127, 134
Operating Manual for Spaceship Earth (Fuller), 286–287
Operation Grapple, 24
Orcas (human), 13–15, 16, 272–273
orcas (mammals), 15
Osberg, Sally, 205
Our Common Future report (Brundtland Commission), 166
Overshoot Day, 108

Øvlisen, Mads, 158, 159
ownership, reconsidering best forms of, 216

P

Pacioli, Luca, 213
paganism, 34
Pakistan, 259–260
Pan Yue, 190–191
pantheism, 34
paper industry, 176–177
paradigm shift, 54, 224
Paraíso Orgánico (Costa Rica), 249
Parkin, Sara, 228
Partnering (Oelwang), 127, 134
Patagonia, 131, 171, 204, 240
Payne, Buryl, 90
People, Planet, and Profit (3Ps) formula, 180–183
People's Habitat Festival, 91
The People's Hall, 178–179
PepsiCo, 234
Perez, Carlota, 102
personal impact statements, 225–226
Peters, Tom, 129
Pevsner, Dieter, 89
Phantumvanit, Dhira, 129
Phelan, Ryan, 87–88
Philip Morris, 212
Phillips, Shawn, 63
photography, 64
Physic Ventures, 203
Pilkington, 56
Pinker, Stephen, 247
Pinn, Ingram, 181–182, 264
Plan B 3.0 (Brown), 85
Planetary Boundaries, 108
playfulness, 78–79
The Poisoned Womb (Elkington), 92, 142, 143
politics, 167–168, 221

Polly, Jean Armour, 96
Polman, Paul, 193
Polunin, Nicholas, 122
population growth, 106
Porritt, Jonathon, 189, 228
Porter, Michael, 10–11
The Postman (Brin), 136
power, speaking truth to, 5, 274. *See also* Sharks (human); tickling Sharks
The Power of Unreasonable People (Elkington & Hartigan), 205, 207
Prahalad, C. K., 10
Prakash-Mani, Kavita, 175, 190
predatory quartet, 13–18
Preta Terra, 250
Procter & Gamble Company, 94
Project Breakthrough, 111, 217, 219
public smoking, 175–176
Pullman, Philip, 286
Putin, Vladimir, 25, 162

Q

QAnon, 279
Quin, Jeremy, 247

R

RAF (Royal Air Force), 24, 30, 126
Ramparts magazine, 59
Rancho Margot (Costa Rica), 249–250
Randers, Jørgen, 95–96, 247
Randers, Marie, 95
Rappaport, David, 178
rare earth metals export ban, China, 192
Rattner, Beth, 236
Raworth, Kate, 235
RE100 initiative, 280
Rebuck, Gail, 92
Redford, Robert, 209
Regenerate Costa Rica (Costa Rica Regenerativa), 248

Regeneration (Hawken), 234
regeneration pressure wave, 19, 108–109
  Azzam Alwash in, 240–245
  background of, 233–234
  Costa Rica in, 246–247, 248–251
  Green Swan Awards, 229–230
  growing interest in, 230–232
  and impact agenda, 222
  need for, 86
  open prison, 108–109
  overview, 227–229
  strategies for economics, 235–238
  Ukraine conflict, 246, 247–248
  in value proposition of Volans, 238–241
Reich, Charles A., 79
Renton, Edward, 52
Republic of Frestonia, 177–178
RethinkX, 109, 111, 219
rewilding, 232
Richard the Lionheart, 50
Roberts, John, 72, 119–120
Robins, Nick, 103
Robinson, Kim Stanley, 256
Roddick, Anita, 17, 131, 170–171, 183
Rolls-Royce Merlin engines, 82
Roosevelt, Franklin D., 85
Roosevelt, Theodore, 197
Roper, Louise Kjellerup, 12, 216–217, 239, 251
Rosenzweig, Will, 203, 205
Rothschild family, 72
Rovelli, Carlo, 108–109
Royal Air Force (RAF), 24, 30, 126
Ruckelshaus, William, 168–169
Rushkoff, Douglas, 145
Russell, Dudley, 55
Rustin, Bayard, 5

S

Sabena airline, 165, 166
Sachs, Jeffrey, 10

Saladin (Salah al-Din), 50
The Sales Manager's Letter Book (Frailey), 93
Salzman, Jim, 216
Sandbrook, Richard, 175–177, 228
Sanders, Johnny, 37
Saro-Wiwa, Ken, 183
Saunders, Nicholas, 179
Sauven, John, 170
schistosomiasis, 199
Schmidheiny, Stephan, 169
schools, green audit for, 157–158
Schumpeter, Joseph, 101–102
Schwab, Klaus, 204, 205, 206–207
Schwab Foundation for Social Entrepreneurship, 204–205, 206
Schwartz, Peter, 87
Schweickart, Rusty, 87
science fiction, 60–61, 135–138, 195–196
The Science of War and Peace (Clarke), 88
Scott, David, 139
Scott, Lee, 233
Scott, Peter, 49, 231–232
Scott, Robert Falcon, 231
Scottish Environment Protection Agency (SEPA), 239
SDGs (Sustainable Development Goals), UN, 108, 220
sea lions, characteristics of, 15
Sea Lions (human), 13, 15–16, 273
SeaWorld, 15
Seba, Tony, 219
Secrett, Charles, 228
self-care, when trying to achieve system change, 266–267
self-knowledge, when tackling Sharks, 274
SEPA (Scottish Environment Protection Agency), 239
SERI (Solar Energy Research Institute), 118–119
Seven Bridges to the Future (Elkington), 102, 175
sewage pollution, 96–97

Shafak, Elif, 38–39
Shapiro, Bob, 211
shared value, 11
Shark Heart (Habeck), 14
sharks (fish)
   cannibalism of unhatched siblings, 11–12
   crucial role of, 14
   general discussion, 1–6
   killed by humans, 13
Sharks (human). *See also* tickling Sharks
   flipping Shark-like governments into Dolphin mode, 112
   overview, 3–4, 14
   playing at being Dolphins, 16–17
   risk versus potential, 13–14
   tackling, 271–280
   Trojan, 272–273
Sharp, Dick, 43
Shaw, Richard Norman, 51
Shell, 170, 177–178, 183–187, 202
Shizenkan University (Japan), 269
Shopley, Jonathan, 128–129, 175, 184–185
Shovell, Cloudesley, 53
Siemer, Peter, 66
Silent Spring (Carson), 53, 121
Silicon Valley Bank, 259
Silva, Marina, 149
Simpson, Wallis, 55
Singapore Economic Development Board, 209–210
Sitting Bull, 35–36, 51
Skoll Centre for Social Entrepreneurship, 209
Skoll Foundation, 111
Sloman, Albert, 57–58
Smart Surfaces Coalition, 262
Smit, Tim, 12, 84, 208, 227–229, 230, 263, 285–287
smoking, public, 175–176
Soames, Jeremy, 232
Sobel, Dava, 52
social anarchism, 106

social enterprise, 204–207
Social Stock Exchange (SSX), 102, 212–213
societal pressure waves. *See also* environmental pressure wave; globalization pressure wave; green pressure wave; impact pressure wave; sustainability pressure wave
  analysis and mapping of, 103–104, 107–110
  Greta wave, 108–109, 220–222
  Kondratiev's economic cycle theory, 100–101
  long wave theory, 101–103, 105, 107
  Minsky moments, 105–107
  out of the blue nature of, 98–100
  overview, 95–96
  surfing, 96–98, 110–112
Solar Energy Research Institute (SERI), 118–119
Soleri, Colly, 70
Soleri, Paolo, 40, 69–71, 88
Something Fierce (exhibition), 57
The Song of the Earth (Bate), 161
Sørensen, Ingvild, 217, 219
Sostheim, Juan, 249–250
Soto, Rolando, Jr., 249
"A Sound of Thunder" (Bradbury), 196
Soviet Union, collapse of, 147–148
SpaceShipOne, 217–218
speaking truth to power, 5, 274. *See also* Sharks (human); tickling Sharks
speculative fiction, 137, 138, 256
Spencer-Cooke, Andrea, 181
Speth, Gus, 175
Spielberg, Steven, 1–2, 104
spiral dynamic in life, 261–263
Sprague, Hollister, 40–42
SSX (Social Stock Exchange), 102, 212–213
stakeholders, politicized sense of term, 135
Stalin, Josef, 100–101
Steal This Book (Hoffman), 68
Steel-Maitland, Brenda, 30

Steel-Maitland, Dorothy, 30
Steel-Maitland, James, 30
Steffen, Alex, 161
Steger, Ulrich, 189
Stephenson, Pamela, 152–153
Stockholm Resilience Centre, 108
Stockholm syndrome, 11
Stone, Rosie, 247
Stop, Frank, 66
Storm, Laura, 237
stranded assets, 259
Strong, Maurice, 168
The Structure of Scientific Revolutions (Kuhn), 53–54
student protests and movements, 57–58, 78–80
A Study of History (Toynbee), 53
Sukhdev, Pavan, 237–238
Sun Traps (Elkington), 92, 142
Superfund (Comprehensive Environmental Response, Compensation, and Liability Act) legislation, US, 143–144
supermarkets, environmental practices of, 157
Surfers Against Sewage, 96
Surfin' U.S.A. (Beach Boys), 99
surfing, 96–98, 99, 281–282. *See also* societal pressure waves
Surrealistic Pillow (Jefferson Airplane), 61
SustainAbility, 92, 94
  battle against McDonald's, 153–156
  careful selection of partners and clients, 211–212
  and disruption to companies and supply chains, 156–158
  founding of, 151–152, 169
  The Green Consumer Guide, 151–152, 153–154, 155
  impact projects at, 200–202
  mission of, 169–170
  move to The People's Hall, 178–179
  naming of, 165–167

sale of, 77–78, 172–173
Shell, work with, 170, 177–178, 183–187
success of, 170–172
triple bottom line concept, 180–183
sustainability concept
    history of, 167
    and recall of triple bottom line, 213–214
sustainability pressure wave, 19, 108–109
    business leaders embracing, 192–194
    early champions in, 167–172
    European Commission's Consultative Forum on the Environment and Sustainable Development, 188–189
    ExxonMobil in, 187–188
    governments, working with, 188–194
    opinions of John Elkington during, 177–178
    overview, 165–168
    people serving as inspirations during, 178–180
    Richard Sandbrook in, 175–177
    sale of SustainAbility, 172–173
    Shell in, 170, 177–178, 183–187
    sustainable development concept, birth of, 174–175
    triple bottom line, 180–183
sustainable development
    birth of concept, 174–175
    early champions of, 167–169
    in mission of Environment Foundation, 145–146
Sustainable Development Goals (SDGs), UN, 108, 220
Sustainable Eel Group, 262
Sutcliffe, Theodora, 138
Suzuki, David, 145
swans, 229
system change agenda, 223–225, 226
    economies, dark side of, 258–260
    Farewell Spit as model of, 257–258, 259
    health, fractal vision of, 267–270
    and impact agenda, 207–208
    pushback against, 255–256

self-care needed to achieve, 266–267
spiral dynamic in life, 261–263
tackling Sharks, 271–280
tapping into wider sources of wisdom, 263–265
tickling Sharks, 260–261
and triple bottom line, 215
SYSTEMIQ, 111

T

tackling Sharks, 271–280
The Tao of Love and Sex (Chang), 89
taxation, 85
teasing, 275
Tennant, Tessa, 131, 159–161
Teo, Kevin, 208
TEPCO, 130
Tereshkova, Valentina, 139
Terkel, Studs, 90
TEST (Transport & Environment Studies), 72–73, 119–120, 188, 198–200
Thailand, 129
Thaler, Pierre-François, 224
Thatcher, Margaret, 143
The Other Economic Summit (TOES), 125
Thesiger, Wilfred, 241
The Third Wave (Toffler), 103, 181
Thirteenth Amendment (US), 81
"This Be The Verse" (Larkin), 23
Thomas, Patrick, 210–211, 215
Thomson, Adam, 67
3M, 7–8, 270
3Ps (People, Planet, and Profit) formula, 180–183
Thunberg, Greta, 220, 266
Tickell, Crispin, 139–140
tickling Sharks
    development of book title, 12
    during environmental pressure wave, 134–137
    overview, 3–9
    Stockholm syndrome, 11

tips for future of, 260–261
tikkun olam concept, 137, 240
Tilikum (orca), 15
Tillerson, Rex, 187
Timberlake, Lloyd, 176
Tinker, Jon, 120
tipping cascades, 111
Todd, John, 90
TOES (The Other Economic Summit), 125
Toffler, Alvin, 90, 103, 181
Tomorrow's Capitalism Forum, 261
Toulmin, Camilla, 176–177
Townsend, Peter, 58, 66
tow-surfing, 99
Toynbee, Arnold, 53
trade unions, 127
Transport & Environment Studies (TEST), 72–73, 119–120, 188, 198–200
Trident nuclear deterrent program, 25
Trinel, Frédéric, 224
triple bottom line
  Alvin Toffler, influence on concept, 103
  framing for use, 230–231
  Novo Nordisk, rechartering around, 159
  recall of concept, 213–216
  Shell's embrace of term, 185
  in sustainability pressure wave, 172, 180–183
Trojans, 272–273
Trotsky, Leon, 280
Trudeau, Garry, 90
Tudor, Andy, 60
Tuersley, Nigel, 149–150
Turner, Charlotte, 42
Turner, Clark, 42
TV programs on nature, 116–117
2052 (Randers), 247

U

UCL (University College London), 40, 69–70, 72, 198, 233
ugly ducklings, 179, 217

Ukraine conflict, 162–163, 246, 247–248, 259
UN. *See* United Nations
Undercurrents magazine, 90
Unilever PLC, 94, 193, 203, 215, 234
United Fruit Company, 248
United Nations Environment Programme (UNEP), 130–131
United Nations (UN)
  Climate Change Conference, 220
  environmental impact studies in Egypt, 119–120
  Global Compact, 111
  Sustainable Development Goals, 108, 220
United States (US)
  CERCLA or Superfund legislation in, 143–144
  Environmental Protection Agency, 168
  Inflation Reduction Act, 162, 220
  Thirteenth Amendment, 81
University College London (UCL), 40, 69–70, 72, 198, 233
University of Essex, 56–60, 62–63, 69, 71
University of Sussex, 56
Uranus myth, 115
urban planning and development, 69–71
urban regeneration, 71, 233
US. *See* United States
US Agency for International Development, 129

V

van Beurden, Ben, 187
vaping, 212
Varlamos, Giorgos, 63–65
venture investment, 203
A Very Civil War (Elkington), 40
Victor Gollancz, 146, 154
Vietnam War, 25, 41, 59–60, 78
Villeneuve, Denis, 136
violence, 246–248, 272
Virgin Galactic, 217–218

Volans Ventures, 92, 111
   advisory boards, 265
   careful selection of partners and clients, 212
   creation of and impact agenda, 207–211
   embrace of Acceleration Agenda, 269
   exponential change agenda, 216–219
   Green Swan Awards, 229–230
   Green Swan Day, 231
   language of impact, 222–225
   regeneration in value proposition of, 238–241
   Tomorrow's Capitalism Forum, 261
Volkswagen, 16–17, 66–67
von Weizsäcker, Ernst Ulrich, 189
vultures, 230

W

Wackernagel, Mathis, 95–96
Wahl, Daniel Christian, 237, 239
Waite, Stanley, 57
Walmart, 8, 233, 234
wars
   Cold War, late stages of, 147–148
   English Civil War, 57
   history and future of, 246–248
   Vietnam War, 25, 41, 59–60, 78
   World War I, 62
   World War II, 27–29, 62, 67, 82, 85–86, 107, 124, 126
Warshall, Peter, 87
The Water Knife (Bacigalupi), 138
water scarcity, 138, 244–245
water-based sports, health benefits of, 281
Waterman, Bob, 129
Watts, Phil, 186–187
The Wave, 281–282
The *Wave* (Casey), 98
waves. *See* societal pressure waves
Wazed, Hasina, 221
WEF (World Economic Forum), 79, 84–85, 111, 163, 205–206, 220

Weinstein, Harvey, 73
Welby, Justin, 46
Wells, H. G., 198
wetsuits, 281–282
Wharton School, 268–269
What Is History? (Carr), 54
whispering truth to power, 135
whistleblowers, 277
White, Allen, 131
"White Rabbit" (Jefferson Airplane), 61
Whole Earth Catalog (Brand), 61, 86–87
Wibberley, Gerry, 70
Wildfowl & Wetlands Trust, 232
Wildwood House, 89–90, 179
William, Prince of Wales, 118
Williams, Heathcote, 178
Wilson, Brian, 227
Wilson, E. O., 59
Wingate, Orde, 26
Wired magazine, 219
wisdom, tapping into wider sources of, 263–265
Witter, Clara, 81
Wolff, Heinz, 153
Women's Environmental Network, 202
Worcester, Bob, 185
World Business Council for Sustainable Development, 193
"World Conservation Strategy" paper, 174–175
World Economic Forum (WEF), 79, 84–85, 111, 163, 205–206, 220
World Resources Institute (WRI), 175
World War I, 62
World War II, 27–29, 62, 67, 82, 85–86, 107, 124, 126
World Wildlife Fund (WWF), 49, 75, 200, 231–232
Worldwatch Institute, 83
Wotton, Henry, 225
WRI (World Resources Institute), 175
Wright, Frank Lloyd, 70
WWA, 281

WWF (World Wildlife Fund), 49, 75, 200, 231–232
Wye College, 70

X

Xi Jinping, 221
XPRIZE Foundation, 217
XR (Extinction Rebellion) protests, 221

Y

A Year in the Greenhouse (Elkington), 149, 154

Young, Daphne, 71
Young, Gavin, 72, 241
The Young Green Consumer Guide (Elkington), 157–158
youth movements, 220, 222
Yunus, Muhammad, 206, 207, 221

Z

Zadek, Simon, 174
Ziantoni, Valter, 250
Zollinger, Peter, 175

Curiosity was there from the get-go.
(source: Tim Elkington, 1950)

Three score and twelve years later: speaking at a dinner in Luxembourg,
October 2022 (source: IMS, 2022)

Tim Elkington, our father, during the Battle of Britain
(source: Air Ministry, 1940)

Pat Elkington, our mother, listening to my tape of her account of being
haunted by a poltergeist as a child (source: John Elkington, perhaps 2010)

A Cyprus home-from-home: HMS *Fiskerton*, seen refuelling, probably in 1962–63, during her role in the so-called "Indonesian Confrontation" (source: Ton Class Association)

Great Aunt Brenda's Dior waistcoat makes it to Ibiza. (source: author's collection, 1968)

Our family Land Rover catching its breath in the Peloponnese during our Greek odyssey (source: author's collection, 1970)

Wed at St. Peter's Church, Little Rissington, with Ian Keay as best man and my sister Caroline as bridesmaid. Elaine's patched veil was first worn at a ball in Brussels after the Battle of Waterloo. (source: author's collection, 1973)

Alternative technologists inspired by John Todd's New Alchemy Institute: Robin Clarke's BRAD (Biotechnic Research & Development) in the early 1970s (source: Undercurrents collection, photographer unknown; see "The Ecologist and the Alternative Technology Movement," https://www.gla.ac.uk/media/Media_102865_smxx.pdf)

ENDS cofounder Max Nicholson, with his Desert Island Discs luxury: a pair of binoculars (source: photo by David Hosking, FLPA, Minden Pictures, around 1970)

ENDS cofounder David Layton with editions of The ENDS Report from 1998 and 1978 (source: John Elkington, 1998)

Gaia at the Strawberry Hill House Flower Festival—where her huge, room-sized Arachne exhibit was a runaway (or perhaps scuttle away) success—seen here against a backdrop by Sophie Powell, a.k.a. Unidentified Floral Object (source: photo by Adam Parker, Woodenzone, 2023)

Hania at the launch of her Netflix series, *The Innocents*, cowritten with Simon Duric (source: Peter Searle, 2018)

SustainAbility team in The People's Hall days; Julia Hailes, booted, center (source: author's collection, 1991)

Management team, slightly later, when Geoff Lye (third from left) had joined (source: author's collection, probably 1993)

Growing team in Bedford Row office (source: author's collection, around 2007–8)

Green politics: Petra Kelly (source: photo by Engelbert Reineke via Wikipedia, 1983, Bundesarchiv, B 145 Bild-F065187-0014)

Sustainability-oriented politics: Gro Harlem Brundtland (source: photo by Luiz Munhoz via Wikipedia, 2014)

Change partner one: Anita Roddick, founder of The Body Shop International (source: The Body Shop International, 1989)

Change partner two: Mads Øvlisen, former CEO and then chairman, Novo Nordisk A/S (source: OECD, 2007)

Change partner three: Bill Ford, CEO and then chairman, Ford Motor Company, 2012 (source: Ford Motor Company via Wikipedia, 2012)

Change partner four: Sir Geoffrey Chandler, a pioneering conscious capitalist (source: photo by John Elkington, author's collection, around 2006–7)

Great White Sharks: Exxon CEO Rex Tillerson (left) greets Vladimir Putin. (source: photo by Igor Sechin via Wikipedia, 2012)

Schooling Dolphins: Ben & Jerry's board meeting in evacuation boat as Hurricane Floyd roared in; I am bottom center. (source: author's collection, 1999)

Pamela Hartigan, my co-author on *The Power of Unreasonable People* (2008) and cofounder of Volans (source: Thinkers 50)

Some of the Volans team in Bloomsbury Place days; (left to right) Amy Birchall, Sam Lakha, Amanda Feldman, Richard Johnson, Char(mian) Love, Jacqueline Lim, and me (source: author's collection, 2010)

Early days at EcoVadis, Paris, with founders (left to right) Sylvain Guyoton, Fred Trinel, and Pierre-François Thaler; they went from half a dozen people when I joined to 1,700 by the time of writing. (source: EcoVadis, 2009)

B Team event in Amsterdam; having just done a keynote, I'm in there somewhere. There were well over 8,000 B Corporations worldwide by the time of writing. (source: Jurre Rompa, 2019)

A country on the brink of disintegration;
Elaine and I in Syria (source: author's collection, 2002)

Regenerator one:
Azzam Alwash in the
Iraqi Marshes (source:
Stephen Foote, 2010)

Regenerator two:
Elaine and I with
Juan Sostheim at
Rancho Margot,
Costa Rica (source:
author's collection,
2022)

My idea of heaven (source: Apollo 17 crew, NASA, 1972)

Lifelong inspiration: with Sandy and Jim Lovelock in Dorset (source: photo by John Gilbert, 2013)

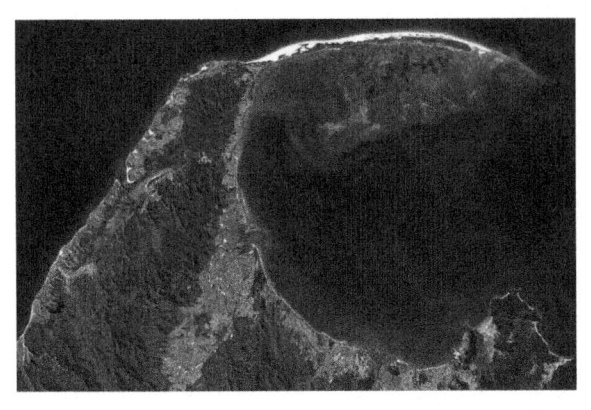

Anyone spot the kiwi? Farewell Spit, New Zealand (source: NASA Earth Observatory, 2001)

Our writing on Aviva's wall at our first Tomorrow's Capitalism Forum; (left to right) Steve Waygood of Aviva, Dominic Hofstetter of Climate-KIC (now with TransCap Initiative), Clara Barby of Impact Management Project (now with Just Climate), and Professor Bob Eccles of Harvard Business School and Saïd Business School, Oxford (source: Volans, 2020)

Change runs on renewables: with Neste in Espoo, Finland, during a session of the energy company's Advisory Council on Sustainability and New Markets. Left to right: Bernice Lee of Chatham House, Geoffrey Weston of Bain & Company, Salla Ahonen of Neste, climate solutions pioneer James Cameron, Vanessa Pérez-Cirera of WWF and then WRI, me, Minna Aila of Neste, Marcius Extavour of the XPRIZE Foundation and then Time Climate 100, and Volans CEO Louise Kjellerup-Roper (source: Neste, photo by Ismo Henttonen, 2023)

Regenerators: Sir Tim Smit of The Eden Project and Andrew Kerr of the Sustainable Eel Group on the first Green Swan Day (source: Toby Adamson, June 23, 2019)

Elaine and I help release 30,000 elvers into the River Severn with the Sustainable Eel Group. (source: photo by Andrew Kerr; author's collection, September 16, 2014)

About the Author

John Elkington, a.k.a. "The Godfather of Sustainability," is an author, advisor, educator, and entrepreneur. He was born in 1949 in a mill cottage by a Thames tributary, on a bed propped up with ammunition boxes. He traveled with his Royal Air Force family until 1959, returning to England as something of an alien. He then added to that alienation by becoming an early environmentalist, helping to pioneer the global sustainability movement. Over time, he led the first wave of activists into corporate boardrooms, introducing concepts like green consumerism and the triple bottom line. He was inducted into the Sustainability Hall of Fame in 2013 and won the World Sustainability Award in 2021.

Among interests listed in his *Who's Who* entry is "thinking around corners." His purpose: to help business regenerate—everything, everywhere, all at once. He is an ambassador for the Churchill Fellowship, the Eden Project, and WWF-UK; has served on more than eighty boards and advisory boards; and is a visiting professor at leading universities. He has cofounded four mission-driven businesses since 1978, all of which still exist in some form. SustainAbility, launched in 1987, was bought by ERM, which in turn was acquired by KKR in 2021. He cofounded Volans in 2008, where he serves as a board member and chief pollinator. *Tickling Sharks* is his twenty-first book, a witness statement on efforts to transform business, markets, and ultimately, the global economy.

Websites: https://johnelkington.com and https://volans.com
Email: john@volans.com

Printed in Great Britain
by Amazon